T0114054

More Praise for *The Economist's View of the World*

"Rhoads has built upon the best explanation I know of how orthodox economists think about choice, markets, externalities and other concepts. The new edition will be valuable to non-economists and economists alike: the former will learn how economists think; and the latter will learn some of the limits to how they think."

Martin Wolf, Financial Times

"America's political class has often exhibited a shaky grasp of basic economic principles. [Rhoads] puts the discipline's core concepts in wonderfully accessible form."

Barton Swaim, Wall Street Journal

"In *The Economist's View of the World: And the Quest for Well-being*, Steven Rhoads updates his classic primer on the theory and practice of economics. His sophisticated insight and practical commentary offer a demystifying guide to what economics has to offer and how we can use that knowledge to build a better world for all."

Arthur C. Brooks, Professor, Harvard Kennedy School and Harvard Business School, and New York Times *bestselling author*

"Since its original publication in 1985, *The Economist's View of the World* was prescient in its clear-sighted recognition of the limitations of contemporary economics. We are now at the end of a period of dominance of these ideas. In this updated version, Steve Rhoads reminds us of some of their virtues as well, in a fair-minded and informative analysis."

Francis Fukuyama, Director of the Center on Democracy, Development and the Rule of Law in the Institute for International Studies, Stanford University

"I think *The Economist's View of the World* is a great book. I think it's extremely important to see the economist's perspective, with its strengths and limitations, in a single place."

Andrew Gelman, Professor of Statistics and Political Science, Columbia University

"A blast from the past that's a breath of fresh air in the current airless, combative environment. The perspicacious Rhoads captures the challenges of government and reminds today's warring factions they have more in common than they know."

Amity Shlaes, chair of the board of trustees of the Calvin Coolidge Presidential Foundation and New York Times bestselling author of The Forgotten Man and Great Society

"The 1985 edition was sometimes ... used as a textbook for a nonmathematical introduction to economics. ... I suspect that the book does a good job of building bridges with those who are skeptical or hostile to what they perceive as the field of economics, because Rhoads is quick to emphasize that economic efficiency and growth are not the only ingredients of human well-being. ... The discussion throughout is based on solid explanations and a wealth of interesting examples."

Timothy Taylor, The Conversable Economist

"This book is unique. It combines in a sophisticated and yet accessible way a standard introduction to the economic way of thinking with a very ingenious introduction to the logic of applied economics and public policy analysis. It is ideally suited as a resource for introductory level courses, while the insightful and sometimes surprising references connecting the concepts and theories presented in the book to classic ideas and thinkers in the tradition of political philosophy and political economy make it an ideal primer for the Politics, Economics and Philosophy (PPE) programs."

Paul Dragos Aligica, George Mason University and University of Bucharest

"I used the first edition of *The Economist's View of the World* with success when teaching at Haverford College and Harvard's John F. Kennedy School. The 35th anniversary edition again enlightens and provides a tool for teaching introductory economics in a compelling way."

Linda A. Bell, Provost, Dean of Faculty and Claire Tow Professor of Economics, Barnard College

The Economist's View of the World

35th Anniversary Edition

Released in 1985, Steven E. Rhoads's classic was considered by many to be among the best introductions to the economic way of thinking and its application to public policy. Now, this anniversary edition has been updated and revised to account for developments in the discipline, as well as political and economic developments – from the greater interest in redistributing income and the ascendancy of behaviorism to the Trump presidency.

Beginning with opportunity cost, marginalism, and economic incentives, Rhoads then explains why mainstream economists – even those well to the left, such as Paul Krugman – still value free markets. The book ends with a critique of economic methods that adopt a strict neutrality between tastes and assume that selfishness rules our behavior. The author's critique of economics is its unbalanced emphasis on narrow self-interest as controlling motive and the route to happiness. He explains the growing interest in virtue ethics among philosophers and positive psychologists' findings that happiness is far more dependent on friends and family than on income or wealth.

This thought-provoking tour of the economist's mind is a must-read book for our times, providing a clear, lively, non-technical insight into how economists think and why they shouldn't be ignored.

Steven E. Rhoads is Professor Emeritus in Politics at the University of Virginia. He received his AB in history from Princeton University in 1961. Steve then spent time in the US Navy, and at the US Bureau of the Budget as the Secretary of the Director's Review. At Cornell University he studied economics, American politics, and the history of political philosophy, receiving his PhD in government in 1973. Steve and his wife Peggy live just outside Charlottesville, Virginia.

The Economist's View of the World

And the Quest for Well-Being

35th Anniversary Edition

Steven E. Rhoads
University of Virginia

CAMBRIDGE
UNIVERSITY PRESS

CAMBRIDGE
UNIVERSITY PRESS

Shaftesbury Road, Cambridge CB2 8EA, United Kingdom

One Liberty Plaza, 20th Floor, New York, NY 10006, USA

477 Williamstown Road, Port Melbourne, VIC 3207, Australia

314–321, 3rd Floor, Plot 3, Splendor Forum, Jasola District Centre, New Delhi – 110025, India

103 Penang Road, #05–06/07, Visioncrest Commercial, Singapore 238467

Cambridge University Press & Assessment is a department of the University of Cambridge.

We share the University's mission to contribute to society through the pursuit of education, learning, and research at the highest international levels of excellence.

www.cambridge.org
Information on this title: www.cambridge.org/9781108845946
DOI: 10.1017/9781108991421

First published 2021
Reprinted 2022
First paperback edition 2023

A catalogue record for this publication is available from the British Library.

Library of Congress Cataloging-in-Publication Data
NAMES: Rhoads, Steven E., author.
TITLE: The economist's view of the world : and the quest for well-being / Steven E Rhoads, University of Virginia.
DESCRIPTION: 35th anniversary edition. | Cambridge, United Kingdom ; New York, NY : Cambridge University Press, 2021. | Includes bibliographical references and index.
IDENTIFIERS: LCCN 2021012693 (print) | LCCN 2021012694 (ebook) | ISBN 9781108845946 (hardback) | ISBN 9781108994071 (paperback) | ISBN 9781108991421 (ebook)
SUBJECTS: LCSH: Economics. | BISAC: POLITICAL SCIENCE / Public Policy / Economic Policy | POLITICAL SCIENCE / Public Policy / Economic Policy
CLASSIFICATION: LCC HB171 .R43 2021 (print) | LCC HB171 (ebook) | DDC 338.9–dc23
LC record available at https://lccn.loc.gov/2021012693
LC ebook record available at https://lccn.loc.gov/2021012694

ISBN 978-1-108-84594-6 Hardback
ISBN 978-1-108-99407-1 Paperback

FOR MARGARET CAMPBELL RHOADS
MY
"PEGGY SUE"
WHO BROUGHT THE SUN BACK OUT

CONTENTS

Preface

In 1975 the University of Virginia promoted me to associate professor with tenure. I think the principal reason was that my department chair needed a graduate student advisor. Apparently, no one else was right for the job, and he believed it would be embarrassing to have an untenured assistant professor in the post. So, wheels were greased for my promotion. At the time, my only publication was a monograph based on my dissertation, and my teaching was mediocre: pretty good for smaller classes and pretty bad in large lecture classes. Few college deans would think this record worthy of tenure. Ten years later my teaching had improved considerably, but my publishing record was still scant; I had added only an edited volume at a commercial press.

My mood was pretty good, though. I had just finished an ambitious book manuscript on how economists think. And one of the best presses in the world was about to publish it. My editor, Colin Day, was enthusiastic and thought it would sell reasonably well in the academic market. Some course adoptions seemed possible. What neither of us anticipated was the book's wide appeal outside the academic market, including with general readers.

The reviews were very good where they appeared, in academic journals and in a few journals of political opinion. The first printing was a couple thousand copies – pretty standard back then. The book sold quickly, and Cambridge went back to press numerous times over the years. It just kept selling. In 2005 a graduate student reviewing on Amazon said the book had been assigned in his public administration seminar. It was gratifying but a little hard to believe that someone was assigning a 20-year-old book about economics and public policy in a graduate course. Sure, there were lots of anecdotes and examples in the book, but they were all at least 20 years old!

Meanwhile, the book had found a sizable readership in Europe and Asia. Tens of thousands of copies were eventually sold, putting the book in the top 1 percent for all books published by Cambridge since the Second World War. There were also foreign-language sales, and *The China Times* (Taiwan) selected the Chinese translation as one of the best books of the year (1991).

I always knew that, when retired, I would want to write a revised edition, since economic issues and economics itself have changed significantly. In 1985 most economists believed that "a rising tide lifts all boats." In the years since, inequality in both income and wealth has increased dramatically. Moreover, 15 percent of prime-age men in 2020 are not even looking for work. In 1985 the economists' belief that satisfying consumers' preferences for goods, services, and leisure leads to happiness went pretty much unchallenged. Now the challenges come from philosophers and psychologists, among others.

Still, the core concepts of economics have endured. In 1985 economists showed great appreciation for markets, emphasized balance between objectives rather than ranking them, considered opportunity costs before making policy, and used the externality concept (effects on third parties) when thinking about an agenda for government. All are as sensible now as then, and I am confident that they will be important to the economist's worldview many decades from now.

I can often generalize about how economists think because ideology is less important in the discipline than one might suspect. The Brookings Institution and the American Enterprise Institute (AEI) are two of the oldest think tanks in Washington. Taken as a whole, Brookings leans left while AEI leans right. But their work in economics is not so different. For most of the first decade of this century an AEI–Brookings Joint Center for Regulatory Affairs was active. More recently an AEI–Brookings Working Group on Poverty and Opportunity put out a joint report (*Opportunity, Responsibility, and Security*, 2016). Also relevant in this regard: Ted Gayer went from deputy assistant secretary for economic affairs at Treasury in the George W. Bush administration to co-director and later director of economic studies at the Brookings Institution!

In this book I present the core of the economist's way of thinking, which affects us all and explains why economics remains the most politically influential of the social sciences.

ACKNOWLEDGMENTS TO THE FIRST EDITION

If this book has any virtues, their genesis was at the Cornell University of the 1960s. As a master's candidate in public administration, I was drawn to Cornell's economics department. There, from Alfred Kahn and Robert Kilpatrick, I learned that the fields of regulatory economies and public finance addressed issues of policy substance in a disciplined and illuminating way.

Many years later, at a chance meeting, Kahn foolishly agreed to look at a manuscript I was working on. When I later deposited 550 pages on his doorstep, he kept any groans inaudible, and, in the midst of a schedule busier than any I will ever know, he produced 22 single-spaced pages of detailed, exceedingly helpful comments. Those who followed Fred Kahn's career in President Carter's administration will not be surprised to learn that at Cornell he was famous for his buoyant energy, wit, and intelligence. They may know less than I do, however, of his astonishingly generous nature.

Toward the end of my study of economics at Cornell, I had the good fortune to encounter another legendary campus figure, Allan Bloom. It was later my privilege to study with this peerless teacher when he was finishing his work on Plato's *Republic* and beginning his study of Rousseau's *Emile*. Like most other graduates of what today pass for good liberal arts colleges, I had never read these, or, indeed, almost any other truly important book. From Bloom I learned of views of the world richer than those of economists. My book would be a far better one if I knew even a few of the great books of political philosophy half as well as he.

After receiving my master's degree, I worked under Charles Schultze at the US Bureau of the Budget. There I was able to see the economist's view of the world as it first began to gain a real foothold in government through the studies that grew out of the old Planning, Programming, and Budgeting System.

When I returned to Cornell to obtain my PhD in government, I was fortunate to be able to work with Richard Fenno, Allan Sindler, and Walter Berns. My efforts here to let economists speak in their own words whenever possible are a tribute to Fenno's more skillful use of this method to bring alive the life of the Congress. In their very different ways, Sindler and Berns provided me with important models of how one can find in political science a source for thoughtful analysis of the issues of American politics. Sindler chaired my dissertation committee and has helped in many ways in succeeding years.

A manuscript that attempts to cover as much as this one does would be riddled with errors were it not for the kindness of readers more expert than I about various parts of it. The entire first draft of the manuscript, or substantial portions thereof, was read by Edward Banfield, Lawrence Brown, Donna Hawthorne Carfagno, James Ceaser, Ward Elliott, Joseph Goldberg, William Johnson, Alfred Kahn, Carnes Lord, Harvey Mansfield Jr., Edgar Olsen, James Pontuso, Abram Shulsky, Allan Sindler, Aaron Wildavsky, Leland Yeager, and several anonymous readers. Although I think my readers' comments have made this version much improved, they are of course blameless if I have made things worse instead.

The graduate students in the public administration classes of 1983 and 1984 were involuntary, but extraordinarily helpful, readers. I extend thanks to them and to my wife, Diana, the only person who has had to read every page of every draft. She is a superb editor, but that is the least of her virtues.

Cathy Dooley, Jim Crane, and Roxanne White were the last of a long line of research assistants who performed important but unglamorous work with skill and good cheer. Barbara McCauley did her usual superb typing job. The Institute for Educational Affairs, the Earhart Foundation, and the Center for Advanced Studies at the University of Virginia provided generous fellowship support that made possible a full year for writing. The university's small grants committee and the Department of Government and Foreign Affairs provided funds to type and reproduce the manuscript. And, finally, Colin Day has been a gifted and helpful editor from the very first. It has been a pleasure to work with him, my excellent copy-editor, Mary Byers, and the rest of the staff at Cambridge University Press.

ACKNOWLEDGMENTS

My friend and colleague in economics, Bill Johnson, has put up with my pestering questions about economics for over 40 years! He has a remarkable knowledge of what is going on in his discipline. Bill read the entire manuscript and offered a powerful and helpful critique.

Thanks also to another friend and colleague in economics, Ed Olsen, for sharing his extensive knowledge of the policy analytic community, and, in particular, his research on housing, which finds its way into my equity chapter.

N. Gregory Mankiw, Deirdre McCloskey, Paul Dragos Aligica, Tyler Cowen, and John Merrifield gave me extensive comments on the whole manuscript. I am most grateful to them.

I'm lucky that my career was at the University of Virginia, which has undergraduate honors students who could have gone anywhere. Better yet, I was able to convince some of the best to be my research assistants. In the last two years, when most of the writing and focused research was done, three have been particularly notable. Brooke Henderson used her facility with data and knowledge of applied economics in many ways but, of particular note, she wrote the first draft of most of the new chapter on economic incentives. Connor Dixon gave special help by becoming truly expert on the founders' views on property rights and the distribution of income. He showed his range by also becoming an expert on the literature on economists and selfishness.

Rebecca Harrington, a major in physics and mathematical economics, showed her versatility in a host of ways. She organized and annotated dozens of EconTalk transcripts as well as several feet of hard copy articles. She rewrote some passages to reflect changes suggested by expert readers. She worked with me until the wee hours during a crunch when I needed to quickly pull together a revised manuscript for a potential publisher. An extremely talented woman, her work on tedious tasks was always accompanied by plenty of energy, a can-do spirit, and a big smile.

At an earlier stage, before taking off for his Rhodes Scholarship, Russell Bogue took the lead in thoroughly updating the old version of my chapter supporting representation and deliberation. Micaela Connery's master's thesis helped convince me of the importance of voluntarism and of President George H. W. Bush's important initiative in that regard. Wendy Morrison helped with research on opportunity cost and infrastructure; Ben Gustafson with equity and the energy efficiency of home products.

Anne Marie Helm, Bradley Katcher, Alexander Mezick, Mary Hickok, and Andy Boyer helped on various assignments early in my research. Thanks go to Lee Coppock, Ken Elzinga, Adele Morris, Andy Rettenmaier, Jay Shimshack, and Todd Zywicki for their help with sources.

The R Street Institute, and in particular Kevin Kosar, provided excellent strategic advice and administrative support.

The first edition of this book came into being after years of effort and some neglect of my family. Along the way I could rely on the nurturing and editing of my late wife, Diana Akers Rhoads, and the usual good cheer of our three active and interesting sons, Chris, Nick, and John.

Jim Ceaser and Blaire French have been good friends and supporters of this project over many decades. Conversations with two of my old students and now old friends, Steve Teles and Steve Camarota, brought sound advice and support. The same can be said of my three amigos: Marc Plattner, Gary Schmitt, and Abe Shulsky.

Anna Sutherland was an excellent personal editor of the early rough draft chapters before her very untimely death. Richard Starr took over the skillful editing of most of the draft, but his ability to find elusive articles and rewrite clunky passages took his portfolio well beyond normal editing. I am most grateful to him.

Robert Dreesen, my acquisition editor, has spearheaded the Cambridge efforts to make my book successful with the general reader as well as academics. His suggestions for tweaking some of the early writing were superb. I have relied on his accessibility, wide publishing experience, and good judgment throughout the publishing process.

In the courtship of my wife Peggy, she repeatedly disproved the theory of diminishing marginal utility. It turns out that the second and third and fourth steak per month do bring successively less pleasure, but with Peggy Sunshine the second, third, and fourth dates per month keep getting better and better. While doing her own writing, she also offered wise strategic advice about publishing this book.

INTRODUCTION

What comes to mind when you think about economics? Nothing good, if you are the reader I most want to reach. You know little or nothing of it and have always found it forbidding. Even if you took an introduction to economics in college (perhaps at your father's insistence), you remember little of it. The class was boring. Depending on your age, you were presented with screechy blackboards with chalk dust flying or whiteboards or slides with diagram after diagram. Your professor, whether droning or excited, would have been telling you that diagrams were the best way to really understand economics.

He was wrong. That is not the best way for you to understand economics. Yet, who am I to make such a declaration? The book jacket says I'm a political scientist, not even an economist.

Early in graduate school at Cornell, I took over 20 hours of coursework in economics. Later, as a professor of politics at the University of Virginia (UVA), I was told that I would be teaching basic economics to graduate students in public administration. As is sometimes the case, UVA's master's program was housed in our politics department. So, I had to think about what, in one semester, future public administrators who knew little or nothing about economics needed to know.

No economics textbook was satisfactory. All those diagrams! What had gotten me excited about economics were wonderful concepts such as opportunity cost and marginalism, which were used to illuminate political issues through cases, examples, and anecdotes. I decided to write my own book.

Absorbing the essence of economics need not be bitter medicine. I think I can make it more interesting and illuminating than you thought economics could be. A George Mason University economist, who previously taught at the University of Virginia, introduced my talk at GMU by saying that "one of my UVA students completing the major told me 'the only economics I remember is what I learned from Rhoads.'"

The editor of *The Concise Encyclopedia of Economics* apparently thought I explained an important concept, marginalism, better than any of his economist peers. He lifted most of the entry on marginalism from a chapter in my 1985 book.[1] He has also written online that he considers the first edition of this book to be one of the ten best books written in economics in the last 50 years. In his review of the first edition, John Brandl, the economist who was the founding dean of the Hubert H. Humphrey School of Public Affairs at the University of Minnesota, called the book "marvelous... Reading it, an economist is taken aback that a person outside the discipline could understand it so thoroughly; and then, precisely because he is not *of* economics, offer new insights into its applicability, and provide a biting critique of its limitations."[2]

There are many books about economics written by distinguished economists. I want you to believe that the best person to teach you about the economist's view of the world may not even have a formal credential in the discipline. No matter who you read, there can be no doubt that some knowledge of economics is essential to good citizenship in a modern democracy. Next to law, it is also the most politically influential subject in a modern university.

If you decide to let me talk to you about economics, you will find that I have a lot of good things to say about markets. Praising markets sounds like something that conservatives do. But, in fact, almost all economists love markets. For example, the politics of Nobel laureate Joseph Stiglitz are well to the left of most economists. He favors many things Bernie Sanders and Alexandria Ocasio-Cortez favor. He thinks our current economic system is not "efficient, stable or fair." But he refuses to join a democratic socialism movement; he prefers the term "progressive capitalism," because it "emphasizes that markets with private enterprise are at the core of any successful economy."[3]

Markets give information to the people who need it and will act on it without flooding "in-boxes." And flood them they will if you try to run an economy without using a market. After all, without a market, how would we decide who should get the sawdust?

Sawdust? Yes, sawdust. In 2008 the price of milk was much higher than usual. An economist asked a dairy farmer, how come?[4] The farmer said his inputs were much more expensive. For example, the price of sawdust had doubled within a year. (Within two years it had gone up by a factor of four for some uses.) He used sawdust to bed his cows more comfortably. They produced more milk when they were more often off their feet. The reason for the increase in the price of sawdust was the sharp downturn in the production of new housing. Since construction of new houses was down, there was less sawdust.

So, imagine you are a politician or a planner trying to satisfy citizens complaining about the high price of milk. Suppose you decide that you could please these citizens by reducing the price of milk in school cafeterias. But another problem citizens were complaining about was homelessness and the high price of affordable housing. Would you realize that using more sawdust to produce milk would increase the price of housing? Probably not. But it would increase housing costs, because sawdust is also the principal component in particleboard, which is used widely in the building industry. It is cheaper than substitutes such as lumber and plywood. You probably wouldn't know that.

Many of your constituents also love gardening, and they would not be happy if the sawdust they use to make their mulch became more expensive because some of it was being siphoned off to help "higher-priority" users. Sawdust is also used in the production of charcoal briquettes and as part of a mix to make a lightweight material for dashboards. It would take a planner a lot of time to decide on the fair and efficient allocation of sawdust. No matter what he decided, many people would think his decision was unfair.[5]

Of course, no politician or planner would have time to worry about sawdust. If there were no entrepreneurs or markets, sawdust would probably be thrown away or used only for mulch; no one would know that the waste product had these other uses. Even if they eventually figured it out, how would they decide which usage was the most important and how much should go to it and how much for the second most important usage?

The lowly sawdust example shows that there is a "dense interconnection" of different kinds of scarce resources.[6] No planner could sort everything out efficiently. This is an important reason why we need markets. If doing something to reduce the high price of milk was so complicated, imagine if you had to plan for a whole economy.

The communist regimes of the twentieth century did not use markets and had poor economic performance. In time they accepted markets to some degree despite their ideological embarrassment. The literature on Maoist China is replete with self-confessions about failures to properly balance capital construction projects with building materials or coal and iron goods with transportation requirements.[7]

Markets can *seem* chaotic. Imagine a 12-year-old prodigy being asked to choose between two economic systems: one in which everyone works as much as they want, at whatever they want, while living wherever they want; whereas, in the second, the best minds in the country work together to decide what should be made, who should make it, and where they should make it. The 12-year-old might say, "Hey, that first system sounds neat." But if he was then asked which system would produce the most economic growth, I think he would choose the second one.

He would be badly mistaken. For one thing, in the second system, political sorts would decide who get to be the planners, and they would be more likely to choose those who will keep them in power than the best economic minds in the country. And, besides, most people could not earn a large income, or even a decent one, if the planners ignored market forces. When I was 12, I thought I wanted to make a living as a professional tennis player. But, in time, I learned that no one would pay to see me play!

The first system actually stimulates planning, but the planning is parceled out; it's within each economic entity. Innovators think of things that people will want to buy and then plan how to get them made at a reasonable cost. Most would-be innovators are no better at this than I was at tennis, and they may end up earning a salary working for others. But, in time, the free-market capitalist system creates economic growth that produces more abundance and leisure than any other system.

In this book we will seldom be talking about macroeconomics, issues that feature the economy as a whole such as inflation and monetary policy. We will be talking about concepts that economists use when studying particular policies that help make up the whole. For example, in the economics department at my university there are courses on education, housing, health care, labor, antitrust, the environment, and antipoverty programs. The teachers of these courses and most of the analytic staffs dealing with these subjects in governments are microeconomists.

Microeconomists feel misunderstood. All the attention goes to their discipline's showy and presumptuous side, macroeconomics, while its larger, more solid, and more elegant better half, microeconomics, remains unseen. Thus, one can find prominent economists calling microeconomics "the Cinderella side of the discipline" or complaining that "macro gives micro a bad name."[8] We all understand that, when navigating, you want to pay special attention to the part of the iceberg that can't be seen. There would be no cause for celebration if we were spending lots of money on all the particular government programs, but the programs were inefficient and accomplishing much less than they could be.

Economics is a discipline full of both marvelous insights and troubling blindness. Most of this book shines light on the insights. But economists place unbalanced emphasis on narrow self-interest as both controlling motive and route to happiness. I demonstrate the weaknesses in the economist's worldview. I also explain how growing systems of thought such as virtue ethics and positive psychology provide an implicit and sometimes explicit critique of the economist's worldview.

Throughout, I evaluate the views of mainstream economists, those whose outlooks have been shaped by the principles discussed in standard microeconomic or public economics texts. As I use the term, "mainstream economist" encompasses a clear majority of economists – liberal and conservative, Democrats and Republicans.

Part I
Useful Concepts

1 OPPORTUNITY COST

Thomas Malthus was a nineteenth-century economist who believed that population would always grow more rapidly than food production, thus dooming people to poverty. His economics was called "dismal" by Thomas Carlyle. Economics is still something of a dismal science, though not for the original Malthusian reasons. As the Nobel laureate Kenneth Arrow noted, the economist's frequent job is to say: "This or that, not both. You can't do both."[1]

There is much talk these days of government programs that do not achieve their objectives. The economist, however, sees a bittersweet quality in even those programs that *do* achieve their objectives. The crowd at the ground-breaking for the new community recreation center finds it a happy occasion that will soon make available wholesome sports for the young and community-building opportunities for senior citizens. The economist broods: "Yes, but by spending the money here and not elsewhere, we give up the remedial reading program that might raise low-income students' test scores a full grade, and the new public park in the underserved north end of town. And what about the recreational opportunities that local families might enjoy if the tax dollars to pay for this center were left in their pockets?"

Economists are sometimes defined as those who "know the price of everything and the value of nothing." In their defense, they point out that a concern with prices or costs is really a concern with values. Our brooding economist was worrying about recreation center costs because he cared about slow-learning children and recreation opportunities in the low-income part of town. Added costs leave us with fewer resources available to pursue values in other policy areas. In other words, whenever the costs of one program increase, the expenditures on and benefits obtained from some other program or from private expenditures decrease.

This is the idea of opportunity cost: the understanding that spending and regulatory decisions that use scarce resources or require their use incur costs in terms of forgone alternatives elsewhere. This idea seems so obvious that one can wonder why it is worth discussing. Anyone who has purchased less expensive food at the grocery store in order to pay the rent on time certainly knows something about opportunity cost in the family context.

As I write the revisions to this chapter, in August 2020, a major opportunity cost situation confronts all parts of the country with regard to Covid-19. Take the issue of in-person versus virtual school learning. Children don't learn as much when they are not in the classroom, and their socialization also suffers. But, if they are in the classroom, they will be more likely to be infected with Covid-19. Moreover, with in-person instruction, infections are more likely to spread to other children and teachers, parents and any grandparents living at home.

How many infections could be prevented by changes in schools' classrooms and routines? How great would be the loss of income in single- and two-working-parent families if someone had to be home with children who were learning online? A variety of partial solutions exist for every Covid-19 complication, and opportunity cost defines the costs incurred, or what we sacrifice, in forgoing alternative options. With Covid-19, most citizens' well-being will be affected by any decision that is reached. It is rare for a public policy decision to affect so many people in such a clear and major way.

Some time ago, a high-ranking city administrator in Virginia described his jurisdiction's recreation policy as follows: "We give primary consideration to the public welfare, but cost considerations are also important." Economists worry about this sort of formulation because it suggests that costs are something other than public welfare forgone in other public programs and in the private sector.

For 60 years output and employment in the textiles and apparel industries have been hemorrhaging in the United States. At the same time, firms in these industries have spent very little on new plants and equipment. Economists do not think these facts are *prima facie* evidence of poor industrial management. Textiles and apparel firms hire large numbers of unskilled laborers, and the wages of unskilled laborers here are dramatically higher than in many developing countries. Our firms cannot compete with foreign competitors in these industries, so it is smarter for the nation to specialize in what it is comparatively good at producing, such as making airplanes, and let China and Bangladesh make the T-shirts.

The opportunity cost to society of taking from expanding industries the scarce investment capital needed to modernize declining textile and apparel industries is likely to be so high that the use of antiquated machinery by declining firms is perfectly efficient. Declining industries are always a sorry sight. Individuals who have not studied economics tend to blame the plight of such industries on their antiquated equipment and on the shortsighted management responsible for it. Economists see the equipment as the effect rather than the cause of the industry's decline.

The economically correct response to steadily declining demand is to continue to operate with existing equipment as long as the firm can cover its variable costs of production. That is, if a company can cover its variable costs, any additional revenue it generates can be used to pay off fixed costs, such as paying off loans, which must be paid whether the firm is operating or not. It should rarely replace old equipment. To modernize equipment with high capital costs would make the firm's plight worse, because costs would rise in the face of declining demand and prices.[2]

Even within the same firm a product might be made with advanced technology in one country but not another. The relative opportunity cost of labor and capital still matters. In less developed countries, capital is scarce and labor is abundant. Thus, David Autor, an economist at the Massachusetts Institute of Technology (MIT), notes that Nissan uses robots heavily when producing cars in Japan but relies more on cheap local labor at plants in India.[3]

Opportunity cost reminds us that we should always think about costs, but it also tells us that the costs relevant to decisions are those that are connected to opportunities. Money already spent and resources already used are "sunk costs." They cannot be recovered, so they have no economic relevance for current decisions. As they say, it's no use crying over spilt milk.

But one sometimes hears people say of a government project that too much has been invested to back out. For example, in 1971

Congressman Tom Steed (D-Okla.) said of the proposed American supersonic transport (SST) airplane: "It is a strange thing why some want to stop now. I ask the question: 'If we stop now, who will benefit?' Certainly not the people, for they are going to be stuck for $1.1 billion."[4] The economist responds: "They will be stuck either way. We should ask if benefits will exceed *additional, controllable* costs. If not, don't send good money after bad."

Economists are convinced that few outside their profession truly grasp the significance of opportunity costs. Thus, University of Wisconsin's Burton Weisbrod has said of his former role in the public policy process, "That which we have to offer is fundamentally very simple and second nature to economists but not to others, and I think it's essentially the notion of opportunity costs."[5] Controversial government-funded infrastructure and transportation projects, many of which I will describe below, offer the perfect lens through which to explore this idea further.

Engineers versus Economists

Engineers and economists were at odds about SST initiatives. The engineers wanted to show what they could do. The economists said, essentially, "Even if you can do it, it's not worth it." The economists were right. In the early 1970s Britain and France, cooperatively, went ahead with developing a state-subsidized supersonic aircraft: the Concorde. In 2003 the Concorde made its last flight; *The Washington Post* summed up the adventure as "a technological marvel but a commercial flop."[6]

In emphasizing opportunity costs, economists constantly find themselves quarreling with other experts and professionals. Engineers, for example, frequently provoke economists' ire, as was the case with supersonic transport. Engineers often ponder costs when considering alternative ways to complete a particular project. But a full calculation of opportunity costs requires more than considering the relative costs of using steel or reinforced concrete when building. It also requires considering ways to solve a problem without building at all.

Examples of this kind of oversight abound. Sanitary engineers have equated solving water pollution with the treatment of municipal and industrial wastewaters while giving little thought to lower-cost solutions, including changing the economic incentives to pollute or merely letting a fast-flowing river clean the water.[7] The Federal Aviation Administration (FAA), an agency in which engineers have great influence, has often favored reducing congestion through costly airport construction projects rather than through pricing changes to encourage use of less congested airports or less congested times at busy airports.[8] A study of Oakland shows that the engineers who run the street and engineering department consider costs only after project decisions have been made on other grounds.[9]

Despite the fact that economists may have more political clout than engineers, it is the engineers who have had reason to smile when contemplating political rhetoric in the last decade or so. During his first term President Obama frequently referred to his interest in a 17,000-mile coast-to-coast network of high-speed trains that would rival the interstate highway system in scope.[10] Joe Biden echoed this proposal when running for president in 2020.[11] Clifford Winston, a Brookings Institution economist, has run the idea by other economists, including some who considered not just speed and convenience but reductions in highway congestion, carbon emissions, and traffic fatalities. He concluded that a national network of high-speed trains could not be justified on economic grounds.[12]

During the 2016 campaign Donald Trump spoke of spending more than $550 billion on infrastructure. In his first speech after the election, infrastructure was the first policy he mentioned.[13] The American Society of Civil Engineers (ASCE) thinks the billions pledged by President Trump would be just a down payment on what is needed. The ASCE gives our current infrastructure an overall grade of D+ and says that it will take $4.5 trillion over the next eight years to bring all the systems up to an "acceptable standard."[14] It may go without saying, but engineers would benefit personally from such a large investment.

The biggest infrastructure program currently under way is a high-speed rail system that is supposed to connect Los Angeles and San Francisco. In a 2008 referendum, California voters approved a bond issue for $9 billion. The rest of the estimated cost of $33 billion was to be picked up equally by the federal government and private investors. But, to date, the federal government has put up only $3.5 billion, and congressional Republicans have vowed to block any additional federal funds. Private investors have indicated that they will provide nothing without a guarantee that they will not lose money.

In March 2018 the state rail authority announced that the cost of connecting Los Angeles to San Francisco would be not $33 billion, but between $77.3 billion and $98.1 billion. The projected cost may rise further, because the estimates for creating 36 miles of tunnels through mountainous southern California are quite uncertain. Jim Frazier, the Democratic chairman of the California Assembly's Transportation Committee, believes that "[w]e still have no realistic way to pay for the project." Republicans have been harsher. One state senator has said: "Initially a rathole, now a sinkhole, soon it will be an abyss in which more and more tax dollars are forever lost."[15]

Even if the necessary funds materialize, will the benefits exceed the high costs? Past precedent suggests the answer is "No." Bent Flyvbjerg is a Danish economic geographer whose research focuses on megaprojects costing $1 billion or more. Looking around the world, he and his researchers found that, in nine out of ten cases, the costs of huge projects are underestimated. Likewise, 90 percent of the time, project benefits are overestimated and schedules are underestimated. Thus, only a very small fraction of projects are completed on schedule, stick to the planned budget, and deliver the promised benefits.

Chapter 4 will provide an argument that economists make as to why the private sector is generally more efficient than governments. This may not apply to megaprojects, however. Privately funded mega-projects are also usually unsuccessful, but no published studies have systematically compared their outcomes with public outcomes. In any case, private boondoggles have one big advantage over public ones: they don't force uninvolved taxpayers to pay for them.

In an EconTalk podcast with Russ Roberts, Flyvbjerg explains why politicians and engineers both love megaprojects. Politicians like the positive publicity that comes with pictures showing them cutting red ribbons with big shots. One of them told Flyvbjerg, "What do you think, Bent, that I would like to point to when my political career is over, that I passed some law that is sitting on a shelf somewhere in a library or I can drive across a bridge or go into a tunnel that I can tell my grandchildren I did this? I decided this?"[16] Support for Flyvbjerg's evidence about politicians comes from a *Washington Post* story on President Trump. His aides told the *Post* reporter that Trump seemed more interested in infrastructure than other subjects. He liked to talk about building and thought "it would be good for him politically to travel throughout the country to promote new projects."[17]

Of the engineers, Flyvbjerg says,

> There's nothing engineers like better and technologists like better than to push the envelope, technologically speaking. So, to make something longer or taller or faster, whatever it is. And, if you are an engineer, what do you want to work on: an average bridge or the longest bridge in the world? Every engineer is clear on that question: they want to work on the longest bridge in the world.

Economists draw the ire of politicians and engineers because, when they contemplate infrastructure projects, they always first ask, "Do we need to build at all?" Maybe we will not need another lane on the Beltway if we discourage driving at the most congested times by charging for it. As Clifford Winston, a Brookings Institution economist and transportation expert, has said,

> Roads have an artificially low price. Cars are not charged for congestion, so they put pressure on peak capacity. Trucks are not charged efficiently for the damage they do to roads; they pay a gas tax when they really need to pay an explicit charge that reflects the damages they do to roads. This underpricing causes road capacity to fill up, causes the roads to wear out a lot sooner. And it generates a demand for more spending.[18]

Winston thinks that the nation's alleged infrastructure crisis is greatly overstated. As its name suggests, the federal "New Starts" program gives money only for new transportation projects. It typically costs the federal government about $2 billion a year. The vast majority of the funds go to fixed rail. But "a variety of cost-effectiveness analyses suggest improvements in bus service generally cost about $1 to $10 per transit trip while rail construction typically costs around $10 to $100 per new trip." Bus service, which the poor are more likely to depend on, typically receives less funding when new rail projects are completed. For example, this has occurred in Los Angeles, Atlanta, and San Jose.

Moreover, rail projects typically do little to get people out of their cars. "In 1980, Portland, Oregon's bus system carried 9.9 percent of the region's commuters to work. By 2010, Portland had built five low-capacity rail lines, a commuter-rail line, and a streetcar line, but transit's share of commuting fell to 7.1 percent."[19] Once one considers the energy needed to build the rail projects, pollution reduction gains from such projects are often nonexistent.[20]

There exists a further conflict between economists' thinking and politicians' thinking. Economists usually want to focus new transportation projects on growing areas that are doing well, because that's where the congestion is. Politicians want to spread the money around the country.[21]

The above passages focus especially on wasteful new infrastructure projects. Infrastructure spending is often, however, about fixing old things up. But, even here, the hype about the necessity for this spending is way over the top.

Bridges, for example, have drawn the attention of both Barack Obama and Donald Trump. In his 2013 State of the Union address, President Obama highlighted "the nearly 70,000 structurally deficient bridges across the country,"[22] and later in the year, in a speech at Knox College, he got lots of laughter when he said, "We've got more than 100,000 bridges that are old enough to qualify for Medicare."[23] When presidential candidate Trump visited the TV show *Morning Joe* early in his campaign, his first example of "our infrastructure disaster" was bridges falling down. Indeed, Trump declared, "61 percent of our bridges are in danger."[24]

The media also echoes the politicians' alarm. For example, *The Washington Post* has published articles with titles such as "Thousands of bridges at risk of collapse in freak accidents" and "US has 63,000 bridges that need significant repairs."[25] In 2010 the construction lawyer Barry B. LePatner wrote a book entitled *Too Big to Fall*, complete with a cover showing a drawing of a large bridge that appeared to have been chopped in half. LePatner noted that nearly a quarter of our 600,000 bridges were either "structurally deficient" or "functionally obsolete." We were "running out of time," and the "risks of continuing to ignore our ill-maintained national infrastructure" were "almost unimaginable."[26] In an interview with one of my research assistants, LePatner seemed more alarmed still, claiming that 8,000 of our bridges were "ticking time bombs."[27]

It should not be surprising that politicians and others interested in ginning up big bucks for infrastructure should focus on falling bridges. Evolutionary theorists believe that a fear of heights is ingrained in us because falling from heights has been a good way to end human life for hundreds of thousands of years. If Americans are asked to picture their fellow citizens dying as a bridge collapses beneath them, they are likely to pay attention.

But here are the facts. According to the Department of Transportation's Office of Highways, "The fact that a bridge is classified under the federal definition as 'structurally deficient' does not imply that it is unsafe." When they remain in use, structurally deficient bridges typically require more maintenance and repair, and they often have weight limits. "Functionally obsolete" is not synonymous with "dangerous," either. "A functionally obsolete bridge is one that was built to standards that are not used today. [...] A functionally obsolete bridge is similar to an older house. A house built in 1950 might be perfectly acceptable to live in, but it does not meet all of today's building codes."[28]

The percentage of our bridges that are structurally deficient has been falling. For example, they represented 20.7 percent of all bridges in 1992, but 11.2 percent in 2011. There has been a similar decline over the last two decades in the percentage of bridges that are functionally obsolete.[29]

How many people die in the United States because bridges collapse? The best evidence comes from a 2014 Utah State PhD dissertation entitled "Bridge Failure Rates, Consequences and Predictive Trends." The author, Wesley Cook, says that about 128 of the more than 600,000 bridges in the country collapse each year, and loss of life occurs only in about 4 percent of collapses.

Are Opportunity Costs Relevant for Lifesaving Programs?

Some readers will reply, "Your analysis shows that bridges do collapse and people lose their lives as a result. Do economists think we should just accept that?" Such skeptical readers will find substantial support among politicians. Congressman David Obey (D-Wisc.) once said, "Quite frankly, I believe that when you're dealing in questions related to human life, economic costs are irrelevant."[30] Several congressional committees have voiced similar sentiments.[31]

In 1986 former Congressman Pete Stark (D-Calif.) wrote for the editorial page of *The Washington Post* in response to a series of articles explaining how a 20-year-old drunk boy's devastating auto accident in Springfield, Virginia, had transformed his family for the worse. Stark wanted auto manufacturers to be required to install airbags and electronic sobriety test equipment in all vehicles.

The articles were as moving as Stark thought they were. But he concluded by advocating a general safety principle that, on reflection, no one could support: auto manufacturers should be required to produce "the safest vehicles that our engineers [can] design."[32] Engineers *could* make cars nearly as safe as amusement parks' bumper cars; the problem is that they would not be very fast, they would get lousy mileage, and they would pollute the environment more. We care about these features as well as safety.

Consider highway safety more generally. Roadway engineers can show that noisy rumble strips reduce traffic deaths when placed on centerlines and shoulders. So too do strong median barriers.[33] If we decide to make all these improvements on the most traveled roads, should we then feel compelled to do it on somewhat less traveled roads, and then on rural roads? Every incremental expenditure would surely save a few more lives. And, if we open the federal checkbook for any program that could save an additional life, doctors, police officers, firefighters, air quality experts, Coast Guard officers, lifeguards, and EMTs, among others, would be at the door with projects that could save lives if we were willing to fund them.

Court awards by juries suggest that ordinary Americans have no more tolerance than bighearted congressional representatives for businesses that put cost-cutting above safety. For example, a Chevy Malibu that caught fire after being rear-ended led to a suit filed by six severely injured burn victims inside the Malibu. An eight-person jury awarded the six burn victims $107.6 million in compensatory damages and $4.8 billion in punitive damages.

This blockbuster punitive damages award was based on General Motors' (GM's) own risk analysis of the vehicle, which concluded that there would be some deaths in accidents because of the Malibu's fuel tank placement. In post-trial comments, one plaintiff's lawyer concluded: "The jurors wanted to send a message to General Motors that human life is more important than profits." Jurors, indeed, echoed this perspective, telling reporters that they "felt the company had valued life too lightly. 'We're just like numbers, I feel, to them,' one juror said."

The GM risk analysis was seriously flawed, but, even if it had not been, the respected cost–benefit ace W. Kip Viscusi concludes that GM would have found it difficult to convince jurors of the desirability of making risk–cost trade-offs. One juror expressed a "zero-risk mentality" in her observation: "There was no evidence that the car they put out there was as safe as what they could have put out there."[34]

If our representatives in Congress put safety above all else, as the jurors seem to want, they would not so regularly divert highway trust funds to provide for bicycle and nature trails, landscaping, and junkyard removal projects.[35]

The behavior of the general public also demonstrates some willingness to trade safety for other perceived goods. In most states, drivers can use cellphones on the road, even though this makes them four times more likely to get into a serious crash.[36] Those who use their phones consider the increased risk more than compensated for by enjoyable, or sometimes urgent, conversation.

More surprisingly, the public regularly forfeits some expected auto safety gains by driving more recklessly once safety features have been installed. For example, a number of studies have found that dual braking systems prevent far fewer accidents than had been expected. Drivers with automatic braking systems drive faster and brake harder. Similarly, people driving cars with studded snow tires drive faster in the snow.[37] Skeptical readers should engage in this thought experiment: suppose your car did not have airbags or seatbelts but, instead, had a dagger on the steering wheel. Would you drive more carefully?

In the addendum to Chapter 6, I will briefly explain the way economists estimate the value of a life saved through risk reduction. All I wish to argue here is that, all other things being equal, programs that can save more lives for a given expenditure should be preferred over programs that would save fewer. In 1994 a group of economists compared the cost-effectiveness of various lifesaving interventions. Overall, they found that the median medical intervention cost $19,000 per year of life saved; the median injury prevention cost $48,000 per life-year saved; and the median toxin control intervention cost $2.8 million per year of life.[38]

It seems obvious that shifting funds from some toxic control interventions to injury prevention ones would save lives. Yet, when economists delve into quantifying the lifesaving effects of particular projects, their work often draws controversy. One study tried to put radiation-induced deaths at Chernobyl in the Soviet Union in context by expressing them as a small fraction of the cancers that probably would have occurred in the affected region even without the disastrous 1986 accident. Likewise, the coal-fired plants that nuclear energy would replace cost more lives per year than Chernobyl cost one time only.

Thomas Cochran, a nuclear physicist with the Natural Resources Defense Council, called this a "time-honored way to minimize adverse health effects. [...] It's a common way to hide the truth."[39] Economists, and even many physicists, would disagree. In their book *Risk–Benefit Analysis*, physicists Richard Wilson and Edmund Crouch estimate, for example, that over a five-year period, if every person in the United States were to receive a single chest X-ray, 15,000 would develop cancer from the X-rays, whereas if every person in the country were to live within 20 miles of a nuclear plant under normal operation, one person would develop cancer. For another point of comparison, if everyone in the United States was exposed to the level of cosmic radiation that naturally occurs in high-altitude Denver, over a five-year period more than 25,000 people would develop cancer as a result.[40]

If readers absorb the information in Wilson and Crouch's book, I think they will become less worried about nuclear energy, a form of energy that, besides its other benefits, does not contribute to deaths from exposure to the air pollution caused by carbon fuels. The many deaths from exposure to a nuclear power disaster surely cause more damage to the public's confidence than do the thousands who die of cancer caused by a wide range of other factors. Still, we have never had a nuclear reactor accident as bad as Chernobyl, and efforts to avoid one should not always take precedence over other ways of combating cancer.

It is not just natural but appropriate for auto regulators to care deeply about the safety of cars, for doctors to care most about fighting disease, and for the Natural Resources Defense Council to fight environmental pollution. But surely, when we must allocate limited funds to various lifesaving interventions, it is helpful to have a group that looks at the big picture. Economists play this role, and they are not "hiding the truth" when they practice their discipline.

Opportunity Costs When Preserving the Natural Environment

In 1972 the Government Accountability Office (GAO) published a very critical review of Potomac River cleanup efforts in the national capital region. In the preceding ten years more than $1 billion had been spent, $128 million of which was completely wasted, going "to plan, design and construct facilities which were either not built, not needed or are minimally used."[41] None of the communities surrounding the Potomac wanted new waste treatment facilities in their area. Coordination among the involved governmental jurisdictions had been poor. Costs had been much higher than anticipated and benefits far fewer than expected.

There was one major unsolved problem. To get the river cleaner meant accumulating much larger amounts of sludge residue, which themselves posed public health risks. It was not clear what was to be done with the sludge. Federal laws and regulations controlling land disposal practices and incineration had become more rigorous, and ocean disposal had been prohibited by federal regulations. Was the improved wastewater treatment worth the public health risks from the increased sludge? The Government Accountability Office reported the National Academy of Science's belief that the benefits of cleaning our rivers could not be assessed without answering the sludge question. The GAO concluded that the cost of the decade-long cleanup had exceeded the benefits, and no further efforts were justified unless a better effort was made to compare costs to benefits and resolve coordination problems.

When Angus Phillips, *The Washington Post*'s "outdoors" columnist, read about the GAO report, he hit the roof. "The GAO balance sheet boys" nowhere acknowledged that the improved river water has created "a recreational and aesthetic magnet for hundreds of thousands of people," he wrote, including fishermen, picnickers, water skiers, canoers, and kayakers. The GAO "accounting wizards are too tired from staring at numbers to glimpse the broad view." "The Potomac is the people's river. [...] It is inconceivable that anyone will convince them to let the river be destroyed again to save a few pennies in their tax bills."[42]

It is certainly true that the GAO report did not focus on recreational and aesthetic benefits from the cleanup. But economists would be unlikely to jump on Angus Phillips's bandwagon. Phillips thinks he has the broad view because he really understands the benefits, but, since he refuses to seriously consider costs, his view is in fact quite limited.

Looking ahead, the costs of coordination are not going to get any easier. There will still be no jurisdiction that wants a waste treatment facility in its area. And what about the health risks and other costs of disposing of the sludge? Would the financial costs be merely pennies in the tax bills of Washington, DC, locals? A few pennies collected from such folks won't reach a billion dollars. Phillips claimed hundreds of thousands of people benefit from the improved recreational and aesthetic features of a cleaner Potomac River. Let's assume 200,000 people get a large benefit from the *somewhat* cleaner Potomac – a generous assumption, I believe. The benefit would have to be worth $5,000 for each of them if it is going to justify spending $1 billion.

Protecting animals also involves often overlooked opportunity costs. Two economists writing on the Endangered Species Act noted that their profession has "not been especially welcome in this debate about the natural world. Many natural scientists and ecologists view the methods and mindset of economists with grave suspicion."[43] This is surely true. Two world-famous biologists, Edward O. Wilson and Isaac Ehrlich, have suggested that we "cease developing any more relatively undisturbed land."[44] They fully support the principles of the Endangered Species Act, principles declaring that there should be no development that threatens extinction of any species in its natural habitat. But economists are all about trade-offs: trade-offs with other goals. The Endangered Species Act, likely cheered on by a majority of ecologists, does not want to discuss trade-offs. No thinking about opportunity costs, or benefits forgone elsewhere.

The utilitarian argument for this absolutism has weakened over recent decades. It is surely true that study of obscure species has led to the development of medicines that protect human health.[45] But now we can save the DNA of threatened species and avoid the costs of preserving them in their natural habitat.[46] Moreover, in general, species diversity is not declining. In any case, species diversity is not always helpful to humans. For example: "Infectious diseases are most prevalent and virulent in the most diverse tropical areas."[47] Evolution has always obliterated species, and only constant assistance by humans can save some animals, such as New Zealand's flightless birds.[48]

The biologists Wilson and Ehrlich mention the trade-off between preserving nature and building another California shopping center. But sometimes we must make trade-offs between two high-minded uses. In the 1980s the University of Arizona wanted to put three telescopes on the top of Mount Graham. Ecologists thought that this could endanger the habitat of the red squirrel on the mountaintop. Approval for the telescopes was eventually achieved, and the red squirrel population has risen some years and declined more often. An Arizona field supervisor for the wildlife service believes that extirpation of the squirrels in the wild is still possible.

Should no development be allowed if there is any reasonable possibility of a local animal's extinction? If so, the telescopes should never have been constructed. But isn't the human desire to explore our universe also a high-minded goal that deserves to be traded off against some risk to the red squirrels on Mount Graham?[49] Should we spend whatever is needed to ensure that there is no risk at all for *every* endangered species? Economists are more likely than ecologists to take a human-centered approach.

William Baxter, a lawyer who has clearly been influenced by his study of economics, argues that people like to see penguins walking around on rocks, and that's reason enough to promote the survival of penguins.[50] But most people do not have warm feelings about the 200 species of poisonous vipers or the AIDS virus, and Baxter would say we should not feel selfish about our lack of interest in them. The biologist R. Alexander Pyron agrees. He notes that, when beavers make a dam, they cause the extinction of numerous local species. "Humans should feel less shame about molding their environment to suit their survival needs [as the beavers do]."[51]

A society's moral principles sometimes change, but we should at least recognize when they have and be sure that we like the change. In his debates with Stephen Douglas, Abraham Lincoln insisted that human beings had a dignity that other animals lacked. They could make moral choices. They had special talents and responsibilities. "[T]hey are endowed by their Creator with certain unalienable rights, ...among these are Life, Liberty and the pursuit of Happiness."

Douglas maintained that it was no business of others whether a man wanted to bring a pig or slave into the territory of Nebraska. But Lincoln said that, in "the bosoms of the southern people," there was an understanding of the wrong of slavery and of "humanity in the negro." "In 1820 you joined the North, almost unanimously, in declaring the African slave trade piracy" and punishing it with death. "If you did not feel that it was wrong, why did you think men should be hung for it? [...] You never thought of hanging men for catching and selling wild horses." Among you, Lincoln continued, are "native tyrants, known as the 'SLAVE DEALER.'" You will deal with him if you must, but "you despise him utterly... Your children must not play with his; they may rollick freely with the little negroes but not with the slave-dealers' children. [...] Now, why is this? You do not so treat the man who deals in corn, cattle or tobacco."[52]

As Lincoln pointed out, and as Southern whites of that era half acknowledged through their actions, humans are fundamentally different from the rest of the natural world. We should never discount the health of plants and animals; but we should not underestimate the cost of the protecting them, or unthinkingly put their interests above our own.

The bulk of the argument above is certainly not conclusive. Lincoln aside, the core value expressed is submission to the preferences of humans whatever they may be. I believe most economists would be comfortable with that core value. But one Harvard economist, the late Robert Dorfman, thought it insufficient. In this regard he agreed with the Harvard law professor Laurence Tribe when the two discussed natural resources policy in the 1970s. Nonetheless, they had important differences, because Dorfman emphasized the opportunity costs of preserving undeveloped nature in a way that Tribe did not. The two were examining a very large infrastructure proposal to build a dam on Tocks Island in New Jersey. Their debate, expounded below, is as relevant today as it was over 50 years ago.

The proposed dam would provide some flood control, water supply, electric power, and a new recreation facility while destroying the local communities: mainly rural countryside, but countryside where suburbanization was already encroaching. Tribe argues that, for centuries, political thought in the West has had at its core an understanding of transcendence. For example, Aquinas "argued that man excels all animals not by virtue of his power but rather by virtue of the faculty of reason through which he participates in the kingdom of heaven." The radical dichotomy between heaven and earth, soul and body, is apt to regard natural phenomena "as appropriate objects of human manipulation."

Tribe argues that we should consider the alternative of immanence as well as transcendence. Environmentalists' thinking rejects the dominant egoistic style and asks for ecological awareness. He asks that we try to synthesize immanence and transcendence, our roles as "sacred observer" and "grand manipulator." Tribe believes we are doing better than we used to in this regard. Torturing animals was once a frequent occurrence; we now feel an obligation to prevent it. We also have laws about the acceptable use of animals in federal laboratories. He wants this process of increasing respect for living things to continue and somehow be institutionalized. "Every assault on domination is an ever-broadening realization of reciprocity and identity." More generally, we understand that, "once the world is seen as man's playground and ultimately his mirror, nothing remains outside himself against which to test his uniqueness or his strength." Reflection on these matters, Tribe believes, means "preserving intact at least some major areas of real wilderness while we convert others into more Walt Disney Worlds and Coney Islands."[53]

Dorfman calls Tribe's thinking "groping upwards," and he subscribes to the same general philosophy. Dorfman shares John Stuart Mill's conviction that an important consideration for any public undertaking is the degree to which it tends to increase the "sum of good qualities" in the people. But Dorfman argues that the Tocks Island dam would not create another Coney Island; instead, it would create consciousness-expanding opportunities for many more people to enjoy several forms of outdoor recreation. The dam would create a reservoir and park of 47,000 acres, which could accommodate 150,000 visitors. It would create a huge, 37-mile-long lake with beaches that could accommodate 59,000 people. It would be easily reached by car from New York, Newark, and Philadelphia. There would be nature walks, rental canoes, picnic areas, and even a 900-acre wildlife preserve. "And, of course, the family picnic is itself an American tradition with some claim to preservation," Dorfman adds.

Dorfman thinks it unclear which use of the Tocks Island area maximizes the sum of good qualities in the populace. "Untrammeled wilderness" reflects higher values, but so does "inexpensive outdoor recreation for city-dwellers."[54] Dorfman clearly believes that Tribe does not fully consider the opportunity costs of preserving the Tocks Island landscape in its present condition.[*]

---

[*] There is no space for a serious discussion of global warming, but it seems clear that opportunity costs are relevant in responding to it. There are currently alternative ways to impact climate change, with special emphasis on solar, wind, and batteries. But it is widely believed that none of these will have a major impact on climate change. A very different alternative would be dramatic increases in research and development. There is current excitement about kelp farms and direct air capture systems that extract CO_2 from the atmosphere chemically. See Sir David King and Rick Parnell, "Saving the planet would be cheaper than battling Covid," *Washington Post*, September 20, 2020. Sarah Kaplan discusses interest in "Bringing the chill of the cosmos to a warming planet: scientists tap into

Further Reflections

Economists like to stimulate thought about opportunity cost with statements such as "There ain't no such thing as a free lunch" (TANSTAAFL). Their point is that someone has to pay for every lunch, even if the payment is just taking the time and shouldering the expense to grow the vegetables for a salad luncheon. When answering survey questions, unless reminded, respondents often forget that supporting new or expanded government programs means higher taxes or increases in interest on public debt.

Thus, polls have shown that 92 percent of Americans support requiring police officers to wear body cameras, but only 55 percent say they would be willing to pay higher taxes in order to outfit their local police department with body cameras.[55] Similarly, 48 percent of Americans support a universal basic income program, but, among those who support it, 54 percent would not be willing to pay higher personal taxes to fund the program.[56] Even when considering questions of basic health care, the same pattern holds. For example, 77 percent favor a provision of the Affordable Care Act (ACA) that requires insurance companies to cover anyone who applies for insurance, even if they have pre-existing medical conditions, but only 40 percent favor the measure if it means their taxes will increase.[57]

Politicians are also inclined to neglect opportunity costs, because unusually strong support for particular programs brings them many benefits. Programs important to a politician's district will, of course, get special emphasis. But, beyond this, politicians will want the electoral support and psychological pleasures that come from standing for something. They want to be introduced amid applause as, say, "Mr. Solar Energy," "Someone veterans can always count on," or "A dependable friend of occupational safety." The legislator who keeps opportunity cost in mind may have to forsake much of that.[58]

I suspect that many readers will agree with my support of economists on opportunity cost – except when the costs are to business profits. A fuller defense of economists' generally benign attitude toward

a law of physics to create innovative cooling systems," *Washington Post*, October 12, 2020. For different perspectives on climate change by two thoughtful economists, see Gernot Wagner and Martin L. Weitzman, *Climate Shock: The Economic Consequences of a Hotter Planet* (Princeton, NJ: Princeton University Press, 2015); and Matthew E. Kahn, *Climatopolis: How Our Cities Will Thrive in the Hotter Future* (New York: Basic Books, 2010). See also the discussion of technological change in Chapter 4 of this book.

profits is provided in Chapter 4. But there can be no doubt that most economists, whether left of center or right of center, believe that costs to business are generally costs to the broader society. Despite the schoolmarmish tone, Charles Schultze (former head of President Jimmy Carter's Council of Economic Advisers) and Allen Kneese get opportunity costs exactly right when asking their readers to consider the costs of overambitious antipollution goals:

> These costs are not simply numbers for accountants or econo-mists to ponder. They represent the value of the resources that must be channeled into controlling pollution and that will not be available for meeting the other wants of society. In the long run their principal source will not be the profits of industrial firms, but the higher prices and higher taxes that all of us will have to pay. Environmental goals therefore are not the simple consequence of decisions about how clean we want the air and water to be or how "tough" the government should be with particular industries. Establishing them confronts us, especially at the highest levels of control, with a set of hard choices between environmental quality and other aspects of living standards, in which the more we want of one, the less we can have of the other.[59]

2 MARGINALISM

Perhaps, when you were growing up, you gave less than your all to some endeavor. Maybe you missed softball practice some, and practiced the piano less than you should have. A teacher, coach, or parent may have taken you aside and told you, "Anything worth doing is worth doing well." You still like softball and the piano. Sometimes you wish that you had spent more time with them when you were growing up and wish that you had taken to heart the wisdom of your elders. Economists think the "anything worth doing" maxim makes little sense, and you should stop berating yourself. To understand why, you need to know what they have to say about marginalism.

Writing in the eighteenth century, Adam Smith struggled with what came to be called the paradox of value-in-use versus value-in-exchange. To illustrate this paradox, let's compare water and diamonds. Water is necessary for existence and is of enormous value in use. Diamonds are frivolous and clearly not essential. But the price of diamonds per ounce, their value in exchange, is far higher than that of water. Smith wondered: what accounts for this discrepancy? What troubled Smith is now explained in the first chapters of every college freshman's introductory economics text; Smith had failed to distinguish between total and marginal utility. The elaboration of this insight transformed economics in the late nineteenth century, and the fruits of the marginalist revolution continue to set the basic framework for microeconomics.

Most choices in life, economists argue, are made "at the margin." You can live without diamonds, but you can't live without water. Economists would therefore say that the total utility or satisfaction of water exceeds that of diamonds. But rarely do we face such all-or-nothing decisions. All of us, unless we're dying of thirst, would prefer to win a prize of a one-ounce diamond rather than an ounce of water. In other words, marginal utility depends on how much of each we already have. Although the first units of water we consume are of enormous value to us, the last units are not. The utility of each additional unit – "at the margin" – decreases as we consume more and more.

Even if we equate diamonds with foolishness and vanity, we would prefer to win a diamond because we could sell it for far more than a bucket of water. The price of diamonds per ounce is higher because people value them and they are rare and hard to find. Because of their high price, many people do not buy diamonds at all, and others stop buying them even though they would very much enjoy having another. Actual choices, then, reflect not just core values or preferences (water is more important than diamonds) but also relative scarcities. They reflect a weighing of the marginal utility and marginal cost of the opportunities at hand.

In economics the term "marginal" is usually paired with another word or phrase. Marginal benefit or marginal utility is the added satisfaction from consuming a little more of a good or service; and marginal cost is the cost to produce another increment of a good or service. Similarly, the marginal tax rate is the amount a person would have to pay to the Internal Revenue Service (IRS) on an additional dollar of income. And the marginal savings rate is the amount we would save rather than spend from an additional dollar of income.

The concepts of marginalism and opportunity cost flow from the same insights. Marginal cost is defined as opportunity cost, and opportunity cost means alternative benefits – alternative marginal benefits – forgone.

Although the two concepts are closely related, marginalism is better suited to illustrating certain mistakes in theorizing about human nature and in framing some large public policy questions. Economists think that most people's private decisions are based on a comparison of marginal utilities and marginal costs even if the comparisons may be only subconscious. But, when theorizing about human nature, noneconomists often miss the common sense of marginalism.

Human Needs and Marginalism

A. H. Maslow was a psychologist whose work on human motivation has been influential in fields such as industrial psychology. Maslow argued that basic human needs can be catalogued and ranked according to their importance in providing motivation and influencing behavior. He saw physiological needs such as water, food, sex, and sleep as the most fundamental and powerful. When the physiological needs "are relatively well gratified, there then emerges a new set of needs" pertaining to safety. Once the safety needs of security, order, and protection are "fairly well gratified," there then "emerge" love, affection, and belongingness needs. When these have been satisfied, needs for esteem (achievement, reputation, prestige) take over, and these, when satisfied, are replaced by the need for self-actualization, "the desire to become more and more what one is, to become everything that one is capable of becoming."

Maslow did not hold rigidly to this ordering of needs. He said there will be exceptions and that a need does not have to be satisfied 100 percent before the next need emerges. Nevertheless, the view that at any point in time a person is dominated by the most powerful of the unsatisfied needs is his clear theme. Here is how Maslow summarized his argument:

> We have seen that the chief principle of organization in human motivational life is the arrangement of needs in a hierarchy of less or greater priority or potency. The chief dynamic principle animating this organization is the emergence of less potent needs upon gratification of the more potent ones. The physiological needs, when unsatisfied, dominate the organism, pressing all capacities into their service and organizing these capacities so that they may be most efficient in this service. Relative gratification submerges them and allows the next higher set of needs in the hierarchy to emerge, dominate and organize the personality, so that instead of being, e.g., hunger obsessed, it now becomes safety obsessed. The principle is the same for the other sets of needs in the hierarchy, i.e., love, esteem, and self-actualization.[1]

The economists Richard McKenzie and Gordon Tullock have used the insights of marginalism to criticize Maslow's theory.[2] They agree with Maslow that the individual can rank his needs and wants and that he will pursue those avenues that give him the greatest satisfaction. They also note that Maslow seemed to accept the principle of diminishing marginal utility; as hunger and then safety needs are increasingly met, they cease to motivate, and other needs emerge. But Maslow mistakenly thought that one can predict human behavior by looking at the relative strengths of the needs without considering the relative costs of satisfying them.

Even if one assumes that, in some total or absolute sense, the demand for satisfying a basic physiological need is greater than that for satisfying a belongingness need, say, there is no reason to believe that a higher proportion of the physiological need will actually be satisfied. In developing countries there are many people who satisfy a higher percentage of their total love and belongingness needs than of their physiological or safety needs.[3]

The same could probably be said of some low-income families in the United States – or, for that matter, the members of a properly motivated military unit. And many who strive for esteem nevertheless feel vulnerable and unsafe, worried about their health, nuclear destruction, global warming, or violent crime. Such worries, even if fairly strong, may not dominate behavior, because people do not think they can do much to alleviate these concerns at reasonable cost.

The demand for satisfying needs, in other words, is not completely insensitive to price. How much we try to satisfy our total need for anything will, in every instance, depend on the costs of doing so, as well as on our fundamental needs and beliefs. Moreover, our needs are not considered separately but in conjunction with each other. A need for belonging may lead you to consume kosher food or to put on a Chicago Cubs cap.

In some cases, a comparison of the marginal utility and marginal cost of different alternatives may lead us to give priority to a relatively small "total utility" need rather than a relatively large and powerful one even though the latter is not close to being fully satisfied. And, if the costs of meeting needs change sufficiently, choices and behavior can change substantially while basic needs and preferences remain the same.

Health Needs and the Demand for Medical Care

The marginalist insight can illuminate some weaknesses in the health policy outlook of those whose position is determined by the idea of medical needs. One view of medical needs holds, in the spirit of

Maslow, that they dominate behavior. Doctors are not like books and movies; they give no positive pleasure. No one *wants* to see a doctor. But if a person is sick and needs to see a doctor, it is often said, nothing will keep him from seeing one. In this view, demand is almost completely insensitive to price; it is either there, or it is not. Thus, changes in insurance-deductible provisions or the coinsurance percentage rate paid by consumers will not effectively limit demand; nor should they.

The available evidence gives little support for such a position. From the point of view of the consumer at least, a significant portion of demand for medical care gives small benefits. The benefits are poorly indicated by thinking about total utility – that is, how important health is.

Economists have observed the effects of insurance policy changes on the demand for health care. One experiment asked a group of California Medicaid beneficiaries to pay $1 for their first two office visits each month, while a similar group continued to receive completely free service. This modest charge reduced office visits by 8 percent.[4] Other studies have found that even small changes in time cost can have an effect. For example, when the health facility at one college was moved so that it took 20 minutes rather than five to ten to walk there, student visits fell by nearly 40 percent.[5] Whether the health services forgone in these cases were necessary remains an open question, but surely the behavior of the potential patients was not dominated by their health needs.

A more sophisticated version of the medical needs position holds that certain fundamental goods such as "health, education, food, housing, and clothing" are "essential needs," to which there should be "a social, institutional right."[6] The Harvard law professor Charles Fried has made this argument well. Fried believes that the economist's tendency to talk about ethics only in terms of the individual's right to a societally determined fair share of general resources is inadequate.[7] He maintains that

> distributional schemes would not (if equality were our canon of just distribution) be satisfied by an equal distribution of money with which the chronically ill could purchase medicines while others purchased holidays, opera tickets, or other luxury goods. Good health is a need precisely in the sense that we have or we seek objective measures of good health. We try to assure this

objective good, the satisfaction of this objective need apart from, or without prejudice to, the balance of an individual's distributive share.[8]

Fried seems reluctant to say that health and other fundamental needs deserve absolute priority over other goods. He also acknowledges that there will be great complexities in working out the details of his idea. Still, he treats the health need as far easier to define than seems warranted. Fried seems to think of serious, medically treatable illness when he pictures health demand and medical expenditures. So too does the president of a religious association who has written that health care is an "essential community service. It is essential because persons requiring healthcare have no options other than to seek healthcare."[9]

But, again, those who have looked closely at the question find that the marginal utility of much spending for medical services does not belong in a fundamental need category. The problem, moreover, is not just patients' unnecessary use of a heavily subsidized system, but doctors' disagreement concerning the presence of a health need.

Michael Cooper, a British economist and a pioneer in the development of health economics, found that hospital surgeons in the United States referred twice as many patients for surgery as did their British counterparts. In the United Kingdom, decisions about referring patients to a specialist or for hospitalization also showed inexplicable variation between regions. Cooper presented this information as part of his assessment of the 1946 socialized British Health Service Act, which established access to health care resources as a "human right" of every person doctors believed had a need. He concluded: "The conception of sickness as an unambiguous and absolute state led to the false hope that unmet need could be abolished. In practice, sickness has been found to be a relative state capable of almost infinite interpretation by both potential patients and the medical profession."[10]

Indeed, from the patient's point of view, the potential for entry into the category of need is enormous. Large numbers of people do not feel entirely well. An English study found that 95 percent of the people in one community considered themselves unwell during the 14 days prior to questioning. A survey in Rochester, New York, found that adults suffered from at least one disorder on 20 percent of the 28 days covered.[11] In the absence of money costs, queues, or other allocative devices, many of those who are not now seeing doctors would do so.

Doctors know that their science is uncertain, and, if there is no cost to them or their patient, many will do something. After all, further tests *might* find something, and extra days of hospitalization *might* prevent complications.

Cooper noted that both demand and need tend to grow in line with provision. Doctors react to any expansion in supply by realigning their conception of need. Thus, one study of acute care hospitals found that both admissions and length of stay increased with bed availability. It could not discover a level of bed provision that would have fully satiated doctors' demands.[12]

Some of the studies discussed here are old. But human nature hasn't changed, and the insights of marginalism are just as important today. According to the economist Robin Hanson, "We see at best only weak aggregate relations between health and medicine, in contrast to apparently strong aggregate relations between health and many other factors, such as exercise, diet, sleep, smoking, pollution, climate, and social status. Cutting half of medical spending would seem to cost little in health, and yet would free up vast resources for other health and utility gains."[13]

In an article published in the *Journal of the American Medical Association* in 2012, the midpoint estimate for waste in the US health system is 34 percent of total spending and the high end is 47 percent.[14] The Institute of Medicine puts the level of waste in context by comparing it to total expenditures in other areas: "Unnecessary health care costs and waste exceed the 2009 budget for the Department of Defense by more than $100 billion" and "could pay the salaries of all of the nation's first response personnel, including firefighters, police officers, and emergency medical technicians, for more than 12 years."[15]

In 2008 Oregon decided to expand Medicaid but received far more applications than it could accept. It randomly chose some of the applicants to receive Medicaid coverage. This made possible a powerful natural experiment in which the Medicaid "winners'" medical care usage and health outcomes could be compared to those who were not selected.

A leading article in the *New England Journal of Medicine* found that the "winners" used about 35 percent more medical service than the "losers," who did not receive Medicaid. Financial strain was reduced for the winners, but there was a very modest difference in health. For example, the study found "no significant effect of Medicaid coverage on the prevalence or diagnosis of hypertension or high cholesterol levels or on the use of medication for these conditions."[16]

A number of people believed that passage of the Affordable Care Act ("Obamacare") would lead many patients who used expensive emergency rooms for health care to instead see primary care physicians. President Obama himself often used this argument when promoting the Affordable Care Act, evidenced in 2009 remarks on the need to make sure that people are getting "the care they need and the checkups they need and the screenings they need before they get sick – which will save all of us money and reduce pressures on emergency rooms all across the country."[17] This did not happen in Oregon. Instead, the winners used emergency rooms 40 percent *more* than the losers did. It seems that, "when people are insured, they use *all* types of medical services more often."[18]

Nothing said so far is meant to argue that the concept of medical need is meaningless. Good health is not simply subjective, and, like water, it is more important than diamonds. As Fried argues, when physicians can significantly help the seriously ill, the needs of such patients should have a special claim on resources. But most of the time they already do. In any case, when considering whether all those with medical complaints should have free and immediate access to physicians, one should not think mainly about a catastrophically ill patient with low income. The problems that such patients face are very real, but they could be resolved with coinsurance for all but the destitute.

The more typical patient, whose demand would be restricted by coinsurance or deductibles, is one who suffers from a fairly minor disorder, who has an ailment with uncertain causes, or who faces slim odds of successful treatment. When younger, I was such a patient, and I would frequently see a sports medicine doctor and a physical therapist about my tennis elbow. They would subject me to electrical stimulation and therapeutic ultrasound therapies. I was never sure that either did anything to get me back on the court any sooner. But I loved tennis, and it was worth $10 a visit (my co-pay) if it might speed up the natural healing process. I would never have paid the full cost of the treatment. My fundamental health was never at issue.

Many doctors will want to use scarce resources to the point where the marginal utility of further expenditures equals zero ("everything possible for my patients"), not to the point where it equals opportunity cost. One should encourage doctors to do so only if good health is the only important component of a good life and if greater access to physician services is the only route to better health.

Setting Priorities and Marginalism

Government leaders and agency heads often talk of the need to set priorities so as to give direction to their activities. Even though the setting of priorities is seen as little more than common sense, it often violates marginalism.

Economists believe that even good answers to certain grand questions give little guidance for rational policy choices. What is more important: health or recreation? Clean air or economic growth? Natural-setting recreational opportunities for some or developed recreational opportunities for far more? Marginalism suggests that our concern should be with proportion, not rank. If forced to choose, everyone would find health more important than recreation, but this finding does not imply that all swimming pool diving boards should be removed because a few people die in diving accidents. Similarly, we want cleaner air *and* economic growth, natural-setting recreational opportunities *and* developed ones. Reasonable policy choices require knowledge of how well we are now doing in all these areas and of the alternative opportunities available.

In addition, costs must be taken into account. Even the biggest *remaining* problem may not deserve most of the extra money. One writer, for example, argues that early deaths of the young are our greatest lifesaving problem, and therefore the health budget should emphasize preventing the largest killers of the young, such as accidents and suicides.[19] But, even if one accepts this writer's values, his policy conclusions do not follow.

We may not know how to prevent accidents and suicides at reasonable cost, but perhaps a medical breakthrough has made it possible to cure at low cost a disease that is the sixth leading cause of death among the young. We would then save more lives among the young if we devoted more of our resources to their sixth largest health problem rather than their first or second. Marginalism requires looking into the details – looking into the costs and benefits of particular opportunities.

Social scientists who are not economists sometimes want a community's budget policy to be heavily influenced by poll results about the major problems facing the community or the functional areas the public thinks should be cut in times of fiscal stringency. Economists are skeptical. When consumers are asked such questions, they are almost never provided with detailed information on probable effects and costs. Thus, respondents usually look to total utility when giving their answers, and cuts in lifesaving departments such as police and fire receive almost no support.

In 1978 California voters passed Proposition 13, which severely limits the magnitude of legal property tax increases; a poll at the time found that only 8 percent of Californians thought that any cuts should be made in police budgets, and only 6 percent wanted any cuts in fire departments.[20] But perhaps cuts in the police budget could be accomplished by replacing police officers doing desk work with less expensive clerks, and fire department cuts may involve replacing some full-time firefighters with supplementary reservists, fully trained and paid a monthly retainer and an hourly wage while fighting fires. The public cannot be expected to be aware of these possibilities, and thus the most common types of polls will tell little about their true preferences.

In 1974 the Federal Aviation Administration had new leadership eager to take charge of the agency by reshaping priorities, setting and achieving quantitative objectives, and systematically using cost–benefit analysis when deciding levels of program funding. The FAA implemented the changes in a way that placed the priority- and objective-setting processes in conflict with cost–benefit analysis, a fact that went unrecognized because of the neglect of marginalism.

The FAA first developed objectives it thought could be achieved over the next two years, such as reducing air carrier accidents by 6 percent, general aviation accidents by 10 percent, delays by 25 percent, and noise by 10 percent. But, in order to be consistent with marginalism, the establishment of even one such objective or priority would have to be preceded by some weighing of the marginal gains and marginal costs of expanding each of the programs dealing with the objective in question as compared to the marginal gains and costs of expanding programs advancing other agency objectives. We can know how high to set any one objective only if we know what we give up in progress toward other objectives.

Moreover, it makes little sense to say that achieving one of these objectives has a higher priority than achieving another. Think back to Maslow's hierarchy of needs, and the economists' criticism of it. Chances are that some of the programs aimed at all three of the principal problems – safety, congestion, and noise – will provide high marginal benefits compared to marginal costs. Thus, a list of priorities guided by the marginalist insight would have to be incredibly detailed.

The highest net benefit program, or the one with the highest ratio of benefits to costs, might aim at congestion, the second highest at safety; the third might aim, again, at congestion, the fourth at noise. The resulting list of agency priorities would thus be terribly complicated: "Our top priority is reducing congestion by about 0.4 percent" (by implementing the highest net benefit program, say by charging more for peak times for takeoffs); "our second-highest priority is reducing general aviation accidents by 0.8 percent" (by implementing the second-highest net benefit program); "the third-highest priority is reducing congestion by another 0.9 percent" (by implementing the third-highest net benefit program, which is also the second-best congestion program). Although this second-best congestion program reduces more than twice as much congestion as the best, it is ranked second because it costs four times as much as the best, and so on.

Once objectives were set, they would have to be updated continually. If the traffic at an airport that was supposed to get a landing aid should fall substantially, the cost of the landing aid might then exceed the benefits. It would mean the landing aid was no longer justified. When it was abandoned, safety, and perhaps delay reduction, goals would fall and priorities might have to change to take account of the abandonment of this project. Similarly, if an increase in development costs should make a planned piece of equipment inadvisable, again, goals and priorities would have to change.[21]

Economists want program goals that can be changed easily as circumstances change. It is not a philosophy likely to appeal to politicians, because, to the public, it suggests weakness and indecisiveness. At the start of his presidency, Jimmy Carter faced both high unemployment and rising inflation. At first he supported a $50 tax rebate so as to address the unemployment problem; but, less than three months into his presidency, his economists became much more alarmed about inflationary pressures. So Carter dropped his support for the $50 tax rebate.

In a press conference after this decision, reporters noted that Democrats in Congress were left with "political egg" on their faces by this reversal; some had succumbed to pressure to support the rebate and then a few months later had to explain to their constituents why they had reversed their position. Republicans in Congress piled in by supporting a permanent tax cut rather than the temporary rebate that Carter had proposed. They could say that they were not wishy-washy like the Democrats.[22] But Carter was doing what economists want political leaders to do; he was willing to change policy as circumstances changed.

The Costs of Marginalism

There are costs to the kind of calculation inherent in marginalism, costs apparent to the most thoughtful of economists. Kenneth Boulding once observed that it is profoundly unromantic: "No one would want his daughter to marry an economic man, one who counted every cost and asked for every reward, [and] was never afflicted with mad generosity or uncalculating love."[23] Marginalism is also unheroic. The military's motto, "Theirs not to reason why, theirs but to do and die," is very far from the economist's view of the world. So too is the prayer of Saint Francis: "To give and not to count the cost, to labor and ask for no reward." Boulding reminds us of the powerful critique of marginalism in Wordsworth's sonnet, "Inside of King's College Chapel, Cambridge":

> Tax not the royal Saint with vain expense,
> With ill-matched aims the Architect who planned –
> Albeit labouring for a scanty band
> Of white-robed Scholars only – this immense
> And glorious Work of fine intelligence!
> Give all thou canst; high Heaven rejects the lore
> Of nicely-calculated less or more;
> So deemed the man who fashioned for the sense
> These lofty pillars, spread that branching roof
> Self-poised, and scooped into ten thousand cells,
> Where light and shade repose, where music dwells
> Lingering – and wandering on as loth to die;
> Like thoughts whose very sweetness yieldeth proof
> That they were born for immortality.

In principle, economic welfare theory offers no objection to uncalculating dedication to a single end. As we shall see in Chapter 7, it has nothing to say about the best end or ends for individuals to pursue. But marginalism and opportunity cost show their full power only when the ends are plural, and for most people they are. Because economic calculation is so useful most of the time, it can become a habit. And, despite its many uses, the habit of looking at the world through the eyes of marginalism and opportunity cost could lead us to forget that single-mindedness, though uncommon, can produce great results. A society without some single-minded people loses sight of an important aspect of human nobility.

As Alexis de Tocqueville noted, democratic, egalitarian societies are quick to tax with vain expense those who give all they can. There are not, as in aristocracies, tight groups of artisans who honor the most skillful of their number, nor persons "who derive from their superior and hereditary position a taste for what is extremely well made and lasting." Instead, there is "a multitude of persons whose wants are above their means and who are very willing to take up with imperfect satisfaction rather than abandon the object of their desires." Artisans and artists soon learn to be "sparing of their powers," to "remain in a state of accomplished mediocrity" far from the limits of their art.[24]

David Ramazani, a Charlottesville craftsman, was lucky enough to find a wealthy investor who wanted him to build the most beautiful desk he could. Ramazani found a 400-pound piece of walnut – 6 feet 3 inches wide, 9 feet long and 2 inches thick. After building the desk, he spent 50 hours hand-rubbing 23 coats of antique oil into it. His shoulders became so sore that he had a hard time sleeping, but "having the time to find that deep beauty has given me great joy." The top was "the most magnificent piece of wood I've ever seen. [...] I couldn't build it better. The one thing that drove me crazy when I was working for other people was that they would always try to restrict the amount of excellence I could put into something. It was always cut corners and rush it out."[25]

A person totally dedicated to philosophy, to art, or to the worship of God has no need of marginalism. Although he must manage his time and resources, food, for example, is not an end but a constraint that must be satisfied so that he may continue his only valued activity. Tocqueville reflects on Pascal's ability

> to rally all the powers of his mind...for the better discovery of the most hidden things of the Creator. When I see him, as it were, tear his soul from all the cares of life to devote it wholly to

these researches and, prematurely snapping the links that bind the body to life, die of old age before forty, I stand amazed and perceive that no ordinary cause is at work to produce efforts so extraordinary.[26]

Tocqueville doubted that such passions, "at once so rare and so productive," would grow as easily in democratic communities.

Further Reflections

The costs of nicely calculated less or more suggest that a good education should include much more than economics. Reflecting on these costs may have other implications for public policy as well. On occasion, statesmen may want to carve out some projects for which they abandon nicely calculated less or more and tell their artists or professionals, "Forget your budget; make it as beautiful as you can."

We should not feel the need to cut corners in deciding on the size of the Lincoln Memorial. Nevertheless, whatever its limited usefulness for philosophers, artists, and members of religious orders, marginalism must be one important part of a policy analyst's or statesman's perspective. The statesman's art is prudence or the use of reason and forethought to skillfully select and use the best means to achieve good ends.

And, for the statesman in peacetime, the ends must be plural. Politics remains the architectonic art. The engineer, naturalist, librarian, prison doctor, and traffic safety expert still come to the politician with their competing claims for resources. The politician who distinguishes marginal and total utility will do a better job of judging these claims.

The temptation not to distinguish the two will be very great. When thinking about government programs, the public is likely to ignore opportunity costs and see the policy world through the lens of total utility. The people will oppose cuts in the police and fire department budgets, will believe that environmental standards cannot be too high, and will support further environmental improvements regardless of cost.

It is unlikely that the voters will ever be deeply knowledgeable about public affairs. The politician who sets his priorities, who focuses on and accomplishes a few things, will not only get reelected but will boost public morale and give people more confidence in their ability to control events. The complexity of the marginalist perspective and the necessity to qualify, to back and fill as circumstances and technology change, would, if presented unadorned, leave the people with a demoralizing sense of governmental drift and indecision. The tension between marginalism and politics requires that the statesman's art include rhetoric. The statesman must not ignore marginalism. Even accomplishing a few publicly supported objectives will not yield reelection if it is accompanied by significant deterioration of other public services or by a substantial increase in taxes or prices.

The principal problem to date has not been the lack of rhetorical skills through which knowledgeable politicians could make their marginalist insights compatible with public misunderstanding. The principal problem has been politicians' own ignorance of marginalism. Unfortunately, institutions that are potentially capable of overcoming this ignorance are poorly equipped to do so. Allen Kneese and Charles Schultze have noted that most congressional staffs are chosen for their negotiating skills, and few have much knowledge of economics.[27] And Washington political reporters do not have much knowledge of the subject either.

The Nobel laureate James Buchanan suggested that an economist can be distinguished from a noneconomist by his reaction to the maxim mentioned at the start of this chapter.[28] Another economist actually polled a group of economists to judge their agreement or disagreement with this and four other maxims. "Anything worth doing. . ." was by far the least popular, with 74 percent of respondents disagreeing.[29] Thus, it was a keen appreciation of marginalism that led McKenzie and Tullock to entitle a book chapter "Anything worth doing is not necessarily worth doing well."[30] A careful weighing of marginal cost implies that we should use well the time and money we devote to a task, but we should rarely do as much as interested professionals think necessary.

So, to return to our beginning, you may have been wise to miss your softball practice. Your softball may already have been pretty good, but your piano playing needed a lot of work. You could not *maximize* the time you devoted to *each* activity. In any case, you might remember that you had come to love tennis, and those teammates wanted you on the court more just as your softball pals wanted you on their field more. At the time, your marginal utility from an extra hour on the tennis court was greater than your marginal utility from an extra hour on the softball field.

3 ECONOMIC INCENTIVES

with Brooke Henderson

Economists can provide insights into two main areas of policy design. The first, whether the benefits of certain laws and regulations outweigh their costs, is briefly discussed in the addendum to Chapter 6. In this chapter, we focus on the benefit of using incentive-based approaches to achieve policy goals.

A landmark showing this orientation was Charles Schultze's Godkin Lecture series delivered at Harvard University in 1976. The lectures attracted the attention of the newly elected president, Jimmy Carter, and helped convince Carter to make Schultze the chairman of his Council of Economic Advisers. They were later turned into an influential book, *The Public Use of Private Interest*, which nicely synthesized an important theme in contemporary economists' criticisms of a host of current government policies.

In his Godkin Lecture series, Schultze argues that the growing industrialization, urbanization, and interdependence of society have generated problems that require a more active government than we have known throughout most of our history. To perform these new tasks we have passed detailed laws and adopted detailed bureaucratic regulations. Such "command-and-control" methods worked well when the typical governmental task was to build a dam or mail out a check, but they are a costly and ineffective way to deal with pervasive problems such as air and water pollution.

Schultze notes that we have largely ignored an alternative method of collective intervention: market-like incentives, such as taxes and subsidies, that make private interests more congruent with public goals. We acknowledge the power of markets and economic incentives to foster steadily improving private-sector efficiency and a higher standard of living. And "we would laugh if someone suggested that the best way to reduce labor input per unit of production was to set up a government agency to specify labor input in detail for each industry. But that is precisely how we go about trying to reduce environmental damage and industrial accidents."[1]

Economic Incentives and the Environment

Weaknesses in the Current Regulatory System

The environmental movement of the 1960s led to legislation that set strict standards and rigid deadlines to be enforced by the Environmental Protection Agency (EPA), established in 1970.[2] Since then, however, the Congress, the courts, and the EPA have continually ignored or postponed deadlines and revised timetables for motor vehicles, stationary sources, and overall air quality. Lester Lave and Gilbert Omenn note that this "charade reached its culmination in the conclusion of the National Commission on Air Quality that stringent standards should continue to be set without regard to costs or feasibility but that federal deadlines should be removed altogether!"[3]

To illustrate the complexity of trying to protect the environment through laws and standards, consider the following. Within 15 years of the establishment of the EPA, it was tasked with regulating more than 200,000 existing stationary sources subject to air emission limitations. In most cases, these firms were certified as compliant on the basis of their own reports. Not in compliance were over 1,400 major sources of serious pollution. These uncertified major sources used the courts to fight the EPA regulations with great vigor.[4]

The command-and-control approach to regulation was as complicated for water as for air pollution. This legislation mixed tens of billions of dollars of grants for the construction of municipal waste treatment plants with the same sort of detailed effluent emission standards for individual sources as in the clean air program. It was originally hoped that the EPA could avoid setting standards for individual plant processes by setting national standards differentiated by industry. But the National Commission on Water Quality noted that there was too much complexity, variation, and change within modern production processes for this to have been possible. The result was "a staggering array of technical distinction and subcategorization which has still been inadequate to make the guidelines the kind of equitable, unchallengeable regulations the framers of the law anticipated."[5]

For example, the promulgated guidelines for the Canned and Preserved Seafood Processing Point Source Category contained 33 subcategories for items such as conventional blue crab, mechanized blue crab, and nonremote Alaskan crab meat. There were also 35 subcategories for iron and steel manufacturing and 66 for canned and preserved fruits and vegetables. Despite the elaborate subcategories, the EPA has still had to tell its regulators that "these limitations should be adjusted for certain plants in the industry."[6]

Senator Edmund Muskie played a central role in passing the United States' first environmental standards and subsequent amendments in the 1970s. Bernard Asbell shadowed Senator Muskie during the year the landmark 1970 environmental law was created and wrote a book about this experience. In the negotiations over one of the relaxations of the congressionally mandated standards for new automobiles, evidence that the auto companies' technical staffs withheld information at the behest of their policy staffs was clear.

At one meeting a Chrysler vice president was surprisingly candid: "They're all – all the companies including us are trying to tell you we're making progress. But we're afraid to say it. We're all worried that if we sound hopeful, what will the damned standards be tomorrow?" Although Muskie was a "get tough" type and had reports from the National Academy of Sciences and other sources at his disposal, it was clear that he did not believe he knew as much as auto company executives. At one meeting he told their representatives, "You fellows in the industry have got to look into your own hearts and ask yourselves what you can really do and how we can devise something that will really give assurance that you'll do it."[7] The EPA's knowledge disadvantage on most of the thousands of smaller decisions that they have to make is even greater than it is on the auto pollution question.

The Promising Power of Incentives

Economists suggest two approaches to pollution control, either of which would be preferable to the administrative quagmire of the original system. One is to tax pollution. A tax per pound of sulfur (or other pollutant) emitted could be imposed on power plants and other industrial firms. A tax could also be imposed on automobile emissions, based on each car's expected lifetime emissions or on actual emission levels (as judged by periodic inspections) multiplied by the number of miles driven. Many economists would argue that the tax should be set at a level that approximates the harm a marginal unit of effluent does to the public.[8] But the tax could be set higher, without compromising the efficiency advantages of achieving more pollution reduction for a given cost (or, if one prefers, the same reduction for less cost) that this approach provides over regulatory mandates.

The second suggested approach is tradable discharge licenses, also known as cap-and-trade. The regulatory authorities could determine the total amount of emissions to be allowed in an air shed or river basin and then issue permits or licenses for such emissions. The permits would be bought and sold like industrial property. Those planning to build a new plant would negotiate to purchase discharge licenses from existing firms the same way they now negotiate to buy the property for the plant. Under this method, regulators can still set a maximum allowable level of pollution for a particular region while using market forces to incentivize pollutant reduction.[9]

Both of these mechanisms have an overwhelming advantage over a command-and-control system like the one set up in the 1970s, thanks to their ability to rechannel self-interest so that it becomes congruent with the public interest. Emissions become costly to a firm. They result either in higher taxes (under the first scheme) or in tying up money in costly emissions permits (under the second). Even firms that already own emissions permits would be incentivized to decrease their pollution in order to gain revenue by selling or leasing the unused portion of their emission permits.[10]

With such economic incentives, many firms would find it more profitable to clean up than to delay cleaning up by fighting the EPA on questions on which the firms have a knowledge advantage. Recognizing this advantage, the EPA has gradually increased its use of incentive-based programs. But the EPA's website acknowledges the inefficiency of its current mix of programs, saying: "Hybrid approaches are not always the most economically efficient approach because either the level of abatement or the cost of the policy is greater than what would be achieved through the use of a market-based incentive approach."[11]

The United States encourages so much litigation about regulatory matters that it would be folly to assume that all the litigation costs in the current administrative snarl would be eliminated with effluent taxes or marketable licenses. But at least things should improve. As it stands now, if delay saves a company more than it loses in court costs, the company has an incentive to appeal at every stage even if it thinks it will finally lose. Under the tax scheme it would owe back taxes if it lost. There would also be less to litigate.

Since the EPA would not be requiring each firm to meet a certain standard for emission or to install a particular technology by a particular date, the courts would not have to determine whether the EPA's rules for each firm were reasonable. The court need simply find that the tax reflects the agency's or Congress's best judgment about the harm done to society by the firm's pollution, and it would be up to the firm to decide whether it wishes to eliminate some or all of the effluent or pay the tax. Alternatively, the court might find that the Congress has determined that it wants air or water of a given cleanliness, and to achieve that level of cleanliness requires limiting emissions to the level indicated by the emissions licenses. If a firm believes it must go to unreasonable and disproportionately great expense to clean up, the court can point out that the firm has the alternative of buying a marketable license from one of the firms with proportionately lower cleanup costs.[12]

As Kneese and Schultze argue, for any given level of tax or effluent licenses,

> firms with low costs of control would remove a larger percentage than would firms with higher costs – precisely the situation needed to achieve a least-cost approach to reducing pollution for the economy as a whole. Firms would tend to choose the least expensive methods of control, whether treatment of wastes, modification in production processes, or substitution of raw materials that had less serious polluting consequences. Further, the kinds of products whose manufacture entailed a lot of pollution would become more expensive and would carry higher prices than those that generated less, so consumers would be induced to buy more of the latter.[13]

Some studies have found that such incentive-based schemes could achieve equivalent air quality for as little as 10 percent of the costs of existing methods. These findings are perfectly plausible. For example, one study in St. Louis found that particulate emissions could be removed from one boiler in a paper products factory for $4 a ton whereas to remove a ton of emissions from one brewery's boiler would cost $600 per ton. Similarly, one St. Louis power plant could remove emissions for $5 a ton, but for another the cost was $909 per ton.[14]

In these situations, the paper products factory and the first St. Louis power plant would be motivated to pay $4 and $5 per ton to reduce their pollution in order to sell their emission permits to the brewery and the second power plant, which would value these permits up to $600 and $909 per ton, respectively. In a tax scheme instead of a permit system, the low-cost companies would find it cheaper to reduce pollution while the high-cost companies would find it cheaper to pay the tax. In the end, the companies end up reducing pollution while paying money that can then be used to society's benefit elsewhere. Additionally, all four companies make these decisions on their own without the need for costly government analysis, regulation, and court adjudication, or inefficient mandates that view all four companies as the same.[15]

Economists explain that there is evidence that pollution taxes will not just be paid and passed on to consumers, leaving all the firms to pollute as before. Such taxes will reduce pollution.[16] Economists wonder how they could help but do so. Business leaders will sell more of their product and make more money if they can keep costs and prices down. If a business can avoid $1 million in annual taxes by making a technological change that costs $2 million, it will do so because the investment will very soon have paid for itself.

Just as a business looks for ways to minimize what it must pay for electricity or raw materials, so it will look for ways to minimize expenses from dealing with the pollution problem. If it blithely pays the tax and passes the expense on to consumers even though it would be cheaper to clean up, it risks losing business to competitors whose prices can be lower because they behave more efficiently. Furthermore, investors are increasingly considering environmental sustainability when making investment decisions.[17]

At this place in the argument, my students often say: "But you have chosen convenient numbers. Suppose the cost of technological changes is $20 million, not $2 million. Then the taxes will not induce the firm to clean up; it will just pass the tax on to consumers." So it will. But the absolutely crucial element the St. Louis firms' cost figures clearly demonstrate is that no two firms are the same. For some firms, my example will be more appropriate; for others, my students' will. But taxes will definitely lead some firms to clean up.

These firms will be the ones whose costs to clean up are low. If not enough firms clean up, we can raise the taxes. Under the tax scheme, the high-cost firms will, it is true, just continue to pollute as before. They will have purchased a "license to pollute." But, after all, even under the current standards approach, firms have the right to emit pollutants up to the standard; they are already, in effect, given a license to pollute. Economists ask why environmentalists should object to having businesses pay for the polluting they still do rather than letting them do it for free!

The rigidities in the "legislate and mandate" approach were illustrated in the case of Procter and Gamble's Port Ivory plant. In 1980 the company wanted to save 9 million gallons of oil a year by replacing its existing boilers with ones that would burn wood waste. Because of difficulties in proving that the area's carbon monoxide level met the national air quality standards, the EPA did not give final approval for the project until February 1982. Not in dispute was the fact that, although the new plant would emit more carbon monoxide, it would emit fewer sulfur oxides and nitrogen oxides. But the either/or EPA thresholds do not give the flexibility to take this into account, nor do they allow for consideration of energy conservation gains or Procter and Gamble's losses from the delay in its cost savings (over $1 million).[18] The two incentive schemes would give this flexibility without the need for a special EPA determination in this or other particular cases.

In the long run the pollution problem will become overwhelming without improved technology. New technology is even more crucial to address climate change. But, under a command-and-control system, the polluting plants' owners have no incentive at all to develop a fundamentally cleaner manufacturing process since they would thereby hand regulatory authorities the means to impose higher costs on them. Existing standards allow older plants to emit more pollution because the costs of controlling that pollution are much higher for them than for newer plants.

Because of this disparity in standards, plant owners have an incentive to fix up old plants instead of building new plants, which delays the implementation of even improved *known* technology. Once they are in compliance, plant owners have no incentive to further reduce pollution. With the incentive schemes, the possibility of increasing profits by reducing pollutants remains as long as any taxes are paid or capital is tied up in marketable effluent licenses – that is, as long as any pollutant remains. Moreover, the standards approach also discourages innovations because it provides no incentive to develop something that might bring cost savings and dramatic reductions in two effluents if it also entailed an increase in the amount of a third. The incentive systems are flexible enough to encourage a firm to proceed with such innovations.

The incentive schemes would not be simple. Monitoring of important sources of pollution would have to improve. Some variation in taxes or licensed levels depending on location and time of year would probably be advisable.[19] But parallel political and monitoring problems have also plagued the standards approach. And, if opportunity costs are to count at all, the standards too should more closely reflect location and seasonal differences than they have in the past.

Reasons for the Slow Adoption of Incentive-Based Approaches

The business world knows that some environmentalists act as if they prefer a pure law to pure air. And they know what to say to them and to their supporters. Thus, with big, wide eyes, Dan Cannon of the National Association of Manufacturers told a 1976 congressional seminar that "industry needs clear, precise standards that tell us we must maintain a certain quality of environment to maintain health. Surely you wouldn't let a guy violate public health standards by paying a tax?"[20] With the prevalence of the "purity test" in today's political climate, inefficient decisions continue to flourish.

In 2019 *The New York Times* reported that 97 percent of climate scientists believe that the burning of fossil fuels is contributing to an accelerating warming of the global climate.[21] Accordingly, many environmentalists call for a rapid end to the use of gasoline-powered cars. The United Kingdom, France, India, and Norway have plans to completely ban the sale of new gas or diesel vehicles by 2040 or sooner, with at least eight additional countries also setting sales targets for electric vehicles.[22]

Such laws are not favored among economists. As with other standards approaches, there are no incentives to surpass the standard. These kinds of laws do not reward companies or consumers for getting rid of gasoline vehicles before 2040, and by 2040 electric vehicles may not even be the best way to reduce pollution. A tax on pollution – it is pollution that the public is concerned with! – primes the market to seek pollution reduction in efficient ways without government bureaucrats picking one pollutant reduction method to support.

Following such a single-focus approach, a "green" bank in San Francisco, committed to financing environmentally conscious ventures, refused to provide a loan to a gas station to fund the installation of solar panels.[23] But expecting all gas stations to rapidly cease functioning seems costly and unlikely; shifting to solar power to run the pumps of some may be a feasible change, however, and with proper economic incentives many more companies would be incentivized to search for such changes.

Political Feasibility of a Carbon Tax

In early 2017 representatives of the Climate Leadership Council met with White House officials to propose replacing the majority of climate policies enacted during President Obama's administration with a national carbon tax. This tax would start at $40 per ton of carbon emitted, and its revenues would be returned to the American people via quarterly checks from the Social Security Administration. Although the Climate Leadership Council includes three former GOP cabinet secretaries – James A. Baker, Henry Paulson, and George P. Shultz – and two former GOP Council of Economic Advisers chairs – Martin Feldstein and Greg Mankiw – this policy faced great opposition from congressional Republicans opposed to *any* tax increases and a Republican president, Donald Trump, who publicly supports an increase in the domestic extraction of fossil fuels.[24]

Historically, Democrats and environmentalists have also been opposed to pollution taxes. The flavor of the opposition of most environmental lobbyists to the tax approach is best seen in the way they scornfully say, "I want to get rid of pollution, not license it."[25] Senator Muskie spoke for this view on the floor of the Senate in 1971 when he said, "We cannot give anyone the option of polluting for a fee."[26]

In his book *What Price Incentives?*, Steven Kelman argues that the environmentalists' "license-to-pollute" retort reflects incompletely developed intuitive concerns that the economists' responses cannot so quickly dispose of. Kelman notes that environmentalists are quite concerned with developing an environmental ethic. They want to heighten the public's environmental consciousness. For these reasons, they want to stigmatize polluting behavior and avoid doing anything that might lower the value the public places on clean air and water. But a price for pollution may end the stigma by saying, in effect, "It's okay to pollute as long as you pay a fee." And the price itself may make it impossible for us to see unspoiled nature as priceless.[27]

Kelman convincingly shows that an extremely strong environmentalist has reasons to have reservations about pollution taxes. Kelman may be wrong, however, to suggest that a pollution tax would remove the stigma from pollution. Although we tax and license many things about which we have positive or neutral feelings (driving, marriage), we do the same for others of which we do not wholly approve (gambling, liquor, cigarettes). It is not likely that people will stop having negative attitudes toward pollution merely because it is taxed. Some environmentalists, however, argue that we do not just tax murder or "rape, pillage and burning," and some say that they feel the same way about polluting behavior ("crimes against nature") as they do about these ("one day a courageous district attorney will prosecute these people for murder").[28]

Opportunity cost becomes relevant here. If it is impermissible to sanction any polluting activity that places others at some risk, then industrial society must end, because even the best technology leads to some deaths among those with serious respiratory problems.[29] And, if all pollution is a crime against nature, the crime problem is truly pervasive. All humans inhale air with 21 percent oxygen and exhale it with 17 percent and drink water with about 200 parts per million dissolved solids and release it with perhaps 20,000 parts per million.[30]

If opportunity costs are relevant and some balancing of multiple goals is necessary, one is forced to think again about the nature of the stigma that should be attached to polluting behavior. It is not like murder. If all murderers were suddenly willing to do what we asked them to do, we would ask them to stop killing people immediately. If all industrial polluters were equally malleable, few, with knowledge of the consequences, would ask them to stop all pollution immediately. The quality of our lives would suffer too much. So would their length, as the hospital equipment fueled by all those power plants shuts down. And, if balancing with other goals is necessary, then some reduction in the value placed on a clean environment, to a level below priceless at least, is inevitable whether it occurs with taxes, effluent licenses, or nonzero standards.

Support for a carbon tax has grown among the left, and many of the 2020 Democratic presidential candidates were vocal with their support. At the MSNBC climate forum, Democratic candidate Andrew Yang said, "Companies can be trusted to do the right thing for their bottom line. That's the only thing they can be trusted for. They have a singular incentive." By way of a carbon tax we make it necessary for businesses to seek to reduce pollution because only by doing so will their profits increase. Yang concluded, "If you want companies to move in the right direction on climate change, you have to hit them where it hurts – in their wallet."[31] The presidential candidate from South Bend, Indiana, Mayor Pete Buttigieg, also affirmed his support for a carbon tax, saying, "I think we need to make sure that the entire economy is trending towards climate justice and climate action." Buttigieg also acknowledged the political difficulty of passing a new tax, however, saying at a previous town hall, "I know that you're not supposed to use the T-word in politics."[32]

One roadblock to unified Democratic support for carbon taxes is disagreement about what to do with the revenues from these taxes. A proposed carbon tax failed to pass in a ballot initiative in Washington State because some supporters wanted the money reinvested in clean energy or social causes while some wanted all revenues returned to the consumer.[33] Meanwhile, leading left-of-center environmental groups such as the Natural Resources Defense Council are adamantly opposed to any deal that substitutes a carbon tax for the climate rules established by the Obama administration.[34]

On the national stage, conservatives who support a carbon tax demand its implementation be paired with the end of many existing command-and-control-style environmental regulations. Other conservatives dislike the thought of increasing taxes in any form and air concerns about the impact of a carbon tax on real incomes, especially for the middle class. The president of the conservative American Energy Alliance, Thomas Pyle, writes,

> A carbon tax would punish users of natural gas, oil, and coal, which make up 80 percent of the energy we consume. This means that all American families would face higher electricity bills and gasoline prices. In fact, it's estimated that the Leadership

Council's carbon tax would hike gasoline prices by 36 cents per gallon. While everybody will pay more, these hikes would have a disproportionate impact on poor and middle-class families, who spend a higher percentage of their income on energy.

Pyle's argument assumes that carbon tax revenue will not be recycled back to citizens – perhaps to poor and middle-class families in particular. Pyle doubts that such recycling will ever occur:

> The idea that Washington politicians would perpetually refund a massive new revenue stream is incredibly naïve... The more likely scenario is that the government would eventually begin to spend the new revenue on federal programs, saddling Americans with yet another new tax while diminishing America's competitiveness in the process. Sounds like big-government liberalism to me.[35]

Former Al Gore advisor Kalee Kreider suggests that proponents of a carbon tax should focus on the benefit these tax revenues will provide to voters. She says, "People are sensitive to taxes, but they will approve them if they're perceived to be getting value, whether that be a road, a hospital, a school. Where I think environmental groups struggle is they approach carbon pricing in terms of environmental performance." Instead, Kreider recommends environmentalists answer the question "What service are they providing to the taxpayer?"[36] Following this advice, several states have successfully passed gas tax increases by positioning them as vital funding sources to repair aging infrastructure.[37]

President Trump faced outrage in 2018 when he rolled back Obama-era CAFE (Corporate Average Fuel Economy) standards. These standards are designed to reduce fuel consumption in the United States by dictating the average fuel efficiency an automaker must meet for all its new cars sold in any year.[38] The Obama administration had increased dramatically the CAFE standard to 54.5 miles per gallon by 2025. For comparison, the 2014 average was only 25.4 miles per gallon.[39] The policy under President Trump set CAFE standards at about 40 miles per gallon by 2026.[40]

Democrats and environmentalists were outraged by Trump's decision. Democratic Senator Tom Carper said in a press release, "[The EPA] has continued its relentless march to weaken or repeal rules that were designed to remove greenhouse gas, soot, mercury and other pollution from our air. While the rest of the country works around the clock to combat and overcome this deadly respiratory pandemic, the Trump EPA has been spearheading a pandemic of pollution."[41]

Economists, on the whole, aren't as critical of the CAFE standards rollback and have been arguing for years that a gasoline tax would have a much greater impact on fuel use. A full 92 percent of economists "would prefer a gasoline tax over raising fuel economy standards."[42]

Economists see three major flaws in the CAFE standards approach. First, there is a rebound effect; "[P]eople drive about 10 percent more when they switch to a vehicle that is twice as fuel efficient." Second, the technology to increase fuel efficiency increases the price of new cars, which leads to longer use of used cars as people delay the more expensive purchase. Economists have found that 15 percent of emission reductions from higher CAFE standards are offset by the extra time these standards leave older, less fuel-efficient vehicles on the road. With 94 percent of US vehicles over one year in age, a gas tax that applied to all vehicles would be a much more efficient way to address fuel consumption than standards that apply only to new cars.[43] Finally, CAFE standards do nothing to incentivize less driving after a car purchase is made. A gasoline tax would increase the personal cost of each additional mile driven, and those who drive more would have an extra incentive to purchase a more fuel-efficient vehicle. Although the idea of high fuel efficiency across the US fleet may sound wonderful, such standards lack the teeth necessary to create great change. Congress will never let Detroit shut down, because companies such as Ford can't meet mileage standards.

In 2013, when 40 percent of its electricity was generated by burning coal, the United Kingdom implemented an additional tax on carbon beyond the price companies already have to pay to purchase EU carbon permits. By September 2019 only 3 percent of UK electricity came from coal-burning plants![44] Carbon pricing in most of the world has not had dramatic effects, however. Over 40 governments worldwide have implemented some form of carbon pricing, but political backlash has weakened several initiatives, notably in France and Australia; and most systems have priced carbon too low to have the sizable effects economists and environmentalists have hoped for.[45]

In the United States the incentive approach to environmental progress that has been most successful is the cap-and-trade solution to acid rain. In 2018 the Environmental Defense Fund described the program's success as follows:

> It required cutting overall sulfur emissions in half, but let each company decide how to make the cuts. Power plants that lowered their pollution more than required could sell those extra allowances to other plants. A new commodities market was born. Sulfur emissions went down faster than predicted and at one-fourth of the projected cost. Since its launch, cap and trade for acid rain has been regarded widely as highly effective at solving the problem in a flexible, innovative way.[46]

Many economists hope to one day say the same about reducing human-influenced climate change through a market-based carbon approach.

Flood Control

The National Flood Insurance Program was created in 1968 to fill what the federal government saw as a gap in the private market. Private insurance companies refused to sell policies to homeowners living in flood zones because of the unpredictability and wide-ranging impacts of flooding events. Frankly, private companies saw bets on properties built in flood zones as too risky, because, when one property suffered, many other insured properties often suffered at the same time.[47] So why do homeowners choose to build and buy in these risky locations? Simple: the land is cheaper and building costs are lower on the already flat ground of floodplains.[48] With the added guarantee of the federal government bailing homeowners out each time they suffer a flood, the personal cost of that flood risk is much lower than it would be in the absence of government intervention.

With private insurance, premiums are designed to reflect the risk to an asset. In that way, by paying the equivalent of the risk in the form of a yearly premium, homeowners internalize the cost of living in an area with a high risk of floods. Homeowners will continue to buy and build in areas of high risk only if the risk, and the associated premiums, remain low enough to make it worthwhile to live in that location. The premiums homeowners must pay as a part of the National Flood Insurance Program (NFIP) are much lower, however, than those private insurers would charge. The effect of this is twofold.

First, the NFIP does not take in enough revenue in the form of premiums each year to offset the claims it must pay out when floods occur. For this reason, the program has had to borrow $30 billion in taxpayer money from the US Treasury.[49] This is a debt that practically all experts, and the director of the National Flood Insurance Program himself, say the program will never be able to pay back, leaving all American taxpayers footing the bill.[50] Second, lower premiums mean that homeowners do not fully take flood risk into account when making home-purchasing choices. Considering the impact of incentives upon behavior, the result is predictable: homeowners continue to buy and live in extremely risky locations in much higher numbers than would occur without the NFIP.

Let's look at the case of Florida. From 1851 to 2015 Florida got hit by more hurricanes than any other US state.[51] In 2017 Hurricane Irma damaged almost every major city in Florida while the entire state was under a hurricane warning.[52] The threat to Florida is predicted to increase as a result of rising sea levels; a mere 6-inch increase in sea levels would nullify the flood control benefits of Florida's extensive network of canals.[53] Despite these extensive threats, development in Florida has continued to grow at a rapid pace, with seemingly little thought to threats of flooding. More of Florida's population lives on land less than 4 feet above the high-tide line than in any other state.[54]

The state has grown from the least populated Southern state in the middle of the twentieth century to the third most populated.[55] A hurricane that hit Miami in 1926 caused $1 billion of damage valued in today's dollars; after all the development of the past near-century, the same hurricane would cause $124 billion in damages if it were to hit again today.[56] Yet the federal government continues to provide discounted flood insurance across the Florida peninsula. Why should the rest of the nation pay for some people to continue to build and live in flood-prone Florida?

The American people often mistakenly believe that a flood can happen to anyone. Laura Lightbody, spearheading a Pew Charitable Trusts program on flood risks, echoed a common sentiment when she said, "Where it rains, it can flood, so no one in the country is insulated. It touches all 50 states."[57] Certain areas are much more prone to flooding than others, however, because of factors such as elevation, proximity to a waterway, and surrounding development.

In the United States, the worst floods occur around the Mississippi River, the Gulf Coast of Louisiana and Texas, and the majority of the Atlantic Coast (including Florida).[58] Even within these broader regions, certain neighborhoods and properties are at much greater risk than others. Traditional flood control measures, such as dams and levees, are criticized for providing a false sense of security and simply shifting flooding problems to other properties.[59] As former president of lobbying group American Rivers Kevin Coyle said, "The whole thing is like dueling banjos. You build a levee at 20 feet, and someone across the river builds a 24-foot levee. Now *you* get the flood, so you build higher."[60]

If one looks at the history of the National Flood Insurance Program, about 25 percent of all claims paid out have gone to a mere 1 percent of insured homes.[61] National Public Radio (NPR) reported on one homeowner, Jennifer Bayles, who purchased her house for $83,000 in 1992. By 2017 Bayles had received a total of $400,000 from the NFIP for flood damage to her home.[62] In another report, NPR spoke with homeowner Bill Pennington, whose house, purchased for $525,000, had cost the NFIP over $878,000 prior to Hurricane Harvey. After Hurricane Harvey that amount would increase to over $1 million.[63] Another home in Houston, currently valued at only $72,400, has received more than $1 million in payouts from insurance.[64]

The National Flood Insurance Program is not allowed to deny flood insurance to a home such as Bayles's or Pennington's on the basis of it being "too risky" to insure. If the NFIP was able to raise premiums to accurately reflect risk, this would not be a problem; with rates set by Congress, however, and congressmen elected by citizens who dislike paying higher rates, reelection incentives once again win out and premiums do not increase. A senior policy analyst at the Natural Resources Defense Council, Rob Moore, has said, "No congressman ever got unelected by providing cheap flood insurance."[65]

The effect of incentives on elected politicians leads to another issue. It is morally and politically distasteful to deny aid to victims of disaster. After massive floods in 1993, congressmen from flood-ravaged areas accused opponents of "nickel and diming" the victims.[66] Citizens themselves raised $4.3 million for flood relief during a one-hour telethon, indicating a strong public desire to aid victims of such disasters.[67] In 2011, during debates over whether to cut automobile subsidy spending in order to increase disaster relief spending, Speaker of the House

Nancy Pelosi said, "We shouldn't even be having this conversation. The fact is when natural disaster strikes, the American people are in need... They don't need to have the fear that there's going to be a debate over how this is going to be paid for."[68] In 2019 Representative Nydia M. Velázquez tied disaster aid for Puerto Rico to issues of morality and core American values, and 34 House Republicans joined Democrats, in contradiction to President Trump's wishes, in order to pass a $19.1 billion nationwide relief package.

When faced with a disaster, such as devastating floods, American politicians and the American public *will* provide aid to the victims. Anyone living in a flood-prone community knows this, and this expectation of aid affects calculations of the financial risk of a flood. In 1993 only 20 percent of properties mandated to have flood insurance as a qualification for their federally backed mortgage actually had flood insurance.[69] After severe floods the Federal Emergency Management Agency (FEMA) still provided money for people without flood insurance to rebuild their homes as long as they bought a NFIP policy after the flood![70] With such incentives, why would anyone pay flood insurance premiums during the years between disasters?

Don't be fooled that the National Flood Insurance Program serves mostly the poor. The General Accounting Office calls the NFIP a "safety net" for coastal development, and coastal property-owners tend to be of a higher socio-economic class than the average American whose taxes subsidize the program.[71] A program targeted to aid the poor directly would be a much more efficient vehicle for decreasing economic inequality.

A case study of a small town in Virginia illustrates the extreme inefficiencies of usual flood control practices. Scottsville is a town set on a floodplain of the James River that suffered severe floods in 1969, 1972, and 1985.[72] As businesses began to flee and newcomers were afraid to own homes or businesses downtown, Mayor A. Raymon Thacker feared Scottsville was soon to be "a ghost town of utter destruction and disheartened people."[73] To qualify for federal flood insurance, preventative measures would have to be taken before any new building or reconstruction could begin downtown.[74] As local drug-store owner Richard Sago put it, "Anybody in their right mind wouldn't want to build in the flood plain."[75]

In a perfect world, these opinions would be signs that it was time to move to higher ground, perhaps the shopping center just north of Scottsville to which some businesses had already relocated.[76] After heading a university study on Scottsville, professor of architecture Garland Okerlund gave a very different recommendation:

> There will be no insurance against floods until a flood wall is built. Right now, however, the federal government does not seem overly inclined to spend $2.5 million in a town of about 300. But, if the town were built up – and if more housing were brought in – the town would have a more persuasive argument for the federal funds and need for the flood wall.[77]

To be clear, the proposed solution to a location being too great a flood risk was to bring in *more* homes and businesses, so that the potential destruction was so great that the federal government would be strong-armed into stepping in. But it turned out that the federal government sent $4 million to protect downtown Scottsville even without waiting for a surge in building on the flood plain.[78]

So, how do economists propose addressing this issue? One suggested solution is to increase burden sharing with state and local governments to incentivize those governments to take steps to prevent flood damage. According to the National Institute of Building Sciences, each $1 spent on flood mitigation strategies decreases future flood damage costs by $5.[79] With the federal government often sweeping in and covering 90 to 100 percent of disaster relief costs, state and local governments find it cheaper to spend $0.50 per $5 of flood damage than to spend the $1 to prevent that damage in the first place.[80]

If the federal government set a lower maximum percentage of flood damage that it will cover, state and local governments would have a greater incentive to mitigate that damage before it occurs. A 2016 FEMA proposal to implement a deductible that states must cover out of their own budgets before federal aid steps in would have a similar effect in increasing the incentives for state governments to mitigate flood damage.[81]

Another popular proposal among economists is to prioritize *relocation* away from the riskiest of properties. After the Great Flood of 1993, which devastated states such as Missouri, Iowa, and Illinois, the federal government spent $121 million to buy out flood plain properties, relocate buildings, and flood-proof other buildings.[82] Estimates suggest that this saved $600 million in later flood damages.[83] In Missouri alone, a flood in 1995 that covered 85 percent of the same area as the flood in 1993 caused 99 percent less damage thanks to relocation and buyouts.[84] In Charles County, Missouri, buyouts were the difference between $26 million in damages in 1993 and a mere $300,000 in damages in 1995.[85]

The properties that the government buys don't have to sit as empty land. There are many potential flood-tolerant uses that would provide benefit to local communities such as creating parks, wetlands, and conservation areas.[86]

Buyout and relocation programs can cause animosity and anger among the property owners who are forced to move, but others embrace this opportunity to avoid future flood damage. About 500 residents located on the edges of Staten Island applied for buyouts after Hurricane Sandy hit in 2012.[87] Hopes are that wetlands will return on these properties and better buffer the rest of Staten Island from future storms.[88] In 2017 *The Washington Post* suggested offering discounted flood insurance premiums to homeowners in the highest risk areas only if they agreed to accept a buyout instead of repairs when future flood damage occurs.[89]

Congestion

It is 6 p.m. and you are sitting in your car. Traffic is almost at a standstill, as thousands of commuters are making their daily trip home. Congestion causes the average American commuter to waste 54 hours each year.[90] In 2017 alone such congestion wasted 3.3 billion gallons of fuel and cost the US economy $166 billion.[91] Emissions from time spent in congestion also have significant public health impacts. In 2005 such emissions led to approximately 3,000 premature deaths and $24 billion in public health costs.[92]

Although drivers consider the impact of driving during peak hours on themselves – longer commute, stop-and-roll traffic, higher risk of crashes – they do not fully take into account the effect their decision has on every other driver on the road. Here's a quick example. Say you have 999 drivers on road A at 6 p.m. If driver no. 1000 decides to use that road at the same time, he considers the extra 30 minutes this decision will cost him. He has no incentive to consider the extra 30 seconds that this costs each of the 999 drivers before him. The total cost of driver no. 1000's decision to drive on road A at 6 p.m. equals the

30 minutes it costs him *plus* the 500 minutes of driving time added by keeping 999 drivers on the road for 30 seconds more.

In the private market, pricing is used to regulate the number of consumers attempting to use a particular good or service at one time. But, across much of the United States, the most congested roads are not priced according to demand. Politicians and environmental activists love to propose expanding public transportation as the shining solution to congestion ills, but, as long as road usage isn't appropriately priced, commuters will continue to choose to sit in congestion because the private costs of congestion to them are much less than the total cost of congestion to society.

Congestion pricing tends to be extremely unpopular at the outset. In the spring of 2019 63 percent of residents of the Washington, DC, metro area and 54 percent of New York City voters were against proposals to implement congestion pricing in their cities.[93] Studies of public opinion in Europe show that attitudes tend to change once the benefits of congestion pricing are readily visible. In London, 40 percent of residents favored congestion pricing before its implementation; less than a year later that number had grown to nearly 60 percent.[94] In Stockholm, 30 percent of residents supported congestion pricing; after implementation, support grew to 52 percent.[95]

In London, Singapore, and Stockholm – three cities with notable congestion pricing systems – the fees on drivers made up for the initial cost of implementing the system, and have raised millions of dollars in net revenue ever since.[96] Economists would argue that, if these revenues are enough to pay for the construction of an additional lane, only then do we have proof that an additional lane might truly benefit society. As long as roads remain unpriced, inefficient transportation decisions will continue to be made.

Further Reflections

The fruits of thinking about "the public use of private interest" are by no means limited to applications involving profit-seeking firms. Both theory and evidence have convinced economists that, if the price of something valued goes up, some people will consume less of it, and, if the price goes down, some will consume more. Economists thus spend considerable time thinking about the public-sector applications of simple supply and demand curves. Because air travelers, tennis players, and electricity users respond to economic incentives, higher prices at periods of peak use can spread out demand and thus avoid expensive capital investment. Because many uses of water do not have high value to consumers, an increase in price for such uses could make a large difference in demand. Yet one study of the water use forecasts prepared for nine large American cities found that none of them considered the possible effects of changes in water price on expected demand.[97]

To be sure, policy makers should be careful not to just implement the first incentive that comes to mind. To do so means to risk the fate of the poor little town of Abruzzi, Italy. The city was plagued by vipers, and the city fathers determined to solve the problem by offering a reward for any viper killed. Alas, the supply of vipers increased. Townspeople had started breeding them in their basements.[98]

Before laughing at such rustic ignorance, note the way in which the urbane Senator Abraham Ribicoff reacted to proposals for taxes on oil products coupled with a general tax rebate to maintain purchasing power. Such a scheme would conserve oil by raising its relative price and inducing (some) consumers and businesses to spend less on oil products and more on other goods or factors of production. This is not just elementary economics but pretty close to chapter one elementary economics. Yet Ribicoff ridiculed the notion that you could conserve anything by raising taxes on it and then giving the money back to the same people. When the idea was first presented, Ribicoff complained that some economist must have "dreamed this up." Economist Alice Rivlin reports that many other congressmen were also mystified by the proposal.[99]

Part II

Government and Markets, Efficiency and Equity

4 GOVERNMENT AND THE ECONOMY

Contemporary texts in public finance often begin by discussing three separate functions of government in the economy: allocation, distribution, and stabilization. Allocation questions ask whether particular government tax, expenditure, or regulatory programs improve the mix of goods and services produced by the economy. Distribution questions ask who benefits and who is harmed by such policies. Stabilization questions ask what effect all taxes and expenditures, together with monetary policy, have on aggregate employment, output, and prices.

Policies centrally concerned with one of the three functions will affect the other two. For example, US environmental policy seeks to shift resources from making products to making cleaner air. But this allocation effect is accompanied by a distribution one, as some firms' owners and employees gain and others lose. Similarly, a decision to build a highway will change the allocation of resources but will also provide more income for manual workers, and it may reduce unemployment or increase inflation.

Although the three separate functions of government are never isolated from one another, economists argue that we should not let particular allocation decisions be unduly influenced by any spillover effects on the other two functions. If, for example, a highway is a better use of resources than alternative public or private opportunities, then the highway should be built even if inflation is a serious problem. To cope with inflation we can tighten monetary policy, cut other expenditures, or raise taxes. On the other hand, if the highway is not a justifiable project, it should not be built anyway, regardless of its favorable effects on unemployment. Expanding more needed government programs or cutting taxes can help meet employment goals without wasting resources on a low-priority highway.

Stabilization policy is at the heart of macroeconomics and will not be further discussed here. Chapter 5 will cover distribution. This chapter, together with Chapter 6 and the addendum to Chapter 6, will be centrally concerned with the heart of microeconomics, allocation, as well as with the allocative standard economists most frequently use: economic efficiency.

Consumer Sovereignty, Welfare Economics, and Utilitarianism

Most economists look to welfare economics for principles to guide government when it concerns itself with questions of resource allocation. The word "welfare" here signals no special concern with public welfare programs aimed at the poor but, rather, welfare more generally: societal welfare. Welfare economics is an outgrowth of old-fashioned utilitarianism. Its concern is with the consequences of policies, not the policy process or political institutions.

Welfare economics rests on two fundamental normative assumptions: that societal welfare depends only on individuals' subjective senses of satisfaction; and that satisfaction is best achieved by letting individuals' preferences determine the use of societal resources. Welfare economics has no room for any policy standards that limit or guide human wants. The basic starting point is individuals, with their bewildering variety of idiosyncratic preferences. Welfare consists of having what one prefers.

What is most distinctive about modern evaluative microeconomics is this radical individualism, not simply a concern with narrowly economic ends or the materialistic side of mankind. Adam Smith explored *The Nature and Causes of the Wealth of Nations*, and modern macroeconomists continue to do so. But, as the name suggests, the welfare economist's concern is welfare, not just wealth. His concern is not so much with quantities of goods and services as with the subjective sense of satisfaction they and other things bring. Economists, of course, notice that many people seem to have a strong preference for more wealth. Chapter 7 will argue that, in practice, many economists do overemphasize money as a human motive and source of human happiness. But, in principle, a welfare economist is concerned with anything that any individual values enough to be willing to give up something for. Fulfilling people's environmental, aesthetic, educational, or charitable desires is an economic benefit just as much as is a new car.

Welfare economics makes no claim to be able to make interpersonal comparisons of intensity of satisfaction or of levels of welfare. Thus, it abandons any attempt to develop a hedonistic calculus that could yield an unambiguous societal optimum. In welfare economics, the preferences of individuals are all that count, but, as argued in the following chapter, welfare-economic principles cannot tell economists whose preferences should count the most.*

Economic Efficiency

If a society accepts a subjective sense of satisfaction and consumer sovereignty as its standards, economists can show that it should be interested in achieving economic efficiency. The word "efficiency" brings to mind manufacturing, engineers, getting the same output with less input, keeping costs low. Like the word "economic," it sounds narrower than it is, and is thus a source of much confusion. In fact, like "economic," it in principle includes everything that anyone cares about. When the nutritionist Jean Mayer suggested that it would be more efficient to produce calories through cereal grains than through meat, the economist objects because the subjective standard of economic efficiency is ignored: most consumers value a calorie of meat more highly than a calorie of grain.[1]

An understanding of economic efficiency begins with Pareto optimality. A Pareto-optimal allocation is one in which we cannot reallocate resources to improve one person's welfare without impairing at least one other person's welfare. Pareto improvements are

---

* Economists' historic reliance on individual preferences or consumer sovereignty has been challenged by a new school of the discipline: behavioral economics. The school shows that individuals make mistakes in their choices, especially if benefits occur principally in the distant future. The school has not had significant impact on the way introductory courses in economics are taught, and this is a book introducing readers to economics. Later sections of the book discuss the influence of behavioral economics – favorably in Chapter 7 and very unfavorably in the addendum to Chapter 6. I do not think it provides a framework that has or should have replaced the framework I outline in the first part of this chapter.

those in which a change in resource allocation is preferred by one or more members of society and opposed by no one. It is an extremely strict criterion for improvement, and is almost never met; obviously, such changes are very hard to find. If any single person objects to changing the status quo, then the Pareto improvement criterion gives no unambiguous public policy guidance. The existing situation may be Pareto-optimal. But there are a nearly infinite number of other non-comparable Pareto optimums, and the concept is of little policy use.

Economically efficient allocations are always Pareto-optimal allocations. But, if the initial allocation is inefficient, the achievement of economic efficiency does not require that no one be made worse off before a change can be recommended. Economic efficiency requires only that recommended changes use resources in such a way that it would be theoretically possible – assuming costless transfers of income between gainers and losers – to make some better off and no one worse off. Suppose that most people would gain from some change, but some would lose. If the gainers gain enough so that they *could* fully compensate the losers with money or goods and still have an improved situation themselves, the change meets what some economists call the "potential Pareto" criterion and would improve economic efficiency even if the transfer to the losers does not actually take place.[2]

Thus, as we will see in Chapter 5, changes that improve economic efficiency may fail an equity standard. But the concept is not useless. Politicians understand that changes never benefit everyone. Some of them may find it helpful to know when the gainers from a change gain enough so that they could fully compensate losers and still be better off. If politicians can find a way to make the potential compensation actual, they can create a better situation from the points of view of all parties concerned.

Free Markets and Flexible Prices

Economists believe that, in most situations, free markets come closer to achieving economically efficient outcomes than do alternative institutional arrangements. As Kenneth Arrow and Frank Hahn note, to one unschooled in economics an economy motivated by individual greed and controlled by a very large number of different agents brings to mind chaos.[3] But, in fact, free markets with flexible prices coordinate the activities of millions of people in different countries in a remarkable way.

Consider a simple wooden pencil. To produce it, people must cut down trees, and this alone requires saws and trucks and rope, which in turn require "the mining of ore, the making of steel and its refinement into saws, axes, motors; the growing of hemp and bringing it through all the stages to heavy and strong rope; the logging camps with their beds and mess halls," not to mention the thousands who have a hand in every cup of coffee the loggers drink.[4] And still to come is the millwork to convert the logs to slats, the graphite from Sri Lanka that much later becomes pencil lead, the brass made from zinc and copper that holds the rubberlike eraser, which is made by reacting Indonesian rapeseed oil with sulfur chloride.

A single person acting alone could not have the time and knowledge to make a pencil of today's quality in a year, perhaps not in a lifetime. Yet one can buy a pencil for a few cents. Economists explain why. Markets permit a productive division of labor by efficiently transmitting information. When consumers decide that they want more pencils, no central authority has to tell everyone involved what to do. Retailers order more from wholesalers, and wholesalers in turn order from manufacturers. The manufacturer orders more wood, brass, and graphite. As Milton and Rose Friedman say, "A major problem in transmitting information efficiently is to make sure that everyone who can use the information gets it without clogging the 'in' baskets of those who have no use for it. The price system [free markets] automatically solves this problem."[5] The pencil manufacturer, for example, does not have to worry about whether he should hire more loggers or instead use more powerful, expensive saws to fell and process the additional trees needed. Similarly, the producer of wood does not have to decide whether, in light of the temporary shortage of rapeseed oil, eraser size should stay the same while price goes up or price should stay the same while eraser size goes down. Indeed, the producer of wood may not know or care that the increased demand for his wood has anything at all to do with pencils.[6]

Free markets, with their flexible prices, provide more than the right information. They also give people an incentive to act on it. Economists find that the desire for wealth is a sufficiently common goal to ensure that resources will shift when financial incentives do. When consumers start to demand more pencils, the price of pencils goes up to ration the limited supply. The higher price induces the least eager (or the poorer) buyers to drop out of the market, or induces pencil buyers to use them less. The higher price also makes retailers quick to want to increase their supply of pencils so they can take advantage of the new demand and high price. They put pressure on their wholesalers, the wholesalers on their manufacturers, their manufacturers on the producers of wood. Each offers to pay more if necessary; they can do so and still increase profits given the higher price for pencils. The wood companies may, in turn, pay overtime to their employees to get an increase in production or cut back sales to other manufacturers whose consumers are less eager to buy and who therefore cannot afford to pay as much. When consumers are especially eager and drive up the price further and faster, businesses are more eager to meet their demand, and they respond more quickly.

Firms that thrive do not often respond clumsily to consumers' demands. Those that waste scarce resources when making their product have difficulty matching the price and quality of firms that do not. Firms with an inefficient scale of operation come under pressure from those of more optimal size. And firms that guess wrongly about whether consumers would prefer a higher pencil price or a smaller eraser lose business to competitors.

Consumers bid for various goods and services, and businesses bid on their behalf for the resources needed to provide the goods and services. Given scarcity, all consumers cannot get all they want at a low price. But, in the market, resources flow toward those goods and services for which the consumer dollar votes are greatest. If consumers prefer more pencils and fewer toothpicks, they can get what they want by bidding up the price of pencils. This enables pencil manufacturers to make a normal profit – or, temporarily, even better than normal – while still paying a higher price for wood if necessary. Pencil manufacturers expand, and the added supply then eradicates most, if not all, of the price increase. The toothpick manufacturers contract, since they can no longer make the profit needed to maintain past production while paying the new and higher opportunity cost of using the scarcer wood. The costs of providing a commodity thus reflect the competing offers of other producers for the services of the factors to produce it. Consumers, through their demand, determine what those competing producers will offer, and thus, given the distribution of income, the market satisfies consumers' desires as well as scarcity will allow.

Market Failure

If you like consumer sovereignty, you should be interested in achieving economic efficiency. If you care about economic efficiency, you should like free markets. Almost all economists would find these propositions fundamentally persuasive. But they also believe the second one should be qualified. In addition to its stabilization and distribution functions, government will be needed to correct for market imperfections that prevent the allocation of resources in accord with consumer valuations. These imperfections may include concentrations of market power (monopolies and powerful labor unions), externalities, and public goods.

The case for government intervention is strongest for public goods. A public good is not everything that government now provides, or even everything that government should provide, and the term is thus somewhat misleading. The term "collective consumption good" more accurately captures the phenomena that economists wish to distinguish.

Public or collective consumption goods are goods for which consumption is nonrival (i.e. a number of people may simultaneously consume the same good) and for which it is either prohibitively expensive or impossible to confine the benefits of the good to selected individuals. Only the person who consumes a steak enjoys it; his neighbors do not benefit from it. But an individual building a levee to protect against floods benefits no more than do his neighbors. Any individual may thus wait for one of the neighbors to build or pretend to lack of interest in the projects if the neighbors decide to take up a collection to perform the tasks (economists call such individuals "free riders"). Almost everyone might benefit from the projects by more than the proportionate cost he incurs, but each may benefit still more if others pay all the cost. As a result, the projects may not be undertaken unless government steps in and ensures that all pay their fair share through compulsory taxes. The chances of voluntary agreement without government involvement become close to zero for national defense and pollution abatement, where the benefits flow far beyond a single neighborhood.[7]

If economic efficiency is to be obtained, public goods should be provided only if consumers are collectively willing to pay more than the opportunity cost of provision (i.e. the consumers' gains from forgone alternatives elsewhere). Economists' efforts to determine willingness to pay for public goods is one goal of cost–benefit analysis, discussed briefly in the addendum to Chapter 6.

Externalities or spillovers are more common examples of market failure that may justify government intervention. Externalities are effects on third parties that are not transmitted through the price system and that arise as an incidental by-product of another person's or firm's activity. They may be positive effects on others, such as education, or negative, such as pollution. Sending a child to school benefits the child and his parents, but others also benefit somewhat if the child becomes a more informed voter and a more reliable taxpayer. The private market can capture only the dollars the parent or child is willing to pay for the child's education. The numerous external beneficiaries cannot be charged. As a result, without government subsidies the market is likely to provide less education than the community as a whole wants and is willing to pay for. Negative externalities represent the cost side of others' actions. Pollution, for example, hurts the community at large, but, if the costs do not appear on the firm's profit and loss statement, they are usually ignored. The community then gets more pollution-causing production than it desires. As argued earlier, a tax on effluents can internalize the external cost and help us produce a lower, more satisfactory level of pollution.

Externalities are everywhere. Flu shots, newly painted houses, and newly planted flowers benefit many people besides those directly involved. Crabgrass, loud radios, and fancy sports cars bought by those with emulating, or merely envious, neighbors all impose incidental costs on others. And honking horns, flashy ties, and short skirts produce external benefits for some and costs for others. The externality concept is both terribly useful and terribly troublesome, and will be explored further in Chapter 6. What should be noted here is that it can be used to justify an extremely pervasive government role in the economy. Most economists do not think externalities should justify such a role. The concept of government failure helps to indicate why.

Government Failure

Sixty years ago economists wrote about market failure, but rarely about government failure. Today they consider both. Imagine a perfectly democratic New England town meeting in which all citizens participate. Economists show that, whatever its other virtues, such a meeting possesses no inherent tendency to allocate resources efficiently. When the citizens vote two to one against an addition to the local public school, that does not necessarily mean that the losers from the addition would lose more (in taxes) than the gainers would gain (in net benefits) or that there is not collectively enough willingness to pay to cover the costs of the addition. The question put at the town meeting was "Should all taxes be raised 5 percent to pay for the addition?" But perhaps the minority would have been willing to pay 15 percent more. Or, more realistically, some of them might have paid 30 percent more, some 10 percent, and even some of the naysayers 2 percent, to obtain the addition. In either case, there may be enough people willing to forsake other goods to pay for the addition. Yet the local newspaper says the people have spoken and have decisively rejected the project.

The problem here is that voting is not a finely tuned device for gauging public preferences. In particular, it ignores the intensity of preferences. This can lead to too much, as well as too little, spending. The vote might have been two to one for a project that enjoys mild support among the majority but is considered useless, perhaps even perverse (for instance, sex education), by the minority.

The town meeting is likely to encounter a second problem as well: the tendency of voters to be "rationally" ignorant of the consequences of their choices. Most economists believe that voters have good reason to be less informed about political decisions than about comparable market decisions. Because it takes time to acquire information, few consumers take the trouble to obtain all possible information on even their major private purchases. But, if one is deciding whether to buy a new car or repair the old one, there is a strong incentive to learn a good bit about the alternatives, because the potential gains or losses of the decision for the individual are great. They are less great if the decision is the public one of whether to replace all the old school buses. Here, the costs of a bad decision and the gains from a good one are spread among all citizens. Since the personal stakes are less, citizens who do not find politics intrinsically interesting, and are not unusually public-spirited, will not be as well informed. This tendency will be magnified because the individual gains from the correct decision on the buses are not assured once one takes the time to get good information. Once an individual decides that he should buy a new car, he can do so. But taking time to decide if the town should buy a new bus does not ensure that the bus will be purchased. A majority may disagree.

Whatever the economic efficiency problems in a town meeting setting, those flowing from decisions made by representative political institutions and by governmental bureaucracies are potentially much greater. A school of economics called "public choice" explores them. Assuming that people in political organizations are moved by narrowly selfish motives just as they are in markets, public choice scholars predict that a government bureaucracy will have little interest in efficiency or in satisfying citizen preferences. A federal administrator who spends more money on his program will find this has almost no effect on his tax bill. But it may help him in other ways. His salary, his power, his public reputation, and his perquisites of office (free parking, cheap lunches, etc.) are all likely to be greater if his budget is large and he has a lot of people working for him. What incentive is there then to run a lean and efficient bureau?

If one responds that we elect representatives to make certain that bureaucrats do not behave in this way, the public choice economist points out that many government bureaus have a monopoly on performing their function, and thus the representatives will have little real knowledge about whether the bureaus for which they appropriate money could do things more cheaply. More importantly, they will have little incentive to get good information. Politicians know that they get votes by talking about efficiency in government, but they also know that few voters will know if they do anything besides talk. More votes and campaign contributions can be obtained by keeping in touch with groups in the district than by spending time in Washington carefully studying agency budgets. Politicians will tend to vote for programs with visible, immediate, and concentrated benefits and hidden costs. They will shy away from programs with long-term, diffuse benefits and concentrated, visible costs.

Politicians can find economically inefficient programs the best path to reelection because of a "rational voter ignorance" problem many times greater than that explored in the town meeting setting. A typical voter will have little interest in deeply studying how he would be affected by a policy proposal. More information on that issue will probably not lead him to change his mind about whom to vote for in an election in which the candidates differ on many other issues as well. Moreover, his vote and campaigning almost certainly will not decide the election; nor will his representative's vote often be decisive in the legislature.

In his much-praised *The Myth of the Rational Voter*, Bryan Caplan presents evidence that voters vote symbolically. Since their single vote will not change outcomes, they vote for feel-good policies. They feel more compassionate when they favor programs that "save jobs," and more virtuous when they favor policies that favor a cleaner environment regardless of the cost. "If you think the right answer you feel insensitive and unpatriotic; if you say the right answer, you feel like a pariah. There's about as much intrinsic motivation to understand economics as there is to take out the garbage."[8]

Public choice is just one school of economics. As argued in Chapter 7, its narrowly self-interested motivational assumptions are too simplistic to explain much government behavior. By themselves they have a hard time explaining why people vote at all, or why some programs grow much more rapidly than others. But the work of public choice economists has produced useful insights, and it has had influence on the profession as a whole. Moreover, a belief central to public choice – that governmental processes do not have mechanisms for promoting efficiency that are as powerful as the market's – is widely shared by most mainstream economists. This belief has been strengthened by empirical findings from a number of studies.

Market and Government Allocation: Comparing Efficiency

Among the most interesting of these studies are those that compare the relative efficiency of government agencies and their private-sector counterparts. Public choice theory would predict greater private-sector efficiency because of competitive pressures and the greater ability of private firms' managers to reap the rewards of efficient behavior.

One of the most systematic of the comparative studies looked at residential refuse collection. The study found that, on average, US cities with over 50,000 residents get roughly 30 percent cheaper service when they hire firms to pick up refuse than when a city agency performs the work. Reasons suggested for the differences included higher municipal employee absentee rates (12 percent versus 6.5 percent); larger municipal crews (3.26 workers versus 2.15); and the longer time it took the municipal crews to service each household (4.35 work-hours per year versus 2.37).[9]

A study contrasting federal agency efficiency with private firms was carried out by the General Accounting Office in 1975. It found that it costs the government nearly twice as much as it costs private insurance carriers to process each medical claim. The government was also found to be slower in paying claims. The cost results were explained by higher government salaries and lower government productivity. For example, federal accountants and auditors averaged $21,600 in wages and fringe benefits, compared to $18,000 for Blue Cross of Chicago, $17,300 for Blue Cross of Maryland, $13,800 for Travelers, and $13,700 for Mutual of Omaha. Similar salary differences existed for claims examiners and nurses. Despite higher wages, federal employees processed an average of just 2500 claims a year, compared to 3900 for Travelers, 4200 for Mutual, 5700 for Blue Cross of Maryland, and 6600 for Blue Cross of Chicago.[10]

Other federal government surveys have shown average savings of 30 percent when various services (for restaurant workers, mechanics, security guards, etc.) are contracted out to private firms.[11] At the local level, in addition to trash collection, cost savings have been found by contracting out for other services such as firefighting, utility billing, tax assessment, and municipal transit.[12]

Privatization

The movement toward privatization increased after 1980. "Between 1982 and 1992 contracting increased by 121 percent in the 596 cities where comparable data were available." Even so, "[t]he average common municipal service is contracted out by [only] 27 percent of cities." New York City under Mayor Rudy Giuliani and Indianapolis under Stephen Goldsmith were among the leaders in large cities.[13]

Politically, it is harder for Democrats to privatize than it is for Republicans, because municipal unions are so important to the Democratic base. Still, when he was mayor, Ed Rendell made real progress in Philadelphia.[14] My hometown of Charlottesville is dominated politically by liberal Democrats. Nonetheless, in 1999 Charlottesville saved $80,000 a year by contracting out for trash collection.[15] Ongoing competition for contracts is essential to privatization. It won't do to have one competition, and then give the low-bidding private company a monopoly in later years.

Often municipalities try to promote greater efficiency by developing metrics. But some metrics turn out to make policy worse. For example, officials in Fairfax County, Virginia, decided they had made it too easy for employees to get government cars. They decided that workers should lose their government car whenever their odometers showed fewer than 4500 miles per year. A lieutenant in the fire department kept careful track, and near the end of the year he arranged for an investigator who lived far from headquarters to switch cars with one who lived near headquarters, so that both odometers could show that they drove more than 4500 miles in a year.[16] An early effort to increase efficiency in New York City was based on the determination that performance and bonuses in its highway department should reflect the number of tons of asphalt laid per worker. Tons rose dramatically in one year. Its employees had "applied a much thicker overlay than was standard." Worse yet, some dumped the asphalt in vacant lots.[17]

Federal government privatization initiatives also increased after 1980. Under the Clinton administration, the defense secretary, William S. Cohen, launched a major initiative putting up for competitive bidding jobs in janitorial services, payroll, personnel services, and property management. As in a number of municipalities, the public sector has been allowed to bid against private companies. After reducing their costs, they have won a number of competitions.[18] Under the George W. Bush presidency, 20,000 to 40,000 jobs were put up for competition or directly converted to the private sector.[19]

The privatization movement has an important international dimension. My colleague in political science, Herman Schwartz, has brilliantly explained why, in the 1980s, Sweden, Denmark, Australia, and New Zealand all took major steps to weaken the power of "unresponsive bureaucratic service producers." In each country there was a successful effort to subject "state agencies and local governments to market discipline."[20]

Systemic Agency Inefficiency

Economists oppose *most* of the activity of many agencies. For example, Amtrak loses money on 41 of its 44 routes.[21] This is partly Congress's fault. It requires that Amtrak spend money on improvements to lightly used long-distance routes. Deirdre McCloskey and Art Cardin also point out that the Cardinal Amtrak train from New York to Washington to Chicago has 31 stops, of which more than a quarter are in West Virginia. They wonder: does this have anything to do with

Robert Byrd, former senator from the Mountain State, serving 51 years – longer than any other senator in history?[22]

Spending on these routes fails to provide public benefits commensurate with the billions of taxpayer dollars needed to buy new trains and improve fixed infrastructure. Such wasteful spending leaves little for the heavily trafficked routes that do indeed require capital improvements, and costly security arrangements in an age of terrorism.[23]

The Bureau of Reclamation projects providing water in western states often have costs that far exceed benefits. Farmers are the largest beneficiaries, and receive water way below market value – often at 10 percent of market value. This artificially low price encourages overuse of water, thereby exacerbating water shortage and depletion problems in the West. Once again, Congress shares responsibility with the administrative entity. "Every Senator...wanted a project in his state; every Congressman wanted one in his district; they didn't care whether they made economic sense or not."[24]

Many of us who have been in the armed services know how wastefully the government can spend money near the end of a fiscal year. If an agency does not use up its budget in the current year, legislators looking for places to cut are likely to assume their budget can be cut next year. If the agency spends all its budgeted amount, it can make a plea for the same amount, or even more next year. At the end of fiscal 1978 the Department of Housing and Urban Development ordered $65,000 worth of furniture, and then spent $800 per month to store it because it was surplus.[25] A year later The Washington Post had a story about surplus furniture dealers who obtain many of their wares by sifting through items federal agencies throw away at the local landfill.[26] There are no easy solutions to these problems.

Wasting Money

The way that some federal agencies treat government money is hard to believe and sad to contemplate. For over 20 years Professional Carpet Service was paid twice for work by departments such as Defense, Agriculture, Justice, Labor, and Commerce. The company would often send a bill, which would go unpaid for several months. So Professional Carpet Service would send out a second bill. Eventually the departments would end up paying both the first and the second bills. The owner of Professional Carpet Service dutifully sent refunds for the double payments. But at one point she became angry and sent 21 refund checks to the Director of the Office of Management and Budget. She also went to the press. Still, she had reservations about doing either. She thought that disclosure of the overpayments could hurt her firm. "Instead of receiving thanks for honesty, she said, most agencies have reacted 'strangely' when she sends the money back. 'It's like they don't like me pointing it out. [...] I'm convinced they will stop giving us their business.'"[27]

Consider also a wasteful practice of the Federal Energy Regulatory Commission (FERC). It regularly puts out for bid a contract for printing transcripts of hearings before the commission. The bids kept getting lower and lower, because hearing transcripts were voluminous and there were so many interested parties – "energy companies, utilities, pipelines, industrial customers, environmentalists, states and countless lawyers" – that printing companies found they could make a killing on resales to these interest groups. One year a company said it would print the transcripts for nothing. Other companies matched that bid the following year. So one firm, Ace-Federal Reporters, Inc., submitted a proposal to pay the FERC $1.25 million over five years for the privilege of printing all the commission's documents.

The FERC's procurement director said such negative bidding would not be accepted. In a letter he observed that the money was "no inducement" because the FERC couldn't keep it anyway. Federal law would require it to go into the US Treasury. A FERC spokesman further explained that the money would be burdensome to administer. A new solicitation for bidding went out indicating that so-called "bonus bids" would be not be allowed. Ace-Federal Reporters, Inc., took the FERC to court, and the judge required the commission to take the money offered by Ace.[28]

Worse than either of these two mind-boggling examples is the cavalier way that congressional representatives and senators get away with not paying fines assessed when convicted of felonies. For example, in the years after he served jail time for bribery and conspiracy, Michael J. Myers (D-Pa.) still owed a $20,000 fine. No effort was made to collect the fine. In these sorts of cases "everyone points the other way... [F]ederal judges say it's up to the courts to collect fines, but the court says it's the US attorney's job. The attorneys claim the Bureau of Prisons have to do more but the Bureau points its finger at the US parole commission."[29] Obviously, the address of the scofflaw is crucial for collection, but, for Myers, it wasn't even required on the document court clerks filled out after a defendant was sentenced. One overworked attorney, Kathleen Haggerty, found that Myers had gone back to his old neighborhood. "But the resources of the federal government could not find him," even though he reported regularly to a parole officer in the US courthouse there.[30]

These are, no doubt, unusually bad cases of government inefficiency. But we talked about a quite ordinary one in Chapter 1's discussion of new, underused urban rail systems. If there were an unlimited amount of space, I could talk about others; for example, one finding of the General Accounting Office: over a period of six years the Department of Defense never sought refunds for $100,000,000 in airline reimbursable tickets that had never been used. The department compounded the problem by reimbursing employee claims for tickets the Pentagon had in fact bought.[31] Or I could discuss the Internal Revenue Service, which routinely abandons billions of dollars in unpaid taxes. A deputy treasury secretary claims many scofflaws would pay up if they simply got a phone call. He urged using private collection processes to help.[32]

Would there be as much waste in the private sector if the press regularly went looking for it? I very much doubt it. A private-sector manager who corrected such waste in his department would have a better chance of getting a bonus or promotion. If the whole business was using resources poorly, it could not keep up with competitors or it could be taken over by investors who were confident they could do better.

The Troublesome Nature of National Industrial Policies

Industrial policy is not a well-defined idea. Still, the most talked about proposals involve substantial new government involvement in directing capital investment toward some firms or industries and away from others.[33] Economists oppose these measures.

Industrial policy advocates often see themselves as supporters of the capitalist system – but supporters see no reason why government should not *help* businesses rejuvenate depressed areas and grow the industries of the future. Proponents think government help should come by directing new capital investment toward firms, industries, and locations thought to be especially important in meeting these two goals. Such policies have been prominent in all recent Democratic presidential campaigns and subsequent administrations. Mainstream economists seem pretty much united in their opposition to these industrial policies. As we will see later, this has led prominent Democratic economists to sharply criticize prominent Democratic politicians' industrial policy proposals. A quick survey of industrial policy failures in Democratic and Republican administrations will help explain economists' opposition.

President Carter promoted the Synthetic Fuels Corporation (SFC), calling it the "keystone" of US energy policy; in 1980 Congress authorized $17 billion for it to act as a sort of investment bank, funding projects that would turn plentiful US coal and shale into oil and gas. Carter predicted that it would be America's most ambitious peacetime industrial mobilization, a project "greater than the sum total of the interstate highway system, the Marshall Plan and the space program all combined."[34] But, as of July 1985, "SFC had committed only $1.2 billion toward three projects – and they would yield less than 2 percent of that 1987 production target Congress had set." Two billion dollars was spent before the corporation was closed down in 1986.[35] In the last three decades, as concerns about air pollution and global warming have sharply risen, the high environmental costs of synfuels have loomed large.

President Clinton was full of industrial policy ideas. A *Washington Post* reporter noted that during his 1992 campaign he spoke "constantly of using government to help 'organize' the American economy." In one speech in Philadelphia, he said "he would spend – or, as he preferred it, 'invest' – $50 billion a year in new environmental systems, new transportation systems, new communication systems."[36] Later, in his first year in office, he proposed a joint government/auto industry project that in ten to 15 years would produce a car that would pollute less than current cars, cost no more and get 70 miles to a gallon of fuel. He said it would be "a technological venture as ambitious as any our nation had ever attempted."[37]

The above and what is to come below illustrate that economists have no interest in having our government organize our economy – an economy that they think is remarkably well organized by markets. More than 25 years have passed since the Clinton administration; in that time we have been producing cars that pollute significantly less. But there is still no large market for high-priced cars that achieve 70 miles to a gallon, and many economists dislike the federal policy that grants a $7500 federal tax credit for people – almost always rich people – who buy Teslas. Most state governments have also forced Tesla to use dealers when they would prefer to sell directly to consumers at a lower price.[38]

President Obama's industrial policies placed a heavy emphasis on clean energy. I have not seen a systematic assessment of the costs and benefits of the various projects. There have been well-publicized failures, however; Solyndra, a solar energy company, has been studied most thoroughly. Solyndra received the first guaranteed loan, for $535 million, in 2009. It went bankrupt in 2011. True, the company had some bad luck; for example, the price of polysilicon, a key ingredient for most competing technologies, dropped by about 89 percent. But there was also extravagance in the new $733,000,000 plant, with whistling robots and spa showers,[39] and the Department of Energy's inspector general concluded that Solyndra had misled the department in its characterization of the sales contracts it had in hand.[40] Further, there were charges of crony capitalism from the start. George Kaiser, a key Obama fundraiser, had a financial stake in Solyndra. The company's two top executives made 20 trips to the White House while the loan application was being considered and then invoked the Fifth Amendment rather than answer questions of the House Energy and Commerce Committee.[41]

The billionaire entrepreneur Peter Thiel has noted that 40 solar firms went under in 2012 alone. He believes that successful technology companies need "proprietary technology an order of magnitude better than its nearest substitute." Solyndra's novel cylindrical solar cells were *less* efficient than flat ones.[42] Thiel goes on to argue that the general idea of green energy should not have implied

> an overwhelming business opportunity for cleantech companies of all kinds. [...] Great companies have secrets: specific reasons for success that other people don't see. [...] Doing something different is what is truly good for society. [...] The best projects are likely to be overlooked, not trumpeted by a crowd; the best problems to work on are often the ones nobody else even tries to solve.[43]

Solyndra aside, the Department of Energy's $36 billion subsidized loan program for clean energy was widely criticized. The left-of-center *Washington Post*'s editorial page sounded like an economist when it called the whole program a "scandal." "You can call it crony capitalism or venture socialism – but by whatever name, the energy department's loan guarantee program privatizes profits and socializes losses." The *Post* continued by quoting from a 2010 Internal Office of Management and Budget email: "'What's terrifying,' one staffer wrote, 'is that after looking at some of the ones that came next, this one [Solyndra] started to look better. Bad days are coming.'"[44]

The *Post*'s criticism was echoed by an energy expert who was a friend of the Obama administration. Dan Carol, who worked on Obama's 2008 campaign, sent a "blistering" email to senior White House officials. He complained about the number of Department of Energy "deals that have gone to Obama donors and have underperformed."[45] Furthermore, the energy department rushed to get solar guaranteed loans out before the end of the fiscal year, when its authority to grant loans would expire. Indeed, $4.7 billion was committed just hours before the programs' funding expired.[46]

Republicans are more likely than Democrats to have a philosophical objection to "picking winners." For example, President Reagan's administration complained that the Synthetic Fuels Corporation charter – "providing subsidies to private industry for commercial-scale projects – ran counter to free-market principles."[47] Reagan increased defense spending, which, of course, helped defense firms, but he had no policy specifically aimed at building up a firm or industry.

George W. Bush was the Republican who strayed furthest from conservative doctrine against subsidies to particular industries. In his 2003 State of the Union address he called for "a new national commitment" to work toward hydrogen-powered vehicles so that "our scientists and engineers will overcome obstacles to taking these cars from laboratory to showroom." From 2004 to 2008 the federal government spent $1.2 billion on hydrogen vehicle projects. The General Accounting Office later found that about a quarter of the money went to "congressionally directed projects" rather than research and development. The cost of the vehicle that resulted was prohibitive, and the car was never commercially sold.[48]

George W. Bush also supported steel tariffs, which studies showed cost jobs rather than preserving them.[49] Late in his 1992 reelection campaign, Bush's father added a subsidy for wheat exports and dropped his opposition to development of a "tilt rotor" aircraft and a modernized M-1 tank. The Homestead Air Force Base "barely escaped closure" by an independent commission in 1991. After that decision the Florida base was ravished by a hurricane. Keeping the base open meant rebuilding a place that was barely justified even when it was fully built! Florida was crucial to his electoral coalition, and President George H. W. Bush decided to support rebuilding.[50]

Donald Trump's tariff-centered trade policies ended up picking winners right and left based on no particular theory. The favoritism came by way of exemptions from tariffs. For example, exemptions were granted to companies that sold salmon and cod (caught in Alaska and processed in China), and fracking chemicals. The process for granting favors was opaque. Sometimes Trump got directly involved. He consistently helped "companies and workers in key battleground states" he hoped to win in 2020.[51]

Economists are close to unanimous in believing that trade is beneficial to all countries that participate, since it enables all sides to focus on activities for which they have a comparative (relative) advantage. Trade also brings more variety in goods and lower costs through economies of scale and increased competition. Whether you look at Harvard's Greg Mankiw, George W. Bush's Chairman of the Council of Economic Advisers, on the right, or Paul Krugman, Nobel laureate and *New York Times* columnist, on the left, you will find free trade advocates.[52]

This survey is sufficient to show that industrial policies in the United States have not had significant achievements. Similarly, economists think that the European experience has been "terrible" and "conspicuously unsuccessful."[53] Targeted industries, such as aircraft in the United Kingdom, computers in France, and the nuclear industry in Germany, have done poorly. For a time Japan's growth rate was clearly superior to ours. But studies by economists found that government investment was not the secret to their success; in any case, Japan's economic performance over recent decades is clearly inferior to ours.[54]

In the last decade or so China's growth rate has been terrific, but these gains came as China moved toward a free-market system. Some aspects of central planning remain, however, especially in the allocation of financial capital to politically connected businesses. Paul Krugman and Robin Wells's popular introductory economics text concludes its discussion of China by saying "many economists" have commented that this type of inefficiency "must be addressed if China is to sustain its rapid growth."[55]

An economic encyclopedia notes that it was in the early to mid-1980s that discussion of industrial policy was most prominent in the United States. Democratic presidential candidates thought that the nation was in long-term economic decline and could not regenerate itself without "greater government involvement in the restructuring of the economy." The 1984 Democratic presidential nominee, Walter Mondale, was a strong industrial policy proponent who thought that President Reagan's policies were "destroying industry – not building it."[56]

It is remarkable to see how many left-of-center Democratic economists disagreed with Mondale on this issue. MIT's Nobel laureate Paul Samuelson said industrial policy was "not good macroeconomics. And I don't think it's defensible social philosophy."[57] Lifelong Democrat and Carter economic adviser Alfred Kahn is on record as fearing that industrial revitalization policies would provide "a vehicle for business and labor to exert their concerted influence to enlist the government as a great protector, subsidizer and carteliser." Walter Heller was concerned about Democratic presidential candidates' searching for "novelty rather than soundness." William Nordhaus, a member of President Carter's Council of Economic Advisers, believed that "the clearest difference between the Democratic candidates and Reagan" concerned government intervention through industrial policy. "On this [issue]," Nordhaus said, he was "on the side" of Reagan. And Charles Schultze, chairman of Council of Economic Advisers, said, "I'd like to get all these Democratic candidates off this industrial policy kick, which I think is absolute nonsense." Schultze believed that, although the United States has economic problems, "an inability to make the necessary transition from old industries to newer, growing ones is not one of them."[58] More recently, Larry Summers, a prominent economist in both the Clinton and Obama administrations, has said that the government is a "crappy" venture capitalist.[59]

Republican administrations, especially under President George W. Bush, have supported enterprise zones, which give tax breaks and sometimes other assistance to businesses that are located in low-income areas. In principle, economists look more favorably on these than on industrial policies, because the aid goes to any business in the low-income areas, not only those chosen by government. The Obama administration also supported enterprise zones (they were called "promise zones"), but only in low-income areas they designated. A number of studies have found enterprise zones ineffective in stimulating employment in low-income areas.[60] The Trump administration called its enterprise zones "opportunity zones." The 2017 tax cuts provided, for the first time, "unlimited" tax incentives for these zones.[61] It is too early to see if results have been more favorable.

As indicated earlier in the chapter, economists do support government research expanding the base of technical knowledge, which in turn seems likely to lead to profitable innovations in the future. For example, I would think that most economists would support the activities of the Advanced Research Projects Agency – Energy. Funding for this agency has not been large, and, unfortunately, President Trump's fiscal 2021 blueprint for the budget proposed to eliminate ARPA-E. This sort of spending is less appealing to politicians because it does not clearly create jobs.[62]

Theoretical Reasons for Industrial Policy Failures

The Columbia economist Richard Nelson notes that private technological innovation is largely unpredictable. Many seemingly promising developments do not pan out. Other important breakthroughs were unexpected and not supported by most experts in the field.[63] Nelson finds that "in most of the technically progressive industries, like chemicals and electronics, most of the bad bets were rather quickly abandoned, particularly if someone else was coming up with a better solution, and good new ideas generally had a variety of paths to get their case heard." On the other hand,

> military R&D programs since the mid-50's, the civil reactor programs, and the supersonic transport experience are in sad contrast. In all of these areas the early batting average has been dismal. However, there has been a tendency to stick with the game plan despite mounting evidence that it is not a good one.[64]

Nelson suspects that a central plan for technological advance would make things worse, because such advance is not "a clearly plannable activity. [. . .] Only in hindsight does the right approach seem obvious; before the fact, it is far from clear which of a bewildering array of options will prove most fruitful or even feasible."

Nelson favors an active government role in support of basic research and applied knowledge of widespread interest (where non-appropriable public good benefits may be present). But he opposes support for development of particular products that government believes will be commercial winners. Nelson finds that the historical record for such government ventures is "unequivocal. Unequivocally negative."[65] Nelson's studies show that it is essentially impossible to plan technological advance. Other students of scientific advance agree. One says: "If you look at the Nobel laureates in case after case after case the critical event was a surprise."[66]

Some of the greatest inventors didn't have a clue about what they had accomplished. Marconi thought his radio would be used mainly by steamship lines. Alexander Graham Bell's patent for the telephone was described as "improvements in telegraphy." The Nobel-Prize-winning scientist who proved that "bizarre infectious proteins" could cause mad cow disease "endured derision from his peers for decades." The idea that ulcers were caused by a germ was also laughed at until it was proved to be correct.[67] Isaac Asimov put the unpredict-ability this way: "The most exciting phrase to hear in science, one that heralds new discoveries, is not 'Eureka!' (I found it!) but 'That's funny...'"[68]

The winner of a $2.6 million prize for developing a lightweight affordable health kit that could diagnose and interpret 13 health conditions bested 300 entries. He was an emergency room physician working in his home office with the help of his relatives. Many of the runners-up were backed by large corporations. The second prize went to a group of 50 physicians, scientists, and programmers; it was headed by a Harvard Medical School physicist with a 29-page resume. Who would have thought at the start that the emergency room physician would win the prize?[69]

A student at Rensselaer Polytechnic Institute (RPI) had had some experience harvesting mushrooms when he was growing up. "He thought it might be possible to make insulation out of fungi" – and in a class before he graduated he proved he was right. He founded Ecovative Design, which hoped to produce "a mass-market, organic insulation material, which was also a more environmentally friendly...product than Styrofoam, the nonbiodegradable carbon intense material widely used in packing and shipping." Computer giant Dell now uses the mater-ial in its packaging and IKEA and many other companies are exploring its use. No federal grant was needed, nor would any have ever been awarded to an RPI undergraduate.[70]

Far more significant than any of these inventions was George Mitchell's figuring out how to efficiently free natural gas from shale. Hydraulic fracturing was first tried in the late 1940s and was "helped along by Department of Energy research in the 1970s." Through 15 years of failure Mitchell ignored all the doubters and kept plugging along until he found that an injection of a water, sand, and chemical mixture could make fracking commercially viable. Because of the local environmental effects of the drilling, regulation of fracking processes will be necessary. But gas releases half as much carbon dioxide as coal, which is still widely used to produce electricity. In August 2012 a *Washington Post* headline was trumpeting "emissions of CO_2 fall to 20-year low in US." Over the first five years of fracking in the United States the reduction in CO_2 emissions was twice what had been achieved from "the total effect of the Kyoto Protocol and all other climate legislation in the rest of the world over the previous 20 years." Fracking has also reduced energy costs significantly and made the United States an energy exporter.[71] On July 14, 2018, the Associated Press declared that "the idea that the US could ever again become the world's top oil producer once seemed preposterous." Daniel Yergen, an oil industry expert, adds: "A decade ago the only question was how fast would US production go down."[72]

Even if one could predict scientific advance, economists cite evidence that politicians would not put the public's money toward these technologies. The Model Cities program and the Economic Development Administration were both meant to provide selective assistance to targeted areas. But the six test sites for model cities soon became 150, and the Economic Development Administration's aid to economically depressed counties soon went to 87.5 percent of *all* US counties. When our political process has discriminated between winning and losing industries, it has usually favored losers, because they are established industries upon which more voters depend. The steel industry gets a lot of attention; bioengineering much less.[73]

Moreover, even if the government could put federal monies exactly where private investors would, not as much would be gained, because businesses that lose out on federal largess would suspect political favoritism even if there were none. We don't need more cynicism about politics.

But who can believe that politics won't be considered? *Washington Post* columnists spoke to clean-tech companies that got both federal money and President Obama visits and many that did not. Both camps believed that "an image of Obama speaking from a factory floor brings global attention to companies trying to raise capital and best competitors." Orion Energy Systems in Wisconsin "worked political connections for two years to get an Obama visit." The chief executive said that, with customers, "it is huge credibility." The president of Cooper Lighting in Georgia, a Republican stronghold at the time, said his company sells "six times more energy efficient lighting than Orion." He would be happy to host the president but was not waiting by the phone.[74]

What *Are* Economists Worried about?

Economists are certainly worried about increased inequality in income and decreases in male labor supply. The subjects are better discussed in the following chapter on equity, however.

Weaker Economic Growth and Lousy Statistics that Make It Seem Worse than It Is

One of the most common refrains of politicians running for office is "Jobs, jobs, jobs." Economists, of course, like the refrain when unemployment is high. Increases in unemployment reduce economic growth, and the unemployed are more likely to use illegal drugs and to become depressed. But we hear the "Jobs, jobs, jobs" slogan even when the unemployment rate is low by historical standards. President Trump thought we were losing the good manufacturing jobs to Mexico; 24 years earlier the businessman Ross Perot made a serious run for the presidency as an independent. Perot also focused on the harm that Mexican trade caused. He asked us to keep a hand to our ears so as to hear the "giant sucking sound" of jobs heading south. Remarkably, despite several decades of jobs rolling toward Mexico, our unemployment rate has not risen, and the average US worker has increased his level of economic well-being! (Readers may have heard that the average worker has made no economic progress – but see below and Chapter 5.)

For economists, the biggest problem with the "Jobs, jobs, jobs" chorus is that the politicians usually emphasize preserving existing jobs because it is job holders in existing industries who are the voters. Thus,

President Trump put a lot of emphasis on coal miners and steelworkers. Economists want us to understand that, if we want to continue to be one of the richest countries in the world, we have to be willing to work at new jobs at cutting-edge companies. Many of the jobs in older industries will inevitably be lost to labor-saving technologies and countries with significantly lower wages. Economists thus worry when they see evidence that workers are less willing to move for better job opportunities than they used to be.[75]

I think most economists would prefer a mantra of "Growth, growth, growth" to "Jobs, jobs, jobs." Some official statistics say there has been little or no growth in real wages for decades. Politicians claim this is terrible, and they promise to do better.

In a 2018 article entitled "For most US workers, real wages have barely budged in decades," the Pew Foundation sets forth the dismal facts of the usual presentation. The conclusion is: "After adjusting for inflation...today's average hourly wage has just about the same purchasing power it did in 1978." Pew does acknowledge that benefits, especially for health care, have increased substantially in recent decades.[76] But official growth rates underestimate growth because they underestimate improvements in products and the worth of new products. The latest phones are not just phones. When you buy an iPhone you no longer need to buy a camera, a GPS, or a CD player. Official accounting for these types of product improvements misses much of the gain provided. And then there is all the "free" stuff: Facebook, Wikipedia, and search engines such as Google.

Economists have tried to come up with a rough and ready estimate of the worth of these free goods by asking how much people would pay rather than do without them. This is an effort to try and value consumers' improvements in well-being because of the existence of these products. Using this method, some findings are as follows: the median consumer would, if necessary, pay annually $17,530 to avoid the loss of search engines, $8414 to avoid the loss of email, and $3648 to avoid the loss of easy access to maps.[77] These numbers seem awfully high, since, when added together, they reach a level almost as high as median income! But they do serve to show that the public really values these products.

In his book criticizing the rationality of ordinary voters, one of Bryan Caplan's complaints is that voters are too pessimistic about the workings of our market economy.[78] Misleading statements such as those in the Pew report just increase irrational pessimism among the public. If people think the economy is performing very badly, they are more likely to support left- or right-wing populist politicians. Neither type is popular among mainstream economists.[79]

Economists *are* worried, however, about some trends in the economy that they believe reduce growth rates. For example, new businesses are an important source of increasing growth, and their number has been declining in recent decades.[80] The decline in the willingness of workers to move for better jobs also causes a decline in growth.[81] But I believe most economists would agree with Caplan; when they look at the big picture, they think the public is too critical of our economic performance. They are impressed by what markets and our capitalist system have produced over time. There is no agreement about how much official figures on growth should be adjusted to take account of the sorts of economic gains for ordinary consumers that official statistics ignore. But, even without looking at gains from recent technological marvels, more mundane product improvements are not fully accounted for.

In 1970 I paid $350 for a 19-inch color television set. Search engines can quickly tell me that Best Buy now has a 19-inch color television set for $69.99 – of inflation-controlled dollars. The set today would also have better color, better sound, and a remote that would make it unnecessary to get up from a chair to change channels.[82]

Mark Perry compares the cost of a room air-conditioner in 1956 with one today, but, instead of comparing costs in dollar terms, he computes how many hours an average factory worker would have had to put in to buy the air-conditioner in 1956 versus now. The results are 164 hours of work in 1956 and 11 hours of work in 2014. The contemporary air-conditioner was also more than three times as powerful as the one for sale in 1956.[83]

Misinformed Criticism of Some Market Characteristics

Imagine a profit-seeking CEO. Economists, unlike much of academe, find him pleasant to contemplate. The economist imagines the business leader to be just as greedy as his colleagues do, perhaps even more so. But today's economist, like Adam Smith, thinks that, although the profit-seeking business leader does not intend to promote the public interest, by an "invisible hand" he promotes it nonetheless.[84] Higher prices and higher profits induced pencil manufacturers to give the consumer more of what he wanted, and losses made the toothpick manufacturer willing to make available added resources so that the pencil manufacturer could do so. If the consumer demand for pencils remains strong, above-normal prices and profits will lead new firms to start making pencils. This added production plus the increase by the old firms will in turn lead to lower prices and a profit rate from pencils no higher than in other industries. This "normal profit" is the return to investors for being willing to defer consumption (save) and take risks. The risk-taking and deferred consumption (capital) permit investment, and the resulting increases in worker productivity and wages that spread benefits throughout society. Only persistently higher-than-normal profits not explained by greater-than-normal risk or firm efficiency trouble economists.

For economists, profits are not an arbitrary decision to give business owners and managers more money – money that might instead have been transferred to workers. Good management emphasizes cost-cutting, creating and improving products, and accurately predicting consumer demand.[85] Managers who are lousy at these tasks will not just have lower profits; they are likely to go out of business. Competing firms keep the pressure on for good performance.

In one survey the public thought the average return on investment was 32 percent. At the time the profit rate was about 13 percent.[86] Even this 13 percent return is not a cost of doing business that government might avoid if it provided the same good or service. Additional increments of government spending are usually paid by debt (federal spending is the majority of total public spending), and those who lend this capital also expect a return (a "profit"). The tax-free interest on municipal bonds that makes municipalities' borrowing costs lower than industry's does so only by forsaking an equivalent amount of taxes, which means other taxes must eventually be raised.[87]

Some readers will be skeptical: what about the unfair way that companies scoop off profits from the people who actually produce the products? Look at farmers; they get a fraction of the profits from their hard work. What about speculators; what are they doing to earn their profits? What about price gougers who jack up their price for gasoline after a war in the Middle East: why are their excess profits justifiable? How does it help the economy when corporations increasingly use their profits to buy back their stock? The stock is disproportionately owned by the wealthy, so this practice just increases wealth inequality.

Economists offer reasonable defenses for all of these much-maligned groups. Complaints about middlemen come even from US presidents. Alfred Kahn, a distinguished economist who served President Carter at a time of very high inflation, told me that Carter was a good listener, but Kahn was unable to weaken his animus toward middlemen. As a former peanut farmer, he thought he was doing the hard work, but middlemen were getting most of the profits. Farmers can do without middlemen, and some do; they participate in farmers' markets, which are growing throughout the country. But most farmers think they make more money if other people store and transport their product and then sell it in grocery stores. Middlemen are a further development of the wealth-increasing division of labor. If they do not provide services worth their costs, retailers that do not use them will put out of business not just the middlemen but also the retailers they supply.

Some businesses do find that they can make more money by cutting out a middleman; think of the many who sell their products online. Unfortunately, government sometimes prevents attempts to cut out the middleman. They make it hard, for example, for Tesla to sell cars without using an established automobile dealership. But middlemen are not going away – they seem to me to be growing. I love TripAdvisor and OpenTable. Many brides seem to want a wedding planner. Speculation is condemned if it is part of an attempt to monopolize or "corner" a market. But usually it serves a socially useful function and helps stabilize prices for both consumer and producer. When bad weather hurts next year's coffee crop, congressmen howl at the "manipulation" of the market that leads to sharp rises in prices for coffee *this* year, as speculators compete with retailers for the available supply. But speculators hurt consumers this year only by helping them next. They buy coffee only because they think prices will be significantly higher next year than this. If they are right, the higher price means consumers will value the coffee next year even more than this year. Without the speculators, third cups this year might be available only at the expense of seconds next, and the price swings between the two years would be far greater.[88]

When, in 2012, oil prices rose sharply, President Obama felt the need to assure the public that his administration was on guard to ensure that speculators did not "artificially manipulate markets."

Robert J. Samuelson, who enjoys respect from economists for his balanced economic commentary, began a column entitled "The fallacy of blaming oil speculators" with a quote from Obama's speech. Samuelson quoted economists who said the recent spike in oil prices was the result of changes in supply and demand.[89]

Price gougers may just be lucky. Gas station owners did not predict that Iraq was going to invade Kuwait in 1990, but their gasoline and their contracts for future gasoline soon became more valuable than they had expected. They raised their prices and thus enjoyed "windfall profits." But, if we think it's fair to forbid windfall profits, will we also subsidize gas station owners who are unlucky and suffer windfall losses? Economists prefer to emphasize the benefits that price gougers provide. When the price of gas goes up substantially, drivers will drive less, drillers will bring up more oil, and refiners will turn more into gasoline. When faced with price gouging, economists emphasize that a process to overcome shortages has begun. Help is on the way. The higher the gougers gouge, the more will be the conservation and the new production that will appear.[90]

Senator Chuck Schumer and Bernie Sanders sharply criticize the increases in stock buybacks. They promote legislation which would make them illegal unless the corporations first invest in "workers and their communities." Economists say it may well be that the best investment opportunities are not in the corporations that made the profits. Schumer and Sanders seem to think that the increased wealth from buybacks will be spent on luxuries. As will be shown in the following chapter, the much-maligned top 1 percent are much more likely to invest their marginal income rather than spend it.[91]

As these rebuttals indicate, most economists think many major government interventions in the economy that are meant to improve efficiency and growth do more harm not good.

Microeconomic Policies that Need Attention

Licensing of Occupations and Overregulation of Commercial Life

Economists think there is too much regulation of commercial enterprise. One area of focus is the restrictions of the freedom to work. In the 1970s about 10 percent of individuals who worked had to have licenses, but by 2015 about 30 percent of the workforce needed a license to work.[92] Economists know that, if you restrict entry into a profession, the decrease in supply will lead to increased income for practitioners. Many think that the growing credentialism in the United States is sparked by the self-interest of the groups that would benefit from more regulation.

There is no evidence that the public is protected if only dentists are allowed to administer teeth whiteners; but in North Carolina the Board of Dentistry, "mainly elected by dentists themselves," tried to prevent hygienists and beauticians from whitening customers' teeth. It took the Federal Trade Commission and a case before the Supreme Court to keep them from doing so.[93] Similarly, a full review of the literature found "no study that raised concerns about the quality of care offered by nurse practitioners." But in many states they cannot prescribe shoes for diabetics without the approval of a doctor. In California nurse practitioners must be supervised by a doctor, but no doctor may supervise more than four nurse practitioners. The California Medical Association campaigns hard against reform of this law.[94]

In comparison to other countries the US bar associations, composed of lawyers themselves, make it much harder to become a lawyer. They insist, for example, that a three-year law degree is necessary to provide most legal services. The result is more expensive legal service. In fact, the World Justice Project ranks the United States 96th among 113 countries for access to and affordability of justice.[95] Doctors and lawyers represent about one-quarter of the top 1 percent of American earners. They are paid much more here than in the same professions in other rich countries.[96]

Many well-meaning citizens believe that our regulations "were developed to protect citizens from the more powerful" – from "influential non-elected entities [seeking] profit."[97] As noted above, economists increasingly think, to the contrary, that it is the influential nonelected entities that regulate themselves so they can control entry and make still more money.[98]

Even when a licensed practitioner would be likely to provide safer service to a customer, the license requirement may not lead to safer outcomes for customers. As always, economists remind us that incentives matter. Take electricians, for example. An early study found that "accidental electrocutions occurred 10 times more often in states with the most restrictive licensing rules for electricians."[99] This could happen because restrictive entry leads to higher prices being charged by electricians, which, in turn, leads to more self-help work done by folks who would be customers of electricians if their prices were lower.

In many states there are unnecessary, time-consuming, and expensive requirements for less well-paid occupations for which consumers would be able to judge successful outcomes without further supervision. These include florists, travel guides, dance instructors, hair braiders, manicurists, interior designers, and upholsterers. Relaxing these licensing requirements would expand occupational opportunities for low- and middle-income workers and reduce prices for all of us. It would also increase the practitioners' opportunities to start a small business.[100]

Leading politicians agree with economists that there is no public interest justification for many restrictions on the freedom to work. Indeed, both the Obama and Trump administrations encouraged states to scale back onerous licensing regulations.[101]

Of course, much regulatory activity is aimed at businesses, not occupations. Between 1970 and 2008 the number of prescriptive rules in federal regulations mushroomed under Democratic and Republican administrations. In that period the number of prescriptive words such as "shall" and "must" grew from 403,00 to 963,000. Whatever their virtues, both the Affordable Care Act (Obamacare) and the Dodd–Frank financial reform bill led to thousands of pages of new rules.

We saw above that economists emphasize economic growth. Increased regulation is offered as one of the main factors reducing growth and new business expansion. Since small and large companies alike require staff to document compliance with regulations, regulatory costs, as a percentage of all costs, are higher for small than for large businesses. A survey of small firms found that one in five considered regulatory compliance their biggest problem.[102]

Economist Luigi Zingales migrated to the United States from Italy because he wanted no part of the Italian economic system, where far too often success depended on who one knew, not what one accomplished. He and many other economists fear that, by distributing grants to particular businesses, bailing out some banks and financiers, and doling out licenses to particular occupations, we have been moving toward an Italian-like crony capitalism.[103]

The economics profession is especially proud of having led the way in achieving deregulation of many infrastructure industries, such as trucking, railroads, telecommunications, utilities, and air fares.

Economist Elizabeth Bailey argues that "the regulatory movement of the 1930s reflected the view the market failure was pervasive. [...] The deregulation movement of the late 1970s and early 1980s reflected the view that economic regulation of prices and entry was a government failure."[104]

Deregulation has worked well. Five years after the interstate commerce commission started to decontrol the industry, rates for truckload shipments fell about 25 percent. Moreover, service to small communities increased and complaints by shippers decreased.[105] Deregulation of airfares has brought an average decrease in fares of about 30 percent.[106] With the success of deregulation, two government agencies, the Interstate Commerce Commission and the Civil Aeronautics Board, were shut down.

What was remarkable about airline deregulation was not just the overwhelming support by economists but also the coming together of liberal and conservative politicians in support of deregulation. This strong support owed much to comparisons of 1970s fares on interstate routes regulated by the Civil Aeronautics Board with intrastate Texas and California routes of similar length. The fares on the regulated interstate routes were more than 70 percent higher than on equivalent intrastate routes even though the market concentration ratios on these latter routes were quite high. On the Los Angeles to San Francisco route, one of the best serviced, two companies had about 70 percent of the business. This seems to be evidence of considerable market power. Yet even this relatively low level of competition and the threat of more if prices went up kept air fares well below government-regulated interstate levels.[107] Evidence such as this makes understandable economists' skepticism about government's ability to improve upon the performance of imperfect markets.

Economists remain in the forefront of groups pushing regulatory reform. For example, they oppose efforts by many localities to place roadblocks in front of Uber and Airbnb. The University of Chicago's Booth School of Business surveyed a panel of prominent economists about various issues. *All* of them believed that "[l]etting car services such as Uber or Lyft compete with taxi firms on equal footing regarding genuine safety and insurance requirements, but without restrictions on prices or routes, raises consumer welfare."[108] Economists are not surprised to learn that it is mainly the taxi companies and hotels that want laws hindering firms such as Uber and Airbnb, not the ordinary public.

Some readers will be astonished that anyone would be praising airline performance these days. Complaints are everywhere; at the time of this writing it was airplanes' seat sizes that were receiving the most complaints. Passengers felt they were packed in like sardines, with their knees nearly touching the seat in front of them. Seats are certainly less roomy than they used to be. Since 1978 rows of seats have moved three inches closer together, and the width of seats has shrunk by one and a half inches. About a half of male passengers have shoulders that are wider than the average coach seat.

The Federal Aviation Administration says it will regulate only if there are safety issues. Their studies show that smaller seats do not increase evacuation times. If they had read Chapter 1 of this book, they might have added that very few planes crash, and only in a very few of those crashes would shorter evacuation times have made a difference in survival.

The Flyers Rights consumer group says it will sue. The dean of an aeronautics university says: "Airlines will do almost anything to make a buck, I'm sorry to say." She is offended that their pricing system is to stick you in their worst seats and make you "buy your way out" if you want to sit in "economy plus." Representative Steve Cohen (D-Tenn.) "has pushed an amendment through the House Transportation Committee that would require the FAA to set seat sizes."[109]

The above paragraph is based on stories on National Public Radio and in *The Washington Post*. The authors seem almost as upset with the current situation as are the complainers they write about. They seem to think it's completely obvious that it would be in the public interest if the FAA took charge of seat design for our airlines.[110]

Late in 2018 an article in *The Washington Post* described a section of the congressional funding bill for the FAA. The section would allow the secretary of the Department of Transportation to regulate airlines' abilities to add fees for such things as checking extra bags, changing tickets, sitting on the aisle, or having a seat with more legroom.[111] Again, the *Post* news article frames the question in terms of whether Congress would end up doing what the public wanted or what the airline lobbyists wanted. In other words, the public, according to the *Post* reporter, would clearly do better with the regulation of airline fees and seat size.

Economists would want transparency in pricing. A customer considering buying a ticket should know about all the added fees that might ensue. But, beyond this, I think that the airlines' current pricing system would sound pretty good to economists. Passengers who want a little more room can pay a higher price and get it. Passengers who want to save a little money would sit in smaller seats, in the middle of a row, and in the back of the plane.

The beauty of market pricing is that everybody doesn't have to purchase the same form of a product. In the case of airline pricing, the economist considers a 5' 3" mother traveling with a three-year-old. She doesn't need wide seats or a lot of legroom. She would love to give these fringes up to save some money. Both passengers who want to save lots of money and those who want lots of amenities benefit from flying with each other, because they can share in covering the airlines' fixed costs.[112]

I suspect that the congressmen and others who complain would also complain if the airlines raised prices when they were required to have larger seats. But airlines have competitors and don't make exorbitant profits year after year. Here is what *The Wall Street Journal* had to say in 2018:

> Airlines' average profit margin of 9% [out of gross revenue] is about average for a US business. [...] But that average is a leap for an industry that had cumulative losses from 1979 to 2014 of $35 billion and suffered six major bankruptcies in the 2000s. [...] Airline profits last year were squeezed by higher fuel and labor costs..., [and] expanding competition from low-fare carriers has kept fare increases small.[113]

If the airlines can carry fewer people on a plane, their costs will go up and so will their prices. The analysis of pollution pricing in Chapter 3 is also relevant here. The secretary of transportation is told that he or she should make decisions about excess fees based on whether they are "unreasonable or disproportional to the costs incurred." How in the world would the secretary of transportation do this in a rational or fair way? For example, the costs would depend on the configurations of the airline's planes! So, as with pollution, the regulators would have to get into the bowels of *each* airline's cost structure, based on the size of its planes, among other things. We would end up with another morass of arbitrary regulation for no good reason.

Currently some planes have more legroom than others. If airlines think they can get more passengers with still cheaper tickets and still smaller seats, the market will tell them if they are right. And if they are wrong customers will desert them for other airlines. No one complains when restaurant prices are higher for large steaks than for smaller ones. Economists wonder why it should be outrageous if larger seats are priced higher than smaller ones.

I am old enough to remember the "good old days." There were more vacant seats, and planes were less crowded; the airlines, forbidden by the Civil Aeronautics Board to compete with a lower price, would compete, say, by having a famous chef plan their meals. I remember those flights fondly, but I try to remind myself that I'm saving substantial money by forsaking those pleasures. And, by signing up for economy plus on longer flights, I can get a little more room and still pay significantly less than I would have 40 years ago.[114]

Stronger Antitrust Policies?

One form of regulation is antitrust policy. Interventions for antitrust reasons have had some economist support for many decades. Since economists would like to see more new startups and small companies, one might expect them to favor stronger antitrust policies. Also relevant is the large market power of tech firms such as Apple and Amazon.[115]

But economists are split on whether to advocate stronger antitrust policies. Some say tech companies such as Amazon, Facebook, and Google have too much market power and are likely to get more; they should be broken up. Other economists say these sorts of predictions of future market power have been proved wrong over and over again. While the government's monopolization case was pending against Alcoa (1937–51), its share of the aluminum industry fell from 90 percent to 55 percent. While the case against IBM was pending (1969–82), the industry went through two generations of computers, foreign competition increased, and minicomputers able to handle almost all computing tasks were developed and marketed by many smaller firms.[116]

In a survey article in *Regulation* magazine, Alan Reynolds makes the following points. iTunes jumped into the early lead in online music, supposedly creating nearly "predatory" competition for compact discs. But in 2011 Savage Beast went public as Pandora and

Stockholm's Spotify launched its US service. One of the highest market shares is Google's: Google held a 72.5 percent share of global meta-search in mid-2016. But Google was not the first to enter this market. AltaVista, Lycos, Infoseek, HotBot, Excite, and Yahoo beat them there. These early winners were soon trumped, however, by Google, Ask, and Bing. Reynolds also notes that meta-search is only part of a much larger universe that includes specialized vertical search engines such as OpenTable, TripAdvisor, Match, Yelp, and Houzz, not to mention Expedia, and comparative shopping engines such as Amazon, eBay, PriceGrabber, NexTag, and Shopzilla.[117]

Advocates of stronger antitrust policy pay special attention to Amazon because it seeks to dominate in so many areas. Moreover, its competitors often use the Amazon online site. Sears's stock went up significantly when Amazon decided to sell its appliances. Many small retailers feel they have no choice but to use Amazon's platform to reach their customers.

Those opposed to a stronger antitrust policy point out that Amazon doesn't in fact dominate in its new markets. In clothing, for example, where it has made a big push, Amazon accounts for 20 percent of online sales but less than 7 percent overall. Amazon will soon dethrone Best Buy as the largest seller of consumer electronics, but, even there, its overall share will be only 20 percent.[118] I used to think that Amazon was so useful and efficient online that no one could ever catch them. But Walmart thinks it can compete with Amazon's online dominance.

Beyond economics, it is a fair question whether, politically, we want single firms to be as powerful as Amazon and Google. Will they inevitably have more political power than we are comfortable with? This is one of the concerns of Steven Pearlstein, a *Washington Post* economics editor. His "Is Amazon getting too big?" article summarizes the debate and argues for more governmental antitrust interventions. But Pearlstein quotes a former antitrust official who believes that antitrust cases are so complicated and open to argument that "an unconstrained antitrust policy could be an invitation to 'political and ideological mischief.'"[119] Jeff Bezos, founder of Amazon, also owns *The Washington Post*, a consistent critic of Donald Trump as president. Trump threatened Bezos with "a huge antitrust problem" because he was using the *Post* as a "tool for political power against me."[120] Abuse in presidential power is more worrisome than abuse of even an

Amazon's power.[121] Both camps would agree on one thing: markets work well only if there is competition.

Economist Tyler Cowen says there is. He sees too much market power in pharma and hospitals. But, those areas aside, the biggest companies don't act like monopolists. Monopolists restrict entry and raise prices. Google does neither. It provides search services – and Gmail for free. Amazon's platform provides price and quality information on more competitors for goods and services than was ever available previously. The Googles' and Amazons' wages are higher than for small business – even for janitors. The big Chinese companies compete with our big tech companies. Cowen argues that, if the managers of our big companies need to worry about antitrust and public relations rather than competitive business practices, they will lose out to the Chinese.[122]

Economists Warn against the Side Effects of Government Forcing Businesses to Be Kinder to Labor

The subtitle above is a complaint of economists sure to bring outrage from many left-of-center political commentators. "I told you these guys are so wedded to markets that they couldn't care less if the gains of economic growth go only to those at the top."

To head off such complaints, economists don't usually make a *general* argument against attempts to help ordinary workers through government intervention in the economy. But they certainly have reservations, if not opposition. Most would prefer that any redistribution of income toward the poor and middle class be by higher taxes on upper income folks rather than by less targeted and often damaging direct intervention in markets.[123]

The economists' argument here is likely to rekindle in readers stereotypes of economists as unfeeling and inhumane. Remember, though, that it is mainly the consumer's well-being that economists always keep in mind; they know that consumer sovereignty often means that some people will lose their jobs. Consumers would like products to be well made and cheaper. To accomplish this, businesses must reduce costs. Labor is an important cost. One way to reduce labor costs is to improve business procedures or equipment so as to be able to make the same product with less labor.

This may mean firing people, but it need not. For example, some companies that need less labor give large bonuses to longtime employees who agree to take early retirement. And employers can't completely ignore their workers' morale, because there is a market for labor, and businesses that do not offer a competitive wage, fringe benefits, and a pleasant working environment will have a hard time attracting and keeping good workers. For example, when a new restaurant opens in Washington, DC, its managers are seen to frequent area restaurants and pass out their business cards to good waitresses and busboys. (It is important that such competition exist; some states have investigated restaurants that may have agreed to a "no poaching" pact.)[124]

Regardless, economists point to the evidence that requiring businesses to be kinder to their workers does not necessarily mean being kinder to labor in general. Many European countries require employers to offer their employees many fringe benefits. For example, full-time workers in France are guaranteed at least five weeks' vacation, and there are another dozen public holidays; there is paid maternity and paternity leave and workers getting married get four days off.

In France it is very difficult to fire a full-time worker, especially if a firm has 50 or more employees. Businesses are naturally reluctant to hire workers if they know they will not be able to fire them when their business declines.[125] One economist found that France has an unusually large number of companies with 49 employees and an unusually small number with 50.[126] It seems that a number of companies that have growth potential stop at 49 employees so as to avoid burdensome firing rules. Thus, countries that limit businesses' ability to fire workers or that require large fringe benefits tend to have higher long-term unemployment rates.

The unemployment rate in France is typically around 10 percent, much higher than is normal in the United States.[127] Worse yet, the long-term unemployment rate as a percentage of total unemployment is much higher in France (averaging 40 percent from 1998 to 2018) than in the United States (averaging 13 percent from 1987 to 2017). Short-term unemployment is rarely a societal crisis. But the fact that, year after year, 40 percent of the French who are unemployed are unemployed for over 12 months does seem particularly sad.[128] Most people would think we should be especially kind to would-be workers who, over many months, can't find employment of any kind. But it seems that requiring kindness of businesses leads to an increase in hardship for those who most need kindness.

Even left-of-center economists join the chorus opposing European-style regulation of business. For example, although a fan of bigger government and higher taxes on the wealthy, Robert Frank says "there is prescriptive regulation aplenty...in this country, and good reasons for fearing that it does more harm than good." Frank has contempt for "the byzantine regulations of private labor contracts in many European countries," and he calls them "an important factor behind persistent double-digit unemployment rates on the continent."[129] Joseph Stiglitz, former chairman of the Council of Economic Advisers under Bill Clinton, chimes in: "The Europeans seem to be saying, 'We haven't created any new jobs, but if we had created any they would have been good ones.'"[130] Larry Summers, a secretary of the Treasury under President Clinton and a prominent advisor to President Obama, said in 2012 that, once Europe had recovered from its great recession, there would need to be reform to its "sclerosis-inducing regulations."[131]

From the point of view of economic efficiency, government itself is often too kind to its workers. In the Department of Labor, one manager negotiating with the department's union told a reporter: "I don't accept the premise that there has to be an adversarial relationship between management and the union." The negotiator for the union told the same reporter: "We behaved like a union – self-interested – and we achieved accordingly."

In 1962 President Kennedy issued an executive order that brought collective bargaining to the federal government. Arthur Goldberg, head of the Department of Labor, "made it a point of pride that his department would be the first to sign an agreement." His negotiators were told to make whatever concessions were necessary to make this happen. They made unusual concessions, and it happened. One experienced management negotiator at Labor later groused that those early concessions had set a precedent for soft negotiating that continued thereafter.[132]

When the Reagan administration's planned budget cuts included 1270 jobs at the Department of State, the rallying cry among employees at State was "Cut things, not people." An apologetic undersecretary for management noted that earlier cuts had focused on equipment supplies and vehicles, but "we have reached a point where such 'thinning the soup' measures will no longer suffice."[133] Similarly, during tough times governors in my state of Virginia take great pride in announcing that no state employees in any agency will lose their job.[134]

In my class, I once had an employee at a nonprofit organization angrily fight back at the course reading that argued government and nonprofits are less efficient by saying, "We needed to be efficient; our grant was being cut; jobs were on the line." Similar priorities were present in the city of Oakland when tight budgets led librarians to cut books, not librarians. Always giving priority to protecting jobs is not economically efficient, because it is not a policy that best satisfies the desires of consumers or citizens. Cutting books but never librarians, for example, is not what economic efficiency requires because it is not a policy that best helps the reading public.

Of course, as mentioned above, private-sector businesses also try to avoid firing employees, but many times they find it necessary to do so. Faced with intense pressure from Japanese auto companies, the US automobile industry laid off over 200,000 people in a five-year period beginning in 1979.[135] During the same period Ford sliced its North American salaried work force by 25 percent.[136] More cuts continued. For example, in 1991 General Motors announced plans to cut 70,000 employees in the next few years.[137] Large employment cuts such as this in federal budgets are almost unheard of. Princeton economic research has shown that public-sector jobs are safer than private-sector jobs, especially in recessions.[138]

I acknowledge, however, that accommodating policies toward employees may make more sense in the public sector than the private sector. Imagine the outrage that would be directed toward my student if she had fired employees. "Oh yes, Ms. Jones, I hope you feel really great about your efficiency moves. But I know who doesn't feel great. Poor Agnes is a single mom who really needs this job. But Ms. Efficiency says she has to go." Morale among employees who stay is likely to plummet dramatically. Less so in the private sector, where managers can respond to complainers by saying: "Look, this division of GM is losing millions. It can't continue or we will all lose our jobs."

The impulse to try to save people's jobs is a sign of a benevolent fellow feeling. But economists say it hinders growth and hurts most workers in the long run. People would say they are not in favor of "make work" jobs. But they act in favor of them when they hinder techno-logical change that saves on labor costs.

In 2017 economist Larry Summers took Bill Gates to task when he proposed a tax on robots to "cushion worker dislocation and limit inequality." Summers said: why pick on robots? Kiosks that dispense airplane boarding passes, mobile banking technologies, word-processing programs that accelerate the production of documents – all these save on labor. They make industry more productive, which increases economic growth. Let them increase the size of the pie; we can enjoy the extra output and "establish suitable taxes and transfers to protect displaced workers."[139]

Gates's opinion is quite common among ordinary citizens. An important survey of 250 economists and a much larger sample of the general public asked their opinion about some possible reasons why the economy "is not doing better than it is." One of the possible explanations offered was that "technology is displacing workers." Those surveyed could choose between "not a reason at all," "a minor reason," or "a major reason." A substantial majority of the economists said "not a reason at all." The public thought it was a reason, with more saying it was a minor than a major one. The public, but not most economists, also thought it was bad for the economy when a company let workers go so as to increase profits.[140]

Timothy Taylor, the editor of the *Journal of Economic Perspectives*, thinks our political dialogue has gotten things backwards. In the natural order, the private sector would do what it does best: let companies grow the economy by introducing new products and management techniques. Let government take care of workers by way of programs such as unemployment insurance and the earned income tax credit (which supplements low wages). Instead, we encourage politicians to talk about tax cuts and industrial policies that will "grow the economy," and we applaud businesses that give substantial amounts to charities and never lay off workers even though revenues decline year after year.[141] As shown above, economists think the private sector is better able to find and correct for waste. What has not been shown is just how long public-sector inefficiency can go on without being corrected.

The federal government has been building housing for low-income citizens since the 1930s.[142] Since 1974 low-income subsidized housing has usually been built by the private sector. The builders then receive rent from their tenants and a subsidy (usually a tax credit) for each tenant from the government. This policy is unfair, for two main reasons. Unlike other major means-tested transfer programs in the United States, low-income housing programs don't offer assistance to many of the poorest families who are eligible for them. Eligible families that want assistance must get on a waiting list. It is also unfair to many builders who would like to participate in the program. Only some builders are allowed to participate and thus enjoy the federal subsidies of the rentals. Since the lucky builders are not subjected to open competition, they receive excessive profits for their work.

Economists ask: why not give *all* low-income folks a voucher for part of the cost of their housing? Then let them find housing that provides the best value for their dollars, their own and the government's. Why tell low-income people we will help you only if you live in this particular project?

The Department of Housing and Urban Development has a voucher program, but it is funded at a lower level than the less efficient program that subsidizes builders. Over several decades economists have made arguments for vouchers and provided evidence for the inefficiencies of the subsidized building programs. For example, one excellent study found that the "largest program subsidizing the construction of privately owned housing projects indicated an excess taxpayer cost of at least 72 percent compared with housing vouchers that provide equally good housing at the same cost to tenants."[143]

Why has it been so hard to move to a full voucher system? One reason is heavy lobbying by and campaign contributions from the lucky builders selected for participation in the building and rehabilitation programs. This process is particularly ugly in Missouri, where the Republican speaker of the house and several Democratic senators benefit from contributions from one of the largest developers in the state.[144]

Further Reflections

Six decades ago many economists optimistically imagined a federal government that would selectively intervene in the economy to correct for market imperfections once the principles of public finance were better developed and disseminated.[145] Few today have such a vision.

Part of the problem is that even regulatory policy that makes sense can be very easily abused. Rules granting patents to inventors make sense. There would be a great reduction in inventions if company B could copy company A's new production method as soon as A implemented it. But some established firms buy promising patents from inventors and sit on them; by doing so they prevent new technology from interfering with their existing profit-making routines.

Brink Lindsey notes that the "number of patents issued every year is 5 times now what it was back in the early 1980s." Now, especially in patent law, the main function of the law is just to create a legal minefield for innovators, who can be shaken down by so-called patent trolls who buy up portfolios of patents just to weaponize them and litigate on them. So, what should have been pro-innovation policy is, perversely, turned into pro-lawyer policy.[146]

The larger problem, however, is government promotion of policies that economists would never support even in principle. A survey of top economists with past high-level government experience found that most national policy proposals were developed to deal with political necessities and under tremendous time pressures. Careful analysis of the proposals was rare.[147] Alan Blinder, a member of Bill Clinton's Council of Economic Advisers and later vice chair of the Federal Reserve, offers the "lamppost theory" to explain the same phenomenon: "Politicians rely on economic experts for support, not for illumination."[148]

In government agencies, administrators and political appointees will say to their economists "Just give me the best economic argument for my position," and economists will say "There are no good economic arguments for your position." Agency administrators will tend to conclude that they need to begin to hire economists who are less wedded to the market. In time, they find that there are very few to be found.[149]

It is not just conservative economists who have a skeptical view of government efficiency. Readers will note how often I have made the case for this conclusion by quoting left-of-center mainstream economists. Economists like free markets because they stimulate competition. The economic columnist Robert J. Samuelson puts it well: precisely because technological change is so unpredictable, the market may be best equipped to promote it.

> The much maligned "market" is simply a shorthand way of describing a system that allows diversity; that allows firms and people to guess what will work best. [...] It is the threat of failure and prospect of reward, the uncertainty, that drives the constant search for improved products.[150]

Markets don't just lead to better products and services. They also stimulate new institutional innovations that, in turn, lead to better products and services. For example, Kickstarter is a crowdfunding platform that, as of 2018, had raised $3.9 billion and helped launch thousands of companies. It relies on relatively small contributions from a large number of investors.[151]

Also of interest is the X Prize Foundation, which offers big bucks for important innovations, such as $1.4 million for finding a faster way to clean oil spills from the ocean. The Gates Foundation has now jumped on board and is offering prizes. So too has Netflix, which offered $1 million to anyone who could improve on its own algorithms used for online recommendations to Netflix customers. Fifty-five thousand people from 186 countries entered the contest. "The seven members of the winning team, who collaborated online, met physically for the first time when they picked up the prize in 2009."[152] NASA offered a prize for the design of a new astronauts' glove. The winner was not an aerospace firm, but instead "an unemployed engineer who has gone on to form a new company."[153]

The entrepreneur Dr. Peter Diamond, who runs the X Prize Foundation, says he has become convinced that the pursuit of prizes and acclaim "can change the world" by changing "what people believe to be possible."[154] Economists love these sorts of institutional innovations, which bubble up from markets and use economic incentives to encourage development of a better world.

The power of markets is not obvious for many who haven't studied them. But there is an exception to this rule; people who only happen upon the fruits of markets in later life can be every bit as enthusiastic as economists. But even this group often credits a particular store they encounter rather than the market mechanism for the abundance they see.

My colleague Allen Lynch, who studies Russia and earlier the Soviet Union, has told me that "during the 1980's, a visit to Kmart was practically obligatory for visiting Soviet delegations. They were in genuine shock at the routine abundance of everyday consumer items. Many Soviet visitors (usually elites) as well as emigres experienced psychological and even some physical shock at walking into a typical US grocery store."[155]

Similarly, after a Kmart visit, east European visitors sometimes concluded that they should go home and get themselves a Kmart. Some of my readers will not know what a Kmart is, since it has gone bankrupt twice – most recently in 2018. The Soviet and east European visitors could not grasp that it was capitalist competition in markets rather than the sprawling store they saw that produced the abundance.[156]

EconTalk's host, Russ Roberts, relates a case when he went to a store with a Russian visitor. The Russian wanted to buy some yeast but there was none on the shelf. Roberts asked the grocer to see if there was some in the back. There was, and, when the grocer came back and handed it to Roberts, the Russian visitor's eyes lit up. The visitor saw this as a sign that Roberts was a powerful and influential man, rather than an ordinary customer receiving routine service.[157]

Some readers will be slow to believe that the vast majority of mainstream economists could be so skeptical about the efficiency of government allocation of resources. Mainstream economists are not anarchists. They do want an active government role in setting up the legal framework for the market system, in providing for significant public goods, in correcting for externalities and other market imperfections. Many mainstream economists also want active government involvement in improving our educational systems, on macrostabilization questions, and on redistributing income to the poor. In a laissez-faire economy the consensus among economists would be for more government intervention. But in the America of the twenty-first century it is not. The economists have seen the poor results of government intervention and have theory to explain why the results are very likely to be bad in the future as well.

Readers might think they could find many left-of-center mainstream economists skeptical of markets. But consider the two most distinguished well left-of-center US economists, Joseph Stiglitz and *New York Times* columnist Paul Krugman, both Nobel Prize winners. In the introduction, I quoted Stiglitz's belief that "markets with private enterprise are the core of any successful economy." Krugman agrees.[158] In their introductory economics text, Robin Wells and Krugman write in one section: "Markets are an amazingly effective way to organize economic activity." Krugman and Wells then discuss market failures such as externalities and public goods. But they wrap up the discussion of markets with still more high praise for markets. "Even with these caveats, it's remarkable how well markets work at maximizing the gains from trade."[159]

Economists are sometimes criticized for "making a religion out of markets." Words such as "remarkable" and "amazing" don't quite reach the level of religion, but they are pretty strong praise. Maybe noneconomists have something to learn about the reasons for an economic consensus on markets.

China reluctantly and slowly moved toward markets because doing so seemed antithetical to communist ideology. But markets came after they concluded that the terrible consequences of Mao's "Great Leap Forward" required this dramatic shift.

In the United States as well, politicians can sometimes find that efficiency requires moving toward markets even when doing so requires the abandonment of comfortable political stances. In 2008 a *Washington Post* headline read "Senate votes to privatize its failing restaurants." Senate restaurants had lost $18 million over 15 years and expected to lose another 2 million in 2008. To avoid a still larger subsidy from taxpayers, the Senate, controlled by Democrats, decided it had to yield control of the restaurants to a contractor, which would "all but guarantee lower wages and benefits for the outfit's new hires." In a meeting with fellow Democrats Senator Robert Menendez (D-N.J.) said: "You cannot stand on the Senate floor and condemn the privatization of workers and then turn around and privatize the workers here in the Senate and leave them out on their own."

Senator Dianne Feinstein, the chair of a committee responsible for the restaurant, had been "practically heckled" by Democratic senators for deciding on privatization. She blamed "noticeably subpar" food and service for the dire financial situation. The article explained that Senate staffers regularly "trudge across the Capitol" to the privatized basement cafeteria on the House side even though the lines can be long there. House staffers almost never come over to the Senate side. Not only is the food better on the House side, it pays yearly a $1.2 million commission to the House. Eventually senators agreed to the move toward privatization after Senator Feinstein warned that failure to privatize would mean Senate restaurant food prices would be increased by 25 percent across the board.[160]

5 ECONOMISTS AND EQUITY

The previous chapter explained why economists give the market high marks as a mechanism for allocating resources. Some in society may be harmed when others engage in market transactions. Obviously, buggy whip makers did not gain when Henry Ford sold his Model T automobiles. But, in the absence of imperfections, the market achieves potential Pareto improvements – those when gainers gain more than losers lose. Henry Ford and all those who bought his cars would have been able to compensate the buggy whip makers for their losses and still be better off themselves.

But what should we think if, as is usually the case, the compensation does not take place? Although the market responds to the dollar votes of consumers, many feel that those votes are not equitably distributed. The person who buys the pencils (or iPads) is sometimes the most eager to have them, but sometimes he is just the richest. Willingness to pay depends in part on ability to pay. If downtown renewal developers want to buy land now owned by landlords providing low-income housing, any agreement on a sale price suggests an efficient outcome in which the developers speaking for the new occupants are willing to pay more for the new use than the low-income residents were willing to pay the landlord to preserve their housing. But perhaps the developers should be stopped, because low-income tenants seem particularly needy.

One way economists try to dissolve the equity issue is by considering it in a larger context. If a local sandwich restaurant in a rented building is forced to close because the owner of the building can demand a higher rent from a computer sales and repair shop that wants to move into this location, the manager of the sandwich shop loses his job. This development meets a potential economic efficiency standard, because the computer supply business expects far more customers, and thus can afford a higher rent than the sandwich shop owner can. But consider all the market changes that will occur in the future. In the vast majority of them, if we let the "gainers gain more than losers lose" standard be decisive, it will be helpful to the person who had been manager of the sandwich shop, because in most of these other changes the manager of the shop will be one of the gainers who *could* fully compensate losers and be better off. If the potential Pareto optimality standard is decisive in every instance, economic growth will be greater and the restaurant manager will probably gain a higher real income through time. Even if he does not, his children will be born into a larger thriving economy and will reap the benefits. This is a good argument, but it will not convince many people who are especially concerned with equity.

Those critical of the economic approach to public policy often accuse economists of being preoccupied with economic efficiency. Economists are more confident that they draw on their expertise when they discuss efficiency than when they discuss equity. They are thus more comfortable talking about efficiency, and they do consider efficiency more often. Nevertheless, they talk about equity and the distribution of income a great deal. There is an economic literature discussing equity in outcomes between various races and ethnic groups, between men and women, and between the young and the old. Space does not allow discussion of any of these literatures. Economists most often focus on one particular distribution question: the relative shares of national resources controlled by broad income classes. This issue will be my chief focus below. But, before discussing redistributing income, a little should be said about how a well-functioning market distributes income.

In a market system an individual's income depends on the payments received for others' use of his labor, land, and capital. The relative demand for these factors of production depends on the demand for the products that they help make. In the absence of market imperfections, income is determined by how much one's labor and owned resources add to market-valued goods and services. Competitive pressures push wages toward levels that reflect the marginal (last-hired) laborer's additional contribution to output – what that laborer adds by working here rather than elsewhere or not at all. Many managers would no doubt like to pay their employees only a half of what they add to their firm's profitability. But employers would then face pressure from other managers who see extra profits for themselves if they hire the first firm's employees and pay them a little more but still less than their productivity warrants. And the new employers in turn face pressure from firms willing to pay a little more still.

The market income received is a result of both chance and choice. It depends on the sort of family or neighborhood one is born into and on one's intellectual and other capacities. It also depends on one's hard work and foresight. The talented and lazy will not have the income of the talented and hardworking, but they may do better than the untalented and hardworking. And they may do better than the talented and hardworking whose talent is valued little by others (e.g., a buggy whip maker).

Pareto-Optimal Redistribution

On the core value issue of whether market income should be redistributed, economists claim no more expertise than the average citizen. But they do think that they can explain why a certain amount of government coercion for redistribution purposes may be economically efficient. Redistribution to help the poor can be seen as a public good that private charity will provide in insufficient quantity from the point of view of both rich and poor. In the absence of public welfare programs, many of the nonpoor would favor societal efforts to reduce poverty. Some of these might feel that it is their duty to give through voluntary charities, and they would get personal satisfaction from doing so. Others, though, would realize that their personal contribution would not make a dent in the nation's poverty, and they would prefer that others gave to help the poor so that they could enjoy the benefits of a reduction in poverty without spending their own money. If too many people reasoned thus, less would be redistributed to the poor than the nonpoor wished. The nonpoor might gladly give something, however, if they knew their personal contribution would lead to more than a drop in the bucket. By requiring all who are similarly situated to give their fair share, government can ensure that the individual's sacrifice makes a difference. Thus, coercive government taxes may be the only way to get government programs the nonpoor desire and are willing to pay for.

The Pareto optimality argument for redistribution does not help one deal with today's issues. We already spend a good bit of money to help the poor. There is no consensus among the nonpoor that more should be spent.[1] Many of the nonpoor, although not a majority, think that too much of their money goes to "the needy" or to those on "welfare." This does not mean that they are right. It just means that additional redistribution has ceased to be justifiable on efficiency grounds. Economists still allow for a possible societal judgment on equity grounds that the rich have more dollar votes than is fair. If we so decide, most economists are perfectly open to requiring the rich to give more to the poor than they choose to.

How Equal Is the Distribution of Income and Wealth and How Much Has It Changed through Time?

Before I began seriously reading literature about the distribution of income, I had assumed that the figures would be straightforward and that the controversy would be about whether and how to change that distribution. I could not have been more wrong. There is at least as much controversy about how to *describe* the distribution as there is about what to do about it. After reading more and more and becoming more and more uncertain about how to summarize this literature, I decided at the start to rely primarily on two sources: *The Economist* journal and the work of a scholar, Stephen Rose, from the Urban Institute. The AllSides website, which rates outlets for media bias, sees both the journal and the Urban Institute as leaning left but not too far left.

The Economist finds that estimates of inflation-adjusted median income growth between 1979 and 2014 range from "a fall of 8% to an increase of 51%."[2] The journal's cover story on the distribution of income and wealth, called "Inequality illusions," finds the lowest figures "hard to believe," noting that decades of innovation have provided mobile phones, video streaming, and cholesterol-lowering statins.

Stephen Rose has conducted a meta-analysis (one that combines the findings of a large number of studies) and reports that inflation-adjusted median incomes grew by just over 40 percent from 1979 to 2014; the top 10 percent captured 45 percent of growth during this period; the share of the top 1 percent grew just 3.5 percentage points. In a separate study looking at gains between 1967 and 2018, Rose finds that the most striking gains went to the upper middle class (incomes between $108,000 and $380,000). In 1967 only 6 percent of Americans were in the upper middle class; in 2018 33 percent were. The middle class shrunk, but mainly because it moved up, not down.[3]

The Dodd–Frank law requires many companies to publish their CEO-to-labor salary ratio. In the 2020 campaign, Senator Bernie Sanders proposed a substantial increase in corporate taxes for businesses in which the ratio of CEO pay to median worker pay was very high.[4] There may be excellent reasons, however, why company A's CEO earns 50 times as much as its average worker whereas company B's CEO earns only ten times as much. Company B may have 100 workers, most of whom are skilled. Company A may have 2000 workers, most of whom are unskilled. Company A's CEO may be responsible for managing much more capital as well as more workers. His greater responsibility would justify a much larger salary in comparison to his workers than company B's CEO receives. Moreover, if one thinks the top 1 percent have too much income, why focus on docking hardworking CEOs rather than others in the top 1 percent who don't work at all? In any case, it would be easy for many CEOs to reduce their pay ratio by outsourcing low-income labor.[5]

The economist Alex Edmans notes that one often hears the complaint that CEOs' salaries and bonuses often stay about the same no matter how well their firms are doing. Although true, this is misleading. The CEO's income and wealth are linked to firm performance, because if his firm performs poorly the CEO's equity holdings decrease in value. "If the stock price falls by 10%, the average Fortune 500 CEO loses millions of dollars."[6]

Although economists are critical of many laws meant to restrict CEO pay, they are not convinced that CEO pay typically reflects the chief executives' worth to their company. A Booth survey of top economists asked for agreement or disagreement with the following statement:

> The typical CEO of a publicly traded corporation in the US is paid more than his or her marginal contribution to the firm's value.

More than four times as many economists agree as disagree, although the agreed total is matched by an equal number who are uncertain. A great many economists seem to think that boards of directors provide inadequate oversight of CEOs. One who believed this added the following comment, however: "But a bad CEO can do huge damage to a firm."[7]

Most economists agree that wealth is much more unequally distributed than income. A 2018 study by the Federal Reserve found that the wealthiest 10 percent of Americans held 70 percent of household wealth, up from 61 percent in 1989. In this period the top 1 percent went from 24 to 31 percent.[8] But these sorts of figures have been challenged by a recent paper that includes social security benefits as a form of wealth. Doing so yields a conclusion that there's been no increase in wealth inequality in the last three decades.[9] Also relevant is the dramatic increase in shares owned by the middle class. In 1960 retirement accounts owned just 4 percent of American shares; in 2015 such accounts owned 50 percent.[10]

On the other hand, inequality in the distribution of both wealth and income would be larger if one took account of the rise in investments in private equity and hedge funds by the wealthiest Americans. Investopedia concludes that, "despite making tons of money every year, the elite hedge fund and private equity sector enjoy generous tax advantages."[11]

Poverty and Mobility at the Top and Bottom

Economists are somewhat less concerned with poverty than they were 60, or even 30, years ago. The official poverty rate has not declined substantially, but economists say that the official rate does not take into account the child credit or the earned income tax credit. It also ignores all non-cash support: Medicaid, Obamacare, the supplemental nutrition assistance program (the old food stamps), housing assistance TANF (temporary assistance for needy families), school lunches, and the low-income home energy program. The decline in poverty is particularly dramatic if one focuses on consumption poverty. Bruce Meyer of the University of Chicago, a leading advocate for this approach, says consumption shows "what families are able to purchase in terms of food, housing, transportation and other goods and services." By his measure, consumption poverty fell from 13 percent in 1980 to 3 percent in 2016.[12]

The Brookings Institution's Isabel Sawhill has been writing about poverty and income distribution issues for nearly half a century. Sawhill, a left-of-center moderate, also finds dramatic recent reductions in poverty. She ascribes this to the earned income tax credit (EITC), which enables low-income wage earners to receive federal supplements to their wages, and the refundable portion of the child tax credit, which provides low-income folks a stipend for minor children even if they pay no taxes. "In 2017 these credits gave 8.3 million people a path out of poverty, including 4.5 million children."[13]

Although they grant the poverty reduction benefits of these programs, more conservative economists also credit economic growth and welfare reform, which gave many mothers incentives to join the labor force. Conservatives also emphasize that the dramatic reduction in poverty was largely due to government transfers, not the self-sufficiency through work that President Lyndon Johnson sought in his war on poverty.[14]

In the last decade both President Obama and leading Republicans such as former House Speaker Paul Ryan have said that economic mobility has declined. After they spoke, some studies found that this was not true. Economic mobility – up and down – was about the same in every decade of the last half-century.[15]

Mobility in the United States is not as strong as in Canada and much of western Europe, however. The odds of escaping poverty are about twice as high in Denmark as in the United States. At the other end of the wealth distribution, there is considerable mobility at the very top. Forbes's list of the 400 richest Americans finds that the number of entrepreneurs on the list rose from 40 percent in 1982 to 69 percent in 2011. The share of the Forbes 400 that grew up wealthy was cut almost in half in the three decades after 1982.[16]

Moderate left-of-center economists such as Larry Summers also note that there is considerable year-to-year turnover in the Forbes 400. But Summers and most economists agree that there has been a rise in inequality in both income and wealth over the last generation. Summers proposes a host of ways to decrease inequality, such as cracking down on tax dodges and money laundering at the top and funding job-creating increases in infrastructure investment and job training for the working and middle class. Still, he seems to think that the broader forces that produced inequality will not go away: robots will replace labor and "there is the basic truth that technology and globalization give greater scope to those with extraordinary entrepreneurial ability, luck, or managerial skill."[17]

Recently, economists have been most struck by the disparity in mobility *within* the United States. Despite lagging behind Europe overall, some US regions can match the most mobile countries in western Europe. Average incomes in Atlanta and Seattle are similar. But mobility in Atlanta is far weaker than in Seattle. Boston, Salt Lake City, and Pittsburgh have high mobility while Memphis, Indianapolis, and Cincinnati have low mobility.

What are the characteristics of highly mobile cities? The number of universities in a city does not improve mobility, nor do greater extremes of wealth significantly weaken mobility. Mobility is improved when poor families live in mixed-income neighborhoods, when schools are better, and when there is more civic engagement, including membership in religious and community groups. The strongest factor associated with greater mobility is a high proportion of two-parent households.[18]

A number of economists look at the evidence, and say that one of the biggest problems is the substantial reduction in the willingness of struggling workers to leave their communities for more prosperous areas. This reluctance harms their income prospects, since, for example, lower-paid service occupations – think barbers and waiters – command a higher wage when practiced in prosperous, growing cities.

Traditionally, economists have argued against place-based policies – arguing that we should support poor people rather than poor places. In the past this made sense, because low-income people tended to migrate to places where there were more jobs and higher wages and poor areas tended to catch up. Because low-income people, and to a considerable extent most people, now seem unwilling to move for better economic opportunities, three Harvard economists, Benjamin Austin, Larry Summers, and Edward Glaeser, have written a report for Brookings suggesting the need for further thought about the possible benefits of helping regions.[19] But neither their report nor the conference discussing it unearthed enthusiasm for any of the ideas for regional support. For example, the abstract to the report said a ramped-up, targeted Earned Income Tax Credit could "plausibly reduce suffering and materially improve economic performance." The EITC does lead some low income people to *stay* in the labor force once they are in it. But, according to political scientist Lawrence Mead's survey of the evidence, by themselves stronger work incentives do not have much effect on drawing nonworking poor men *into* the labor force.[20]

Glaeser considers the rapid increase in prime-age men (25 to 54) who are neither employed nor looking for work the great American domestic crisis of the twenty-first century. In the 1950s and 1960s 5 percent of men between 25 and 54 were jobless. For much of the past decade 15 percent of these "prime-aged" workers have been jobless for over 12 months. In particular, Glaeser has studied a subset of these men in what he calls the "Eastern heartland" of the country; this subset consists of jobless men who live with others – sometimes partners but more often parents. Their personal incomes are just over $8000 a year, most of it from disability. The total family income in these households is above $42,000, however, on average.

Glaeser, like other economists, thinks the increase in the number of men not in the labor force is significantly affected by the decline in jobs for less skilled men. But he thinks there is much more going on because of the rapid increase in men who are not even looking for work. These men are unhappy[*]; Glaeser believes this is because they lack any sense of achievement or purpose.[21] He recommends squeezing money out of programs that deter employment and moving it into programs that encourage working, such as the Earned Income Tax Credit.[22]

For economists, the EITC is the most popular program to help those with low incomes. It provides income for low-wage workers while encouraging them to work more. But we will see below that the EITC has a high "improper payment" rate (often fraud); and we saw above Larry Mead's research showing that the EITC is not very effective at getting people over the hump to employment in the first place.

Mead recommends more work requirements as a condition for government benefits such as food stamps (Supplemental Nutrition Assistance Program: SNAP). He notes that a start could be made by enforcing work for men "who are already supposed to be working – those on parole from prison or in arrears on child support payments." But, for most jobless men, it is help from parents, grandparents, partners, and friends that provides the most significant income enabling them to be listless about seeking employment.

As we have seen in Chapter 4, most economists strongly support a dynamic growing economy. When more people are willing to move in search of economic opportunity, the economy grows more rapidly and is more dynamic. Thus, it is not surprising that the economist Tyler Cowen seems disappointed that people in all income classes are less footloose than they were in the past: "We are digging ourselves

---

[*] A more difficult problem still is posed by the 21- to 30-year-old jobless men with less than a four-year college degree. Their jobless rate is also up significantly, and they have doubled their time playing video games since 2000. But they are happier than their age cohort was in 2000. See Ana Swanson, "Why amazing video games could be causing a big problem for America," *Washington Post*, September 24, 2016.

in. . .investing in stability." His book *The Complacent Class* is dedicated to "the rebel in each of us."[23] Still, we should remember that the jobless in smaller communities with below-average growth rates are a special case. Certainly, they should be made aware of opportunities further from their homes; but not everyone is jobless in smaller communities with below-average growth rates.

In their research, economists usually assume that more income means more goods and services, and thus more satisfaction/happiness. But it should be noted that the economists who are centrally concerned with studying what factors are most associated with happiness are critical of those economists who, sub rosa, seem to advise the struggling working class to, in effect, "get up and move" to the growing cities that further mobility, both for their own sakes and that of the economy as a whole.

The chief economist at Gallup, Jonathan Rothwell, questions such economists. Rothwell grants that folks working in prosperous growing cities are happier with their jobs. But he presents data showing that parents can be more productive at family life in smaller cities: the housing in a nice neighborhood is cheaper and parents are more likely to agree with statements such as "The city or area I live in is a perfect place for me" and "The house or apartment that I live in is ideal for me and my family." In smaller cities racial integration and voluntarism are higher. Folks living in prosperous cities do score higher on some social measures, but, taken as a whole, "people living in large cities are the least satisfied with their communities." Rothwell thinks it quite possible that families seeking mobility for their children would be wise to stay in a nice neighborhood in a small city.[24]

In their geographical studies, another factor that economists tend to neglect is health. There is likely to be more traffic congestion and less green space in large cities. And studies show that traffic congestion is associated with high blood pressure[25] and that living in or near leafy green neighborhoods or parks reduces stress and cardiovascular risks.[26]

Evidence for the benefits of green space comes in part from a well-designed experiment. In Philadelphia, 541 vacant lots were divided into three groups. In one group trash in the vacant lot was cleaned up, in another grass and trees were also planted, and in the third control group nothing was done. The 342 residents (mostly with lower incomes) were also divided into three groups. Those living near the cleaned-up vacant lots showed no significant improvement in their mental health. But those living near the lots that were turned green showed "a 40%

reduction in feeling depressed and a 50% reduction in feeling worthless compared to the control group." The authors of the study also suggest that further research might find that greening could improve social cohesion, interaction, and feelings of safety.[27]

Redistribution

Economists tend to be utilitarians. They believe that pleasure or happiness constitute the human goal and that the happiness of everyone in society should be treated equally. Most are comfortable with the assumption that, as a general rule, consumer sovereignty will maximize a consumer's happiness or utility. Many are attracted as well to the idea of maximizing the combined utility of everyone in society. They further assume that the rich get less utility from a marginal dollar than those who are less well off. Economists realize that you can't scientifically measure interpersonal utility, but few would doubt that a poor man's happiness increases more than a rich man's when he receives an additional $100. Thus, in principle, they believe in redistribution of income.

They caution, however, that there is a downside to taxation.[28] Both the poor and the wealthy will tend to work less when they don't get to keep their full market wage. Low-income workers receiving food stamps and housing assistance may work less or not at all so as not to lose these benefits. The well off are not likely to quit their jobs, but they may retire earlier and avoid long hours. Doctors who take off Wednesday afternoons to play golf may decide to take off Friday afternoons as well.

Taxes will likely reduce innovation and investment, and higher taxes will reduce them more. Some potential entrepreneurs will decide the risks are not worth the rewards; they may instead seek a management position in an existing firm. Some engineers contemplating an advanced degree may decide that the high marginal tax on the added income made possible by their higher productivity makes it not worth the cost.[29]

More important still, with higher marginal tax rates the well off have greater incentives to think of ways to avoid taxes. Liberal and conservative economists agree that high marginal tax rates have a greater effect on the demand for fringe benefits and other untaxed income than on the supply of labor. As the economist Arthur Okun noted, "High tax rates are followed by attempts of ingenious men to beat them as surely as snow is followed by little boys with sleds."[30] One result is more bartering and "pay me in cash" transactions in the underground economy. Another result is businesses providing top executives with expensive tax-deductible cars and conferences in the Caribbean. Still another result is high incomes for lawyers who help the wealthy find tax loopholes.

Okun's core values were strongly egalitarian: "Abstracting from the costs and the consequences, I would prefer more equality of income to less and would like complete equality best of all." Yet, ultimately, Okun argued that all people, "rich and poor," should be permitted to "keep a significant part of any additional income they earn." As an economist fully aware of economic incentives, Okun kept his eye on the size of the economic pie while arguing for a more equal distribution of the slices.[31] Liberal economists think lowering taxes on businesses and the wealthy will not end many of these abuses and tightening rules can help significantly.[32] Conservatives think that "the fact that relatively little revenue is collected at the highest marginal [tax] rates testify [sic] to their basic futility."[33]

Chapter 4 presented evidence that declines in the growth rate have been exaggerated in most of the press. But there have been declines. In the 1950s and 1960s the average rate of growth in gross domestic product (GDP) was above 4 percent; in the 1970s and 1980s it dropped to around 3 percent; more recently the average rate, for many years, has been below 2 percent.[34] A 2 percent growth rate over ten years raises real (inflation-adjusted) incomes 22 percent; a 4 percent growth rate raises incomes 49 percent. Both liberal and conservative economists think that, historically, economic growth is far more important in explaining the material progress of ordinary people than labor unions or political reform.

From the conservative side, Thomas Sowell says:

> If you read many histories and hear many discussions of social issues, you get the idea that people are no longer in rags or hungry today because various noble reformers refused to accept such conditions and worked to alleviate them. Meanwhile, it was merely coincidental that the gross national product rose by 5 or 6 times over that same span. But if you really want to know

why it is that the poor of the nineteenth century were in rags and those of the twentieth century typically are not, it is because a man named Singer perfected the sewing machine, putting factory-made clothing within the reach of great masses of people for the first time in history.[35]

Liberal Alfred Kahn, writing in 1981, seems to agree completely.

Without growth liberalism could never have achieved its victories. The improvement since the 1930s in the material welfare of President Roosevelt's "one third of a nation" has been made possible far, far more by the material progress enjoyed by all three thirds than by the modest redistribution from the top two.[36]

Although not all the causes of high productivity (GDP per employee) growth rates are well understood, there is agreement that a crucial element is the innovation and investment that lead to capital formation. When workers work with better equipment and machinery, they become more productive. Competition in the labor market then causes their real incomes to rise.[37] Investment requires saving, and the rich save a far higher percentage of their incomes than the rest of us. Society as a whole reaps some of the benefits from the savings of the rich (and of others). Most economists think there is some truth in the "trickle-down" or "filter-down" theory of prosperity. Paul Samuelson, a liberal and the first American Nobel laureate in economics, said that the theory, "so scorned by so many noneconomists," has "a very important element of historical truth in it."[38] And Alfred Kahn asked his fellow (noneconomist) liberals to reconsider

their opposition to any and all policies whose method of producing social benefits can be characterized as "trickle down." The most powerful engine of productivity advance is technological progress, generated in large measure by expenditures on research and development and embodied in improved capital goods and managerial techniques; and it confers its benefits on all of us, precisely, by trickling down.[39]

Left-of-center politicians and commentators have lately linked their scorn for trickle-down economics with support for "middle out" economics. "Middle out" is a macroeconomic theory first proposed by a former speechwriter for Bill Clinton and a venture capitalist. Hillary Clinton mentioned it twice in a debate with Donald Trump, and it came up in 2020 Democratic campaigns as well. The idea is that full employment and growth come from middle-class spending. "Companies don't hire when they have an abundance of profits; they hire when they have an abundance of customers."[40] If unemployment is high, it will be reduced if consumers spend more. To meet the increased demand, companies will need to hire more workers. More workers will mean more growth.

Mainstream economists would say there will always be a certain amount of transitional unemployment, as companies go out of business or workers move and look for new employment. But they ask: once other kinds of unemployment have been eliminated in year A, will there be further growth in year B if workers are doing the same jobs with the same equipment in the same factories? No. To get *growth* in GDP per worker, we need new business procedures, new inventions, new technology, new investments.

The rich can spend only so much on themselves. Their marginal propensity to save is much higher than it is for the rest of us. When they invest in new technology and equipment, we all benefit. Thus, when newspapers tell us how much the rich and the middle class gain from tax cuts, the answers can be a little misleading. We all gain somewhat from the tax cuts for the rich, because the bulk of their saved money tends to go in new investments. The improved products made possible by the new investments benefit the middle class.

Readers may think, "But doesn't the middle class save and invest as well? Why do we need tax cuts for the rich?" Maybe we don't need tax cuts for the rich. The rich saved and invested a lot before the Trump tax cuts. The argument here is only that the rich save and invest much more than other classes. Many in the middle class save only by buying a home, which makes them more invested in the country and its economy. But it doesn't lead to technological breakthroughs. Some of the middle class, of course, save for other purposes. When they save to send their children to college, that will lead to increased growth. But most of those who save to start a business are not likely to have below-average incomes. Taxes will deplete the savings of the entrepreneur who wants to start a business. Investors in startups typically want a would-be entrepreneur to have a significant amount of his own cash at risk.

More Growth or More Redistribution?

An important component of the debate about raising taxes so as to redistribute resources to the less well off concerns the *extent* of the negative effect of taxes on economic growth. The low-tax economists point out that some of the negative effects of high taxes are hard to see but almost certainly exist. For example, there can be an effect on work intensity and quality without affecting the hours of work, because, with high taxes, workers are less interested in getting promotions. These economists also note that many of the labor supply effects of higher taxes will not be seen in the short term. People may emigrate or retire earlier in future years. Or they may do different, less productive, and less pressured work. They may, for example, decide that a pressured, risky life as an independent entrepreneur is not worth the small potential after-tax gains in added income.

Many members of the public are not aware of the costs of redistribution. Economists are. Nevertheless, on utilitarian grounds, most economists think these costs are worth paying. But we have, already, progressive taxes and considerable redistribution toward lower-income families. Is that enough?

Economists, like politicians and the public, are badly split on this question. Both sides of the split provide arguments and evidence. Economists on the left think that much higher taxes on the wealthy will have little or no effect on economic growth. They point to evidence that a more robust welfare state and more equal distribution of incomes are not correlated with weaker overall growth. In addition, more progressive taxes in countries such as France yield similar incomes to those in the United States, but incomes that are much more equitably delivered. Many economists on the left believe that tax rates as high as 70 percent on the top 0.1 percent would yield vast amounts of money that could be used to provide economic resources for those at the bottom of the income distribution. This income would barely be missed by billionaires, but it would provide important assistance for lower- and middle-income families.[41]

These left-of-center economists believe higher taxes will not lead to inefficient businesses and poorly performing CEOs because they think executive pay results largely from politicking within businesses. They believe inattentive boards of directors are too easily influenced by executives' self-serving arguments for higher pay. Stockholders don't have the information or ability to prevent this, so executives are paid much more than necessary to attract their services and much more than they are in other developed countries. The problem is not just that business executives are paid more than they should be. As discussed in Chapter 4, economists on the left and right come together in their belief that regulatory barriers to occupational entry are both inefficient and inequitable. Members of highly paid professions, such as doctors and lawyers, restrict entry and thus restrict the possibility for those not in the profession to perform fairly routine tasks.

In their book *The Captured Economy*, Brink Lindsey and Steven Teles discuss these sorts of market imperfections at length and make the general argument that, taken together, they mean that more equity need not reduce efficiency and growth as much as most economists believe. Getting rid of unnecessary credentialing will increase efficiency and growth *and* improve equity.[42] The problem is not just one of the rich placing barriers in the way of the middle class – e.g., limiting the kinds of work that legal and physician assistants can do. For example, many people have moved from low income to middle by operating food trucks. But they have had to overcome significant regulatory barriers. In some states food trucks are forbidden to park near existing restaurants![43] In addition, state cosmetology boards, often dominated by owners of beauty parlors, have pressured law enforcement officers to arrest African-American women for braiding hair without a cosmetology license.[44]

Critics of those who want more government-directed equality in incomes, however, doubt that these unjustified inefficiencies – whether in executive or professional pay – are typical of most of the economy. Earlier in this chapter it was noted that a survey of top economists found that most thought CEOs were paid more than their marginal contribution to firms' value. But most mainstream economists think that executives do not have the free rein to boost their pay that economists on the left believe. They point out that, in privately held companies, CEOs are paid even more than they are in public companies. But the owners, usually private equity investors, hire the CEOs and determine their pay themselves.[45]

I believe most economists would be puzzled by the view that France can be a model for a well-functioning, growing economy. Economists' criticism of France's labor market rigidities and industrial policy failures were presented in Chapter 4, and will not be repeated here. There also exists an important factual disagreement. France's income per capita is not similar to the United States'. US income per capita is about 30 percent higher, because workers work many more hours. The economist Ed Prescott attributes this difference to higher tax rates in France. He finds that, if France were to lower its tax rates to levels more similar to the United States', its labor supply would also be more comparable to labor supply levels in the United States.[46]

Economists from the right also oppose attempts to dramatically increase taxes on the rich. Equity-oriented politicians are especially critical of the 2017 tax cuts for business. But most economists supported tax cuts for business, since business taxes were considerably lower in countries we compete with. For example, in 2017 Larry Summers was sharply critical of the bulk of the Trump tax cut proposals. But he also said that he would support a corporate tax cut, which would increase incentives for domestic production and "would modestly raise wage income as well as the overall size of the economy."[47]

In addition, if government expenditures rise dramatically, in time tax rates will have to rise as well. Using data provided by Moody Analytics and University of California economists sympathetic to Elizabeth Warren's presidential candidacy in 2020, *The Washington Post* reported that the costs of her universal childcare and prekindergarten plans would be $707 billion over ten years; canceling student loan debt would be $640 billion; tuition-free public universities would be $650 billion; affordable housing would be $500 billion.[48]

Chapter 4 laid out the evidence economists present for the relative inefficiency of government as compared to the private sector. A 2011 paper by Andreas Bergh and Magnus Henrekson estimated that a 10 percent increase in the size of government in rich countries is associated with a fall in the annual GDP growth rate of between one-half and one percentage points.[49]

In summary, on the issue of redistribution of income from the top to those at lower levels versus low taxes/more growth for everyone, economists are split – as are the public. A knowledgeable, politically moderate economist has told me that there are all kinds of data available; by picking and choosing, one can find data to support both left-leaning and right-leaning economists.

Just Deserts

One prominent economist, Harvard's Greg Mankiw, is an out-lier among his peers. He ultimately agrees with the conservative lower-tax economists, but he adds different reasons to the ones they propose.

To a considerable extent, Mankiw agrees with economists on the left. He does not object to a progressive tax system. He thinks that the rich gain more than the rest of us from good roads, good airports, and good education systems that produce skilled workers. They espe-cially gain more from a good legal system. He also agrees that the rich should play a higher proportion of their income in taxes to support infrastructure as well as programs to provide assistance to the poor. But Mankiw thinks it unfortunate that so many Americans don't seem to realize that the rich already pay more – indeed, proportionately more:

> The average person in the top 1 percent pays more than one-quarter of income in federal taxes, and about one-third if state and local taxes are included. Why isn't that enough to compen-sate for the value of government infrastructure? A relevant fact here is that, over time, an increasing share of government spending has been for transfer payments, rather than for pur-chases of goods and services. Government has grown as a percentage of the economy not because it is providing more and better roads, more and better legal institutions, and more and better educational systems. Rather, government has increasingly used its power to tax to take from Peter to pay Paul. Discussions of the benefits of government services should not distract from this fundamental truth.[50]

Mankiw believes that many who say the rich don't pay their fair share have in mind a much-quoted statement by the billionaire Warren Buffett. Buffett said he pays a lower tax rate than his secretary. Mankiw shows that this is clearly an anomaly. The Congressional Budget Office reports that, in 2009,[51] the poorest fifth of the population paid only 1.0 percent of its income in federal taxes; the middle fifth paid 11.1 percent; the top fifth paid 23.2 percent; the richest 1 percent paid 28.9 percent of its income to the federal government.

Mankiw has a more fundamental quarrel with left-of-center economists, however, and perhaps with most economists. He does not think that taxes on the well off should be based on how much of their income we can transfer to the less well off without inducing the wealthy to work and invest much less. Many economists are generally comfortable with this utilitarian framework. Mankiw is not, though. He believes income for the rich should be based on what they deserve.

Mankiw objects when Barack Obama or Senator Warren suggest that someone who started a small business should share the credit with all the taxpayers who built roads, airports, and good schools to support businesses. He might say, "Look, the person who got the idea, who did the work to get the business under way, and got the investors, is the person who started the business. We should start with the belief that he or she deserves what he earned."

In one speech at a 2008 campaign rally, Obama said he wanted to "spread the wealth around." In his article titled "Defending the one percent," Mankiw says, "The single most important difference between the political left and the political right is over the questions of whether, and to what extent, 'spreading the wealth around' is a proper function of government." Mankiw's "just deserts" philosophy of taxation believes it is not a proper function of government.

Mankiw believes that income should reflect contributions. In much of the 1950s the top US tax rate was 91 percent. Mankiw says "using the force of government to seize such a large share of the fruits of someone else's labor is unjust, even if the taking is sanctioned by a majority of the citizenry."[52] In the course of his argument, Mankiw references an article showing that even young children think that merit should be considered when sharing resources with others.[53]

About the time that Mankiw wrote "Defending the one percent," Jonathan Haidt, a social psychologist who studied philosophy as an undergraduate, published the book The Righteous Mind. It provides much more evidence supporting Mankiw's "just deserts" argument.

Haidt and the social psychologists he has worked with had substantial experience living in countries outside America and Europe, in particular India, Brazil, and Japan. They came to believe that left-of-center people in the West had only a partial understanding of fairness. The broader understanding they gradually developed was tested by a 30-item online moral foundations questionnaire. The questionnaire was filled out by over 120,000 respondents.

The results are as follows: political liberals usually place a strong emphasis on equality combined with a strong sense of empathy. This leads them to believe that fairness means embracing and championing groups "that seem to be oppressed, victimized, or otherwise dominated by the strong." In contrast, conservatives think that equality and compassion can be unfair because they often break the link between hard work, self-control, and personal responsibility, on the one hand, and money, respect, and other rewards, on the other. Conservative notions of fairness focus on proportionality, not equality. "People should reap what they sow. People who work hard should get to keep the fruits of their labor. People who are lazy and irresponsible should suffer the consequences."

Influenced by the anthropologist Christopher Boehm, Haidt believes that the origins of morality were in a "gossipy, punitive, moralistic community...that emerged when language and weaponry made it possible for early humans to take down bullies and replace them with a shared moral matrix." He also believes that the propensity to punish is the "key to large-scale cooperation." In experiments people "pay to punish selfish people even though they gain nothing from the punishment." People pay to punish because it feels good. "We want to see cheaters and slackers 'get what's coming to them.' We want the law of karma to run its course, and we're willing to help enforce it."

Conservatives believe that "cheaters, slackers and free riders" must be harassed in some way, or others will also stop cooperating and society will unravel. Haidt seems to agree with them. "Punishment promotes virtue and benefits the group." Haidt says he began writing the book as a liberal and ended it as a political moderate.[54]

What does our welfare state do about punishing cheaters and slackers? Not much. Our welfare state has many, many people getting benefits they are not entitled to. In 2014 the General Accounting Office reported that federal agencies as a whole set a new record for improper payments, shelling out $125 billion in questionable benefits. The figures in these audits are underestimates. As the GAO itself acknowledges, typically the audit reports just use the same data that the agencies have used and sometimes find bureaucratic errors, such as divorced fathers and mothers both claiming the child tax credit for the same child.

Beryl Davis is a director in the GAO's Financial Management and Assurance team. She supervises those who perform financial and performance audits, and regularly testifies before Congress. I had a chance to interview her on November 13, 2015. Davis says the federal government is unable to determine the full extent of improper payments, for several reasons. There are statutory barriers that prevent the federal government from requiring states to estimate improper payments for the new welfare program, Temporary Assistance for Needy Families (TANF). In addition, in some years programs at risk for fraud simply don't report estimates of improper payments. Improper payment estimates for other agencies are not included in the GAO summaries because their estimation methodologies have not been approved by the Office of Management and Budget. Further, agency inspectors generally report that still other agencies are using estimation methodologies that are not statistically valid.

The National Directory of New Hires (NDNH) is used by states to track down noncustodial parents and collect on child support orders. But the Department of Labor can use the directory to determine when people claiming unemployment insurance have now been hired. In 2011, concerned by high rates of improper unemployment payments, the Department of Labor instructed state unemployment insurance agencies to tighten up their systems. The department noted that continuing to pay unemployment insurance to people who have returned to work was the leading cause of improper payments. Yet for over six years California and some other states failed to perform the cross-matches with the NDNH that the Department of Labor regulations required them to do. In 2018 the improper payment rate for unemployment insurance was 13 percent, resulting in $3.5 billion in overpayments. This level of overpayment was actually higher than the level in 2010 (11.2 percent), when the Department of Labor "sounded the alarm" about chronic overpayments.[55]

Not every "improper payment" shows fraud, but many certainly do. Ohio conducted a more thorough study of fraud in its food stamp program. The state auditor "became aware of people selling electronic benefit cards and then seeking another one by claiming it was lost." In 2011 an audit found that 310,000 benefit cards were reissued to Ohio recipients and 17,000 of them received *ten* or more reissued cards. The suspicion is that the cards were sold, not lost. The state auditor's evaluation found that there was no system for identifying and combating fraud.[56]

A few years back Maine started printing photos on electronic benefit transfer cards so as to combat fraud. The Obama administration threatened to cut Maine's food stamp funding, claiming the policy could have a "chilling effect."[57] But Maine has continued to push for reform. "The state's welfare agency discovered nearly 4,000 welfare recipients had won $22 million through the state lottery. Yet they all remained on food stamps."[58] Meanwhile, the number of people receiving federal disability benefits has been doubling every 15 years (while the average age of recipients has declined). Once people go onto disability, they rarely go back to work.

Wasteful incentives for states are widespread. A person on welfare costs a state money, but that same resident on disability would receive 100 percent of his benefits from the federal government. So an NPR investigation finds that states employ private contractors to call people on welfare – trying to "help them discover and document their disabilities."[59]

Economists talk very little about waste, fraud, and abuse in government spending. More typically, they make fun of those politicians who focus on waste, fraud, and abuse, noting that there isn't enough of it to close the budget deficit – that it is really peanuts in the big picture. But one of economists' favorite poverty-fighting programs, the Earned Income Tax Credit, is one of the top three offenders in the GAO's list of government-wide improper payments. In 2014 the credit accounted for $66 billion in spending, $18 billion of which was in error – an error rate of 27 percent.[60]

Haidt's work suggests that there would be great public support for going after welfare fraud of various kinds, but I think there would be more political support if there were also a crackdown on abuse by well-off people. The IRS finds that 60 percent of identified tax debts are *never collected*, and says this is because the service lacks the resources to track down the delinquents. Some of the cheaters are non-filers, some are identified through document-matching programs. The cheaters here include many well-off people. Fifty-six percent of noncompliant tax-payers with incomes over $100,000 get off scot-free. This sort of administrative paralysis was noted in Chapter 4 when discussing the inefficiency of government bureaucracy.[61]

Larry Summers is among many who have called for more resources for the IRS to increase compliance with the existing tax code. He estimates that "in 2020 the IRS will fail to collect more than $630 billion" of tax liabilities – the so-called "tax gap." In a new study with Natasha Sarin, he estimates that 70 percent of this gap "comes from underpayment by the top 1 percent. This contributes to legitimate concerns that our tax system unfairly advantages the elite."[62] Sarin and Summers argue that better-focused audits, raising Internal Revenue Service enforcement to previous peak levels, investing in information technology and broadening earnings reporting could raise more than $1 trillion in the next decade, primarily from very high-income taxpayers. This increased tax revenue exceeds the revenue benefit of raising the top individual rate to 70 percent.[63]

Attacking waste, fraud, and abuse will not balance the budget, but it will save a lot of money, and, more importantly, it will help create a tax and welfare system that the public can believe in – that honors people's moral instincts.

What Would the Founders Say?

The disagreements on distribution seem so fundamental that it is useful to focus on the sort of regime the founders gave us and what they might say about the disagreements.

Turning to the founders for guidance may be more controversial in our generation than in any other. The principal founders from the South owned slaves, and only Washington freed them at his death. Slavery is a significant stain on their reputations, and compromises with respect to it found their way into the Constitution. But Abraham Lincoln, the man most credited with ending slavery in America, had great respect for the founders. In fact, although he himself viewed slavery to be morally wrong, he saw that the Constitutional Convention could not have achieved the good it did achieve – the creation of a union that would last and thrive – if it had not compromised on slavery. Legal research he conducted for his Cooper Union address was meant to show that the Constitution allowed laws to prevent the spread of slavery into the territories. Lincoln believed that by arresting the spread of slavery he would place it "where Washington and Jefferson and Madison placed it...in the course of ultimate extinction."[64]

The Constitution allowed the federal government to ban the international slave trade as of 1808. In fact, Congress passed, and President Thomas Jefferson signed into law, a federal prohibition of the slave trade, effective January 1, 1808, the first day the Constitution allowed such a law to go into effect.

Although in recent years the personal lives of our founders have faced new scrutiny and condemnation, the framework they set forth for our government seems to be more valued than ever. Many people were frightened by what they saw as President Trump's disrespect for the separation of powers, and they relied on that separation to help check him. They also relied on a constitutionally protected free press, which thrives even though Trump talked regularly about "fake news," and they relied on our federal system, which gives states significant power to resist federal government attempts to undermine their independence.[65]

What might the founders say about the issues before us? In his study of the economic thought of the founding generation, Marc Plattner finds that

> [t]he inviolability of the rights of property appears to have been accepted for the full range of American political thinkers of the constitutional era – antifederalists as well as supporters of the Constitution, agrarians as well as proponents of commerce and manufacturing.[66]

Along the same lines, in his second inaugural address, Thomas Jefferson said that equality of rights meant maintaining "that state of property, equal or unequal, which results to every man from his own industry, or that of his fathers."[67] In Federalist 10, the most important work of political theory in the founding period, James Madison said that liberty plus the diversity in the faculties of men leads to economic inequality. The rich are always a minority. The greatest danger to the public is when majority factions of the poor unite to defraud or despoil the rich of their lawfully acquired gains.[68]

This bedrock support for property rights did not mean that the founders were indifferent to extreme concentrations of wealth. This can be seen in their opposition to primogeniture – laws and customs that required all property to be left to the eldest son. Most founders condemned primogeniture as perpetuating a hereditary elite that could undermine democracy and natural equality. Jefferson took the lead in ending primogeniture in Virginia, and celebrated his success as having "laid the axe to the root of the pseudo aristocracy."[69]

Jefferson served as the US ambassador to France. He was appalled by what he saw and laid much of the blame on primogeniture. "I asked myself what could be the reason that so many should be permitted to beg who are willing to work, in a country where there is a very considerable proportion of uncultivated lands?"[70] Seeing the consequences of such inequality, he argued that property rights had gone too far and were now infringing on other natural rights. Besides doing away with primogeniture, Jefferson supported a progressive tax on property.

Although he looked more favorably than Jefferson on considerable inequality in wealth, Madison supported abolishing primogeniture as an example of using the "silent operation of laws" to "reduce extreme wealth towards a state of mediocrity, and raise extreme indigence towards a state of comfort." Madison looked favorably on a healthy middle class – what Benjamin Franklin called a "happy mediocrity."[71]

Among other founders, John Adams thought domestic peace could best be attained by dividing land into small quantities and making its acquisition "easy to every member of society."[72] George Washington also supported the widespread division of western lands. He thought America could become a wonderful place for people of "industry and frugality" while also being "advantageous to the happiness of the lowest class of people because of the equal distribution of property, the great plenty of unoccupied lands, and the facility of procuring the means of subsistence."[73] In the founding era, there were public and private efforts to provide aid for the poor. Jefferson took the lead in crafting legislation, and President Adams signed a bill to fund health care for sick and disabled seamen.

So, the founders fought to control the scope of inherited wealth by abolishing primogeniture; they hoped a healthy middle class would develop; and they supported some assistance for the poor and disabled. In the final analysis, however, they supported liberty. Given the "diversity in the faculties of men," if one wants liberty one must expect and tolerate substantial inequalities in wealth and income.

In contrast to the founders, the economist Arthur Okun believed that the incomes the market yields cannot be considered "fair" or "deserved." He thought it helpful if citizens pictured redistribution in the following way: imagine a bucket filled with the income or wealth of the materially better off. Then assume that it leaks, as argued above, because of weaker incentives to work and invest; splitting national income more equally means having a smaller pie to divide. Okun believed we should think about how much leakage we would put up with rather than abandon redistribution.

Okun was writing in 1974, when the bottom 20 percent of families had an average income of $5,000 and the top 5 percent of families had an average income of $45,000. Okun said he would favor an added tax of $4,000 on the top 5 percent in order to get added income for the bottom 20 percent. Because of leakages, the bottom 20 percent would not get to share $4,000. Okun said he would favor this transfer up to the point where the leakage was 60 percent; thus, he would favor taking $4,000 from the top 5 percent if it meant he could get at least $1600 to share among families in the bottom 20 percent.

Okun then considered another potential transfer: to take money from the upper middle class to give to the lower middle class. He favored this redistribution – but less strongly than that from the rich to the poor. The particular example he gives would take money from those at the 80th percentile of family income to give to those at the 37th percentile, but only if the leakage were 15 percent or less.[74]

Okun's second example shows that the redistributive impulse would affect the incomes of everyone in the society. Helping the poor is a legitimate public policy. That the wealthy should pay a higher proportion of their incomes to meet society's needs is just and compatible with some thinking in the founding era. But calling this tax burden a component of a plan to redistribute everyone's income infringes on property rights beyond what the founders thought was just.

The reasons we give for policies matter. A welfare state – yes. A redistributive state – no. As Marc Plattner argues,

> Having government determine the level of people's income by redistribution can be morally justified only if those who originally earn income have no legitimate right to it. By making the political process rather than the "honest industry" of private individuals the arbiter of each person's income, redistribution undermines the notion of genuinely private property. [...] By making everyone's income directly dependent on government largesse, a policy of explicit redistribution must necessarily polarize society. In effect, each citizen would become the equivalent of a government grantee or a welfare recipient.[75]

Explicit redistributive goals would intensify the conflict between rich and poor that the framers sought to minimize. And, as Okun's thinking shows, the conflict would not just be between rich and poor but between the upper middle class and the lower middle class.

Indeed, the conflicts in a redistributive state would not be based only on class. Given the history of slavery in America, questions would

arise. Should African-Americans be entitled to extra redistribution preferences? Should only those African-Americans whose ancestors were
slaves be so entitled? What about ancestors of American Indians? Given
the history of gender discrimination, should female workers be given
special preferences? The questions and conflicts would multiply end-
lessly, as would the politicization of American society.

The redistributive impulse is nonetheless on the rise. Two of the
strongest 2020 presidential candidates, Bernie Sanders and Elizabeth
Warren, pushed for an unprecedented federal tax on the *wealth* of the
very rich, not just their incomes. Wealth taxes have been tried in other
countries, with poor results. In 1990 12 rich countries levied wealth
taxes. By 2017 only four did, and one of the four, France, scrapped
much of the tax because it "contributed to the exodus of an estimated
42,000 millionaires between 2000 and 2012."[76]

Summers thinks the administrative and compliance costs of the
Sanders and Warren proposals have been seriously underestimated.
Wealth can be hidden overseas and wealth taxes avoided through
complex legal structures. Most economists believe that more progressive taxes on income, gifts, and estates produce more revenue with fewer
costs than taxes on wealth.[77]

Warren's proposal was for a 2 percent annual tax on the wealth
of Americans worth more than $50 million. As the campaign developed
she proposed an additional wealth tax of 4 percent on billionaires. She
told her campaign rallies that, in the absence of the tax, the multimil-
lionaires and billionaires would spend the money on "diamonds,"
"yachts," and "Rembrandts."[78]

In fact, most of the spending of the super-rich goes in more
useful directions. Rafael Badziag is an entrepreneur who interviewed
21 billionaires before writing *The Billion Dollar Secret*. One of his
findings is that billionaires enjoy making money more than they enjoy
spending it. Many have frugal habits. They see money as something to
use to invest and create. Even most millionaires are characterized by
"spending below their means."[79]

The super-rich are also often characterized by their work ethic.
CEOs put in long hours. Two Harvard professors had 27 CEOs track
their activities in 15-minute increments, 24 hours a day, seven days
a week for three months. The average annual revenue of their companies
was $13.1 billion. The study found that CEOs worked an average of
62.5 hours a week. The average American works 44 hours per week.[80]

One way to encourage our wealthiest citizens to spend more frivolously and invest less would be higher taxes on investment income. In any case, most lawfully earned income should go to people who earn the income. Federal tax rates higher than 49 percent can prevent this from happening.

The Jeff Bezoses, Steve Jobses, and J. K. Rowlings of the world have shown that they know how to create products that the public clearly values. The profits they gain are the result of pleasing consumers. Would Congress make better investments with the profits if they were taxed away? A 2018 Georgetown University survey suggests that the public does not think they would. The poll asked a sample of the public how much confidence they had in 20 institutions. Some of the institutions included were big banks, labor unions, colleges, major companies, and philanthropic and religious institutions. The military earned the highest public confidence, followed by Amazon and then Google. The executive branch finished 17th and Congress was dead last.[81]

Redistribution seems to me a much closer question when we consider whether wealthy people's desires to leave all or almost all their wealth to their children should be impeded by law. There is reason to doubt that the children of business titans would have the skill and energy to accomplish with great wealth anything like what their fathers and mothers have. Research by Douglas Holtz-Eakin, David Joulfaian, and Harvey Rosen on the impact of inheritances on the work ethic found "that a single person who receives an inheritance of about $150,000 is roughly four times more likely to leave the labor force than a person with an inheritance below $25,000."[82]

But there seems to have been little support in the founding era for inheritance taxes. Moreover, as noted above, contemporary experience shows that they are hard to enforce, and many countries have abandoned them. Nevertheless, *The Economist* magazine thinks they do less damage to growth than alternatives such as wealth taxes or high capital gains taxes.[83] They would serve to reduce the chances that huge familial wealth would continue through generations – a result that would please most of the founders.

The Republican Party seems intent on calling inheritance taxes "death taxes" and abandoning them altogether. In 2015 the Republican-controlled House passed legislation repealing the federal inheritance tax. The Senate did not agree.[84] In their efforts to repeal the inheritance tax, Republicans argued that it places a special burden on small family farms and businesses. But in 2017, because the first $5.5 million of a person's estate is exempted, there were only 80 small farms or businesses that owed any federal estate tax. The risks that heirs may lose family homes and businesses could be mitigated by allowing them to pay inheritance taxes gradually over a number of years.[85]

I think that the enormous and very unequal wealth at the very top of our society would alarm many of our founders. The distribution of wealth is more unequal now then it was in their era. By one research article's estimate, in the founding era the top 1 percent had 8 percent of total wealth.[86] Today, the top 1 percent has nearly 20 percent.[87] In today's environment, the founders might give greater attention to inheritance taxes.

None of this argument on inheritance taxes is meant to call into question the pro-capitalism arguments offered in Chapter 4. The capitalist churning of income and wealth has brought innovation with material benefits to all classes of our people. Our founders would be surprised by our wealth, but they would not be surprised that a capitalist system with secure, constitutionally protected property rights created it.

Taken as a whole, my book argues that economics has much to offer to the debate about domestic public policy. But, on the largest equity question, redistribution of income, economists are so divided that they have much less to offer policy makers than in most substantive areas. Indeed, I have argued that even their commonly used utilitarian framework for discussing redistribution cuts off consideration of powerful contending frameworks.

There are equity matters on which economists do agree, however, and politicians should pay more attention to them then they do. Two of these areas are explored below.

Who Benefits and Who Loses

Focusing only on economists' differences in the face of conflict between efficiency and growth, on the one hand, and helping those with low income, on the other, does not do justice to their agreement on a number of important, though smaller, equity questions. First, they agree that it is important to find out who really benefits and who loses from existing and proposed policies.

As I wrote the first draft of this section, a number of Democratic candidates for president were supporting free college tuition at public universities. Many supporters of free tuition realize that many students in college come from middle- and upper-class families and do not need to have their tuition paid for. Indeed, a free tuition policy would benefit far more students who would go to college even if they had to pay tuition than it would benefit students who would not enroll without free tuition. But a common argument in favor of the "free tuition for all" policy is that social security is popular because everyone gets it; therefore, free tuition will be popular if the policy applies to all college students.

Economists begin their critique of this proposal by asking the following question: "to make college affordable, should we create a scholarship program that gives the biggest financial rewards to students from rich families?" What is the equity gain from creating a "popular" policy that mainly helps children from well-off families? Equity-oriented economists point out that college students spend more on housing, food, electricity, and the like than on tuition. They ask: why don't we take the money that upper-middle-income families save by avoiding tuition and give it to children of low-income families to support their living expenses while in college?[88]

Equity-oriented economists realize that the money that pays for any government subsidy will ultimately come from taxation, which reduces future economic growth that benefits people at all income levels. They also realize that more students drop out of community colleges than graduate from them. Many of these economists join more growth-oriented economists in their belief that we spend too much money subsidizing college students and, ultimately, colleges, which because of the subsidies have less incentive to be efficient. Many economists wonder why we don't subsidize technical training as well as college. And, as believers in consumer sovereignty, most think it would be better yet if aid to the less well off were in cash rather than through subsidized enrollment in some kind of training.[89]

I would guess that the free tuition policy sounds good to many if not most of the public. They probably believe that subsidies that encourage more people to further their education are obviously good for the country. But I doubt that most of the public understand why most economists on the left and the right would oppose free tuition for everyone. Economists, when looking at who benefits and who loses, oppose the policy.

Economists are likely to be even more opposed to a proposal by Elizabeth Warren to wipe out up to $50,000 of student debt for those with household incomes under $250,000. The Brookings economist Adam Looney calculates that the Warren proposal would give the top 40 percent of households about 66 percent of the loan forgiveness, whereas the bottom 20 percent of borrowers would get 4 percent of the savings. No one would get additional education, but more well-off borrowers would get most of the money.[90]

Many policy ideas that economists do support sound terrible to the public, the media, and many politicians. For decades economists have tried to limit the amount of company-paid health insurance that employees can exclude from their taxable income. Here is how James Capretta summarizes the consensus view:

> Workers pay income and payroll taxes on their cash wages but not on the value of job-based health insurance. This differential tax treatment encourages employers to shift compensation toward generous health benefits. Overly rich health plans encourage consumers to use more health services than they otherwise would, which drives up costs. On average, employer plans cost 35 percent more than they would if health benefits were fully taxed like cash compensation, according to a 2008 study.[91]

More relevant to the theme of understanding who gains and who loses: "It is mainly the better paid workers and executives, with incomes above the national average, who enjoy this fringe benefit – not the poor."[92] Those were the words of the economist Alfred Kahn, who served in several high-level positions in the Carter administration. His efforts to gain support for a "Cadillac tax" on extremely generous health plans were countered by another high-level administration official, who indignantly charged that Kahn was "ask[ing] the poor to bear the brunt of our efforts to limit the painful inflation of medical costs."[93]

When running for president, Barack Obama criticized John McCain for proposing to tax job-based health benefits. But, in time, the Obama administration came to support a "Cadillac tax" for health plans costing above $11,000 per individual and $30,000 for families. The tax was supposed to begin in 2018, but pressure from insurance companies, unions, and health and consumer groups led to a postponement of the tax until 2022. Although a version of a "Cadillac tax" had been supported by Presidents Reagan and George W. Bush, in 2018 Republicans in the House tried to get it postponed even further, to 2023.

Many doubt that the tax will ever be enacted, because the lobbies that oppose it are powerful. More important still, and as shown in Chapter 2, voters will rarely support cuts in "fundamental needs" concerning health unless the opportunity costs of not making cuts are highlighted. It certainly was not the poor who would have borne the brunt of the Obama administration's "Cadillac tax." It "was created as part of the Affordable Care Act largely as a way to help fund benefits to the uninsured under the law."[94]

In a similar vein, when working for the Reagan administration, the prominent Harvard economist Martin Feldstein advocated making unemployment insurance benefits subject to income tax. When word of this reform proposal leaked in the fall of 1982, the political uproar was deafening. President Reagan had to quickly disavow interest in the idea, which the press and congressmen of both parties dubbed "the Thanksgiving turkey." Yet, as the Princeton economist Alan Blinder said, the proposal represented "a sound reform that probably commands the assent of the vast majority of economists."[95] The level of unemployment insurance benefits is related to the level of previous earnings. Higher-salaried employees get higher benefits, and they get them even if they are unemployed for only a few weeks and even if their spouses' income is quite high. Blinder noted that more than half the unemployment insurance benefits go to families with greater-than-median family incomes and 15 percent of benefits go to families with incomes more than double the national median.[96]

The Feldstein proposal to tax benefits from unemployment insurance attracts the support of both camps of economists – those most concerned about equity and those most concerned about growth and efficiency. The equity-oriented economists see that taxing unemployment benefits would alter the distribution of benefits in favor of low-income Americans. The poorest unemployed would pay little or nothing under our progressive income tax, and the richest would pay a substantial amount. The efficiency-oriented economists see that the reform proposal would reduce the incentive to remain unemployed.[97] As Blinder puts it, "This is a case in which incentives are improved by cutting the benefits of the rich rather than the poor – a refreshing change from most supply-side prescriptions."[98]

As these examples show, many of the distributional consequences of government policies are not what they appear to be on the surface. Often this is because the policies shift incentives in subtle ways.

For example, businesses required to pay certain benefits or taxes will adjust so as to shift the real burden elsewhere. Although those in Congress spend much time deciding what proportion of social security and Medicare contributions should be paid by employers and what proportion by employees, their decisions probably have few significant economic effects. As a Brookings Institution study noted, "Economists generally believe that a payroll tax nominally paid by the employer is ultimately borne by the worker in the form of lower wages than he would otherwise receive or in higher prices for what he buys."[99] The shifting of burdens may also occur with the corporate income tax. Although there are economists who dissent, Columbia University's Glenn Hubbard says "recent studies find that labor bears much of the burden of the corporate income tax."[100]

Thus, there is controversy among economists about the incidence of some taxes. But, when economists can provide good information, it may help us resolve thorny issues. Equally, of course, it may not, if the shifting of burdens is so complicated that the public cannot be made to understand, and thus demagoguery by candidates remains politically profitable.

Equity and the Price Mechanism

A second area of broad consensus among economists is their opposition to many politically popular equity measures that involve interference with flexible market-clearing prices. Rent controls are one such measure, and minimum wage laws that hike low-income wages well above market levels are also opposed by many, perhaps most, economists.

In recent years many cities have imposed rent controls.[101] Economists believe the measures are not well targeted toward the economically distressed. New York City has controlled rents for decades. Among those who live or have lived in rent-controlled apartments in New York are famous entertainers such as Cyndi Lauper, Mia Farrow, Bianca Jagger, and Al Pacino. When Farrow's apartment lost its rent control status in the early 1990s, the apartment's rent went from $2,300 per month to $8,000.[102]

Moreover, even though low-income families in controlled apartments may gain under rent controls, low-income families looking for housing lose. A 1990 poll showed that 93 percent of economists agreed that "a ceiling on rents reduces the quantity and quality of housing available."[103] When shortages exist, the poorest citizens will be well represented among those doing without or managing with lower quality. Rent controls also encourage landlords to maintain their profit margins by neglecting maintenance. When property values and the tax base then decline, the poor, who are especially dependent on public services, are particularly hard hit.

Also important is the administrative cost of enforcing rent control laws. Picture an apartment building that has always had a doorman. When rent control comes, the landlord figures he can get rid of the doorman and still rent his units at the relatively low rent-controlled price. Regulators say you can't get rid of the doorman. So the landlord hires a less expensive doorman who is regularly late or absent and sometimes drunk. Or maybe the landlord has always rented an apartment furnished. When told he must continue to do so, he stops refurbishing the furniture and buying new pieces. You need a lot of administrators to successfully enforce rent controls. Landlords have a strong incentive to cheat, and, given the scarcity of rental properties, tenants are often afraid to report the cheating.[104]

Rent controls also magnify housing discrimination. Under rent control, there is usually a shortage of apartments. If the landlord doesn't like African-Americans, he can lie and say he has promised the apartment to someone else. Given the shortage of apartments, he can be sure that he can refuse the African-American and still have people of other races lined up to sign a contract. If there is no rent control, there will be vacant apartments, sometimes for months at a time. The landlord will know that acting on his prejudices may cost him a lot of rent; he will be more likely to accept the African-American tenant, lest his apartment stay vacant for months.

More generally, economists wonder why, if low-income families need to be housed better, the burden should fall on landlords to pay for this? Few landlords are rich. Indeed, landlords often do most of the maintenance themselves for their rental properties. Similarly, most economists think there are better ways to get income to struggling families than by substantial increases in the minimum wage. Many are opposed to the efforts of some cities to move rapidly towards a $15 minimum wage.

There has been a decades-long debate about whether raising minimum wages leads to a reduction in employment of low-skilled workers. All economists agree that there are more workers who gain from minimum wage increases than who lose, but the losers are often losing all their income. The city of Seattle, which began phasing in a $15 minimum in 2015, hired economists at the University of Washington to assess the results of the new policy. The authors of the resulting report introduced methodological improvements over earlier studies by getting data on individual employees. The report found that, on average, low-wage employees lost $125 a month. (A second paper by the authors found the loss to employees was $74 a month, not $125.)[105] The losses occurred because employers cut workers' jobs or hours and put off new hiring.[106] Other studies, however, show that jobs lost because of the rise in the minimum wage are fully offset by increases in jobs paying just above the minimum wage.[107]

Although the media focus most of all on the possible trade-off between jobs lost and wages gained, there are other effects that cut both ways. One study finds that raising the minimum wage by 10 percent could reduce suicides by 3.6 percent among adults with a high school degree or less, and another finds that a 50-cent rise in the minimum wage reduces by 2.8 percent the chance that someone will return to prison within a year.[108]

But those worried about sharp increases point out that, when wages go up, prices will also go up, in time, and the low-income customers who frequent fast food restaurants and Walmart will be the losers. Most economists would predict that the sharper the increase in the minimum wage, the more likely it is that in the long run employers will contain labor costs by reducing hours or employment. Some also wonder why we need a *national* minimum wage in the first place. There is research suggesting that job destruction risks will be reduced if the minimum wage does not exceed about 50 percent of the local median hourly wage. Since the median wage differs substantially among localities, it may be best to have a locally determined minimum wage.[109] To some degree this already occurs; states and cities are allowed to legislate a higher minimum wage than the federal government requires.

Just as landlords adjust when forced to keep rents low, employers adjust when required to pay low-skilled workers more than a market wage. If they have previously offered workers inexpensive insurance or partial daycare coverage, they can discontinue these nonwage benefits. Perhaps more important, they can discontinue on-the-job training. Jacob Vigdor, one of the University of Washington economists who conducted the Seattle study, worries that, by harming employment opportunities for junior workers, we may be removing the bottom rung of the ladder to future, better-paid jobs.[110] Evidence for this process comes from the US construction industry. Many employers there

> have found it less expensive to hire unskilled workers at low wages and train them on the job. By accepting lower wages in return for training, unskilled workers increase their expected future income.[111]

Prominent liberal economists are among those worried about rapid movement toward a $15 minimum wage. Alan Krueger, who would go on to chair President Obama's Council of Economic Advisers, was a co-author of an oft-cited 1994 article finding that raising the minimum wage in New Jersey led to no increased unemployment among restaurant workers.[112] But he has called a $15 minimum wage "a risk not worth taking."[113] Christina Romer, also a former chair of Obama's Council of Economic Advisers, has argued that minimum wage increases are far less beneficial for poorly paid workers than an increase in the Earned Income Tax Credit.[114]

The economic arguments against substantial increases in the minimum wage apply as well to arguments that employers must provide employees a "living wage." Both proposals are not well targeted toward poor people. Many of the benefits go to second earners or teenagers from middle-class families. For example, the Bureau of Labor Statistics finds that almost 32 percent of minimum wage employees are 16 to 19 years old.[115] Arguments about the wage that is needed to raise a family are not in play there.

Although there is controversy about whether higher minimum wages give employers substantially new incentives to cut labor costs, there is no real argument among economists that incentives matter. Chapter 3 illustrated this consensus. Indeed, even pro-minimum-wage economists would be worried about job losses if the minimum wage were to increase to $25 an hour.

If space allowed, I could regale readers with tales of the results of energy price controls in the 1970s. Rising prices usually eliminate shortages, but, if it is illegal to raise prices, arbitrary administrative allocations rule the day. They may not seem arbitrary, but they unavoidably are. For example, in the 1970s gasoline was allocated to areas as a proportion of what they had used in the previous year. Sounds fair enough. But people in the city began to abandon their weekend jaunts to the country, because they feared they would not find gas to get home. As a result, there were long lines for gasoline in the cities and unused, unneeded gasoline in the country.

Few public policy debates appear as one-sided to economists as debates over price controls. But what economists know does not travel far beyond their department in the groves of academe, much less beyond. When increases in the minimum wage are considered at the federal level, dozens upon dozens of witnesses testify; very few are mainstream economists. More typical are representatives of the Amalgamated Meat Cutters and the National Council of Churches, on one side, and the South Carolina Restaurant Association and the Menswear Retailers of America, on the other. It is easy to see why congressmen might see the issue as a simple question of equity between business and labor.

Economics as a discipline has weaknesses, but one of them is not a lack of understanding of how markets work. If economists are convinced that these price control measures are more costly, less effective, and less equitable than alternatives such as wage subsidies or housing vouchers, many others could be convinced as well if they knew what economists know.

6 EXTERNALITIES AND THE GOVERNMENT AGENDA

For those concerned with public policy, none of the concepts in the economist's kit is more important than externality. Externalities are the most pervasive kind of market imperfection that may justify government intervention. When economists discuss "the desirable scope of government," the externality concept is at the center of their analysis.[1] When a government role can be justified, economists also use the concept to determine the level of government that should take responsibility.

Why Externalities May Not Justify Government Intervention

In Chapter 4, externalities were defined as nonpriced effects on third parties that arise as an incidental by-product of another person's or firm's activity and that are not transmitted through the price system. As explained there, externalities are everywhere. External benefits can spring from education or newly planted flowers; external costs are produced by serious air pollution or crabgrass. The parallel concept of government failure helps explain why economists do not believe that every externality requires government intervention. Other elements from the theoretical literature on externalities also support a cautious approach to government intervention to correct for externalities.

First, when property rights are clearly defined and small numbers of people are involved, private action may address externalities without government involvement. For example, if a retailer thinks a run-down neighboring store hurts his business, he can buy it out or agree to pay some of the costs of fixing it up.[2]

Second, many effects on third parties, both beneficial and harmful, are transmitted through the price system and are not real externalities as economists define them. Real externalities occur when the market's price system inefficiently breaks down – that is, when it does not take account of some people's preferences. When a factory dumps harmful pollutants in the river, it creates an inefficient externality, since neither the factory's investors, managers, nor the customers who buy the firm's product take into account the preferences of downstream water users. The cost to downstream users has no effect on profits or product price. The market's price system slips up. On the other hand, when a manufacturer harms his competitors by expanding output and thus forcing down prices, the effect on competitors is not inefficient and is thus not an externality.

The effect is transmitted through the price system, in the form of lower prices, not outside the price system. If the manufacturer who had expanded production was forced to cut back and raise prices again to take account of the adverse effect his actions had had on rival businesses, customers would lose at least a dollar for every one the rival businesses gained.[3] When Henry Ford put buggy whip manufacturers out of business, the effect on them was quite serious, but there was no inefficiency because Ford and his customers gained more than the buggy whip manufacturers lost. Changes in tastes and technology constantly exert both beneficial and harmful effects on employers, employees, stockholders, and even consumers (e.g., when a big, popular chain restaurant with many potential customers buys out a small, struggling eatery with a loyal clientele). Most of these effects are captured by the price system and are not externalities as economists define them.[4]

Third, externalities that are in principle relevant may not justify government intervention in the case at hand. Third parties are affected adversely by noise and positively by education. But noise ordinances and education subsidies already exist to take account of these externalities to some degree. Perhaps the marginal benefits of further efforts along these lines are smaller than the marginal costs.

Finally, government intervention can rarely be justified to take account of small externalities. Many homeowners are very bothered by what they see as a neighbor's negligent yard maintenance. Senator Rand

Paul's neighbor in Kentucky tackled him and broke some of his ribs over just this issue.[5] When I was growing up, one of our neighbors was clearly angered by the crabgrass drifting into his yard from ours. When the weather was right, he hosted croquet contests on his front lawn. To make these more enjoyable, he could often be seen on his hands and knees picking out the dandelions and crabgrass that had possibly originated on our lawn. But we had a big yard for children's baseball and the like, and could not have cared less about crabgrass. If a law were passed requiring us to rid our lawn of crabgrass, we would have felt unnecessarily put upon. And there would have been costs to the public for the inspectors and courts necessary to enforce the law.

Government intervention to correct for an externality can be justified only if the benefits of doing so exceed the costs. And estimates of these benefits and costs should not assume ideal implementation untouched by the types of government failure discussed in Chapter 4.[6]

Externalities and the Desirable Scope of Government

In some cases, the concept of externalities provides fairly clear guidance about the need for government involvement. It can, for example, show the inadequacy of voluntary action for cleaning up pollution and securing obedience to pollution standards.

In the 1980s the Chemical Manufacturers Association advertised widely in an effort to convince the public that government does not need to force the industry to clean up the environment because the chemical industry is already doing what it can to keep it clean. In one newspaper advertisement, Ken Ficek, a water specialist with the chemical industry, is pictured smiling while his wife and two children fish in the background. Ken tells readers that he is working to control water pollution in two ways. First, he helps develop chemicals used by municipalities and industries to purify drinking water and treat wastewater. Second, he is working to make sure that the water his own company discharges is "safe for our rivers." Ken adds that the chemical industry has 10,000 specialists whose sole job is controlling pollution and that he himself has been working to combat pollution for 20 years, starting long before the federal government passed major water quality legislation. He notes that the industry has spent $15.3 billion on projects to protect the environment. His fundamental message is simple: the owners and employees in the chemical industry are concerned about the same things we the people are, because they too must live in the environment they create: "I work at improving water quality all over the country. And here in my own neighborhood...the job we're doing is improving the environment for all of us." According to Ken, because "all of us" want a clean environment, it is not necessary for government to compel industry to clean up. Industry will clean up voluntarily because its interests are our interests.[7]

Anne Gorsuch Burford, the first administrator of the Environmental Protection Agency under President Reagan, seemed persuaded by arguments such as Ken's. She and her top aides continually emphasized voluntary measures. In 1982 her agency was commended by the president's Task Force on Private-Sector Initiatives for its emphasis on "voluntary compliance with environmental laws." Even in the wake of his forced resignation in March 1983, Burford's general counsel, Robert Perry, was telling the press, "It's ultimately voluntary compliance that is going to clean up this nation."[8]

Anne Gorsuch Burford's successor, William Ruckelshaus, was unpersuaded by Ken's argument. Ruckelshaus said there is "no way in the world" that voluntarism can work, because, if even one firm does not comply (and saves money by avoiding the costs of compliance), other competitive firms will not be able to comply, either.

> The only way the free enterprise system can work is if there is a framework for competition that roughly provides the same kind of requirement on everybody to protect the free externalities of air and water and land... So there has to be a regulatory program, and it has to be an effective national regulatory program.[9]

The externality concept suggests that we should side with Ruckelshaus rather than Burford and Ficek. The owners of chemical firms and their employees do not have precisely the same interests as the rest of us. Many of the chemicals dumped in "our rivers" will end up in other people's neighborhoods, far from the homes of chemical industry employees. But, even if all the pollution caused by the chemicals remained in the communities surrounding the chemical plants, the plants' owners and employees would still have different interests from their neighbors. As Ken Ficek notes, everyone would share in the benefits of cleaner water. *But the costs of cleaning up would be far higher for owners and employees than for their neighbors.* If chemical firms devote major efforts to reducing the pollution resulting from their manufacturing processes, their costs will increase significantly. They will thus have to raise the price of their products, causing demand for those products to fall. Profits in the industry will then fall as well. Some employees will lose their jobs as business declines, and others may lose their raises. If allowed to decide for themselves, the chemical companies may conclude that the costs of certain pollution control efforts – costs borne mainly by their management, stockholders, employees, and customers – exceed the benefits. But the overall benefits of cleaning up would far exceed those enjoyed by chemical industry folks. And these members of the relevant communities would not have cleanup costs to balance against the benefits of the cleaner rivers.

Since most of the costs of pollution and the gains from cleaning it up are *external* to chemical firms, the general public's interests are likely to be ignored in the industry's decision-making process. If one considers the benefits of reducing pollution to the entire community, mandatory pollution control efforts might well be efficient and justified.

Well before Burford took office, there was ample evidence of what simple reflection on the externality concept would have suggested: that volunteerism will not get the pollution abatement job done. In the early 1960s auto companies assured Americans that they wanted to limit emissions, but the problem was difficult. In 1963 California got tired of waiting. It set up a board to examine and certify proposed emission control systems. It also passed a law requiring all new cars sold in California to feature such a system one year after the state certified that two practical systems were available at reasonable cost. This law gave equipment manufacturers new incentives. By June 1964 the state had certified four devices, all made by independent parts manufacturers. Emission control devices would thus be required for the 1966 model cars.

As the economist Lawrence White has written:

> The results were startling. Three months earlier, in March 1964, the automobile companies had told the state that the 1967 model year was the earliest that they could install emissions control devices. (It is worth noting that a decade earlier they had told government officials that devices might be installed as early as 1958.) The June certification miraculously speeded their technological development programs. In August 1964

they announced that, after all, they would be able to install exhaust devices on their 1966 model cars – devices of their own manufacture.[10]

As explained above, not all harmful effects on third parties are inefficient externalities. Knowledge of the appropriate limits to government involvement in addressing externalities can also equip one to recognize special pleas for government action that rely on bogus beneficial externalities. Without using the economists' terminology, "general aviation"[11] interest groups have, in effect, used the positive side of the externality concept to argue that benefits to the nonflying public justify the continuation of a subsidy for aviation facilities. The benefits they cite include gains to complementary industries and thus GDP, to defense capability in time of war, to mail service, and to disaster relief operations.[12] Economists argue that none of these benefits justify the existing policy that makes the general public pay many costs incurred by the national aviation system in support of general aviation. Sure, some Americans who don't fly do benefit from the availability of airmail and fresh Hawaiian fruit, but those who enjoy these benefits should expect to pay for them. (You don't benefit when I eat Hawaiian fruit or send my mother a quickly delivered letter.) Although the Hawaiian fruit producers enjoy a bigger market because of air travel, the local ice cream manufacturer finds a smaller one. Both contribute to GDP, and neither should expect transportation subsidies.[13] The general public does benefit from having a fully operational airport and airway system available in the event of war. But, as one government economist has said,

> There is no reason to believe that such benefits differ sufficiently in either substance or amounts from the secondary benefits of a host of other industries, such as steel, chemicals, and electronics – none of which have part of their costs of doing business paid from the general tax revenues of the federal government.[14]

Moreover, we already have an extensive aviation system. When considering whether to subsidize the *further* expansion of aviation, we should think only of the defense and disaster relief benefits to the nonflying public that would *not* be available in the absence of the subsidy. These *marginal* benefits are almost certainly quite small, perhaps less than the additional external costs of noise pollution to which many non-flyers would be subjected.[15]

Subsidies to railroad passengers are also quite large. Amtrak's Northeast corridor covers its operating expenses. The other 22 corridors covering less than 400 miles do not, nor do any of the 18 corridors that exceed 400 miles. The two longest corridors in the Amtrak network – the Southwest Chief and California Zephyr – each lost over $60 million in 2011.[16] The Zephyr's subsidy came to about $130 per passenger.[17] All the losses are far greater if one considers not just operating costs but also fixed costs, such as replacing railroad tracks.

The Reagan and George W. Bush administrations proposed cutting Amtrak's subsidies to zero.[18] President Trump's budget proposal for fiscal year 2019 sought to cut Amtrak funding from $1.495 billion the preceding year to $738 million. Congress ended up making no cuts, and actually increased the subsidy slightly.[19]

Supporters of subsidies for railroad passenger travel point to presumed externalities as their justification. Until it closed down in 1996, the Interstate Commerce Commission (ICC) listed externalities to defend government support, and many congressmen have continued to do so. In 1978 the ICC said that public opposition to proposed cutbacks "has helped demonstrate that human needs, which transcend the simple criteria of profit and loss, may indicate a demand for continued intercity rail passenger service even if that means more federal funding."[20] On other occasions the ICC has been more specific, claiming general public benefits from reduced energy consumption, highway congestion, and automotive air pollution. For particular routes they have been more specific still. It is argued that service between Chicago and San Francisco should be preserved because trains pass through spectacular scenery – "the heart of the Rockies" and "snowcapped Sierra Nevadas." The Zephyr is Amtrak's second longest route, at 2438 miles; total travel time exceeds 51 hours. The train is clearly marketed on Amtrak's website as a scenic route.[21] Trains to the Tampa/St. Petersburg area are essential because it is home to "a large number of elderly and retired people who are especially dependent upon rail service." And service to Mexico City is important to our good neighbor policy toward Latin America.[22]

The externality concept helps us sift through these arguments. Public outcry at the loss of service is not necessarily a sign that a criterion of profit and loss must be missing something. The outcry shows only that the people who use the trains would benefit from continuation of the service when they pay 20 percent of the cost. If most passengers still benefited even if they paid far more, Amtrak would have raised fares long ago. Some passengers might be willing to pay five times as much, but this is not conclusive, either. Most failing businesses have some customers right up to the time they close their doors. They just do not have enough of them to cover their costs.

Reductions in energy consumption, congestion, and pollution all yield benefits to those who do not travel by train. The externality, results not from the positive side effects of train travel, however, but from avoiding the negative side effects of other modes of travel that consume more energy or produce more congestion or pollution. If we subsidize train travel as a means of reducing energy consumption, congestion, and pollution, we will end up devoting an inefficiently large percentage of society's resources to the railroad industry, since fares will be lower than the marginal costs of providing the services. This suggests that the appropriate policy is not a subsidy for railroad travel but, rather, a tax to address the adverse side effects of most forms of travel.

Even as a second-best policy, current subsidies to Amtrak cannot be justified on these externality grounds. A Congressional Budget Office study finds that passenger trains outside the Northeast corridor are *less* energy-efficient than automobiles and far less efficient than buses. The most heavily subsidized trains are outside the Northeast corridor, and they do little to reduce highway congestion. And the potential for pollution reduction is small, since even a doubling of intercity railroad travel would leave trains with less than 1 percent of total intercity travel. If other people traveled by train more often, the pollution reduction gains to the rest of us would surely not be four times greater than the benefits reaped by the train travelers themselves.

The scenery that can be viewed from the Zephyr train does not constitute a positive externality. The scenic benefits of the canyon will not disappear if the trains do, and it is those on the train, not the rest of us, who enjoy the beautiful scenery. This should help Amtrak sell tickets. But the Zephyr takes more than two days to go the 2438 miles from Chicago to San Francisco. For the vast majority of us, trains on this route cannot compete with planes, which get people where they are going much more speedily and, subsidies aside, at far less cost.

Some of my students are at first quite sympathetic to those retirees in Tampa/St. Petersburg who are "especially dependent" on rail service. But even an advocate of some in-kind transfers can find little reason to defend this subsidy. The subsidy (over $100 per passenger for travel from New York) benefits everyone on the train, young and old, rich and poor. Most people on the trains are not elderly. Most of the elderly on them are not poor.[23]

Our poorest citizens rarely retire to Florida and then travel frequently by interstate train. Those who do are not "especially dependent" as long as buses are also available. Some minimum level of food, shelter, and medical care may now be the birthright of every American. But, if we keep opportunity costs in mind, I think we will draw the line before we reach subsidized train service to Tampa/St. Petersburg.

To a noneconomist, the good neighbor policy to Latin America may seem the flimsiest justification of all. But here we have a genuine externality (assuming the discontinuation of train service to Mexico City would in fact produce ill will from Mexico). Everyone benefits from good relationships with Mexico, not just those citizens who travel there by train. When considering whether to continue subsidizing that route, an economist would ask the Department of State if it could think of alternative measures that would do as much for relations with Mexico and cost less than the necessary railway subsidy. If it could, the subsidy would not be justified. If it could not, some judgment would have to be made about whether the opportunity costs of the subsidy or the costs in relations with Mexico were greater.

The externality concept gives useful guidance about the need for government intervention in the aforementioned cases. Often, though, its teaching is less clear. It is easy to show that the problem of market failure is far greater for environmental pollution than for occupational safety. Most of the benefits from reduced pollution go to those outside the firm, whereas most of the benefits from better occupational safety go to the firm's own employees. Still, one could make an externality-based argument for an occupational safety administration. Even if one ignores friends and relatives of firm employees, others are affected by the higher health and life insurance premiums that result from inadequate occupational safety measures. In addition, some feel psychological pain from deaths and injuries incurred on the job by strangers.

Agencies responsible for requiring automotive safety equipment will find that externalities can help justify requiring some safety equipment but not others. For example, a better case can be made for requiring automobiles to have features such as dual brake systems or good tires than for requiring them to have collapsible steering wheels. Drivers and pedestrians outside the car are helped by the former, but not the latter. Indeed, if the collapsible steering wheel makes drivers feel safer it could lead to more aggressive driving. If it does there will be negative externalities for other drivers and pedestrians.

There will also be positive externalities, however, such as those associated with occupational safety programs. Economists are likely to point to more directly targeted policies to address these sorts of pervasive financial and psychological externalities. Some have argued, for example, in favor of more severe penalties for speeding and steeper taxes on alcohol.[24] Others object to the loss of liberty that occurs when we use external costs (such as higher health insurance premiums) to justify coercing people to do something they do not believe is in their interest (e.g., buying collapsible steering wheels or eating more vegetables).[25] Still, the externality case for making collapsible steering wheels mandatory cannot be conclusively refuted. It may help to know that it is less urgent than other measures, but it cannot be ruled out.

Economists discussing agencies such as the Occupational Safety and Health Administration and the National Highway Traffic Safety Administration tend to first show that the market will produce some safety improvements on its own. Because workers and consumers want safe jobs and safe cars, they will demand and receive a certain measure of safety even without government involvement. After making this point, economists then mention the positive externalities discussed earlier. But, in part because the agencies seem certain to survive whatever the theoretical case for their existence, these discussions are often quite brief and inconclusive.[26] Accepting the decision to intervene, economists devote most of their effort to suggesting better methods of intervention.

Externalities and Federalism

Most economists who have thought about the question seem to support a federal system of government whereby national, regional, and local bodies share power. Although the traditional political reasons for preserving local power are sometimes mentioned, economists focus on the concept of externalities or spillovers.

There are external benefits associated with street lights and police services, and external costs associated with fires, noise, and litter. But few of the external benefits and costs flow beyond the local level. This suggests that they should be a local responsibility. Some communities will be more concerned with providing street lights and police services, others with combating noise and litter. Citizens will have different preferences for public goods, and they will tend to live in communities where others share their preferences. Their satisfaction will be higher with local regulations than it would be if the national government were to provide uniform services for all communities.[27]

Although localities should provide services such as police forces, other services, such as water quality management, generate widely shared benefits, and these should be furnished by state or regional administrations. Still other interests, such as national defense, space exploration, and cancer research, should be provided for at the federal level.[28] Unlike water quality management, the benefits of funding these public goods flow beyond any single region. But, when deciding how much to spend on such functions, each state or locality may consider only the benefits that accrue to its residents. The benefits to particular parts of the nation will be less than the total costs for many programs, even though benefits to the nation as a whole may exceed the costs. Thus, without the involvement of the federal government, these goods are unlikely to receive the optimal level of funding.

Incentives more than externalities explain why most economists think the national government should be responsible for redistributive welfare programs. A few economists note that people like to give to neighbors rather than strangers and argue that people's preferences about the desirable degree of redistribution differ between states and localities. They thus believe that all three levels of government should play some role in redistributive efforts.[29] But most economists emphasize that any substantial redistribution on the part of states or localities will lead some rich people to leave (to avoid high taxes) and some poor people to enter the area (to take advantage of higher benefit levels). To avoid this result, which causes a decrease in average per capita income in the locality, state and local governments will tend to make welfare programs less generous than most citizens would wish them to be were it possible to neutralize the incentive effects.[30]

This theoretical argument from incentives has played out in many bighearted liberal cities that have soured on their programs to deal with homelessness. The titles of many news articles suffice to demonstrate this problem.

- "Homeless say booming cities have outlawed their right to sleep, beg, and even sit."[31]
- "San Francisco gets tough with the homeless."[32]
- "Cities get tougher on homeless, as number of street dwellers rises."[33]
- "One city's key to keeping its California paradise: arrest the homeless."[34]
- "Exasperated cities move to curb or expel the homeless."[35]
- "Bussed out: how America moves its homeless."[36]

The other side of the welfare magnet problem is chasing away the rich, an effect recently demonstrated in Seattle. The city council passed a head tax of $275 for every employee in large companies, and the revenue was to go to homelessness programs. Amazon is Seattle's largest employer. Its founder and chairman is Jeff Bezos, one of the wealthiest men in the world, with a net worth of around $190 billion. After passage of the tax, Amazon immediately stopped construction on a high-rise near the company's headquarters building and hinted it would make other moves if the tax were not rescinded. It was. The headline on the story read "Amazon crushes a small tax that would have helped the homeless."[37]

The residential mobility that helped localities reach efficient outcomes for other services can prevent such outcomes for redistributive programs. Placing the responsibility for redistribution at the national level can neutralize most of these adverse incentive effects, since only migration beyond national boundaries would then increase people's benefits or reduce their tax burdens.

This scheme for the distribution of powers is complicated by the fact that few if any government services do not provide *some* benefits beyond city and state boundaries. Most of the benefits of police services probably go to those in the localities that pay for them. But other localities can benefit if one city locks up a thief who would have visited them next, or they can incur costs if the first city's vigilance scares the thieves to their neighborhoods. Californians were surely harmed when, in retaliation for California's refusal to extradite a man wanted in South Dakota, the latter state let 93 people charged with forgery, burglary, and theft move to California rather than be prosecuted.[38] And, these more tangible externalities aside, there are people who feel psychological pain when reading about brutal crimes outside their city or state. Some of these would presumably pay something to reduce the number of such crimes.

When such jurisdictional spillovers seem minor, economists recommend ignoring them. When only two or three jurisdictions are involved, voluntary agreements about services such as fire protection or metropolitan transportation may deal with the problem. But, if the spillovers are significant and a number of jurisdictions are affected, a federal or state matching-grant program may help achieve efficiency without losing all the benefits of decentralized service provision. Economists usually suggest that the state or nation subsidize the benefit-generating, lower-level government in accordance with the value of their services to other jurisdictions. Thus, if 70 percent of the benefits of a municipal waste treatment plant accrue to those in the municipality, the municipality should pay 70 percent of the costs.[39]

Just as there is often room for reasonable disagreement about whether significant externalities exist, so there is often room for argument about whether significant benefits spill over beyond city and state boundaries. Still, the precepts flowing from the externality concept can help establish the level of government that should have responsibility for a certain government function.[40] For example, what level of government should regulate environmental pollution? Externality analysis suggests that much depends on the type of pollution. It is hard to see how states or localities can deal with acid rain, for which the spillovers across state boundaries are massive, but the local nature of most types of noise pollution made the federal government's 1970s intervention in that realm hard to justify.[41]

Even those with only a rudimentary knowledge of American politics will notice that Republicans tend to want a smaller federal government and Democrats a larger government. Using the economists' externality concept enables us to see through the weakest arguments of both parties.

Donald Trump's first EPA administrator, Scott Pruitt, said that he hoped Congress would end the tax breaks for wind and solar energy. As suggested in Chapter 4, I think most economists would agree with Pruitt that we should do away with production subsidies for first-generation green energy. (They would also strongly support ending tax subsidies for fossil fuels, which totaled $41 billion over ten years.[42]) Economists are, however, likely to support "green-energy initiatives focused on innovations, making new generations of technology work better and cost less."[43] Setting aside the notable failures of the subsidies discussed in Chapter 4, economists would remind us that the general public does not receive *external* benefits when, for example, energy is produced by wind power. In fact, it experiences external costs: the huge blades used to capture wind power create unsightly shorelines and dead birds. We don't want more and more wind power any more than we want lots of interstate travel via railroad; what we want is less power from fossil fuels, which produce pollution. Many ways to accomplish this goal don't require power of any kind. We could, for example, have more use of GPSs (thus lessening the frequency of wrong turns) and less traveling by cars.

The problem with Pruitt's stewardship of the Environmental Protection Agency was that he seemed uninterested in forcing polluting industries to clean up. He would sometimes suggest that he wanted to be evenhanded: he wanted wind and solar, coal and oil, to compete in the market. But a fair competition would occur only if subsidies for coal and oil disappeared and if polluting industries were forced to pay for the external costs of their pollution.

Pruitt also said that his most important administrative principle was federalism: "We are going to once again pay attention to the states across the country. I believe people in Oklahoma, in Texas, in Indiana, in Ohio...care about the air they breathe, and they care about the water they drink, and we are going to be partners with these individuals [sic], not adversaries."[44] Here Pruitt suggested his agreement with the chemical companies' advertisements quoted earlier, except that he wanted federal deference to states, not businesses. People in the states want clean water and air, so we should let states set the environmental standards more often. The problem here is that most of the states singled out in Pruitt's talk house a large number of polluting firms. Such states will weigh the costs of cleanup to their industries more highly than most states. President George W. Bush's administration also wanted more cooperative oversight and interventions with state environmental agencies. But, at the time, the pollution policy of the heavily polluting state of Ohio was one of voluntary compliance. This policy has not been effective. One study showed that "72% of Ohio plants and refineries surveyed had violations of the Clean Water Act and 33% were in violation of the Clean Air Act,"[45] because the EPA was not enforcing the Clean Air Act's "good neighbor provision."[46]

Pollution aside, economists would also argue that Republicans' general preference for state and local spending, as opposed to federal spending, may lead to inadequate levels of spending on redistributive programs. As mentioned above, it is unlikely that sufficient income redistribution, from the point of view of consumers, will take place unless the federal government is deeply involved.

So, conservatives and Republicans tend to like federal divestment of powers to states and localities even when that means policies are less likely to take adequate account of wide-ranging external costs of pollution and other problems. Liberals and Democrats, on the other hand, see many problems that government might address, and they would like the federal government to help solve them almost everywhere. Externalities and their scope are rarely considered.

The uproar that accompanied Ronald Reagan's proposed 1986 budget is illustrative of this. Deficits were high, partly because of a large Reagan-supported tax cut. Reagan proposed deep spending cuts in many programs to reduce the deficit. There certainly were parts of his plan that most economists would not approve of – such as cutting the federal contribution to states for Medicaid. Medicaid helps citizens with low incomes; since it is redistributive, economists think the federal government should provide most if not all of the necessary funds. But in the Reagan budget there were also many federal cuts to programs that economists would think were not really a federal responsibility to begin with. For example, Reagan wanted to completely eliminate (over the course of three years) "the Federal revenue-sharing program, which [had] provided $74 billion in all-purpose fiscal assistance" to state and local governments. The New York Times noted that "the money is often used by cities and counties for such basic services as schools, police protection and sanitation."[47] These are indeed basic government services, but economists say, since people outside the cities and counties in question accrue almost none of the benefits, why should the federal government be involved?

Such sorting out of government responsibilities angered many Democratic politicians and prominent liberal columnists. New York governor Mario Cuomo said that the "states and localities [were] being told that there is no room in the federal lifeboat." Cuomo then asked some rhetorical questions, such as: "Is it right that the residents of New Jersey spend their money to subsidize farmers in Iowa? Why do Iowans contribute to mass transit in New Jersey?"[48]

In a *Washington Post* column, Mary McGrory continued in the same vein:

> The underlying assumption has been the regions have different needs... Mississippi needs flood control; California needs water. Eastern states need cops; Western states need forest rangers. The North needs snowplows; the South needs smudge pots. And somehow, while everyone grumbles, we all get approximately what we need because we're one big country and it all evens out.[49]

Economists would say no one should be subsidizing farmers in Iowa, certainly not residents of New Jersey. Smudge pots are oil-powered heating devices placed among fruit trees to ward off frost that comes earlier than expected. Why should any level of government be supporting fruit farmers in this way? Just how many snowplows does the north "need"? If all localities pay for their own, they probably will get enough to clear major thoroughfares within hours of snow falling and less-traveled roads within a day or two. If the federal government funds the plows, the cost to the localities is almost zero, so why not ask for enough snowplows to clear all roads in hours?

It doesn't "all even out in the end." Senior legislators will bring home far more federal goodies than newly minted legislators. Substantive programs with more powerful lobbyists will benefit disproportionately. The public's cynicism about politics will grow and grow.

Further Reflections

The concept of externalities can help expose the weakness of self-serving interest groups' positions on public policy issues. Reflection on the concept sometimes suggests that we should reject arguments for reliance on voluntarism and market forces in the face of clear-cut external costs (e.g., pollution). At other times, a proper understanding of externalities exposes the fraudulent nature of pleas for subsidies based on bogus external benefits (e.g., air and rail transportation). Even when the concept cannot give us conclusive guidance about the appropriate role for government, it can often structure debate by clarifying exactly what is at issue.

Although the externality concept is terribly useful, it is also terribly troublesome. Because externalities are pervasive and often intangible, good judgment in separating the significant from the insignificant is essential.

There are policy areas where the appropriate framework for analysis is not local, state, or national but international. I am thinking of global warming in particular. International organizations have no ability to enforce, whether by regulation or taxes, policies that force reductions in carbon. The free rider problem is pervasive. If we Americans cut carbon substantially, we pay the cost of the reduction, but other nations share in the benefits whether or not they implement carbon reduction policies of their own. Getting other nations to follow through on commitments is an enormous problem. Both mitigation of the damage caused by global warming and stimulating investments in a host of new technologies that *might* yield major reductions in global warming seem important in the short term. The substantive endnote near the end of Chapter 1 explains why opportunity costs remain relevant.

Addendum: Cost–Benefit Analysis

The previous chapter showed how economists can use the externality concept to begin to form an agenda for government. But more is needed before money should be spent. Any proposal to mitigate an external cost should still pass a cost–benefit test, also called benefit–cost analysis.

Determining benefits usually involves two steps. First one estimates the effects of the government program – for example, the number of lives or minutes of travel time saved. Then one values these effects in dollar terms. In estimating benefits (and costs), it is important to look at marginal, not average, figures. For example, when considering the expansion of the interstate highway system, decision makers should want to know not how many lives and minutes of travel time are saved per thousand miles of *existing* interstate but how many would be saved with a thousand *additional* miles. Since the interstate highways (or police or emergency medical units, etc.) are usually put first where they will do the most good, the marginal benefits of expanding a government program will usually be less than the average benefits the program has yielded in the past.

Sometimes cost–benefit analysis can be relatively simple: "Should our agency rent office space, or would it save money if it bought and maintained equivalent office space?" But usually the calculations are much more difficult. Readers may wonder, "How in the world can economists put a dollar value on clean air? And a host of government agencies save lives? How can an economist put a dollar value on a prevented death?"

Economists have been working at these problems for decades, and they have come up with some ingenious ideas that at least approximate a dollar value. With respect to air pollution, when estimating the value of reduced damage to materials and vegetation, or the value of greater visibility, one can look at property values. Pollution reduces property values. One can also look at how property values vary across a single urban area (or among urban areas) with differences in air pollution levels, controlling for other sources of variation. As expected, economists find that, after controlling for other variables such as accessibility to employment centers and structural and neighborhood characteristics, property values are higher where pollution is lower.

Aside from the usual statistical problems, one remaining uncertainty with this procedure is whether the value of health improvements is also captured in the property value results. Some kinds of health effects (e.g., eye irritation and shortness of breath) are easily perceived and, presumably, are reflected in property values. But several major pollutants are colorless and odorless. The effects of these and other pollutants on long-term health may not be known to those buying residential property in polluted areas. But, because most people are aware of some of these effects, simply adding reduced mortality benefits to the benefits from property value differentials will bring about some double counting.[50]

But what about the reduced mortality from reductions in pollution: how is this valued? First, I must emphasize that, when economists talk about the value of a life saved, they are not talking about how much it is worth to save Joe or to save Jill. The coronavirus killed a lot of people, but the policy that every agency in the United States adopted at the outset was to try to quickly ensure that a ventilator and a hospital bed would be available for everyone at risk of dying.

Most agencies' lifesaving programs aim to reduce the risk of death among thousands of people by a very small amount. Economists are particularly attracted to a method that figures out how much workers would pay to eliminate the risk of death on a job. Suppose 10,000 workers in some job each undergo a one in 10,000 chance that they will die on the job. Assume further that each of the 10,000 would pay $900 to permanently eliminate this risk. Ten thousand workers paying $900 each would bring in $9 million. Thus, the benefit of the risk reduction program would be $9 million.

Some readers may think that workers are not aware of such risks. But the literature on the wage premium needed for workers to undertake riskier jobs seems to be roughly the same in studies of various occupations. This suggests that workers are aware of the risks that they take, and they demand a wage premium to work in riskier jobs. For example, in zoos, elephant handling is the riskiest job, and in Philadelphia workers who undertake that task receive a $1000 premium.[51] As of 2016 the Department of Transportation was using a value of statistical life of just under $10 million, well in line with current economic literature.[52]

Monetary valuations of a statistical life have been used by federal agencies such as the Federal Aviation Administration, the National Highway Traffic Safety Administration, and the Food and Drug Administration.[53]

———————

Cass Sunstein is an accomplished Harvard law professor. For the first term of the Obama administration, as head of the Office of Information and Regulatory Affairs, he oversaw cost–benefit analyses offered by most departments and agencies of the federal government. He later wrote a book on cost–benefit analysis.

Sunstein is a strong advocate of this method of assessing proposed regulations and of reassessing regulations' worth after they are implemented. When looking at the big picture, he notes that both Republican (Reagan, both Bushes) and Democratic administrations (Clinton and Obama) have supported cost–benefit analysis. Bipartisan support has been strong enough that he believes that cost–benefit analysis "has become part of the informal constitution of the US regulatory state."[54]

One sign of support for cost–benefit analysis is the fact that it comes up frequently in Supreme Court opinions. In 2015 the court declared that administrative agencies must consider costs when deciding whether and how to regulate. Even in her dissenting opinion, liberal Supreme Court Justice Elena Kagan upheld the importance of cost–benefit analysis, saying, "I agree with the majority – let there be no doubt about this – that EPA's power plant regulation would be unreasonable if [t]he Agency gave cost no thought at all."[55]

Written in 2018, Sunstein's *The Cost–Benefit Revolution* was cautiously optimistic about how cost–benefit analysis would fare in the Trump administration. He did not like the Trump rule that two regulations should be dropped for every new one implemented. But, Trump did not jettison Obama's executive order strongly endorsing cost–benefit analysis, and he specifically endorsed retrospective cost–benefit analysis in his effort to weed out costly regulations that accomplished little.

But, after his book was published, Sunstein called Trump's regulatory agenda "a disgrace," as Trump took to rolling back several Obama administration regulations that even business no longer opposed.[56] This is a fair criticism. In the Trump administration, costs of changes to business systems that have already been made – in other words, "sunk costs" (see Chapter 1) – have been treated as if they were relevant to future decisions! Moreover, Trump analyses consider indirect costs but not indirect benefits! One critic exaggerates only a little when she calls Trump cost–benefit analyses "cost-nothing analyses."[57]

I believe Sunstein's book gets a lot right. He strongly opposes expressivism – the tendency of many to support all environmental initiatives (or to oppose them) so as to show their values. Sunstein thinks support for concrete policies must be based on facts, not ideologies: do the benefits exceed the costs? He also sees, as I emphasize in the following chapter, that a favorable cost–benefit ratio does not necessarily mean that societal welfare will increase if the policy is adopted.

Moreover, even though he is a left-of-center Democrat, he acknowledges that cost–benefit analysis is particularly important when the left is in charge of government:

> In such periods, there is a serious risk that certain kinds of regulatory interventions – worker safety, food safety, the environment – will have the wind at their backs. High-level officials will see these issues in "we vs. they" terms, as if regulations were a kind of transfer from the bad guys (the corporations) to the good guys (the people).[58]

Sunstein goes on to echo Charles Schultze's argument that began Chapter 3:

The real victims of aggressive regulations may be workers (who lose benefits or even jobs), consumers (who pay more for goods, or who may lose access to some goods altogether), or small enterprises (for whom regulation may serve as a stiff tax or even a barrier to entry).[59]

A serious weakness in Sunstein's book, however, is that it gives no hint that there are deep disagreements among economists about important benefit measurements. He writes as if only interest groups and politicians, especially in Congress, were standing in the way of cost–benefit successes. Yet, in fact, in the last decade new methods of estimating benefits have come into play; prominent cost–benefit theorists and practitioners have been strong opponents of these new benefit estimation methods.

New Controversies in Cost–Benefit Analysis

Anyone studying a significant proposed federal regulation these days will come across a regulatory impact analysis (RIA). These formalized cost–benefit analyses are compiled by federal agencies to evaluate the impact of "economically significant regulations" and are supposed to aid agencies in efficiently designing said regulations.[60] Some have their doubts about the usefulness of RIAs. The agency proposing a regulation compiles its own RIA with no outside organization authorized to vet it. Instead of focusing on choosing the best policies, these cost–benefit analyses "often serve as legal documents, running to hundreds or even thousands of pages, prepared by agencies in a defensive posture in anticipation of litigation."[61] But, to some extent, agency cost–benefit analyses have always been defensive documents created without vetting and aimed at ensuring that a proposed regulation will be promulgated. This complaint about agency cost–benefit analysis did not begin with President Clinton's 1993 executive order, which led to RIAs.

Historically, consumer sovereignty has been the guiding principle behind cost–benefit analysis. Analysts have tried their best to figure out how much US citizens/consumers would pay to achieve anticipated benefits from a new program. This is no longer the case. As explained in Chapter 4, behavioral economics is a growing school within economics.[62] It shows that there are situations, such as valuing benefits in the distant future, in which people seem to behave irrationally. Beginning with the Obama administration, these general findings have been used as a justification for substituting analysts' judgments about what is in the consumer's interests for the consumer's own judgments. In addition, benefits to those outside the United States have been counted to the same degree as benefits to US citizens. As a general rule, both these changes are quite unfortunate.

There is no evidence that Americans think benefits to people in the rest of the world should be treated as equal to those of US citizens. In 2019 a Pew public survey asked respondents whether more money should be spent in 13 different policy areas. "Assistance to the needy in the world" finished 12th, with 35 percent favoring an increase in spending. But 28 percent favored a decrease in spending for the needy in the world, which was the highest level of favored decreases.[63]

In the following chapter I show that both evolutionary psychology and most consumers themselves doubt that consumer behavior represents their real preferences with regard to overeating and saving for retirement. But recent cost–benefit analysts assume irrationality well beyond these areas. Economists Ted Gayer and Kip Viscusi are prominent critics of this recent trend:

> [T]he existence of such phenomena does not imply that they are ubiquitous and consequential in all economic situations. Just as one would want to assess whether a pollution externality is trivial or important, it is also essential to document both the existence and magnitude of behavioral anomalies if they are to be used as a justification for government intervention.[64]

In many of the cases when consumer irrationality has been used to justify large benefits of regulation, the regulatory impact analyses provide no evidence to support the assumption that consumers are behaving irrationally.[65] For example, in the case of energy mandates on clothes dryers and room air-conditioners, 79 percent and 70 percent of the respective estimated benefits came from "fixing" consumer irrationality.[66] These regulations limit consumers' product choice by banning the sale of energy-inefficient products that the analysts believe consumers shouldn't want to buy.

President Clinton's 1993 executive order on federal regulation decries this type of intervention. It says,

> Federal agencies should promulgate only such regulations as are required by law, are necessary to interpret the law, or are made necessary by compelling public need, such as material failures of private markets to protect or improve the health and safety of the public, the environment, or the well-being of the American people.[67]

How do federal agents arrive at conclusions about the appropriate product choices for consumers? In part, it is by focusing on policies that are meant to be best for the *average* consumer. But the market is made of non-average consumers, which is why it contains supermarket shelves filled with dozens of types of cereal and milk. Consumers seem to want a wide range of choice for consumer durables as well.

In one survey discussed by Gayer and Viscusi, over 85 percent of consumers were opposed to regulation requiring highly efficient clothes washers. After the energy efficiency and associated lower operating costs were explained, over 70 percent of consumers were still opposed to this regulation. The Department of Energy (DOE) had based its analysis on an average number of loads washed per week that was higher than the actual usage rates of many consumers, so the value to those consumers of the cost savings from buying a more efficient washer was much lower than the DOE thought.[68]

Imagine a consumer who wants a washing machine to use in a cabin that he will visit maybe three weeks a year. He may, quite rationally, prefer a cheap, low-energy-efficiency washer. So too may the 46 percent of Americans with credit cards who were charged interest for carrying over a balance in one or more months in the prior year.[69] With the average credit card interest rate hovering around 17 percent in 2019, it makes perfect sense for economically stressed consumers to buy the cheaper, energy-inefficient option.[70] Unfortunately, it also makes sense that manufacturers focusing on high-end products have lobbied for an outright ban on "inefficient appliances."[71]

Historically, economists have opposed mandates and suggested instead information approaches that preserve consumer sovereignty. There is evidence that information about energy efficiency savings does affect consumer purchases. Federal RIAs often fail to consider the possibility of information approaches and fail to account for the impacts of existing informational remedies when calculating the benefits of potential regulation.

Two federal programs seek to increase consumer interest in energy-efficient appliances by informing them of these efficiency benefits. An "Energy Star" label, a voluntary program, can be found on products (and even buildings) that are more energy-efficient than most of their peers.[72]

There is some evidence that information programs such as these have led consumers to make more energy efficient purchases here, in Europe and in South Korea.[73] In this country the energy guide labels yield more energy efficiency in states with high energy costs than states with low energy costs. This provides evidence that some consumers pay attention to long-term costs when purchasing consumer durables.[74]

In conclusion, for decades cost–benefit analysis has been useful when framing and evaluating potential policy options. In the American political process, filled with tunnel vision advocates of many kinds, the economists with their time-tested cost–benefit studies did more good than harm.

This has not been true, however, in the last decade or so. President Trump had no interest in a calm analysis of benefits and costs. Many of the Trump administration's cost–benefit analyses were biased toward business. More surprisingly, despite Cass Sunstein's stated interest in objective cost–benefit analysis, the product under his and succeeding leadership was quite disappointing. The analysts involved in Obama administration analysis did not much care for the economists' core principle, consumer sovereignty. As we have seen, Americans do not agree that people in other countries have as much claim to US taxpayers' money as they do. They also would not agree that consumers are incapable of making reasonable decisions about which appliances to buy, once having been presented with good information on energy costs.

It used to be that cost–benefit analyses could slow down or even kill programs for which costs greatly exceeded benefits, even when those agency proposals, in Sunstein's words, had "the wind at their back." No more. Ted Gayer, one of the most respected students of cost–benefit analysis, has summed up the Obama era by saying the new methods "shot an arrow through cost–benefit analysis."[75]

Part III
The Limits of Economics

7 THE ECONOMIST'S CONSUMER AND INDIVIDUAL WELL-BEING

Evaluative economics usually assumes that individual welfare is best achieved through consumer sovereignty. Consumers size up their alternatives and make those choices that are the most likely to maximize their utility. But does the market provide consumers with enough good information to know what will maximize their well-being? Do consumers change their minds about what will make them happy? Do many consumers aspire to preferences different from their current ones?

Consumer Choice and Consumer Well-Being

Many noneconomists believe that, through clever advertising, businesses coax consumers into unwise choices. Some economists agree that consumers make unwise choices, but find the flaw is in consumers themselves. These behavioral economists will be briefly discussed later in this chapter.

Most economists are struck by the large amount of good information available to consumers in markets, not its absence. Manufacturers advertise their low prices or the attractive features and comparative advantages of their company's products. Clues about quality also come from the brand names of successful companies with good reputations they are interested in preserving, or from the presence of an item in department stores known for the quality of their merchandise. This sort of information has been available to consumers for decades.[1]

The digital revolution has increased relevant information many times over, however. Online searches are faster and provide much more information without the need to travel to stores. When I was looking for luggage recently, there were comparative details about size and weight, and much else, on several sites. Previous buyers of particular bags rated them and wrote assessments of pros and cons. If one plugs "reviews of luggage" into Google, on just the first page of results ratings pop up from Consumer Reports, Travel and Leisure, Good Housekeeping, Wirecutter, Upgraded Points, USA Today, and Business Insider.

Despite the many available sources of information, consumers are never perfectly informed. But economists argue that they should not want to be. There are costs in time and money of both producing and consuming information. Imperfectly informed consumers thus seek more information only if they judge that the expected value of the information will exceed the costs of acquiring it. Although competitive pressures induce firms to provide much relevant information, they do not always yield important kinds of safety information.

The Brown and Williamson Tobacco Corporation rejected its advertising agency's proposal to promote Fact cigarettes as offering greater protection from gases linked to heart disease. An internal Brown and Williamson document argued that advertising the low-gas benefit would be of little strategic value "until the problem of gas becomes public knowledge through government investigation or media coverage." When the ad agency persisted, the tobacco company later emphatically rejected the idea. It believed that talking about cigarette gases would be counterproductive, because it "would require overt references to the alleged cardiovascular ill effects of smoking."[2]

When the competitive market will not provide information important to consumers, a case for government involvement can be made. Government provision of information deserves some credit for the decline in smoking as well as for the lower tar and nicotine levels in the cigarettes that are smoked. Individual firms may not have sufficient incentives to develop tests for important product characteristics because they realize that many consumers will assume that their testing procedures are biased.

About two-thirds of adults and one-third of children are overweight or obese. Government has been requiring many initiatives meant to combat obesity. Thus, for example, many restaurants must now put calorie totals next to menu items. Unfortunately, research shows there is not much reason to believe that these menu rules lead to healthier food choices. One large study found that, after New York City required menu labeling, 25 percent of diners said they noticed the information and subsequently chose food with fewer calories. In reality, the total calories ordered before and after menu labeling did not change.[3] A larger study of menu mandates in 30 cities found that their effect on obesity was trivial. For example, the weight of a 5' 10" male adult would be reduced from 190 pounds to 189.5.[4]

Despite information efforts and other programs, obesity rates in the United States continue to increase.[5] As a result, many public health advocates encourage governments to prevent behavior that they think harms consumers. For example, evidence shows that shrinking portion sizes reduces consumption. Soda drinks bring lots of calories and no nutrition. So, as mayor of New York City, Michael Bloomberg in 2012 proposed banning the sale of soda in cups larger than 16 ounces.[6]

Economists are likely to be skeptical about the results of this sort of program. For one thing, stores would still be able to offer two-for-one promotions, such as two 16-ounce cups for the price of one. Moreover, because of the value the profession puts on consumer sovereignty, economists tend to prefer coaxing rather than requiring – thus, taxes rather than mandates.

Many financial institutions are required to provide voluminous information. A decade ago, when I opened an account with a new investment company, the company sent me "important disclosures" – a booklet with nearly 500 pages of small-font type. When I opened a bank account, there were four disclosure booklets filled with hundreds of pages in small type. One bank had doubts that the detailed electronic funds transfer disclosure statement, required by law, really provided useful information to consumers. The bank inserted in the midst of the disclosure statement a sentence offering $10 to anyone writing the words "Regulation E" on a postcard and sending it to the bank. Out of 115,000 recipients of the statement not one responded.[7]

Sometimes government information requirements are *worse* than useless. In California, chains that sell coffee are now required to have a cancer warning on their cups. This is because a judge sided with a nonprofit organization that was suing major coffee chains. California's Proposition 65 requires businesses to disclose carcinogens, and a branch of the World Health Organization had noted that coffee contains acrylamide, a "probable carcinogen." But, in 2017, a major review of 201 studies concluded that coffee drinking was associated with a lower risk of at least five different kinds of cancer.[8]

When the first edition of this book was being written, there was controversy among economists about whether the federal government should continue to publish *The Car Book*, containing information on fuel efficiency, crashworthiness, and maintenance costs for different models. It would certainly be harder to make a case for government publication of such a book now. There is information on these and many other features on sites such as J. D. Power and Consumer Reports.

If government were to provide a new and improved car book, there is little chance that it would include information central to the purchase decision a friend of mine made a couple of years ago. He wanted a car that could make a U-turn on his cul-de-sac without backing and filling. That meant a turning radius of less than 36 feet. With a quick search online at his desk, he found a database ranking all available cars by that metric. Other consumers would need detail on other features of little interest to him or most car buyers.

Much consumer information about products comes from businesses' advertising. Contemporary economists are qualified supporters of advertising. They find that, although advertising can help create monopoly power, it can also help break down such power. Moreover, heavy advertising for new products can make possible economies of scale in production and distribution, and thus lead to lower prices. Even for mature products, advertising can help medium-sized firms achieve scale economies.

There are cases in which advertising seems to raise costs to consumers, such as aspirin, detergents, and breakfast cereals. But many empirical studies have found cases in which it has reduced prices. By "preselling" customers, advertising makes low-service, low-price discount stores possible. When heavy advertising of toys began in the 1970s, retailer prices and profit margins went down as sales increased. A study of eyeglass providers found lower prices where more advertising prevailed.

Almost all economists would agree that there should be laws against false advertising. But there can be disagreements about whether an advertisement is false. Kellogg paid a fine for claiming its Kashi line of cereal contained "all natural" ingredients. The cereal had included synthetic versions of three of its "natural" ingredients.[9] A cereal may claim it contains "12 essential vitamins and minerals," but the amounts may be a tiny percentage of what a person needs.[10]

The literature on the economics of information has been theoretical for the most part, and it has not yielded useful cost–benefit studies on real-world policy issues. For example, one article that purported to make "welfare comparisons of policies concerning information and regulation" concluded by noting that "proper evaluation requires considerable information on consumer tastes which is difficult to acquire, not only in practice but even in principle."[11]

As noted above, economists generally prefer providing consumers with information on risks rather than completely banning products. But it is not sensible to expect consumers to decide for themselves about all dangerous food additives. Steven Kelman reminds us just how little we know of the safety characteristics of some components of food:

> The reader may ask himself if he would feel confident identifying which one of the four following substances that may be present in food is far more risky than the other three: calcium hexametaphosphate, methyl paraben, sodium benzoate, and trichloroethylene. [...] If he does know, how confident does he feel that he understands the risks associated with various levels of the substance? Is five parts per million of benzene hexachloride a lot or a little? If the bacteria count in frozen egg is one million per gram, should we be alarmed?[12]

Detailed labels or information packets for all risky products would add to their price and require substantial amounts of consumer time if they were read at all. Thus, an economist, Richard Nelson, draws the same conclusion as Kelman, the critic of economics:

> All of us might jointly agree that writing and reading long complete labels is too costly as a general matter. We might agree that safety in a regime of incomplete and quickly read labels requires certain product restrictions, the cost of which is offset by a lower cost general signaling system.[13]

Changing Tastes and Preferences

A more significant problem for the economist's evaluative framework is its inability to find a satisfactory way of dealing with changes in tastes. With regard to changing tastes, the approach that has gained the most support among economists – cited by 13,000 other articles! – solves the problem by defining it away. Kelvin Lancaster argues that utility is derived from the characteristics of goods, not from the goods themselves.

> In this model, the whole process is extraordinarily simple. A new product simply means addition of one or more activities to the consumption technology. Given the technology (or the relevant portion of it) and given the intrinsic characteristic of the activity associated with the new good, we simply insert it in the technology, *and we can predict* the consequences.

Lancaster goes on to state that, when a consumer replaces an old good with a new one, a welfare improvement occurs because the consumer can now more efficiently "reach his preferred combination of characteristics."[14] Lancaster provides no illustrations of how his model might be used to make predictions, and if one tries to make such predictions it is easy to see why. Where does a personal computer fit into the "consumption technology"?

Many consumers might buy one primarily for games. Some of these consumers might see the computer as preferable to Monopoly, others to an old sound system, still others to the movies. An entirely different set of consumers may see the computer as an educational device for their children, whereas a third set might see the computer as an improvement over their filing cabinet. All these consumers would define the characteristic that the computer adds in a different way.

Economists tend to interpret all events in the world in a way that does not threaten the fundamental assumptions of economics. Thus, the typical economist is quick to say that what appears to be a change in a person's tastes may just be a shift toward the purchase of a product that better suits his unchanged, fundamental preferences.

If a person frequently purchasing product A suddenly stops and begins frequently purchasing product B instead (e.g., religious literature instead of liquor), economists argue that he now has more information and experience and thus can more "*accurately*" order his purchases "*in accordance with unchanged underlying propensities.*"[15] If one insists that tastes themselves sometimes change, not just information or the characteristics of goods, economists may grudgingly acknowledge as much, but they are quick to add that one of the virtues of a free-market system is that it provides incentives for a rapid and full response by suppliers to meet such changes in tastes.

At this point, economists might say, "Look, it makes sense to take the current preference as the real preference; it would be silly to take the consumer's old preference instead of his current preference! And there is no way to tell what his future preference might be." But, controversially, most economists assume that current preferences are seen in actual market behavior. They consider stated preferences only when "revealed preference" can't be observed directly in markets.

And yet there are all kinds of addictive behaviors for which the people involved do not think their *behaviors* represent their true *preferences*. We often do seem to be at war with ourselves, and when we reflect on the conflict we usually decide that reasoned resolution is our better half and the temptations of appetite or animal passion the worse. Our better half may sometimes side with the higher passions. It may tell us to act out of love or compassion rather than selfish calculation. But, since our reflective selves approve of many such acts, they merely show that reason may be more than narrow calculation.

Many who regularly indulge themselves with food, alcohol, cigarettes, drugs, or gambling hate themselves for doing so and would love to be able to stop. Consider gambling. Gamblers Anonymous estimates that there are between 7 and 10 million compulsive gamblers in the United States. Many gamblers acknowledge that they are ruining their lives and those of their families. One reformed gambler said that he had "no time" to drive his wife to the hospital on the day she miscarried. But he had time to drive to the race track that night. "I'd go from Arlington to Charles Town at 90 miles an hour just to make the eighth and ninth races. It would take me six to nine months to pay a bill that was due in 30 days."[16]

For many of these people there is no reason to think that outside intervention of some kind would violate consumer sovereignty if the relevant consumer is the reflective, higher side. One father who carried on an incestuous relationship with his daughter for two years said, "I knew it was wrong. When I was finished, I hated myself. I said I would never do it again, but I had no willpower."[17]

Cigarette smoking is a less lurid example, but most of those who indulge clearly see it as a vice. Thirty-four million Americans are still smoking. Fifty-five percent of them tried to quit in 2018. Only seven and a half percent succeeded.[18] An informal survey I conducted as a graduate student showed that most smokers would not mind some financial coercion to encourage them to stop. I asked 50 smokers (in Ithaca and Philadelphia) the following question:

> If it were determined that the federal government had to raise a certain amount of revenue, and the choice was between raising the income tax or raising the cigarette tax, and either increase would bring in the same amount of total revenue from the population as a whole, which tax would you prefer to be raised?

Thirty of the smokers preferred to raise the cigarette tax, 11 the income tax, and nine had no preference. Ten of the cigarette tax supporters volunteered some reasons, and they are revealing. Four said that, if cigarettes were taxed, "then I'll quit" or "people will quit." The other six made comments such as the following: "It's a habit I can do without. It won't hurt to cut down." "You don't have to pay." "You always contemplate that you will stop." "It's my fault; I might stop."

The MIT economist Jonathan Gruber has been alert to the real preferences of smokers that are revealed in these responses. He notes that smokers trying to quit will sometimes tell others about their decision to stop so that it becomes more embarrassing if they continue to smoke. But people can lie and smoke in secret. He wants economists to see that "higher taxes on cigarettes make smokers better off"; the government is helping them resist the temporary pleasure and "achieve the self-control that they cannot achieve through the private market."[19] A paper using European data finds that bans on smoking in restaurants and bars makes some smokers stop, and they are happier when they quit.[20]

Another compulsion a large number of people would love to be rid of is their tendency to spend more money than they have. The late Irving Kristol recalled his youth "when the only thing more reprehensible than buying on the installment plan was selling on the installment plan; it encouraged 'fecklessness.'"[21] Those days have passed. Although there are businesses that give advice to those deeply in debt, it does not resemble the counsel a good friend would give. In the 1970s, when the prime interest rate was 16.5 percent, a radio station in Charlottesville carried a finance company's advertisement for their bill-payer's consolidation loans. The company promised to send customers away with hundreds of dollars in cash. It concluded, "You deserve that vacation you've always dreamed about."

Although business produces most often and most quickly those things that people will buy with little or no persuasion, this does lead to overemphasis on goods. Yet we seem to regret our susceptibility to the allure of material goods: 84 percent of Americans believe that most people "buy a lot more than they need," and 49 percent believe that they themselves do. By a 79 to 17 percent margin, the public would place a greater emphasis on "teaching people how to live more with basic essentials" rather than on "reaching higher standards of living." By 76 to 17 percent, a sizable majority would stress "learning to get our pleasure out of nonmaterial experiences" rather than "satisfying our needs for more goods and services."[22]

The term "self-satisfied" is one of reproach. Many people are not entirely happy with the preferences they "reveal" through their behavior. They aspire to be better friends, better parents, better teachers, better husbands. The country song "The man I want to be" by Chris Young illustrates my argument here.

Young is

down here on my knees,
Cause it's the last place left to fall.

He asks God for help:

I wanna be your man
and I wanna be her man
I wanna be a good man
A 'do like I should' man
I wanna be the kind of man the mirror likes to see.

The song became a number one hit in 2010; one of its writers, Brett James, has said, "I think that's a message that all guys need to hear occasionally to really stay focused on what's important in life."

People want to improve themselves, through anything from losing weight to spending more time reading or traveling instead of watching television. The average American spends 2.8 hours per day watching television and movies (another 50 minutes is spent on Facebook).[23] Surveys of TV viewers have shown that many are bored. The author of one of the surveys calls a large minority of viewers "compulsive." They were asked "When you're watching TV do you ever feel you'd rather do something else but just can't tear yourself away?" and "About how often do you feel that way?" Twenty-four per cent answered "Occasionally," another 12.5 per cent "Almost always." Yet they continue watching.[24]

This section has argued that a man's behavior does not necessarily indicate his preferences if "preferences" means what he thinks is best for himself or will maximize his well-being. Behavior seen in the market may be even further removed from what the man believes is best for the community. Although a strong proponent of markets, the Nobel laureate James Buchanan nonetheless acknowledged that

> [t]he sense of participation in social choice may exert important effects on the behavior of the individual. It seems probable that the representative individual will act in accordance with a different preference scale when he realizes that he is choosing for the group rather than merely for himself. [. . .] [H]is identification will tend to be broadened, and his "values" will be more likely to influence his ordering of alternatives, whereas in market choice his "tastes" may determine his decision.[25]

The examples expounded above are of behaviors that do not reflect deeper preferences. There are also positive preferences – for retirement savings and weight loss, among others – that are not reflected in many peoples' behaviors. Evolutionary psychology provides a powerful framework for understanding these anomalies.

The evolutionists provide evidence showing that humans tend to behave in ways that would make them successful in hunter-gatherer societies, though not necessarily in today's world. For example, in hunter-gatherer societies, it made little sense to save for retirement. People died much earlier, and there was no mechanism whereby you could give a financial institution money now and receive it back with interest decades later.

Since our modern world has existed for only a brief time by comparison, our minds have not yet evolved to be optimal in present circumstances. People are thus remarkably inclined to want benefits now. In experiments, large numbers of people say they would want $1,000 now rather than $1,100 next week. In one study, only 1 percent of employees said they were putting too much in their 401(k) retirement account; 31 percent said their savings rate was about right; 68 percent said their savings rate was too low.[26]

Evolutionary psychologists would also predict that, in the modern world, far, far more people would eat too much compared to those who eat too little. In hunter-gatherer societies, one could not count on finding adequate food. The best rule was to eat food when you see it. In today's developed world, food is abundant, but the inclination to eat what you see is difficult to overcome. Widespread obesity is the result, and a large number of businesses – Nutrisystem, Weight Watchers, and others – offer diet programs to help fight the tendency to overeat.

Two reformers, a behavioral and Nobel-winning economist, Richard Thaler, and a Harvard law school professor, Cass Sunstein, have worked on ways to overcome both these maladaptations. Their award-winning book *Nudge: Improving Decisions about Health, Wealth, and Happiness* suggests that companies should be encouraged to make enrollment in retirement accounts the default choice for their workers. Employees would have the ability to opt out of such accounts and thereby increase current income.

But evidence shows that many more would keep the accounts if they were automatically enrolled than would make a positive choice to enroll if it were left to them. They would be nudged toward more retirement savings – a circumstance that most employees wish they could accomplish with or without a nudge. Similarly, in cafeterias, fruits and salads could be offered at eye level and at the beginning of the line; cakes and cookies could be at the very end and in the back. Without compulsion, people would be nudged toward the healthier, weight-reducing eating most would like to make a larger part of their diets.[27]

Thaler and Sunstein call themselves libertarian paternalists. They think they are libertarian because they preserve choice. They are paternalists because they "try to influence people's behavior in order to make their lives longer, healthier, and better...as judged by themselves." In his nuanced discussion of *Nudge*, philosopher Will Wilkinson seems open to much of the book, because he doesn't think Thaler and Sunstein are paternalists. He notes that real paternalists don't let the people being "helped" decide for themselves if they are being helped.[28]

It is sometimes said that behavioral economists have completely abandoned the central normative standard of economics: consumer sovereignty. This seemed to be the case in the recent cost–benefit analyses criticized in the addendum to Chapter 6. But Thaler is a leading behavioral economist and *Nudge* manages to preserve consumer sovereignty.

Regardless of thoughts about *Nudge*, evolutionary psychology is influencing economics. David Friedman, son of Milton Friedman and a libertarian, is persuaded that evolutionary forces in fact nudge people in directions that seem to go against their better judgment.[29]

Behavioral economists (such as Thaler) are less interested than evolutionary psychologists in the reasons why people discount the future so dramatically and have such weak willpower when it comes to dieting. But they are very much aware of these human tendencies. They help explain why so many behavioralists give less weight than economists have traditionally to the normative principle of consumer sovereignty.

Behavioral economists also consider interesting policy implications of these shortsighted tendencies. The decline in the US savings rate, for example, is perhaps explained in part by the growth of new financial instruments that have made it much easier to borrow against illiquid assets such as family homes.[30] Still, consumers are not completely irrational about saving, because, in bad economic times, people are more worried about the future and save more.[31] Early in the Covid-19 pandemic the US household savings rate went from 7.5 percent to 33.5 percent (in April 2020).[32]

Economists and the Selfishness Assumption

Another serious criticism of economics is that it makes people more selfish. There is some evidence that it does. On the other hand, maybe economists are not learning to be more selfish in the classroom. Maybe people who choose to be economists are predisposed to be more selfish. After all, if you think the best things in life are free, you're less likely to want to major in economics. Both the learning and predisposition schools present statistical evidence supporting their point of view.[33]

On one matter the learning and predisposition economists are in agreement. They believe that economists are more selfish. Over 1000 randomly selected college professors were asked how much they gave to charity each year; about 9 percent of economists gave nothing. This was more than double the amount of any other profession. Moreover, "despite their generally higher incomes, economists were also among the least generous in terms of their median gifts to large charities like viewer-supported television and the United Way."[34]

The assumption that almost everyone is selfish almost all the time shows up in the economics literature. The late Gordon Tullock put it this way:

> Most economists having observed the functioning of the market and government for some time tend to think that most people, most of the time, have a demand curve, the overwhelmingly largest component of which is their own selfish desires.[35]

And many believe that the most important of these selfish desires involves generating income and obtaining what it can buy.

Economists sometimes suggest that apparently altruistic behavior may just be a more indirect kind of selfishness: the desire to feel good about oneself by helping others. But economists realize that this explanation defines self-interest in such a way that it could explain any conceivable behavior.[36] So some search for a less exalted, narrower form of selfishness.

William Breit points out that malevolence toward the rich could explain desires for redistribution as easily as does pity for the poor. But, although he discusses this and other possible explanations, he seems most attracted to the theory that the middle class want to take from the rich to give to the poor out of a self-interested desire to avoid "rioting, looting, burning and other crimes."[37] Bruce Bolnick points out that philanthropic activity enables one to avoid costs such as social pressures, psychological unpleasantness, and religious pangs of conscience. He thinks the "apparent irrationality" of philanthropy can be seen as an attempt to avoid these sorts of costs.[38]

Microeconomics can be most powerful if money is what matters most to people. Because profits are central for business owners, economists can make useful predictions about their response to a rise in price. The assumption that monetary gain is what people care about makes it far easier to estimate the benefits of government programs. On the other hand, if people vote for programs they think are in the public interest or support programs that provide direct benefits to others rather than themselves, predictions and cost–benefit calculations become very difficult.[39]

Gordon Tullock wants to see if burglars have made "a sensible career choice." He can do so if he assumes, as he does, that money should be central to people and that they should feel the same about illegal income as they do about legal income. Sometimes "conscience" or "reputation" costs of crime are mentioned as unquantifiable factors, but they rarely affect economists' conclusions.

For a crime such as tax evasion, Tullock thinks these costs can be ignored entirely. He gives a formula setting forth "the conditions for an individual's decision as to whether or not he should attempt to evade the tax on a particular portion of his income." The formula "indicates that if the likelihood of detection times the penalty he must pay on being detected is less than the standard [tax] rate, he would be wise to attempt evasion."[40]

If one can assume that money is what people care about, one can get fairly good estimates of the external effects of some government programs. For example, an article by the economist W. B. Arthur in the prestigious *American Economic Review* had one central point: The existing willingness-to-pay estimates for the value of life are inadequate because they ignore the external effects of lifesaving programs on others. But the author did not have in mind a psychological pleasure that people feel when they know a fellow citizen's life has been saved. No such effect was mentioned at all. What W. B. Arthur had in mind was the following:

> Willingness to pay, as currently interpreted, would approve an advance in life from seventy to eighty years if those affected and their kin were willing to pay the cost of the increase. Forgotten, however, is that prolongation of life is not costless, to wider society: those who live longer, consume longer, and this extra consumption must be financed by the production of those at younger labor force ages. Proper accounting, we would suspect, should include intergenerational transfer costs, felt in this case as a heavier social security burden on the young.

Arthur saw an important question of equity here:

> Where altered mortality risks strike the population unevenly, or the mortality change comes suddenly..., some people may reap the benefits of increased life and production, while others bear the consumption costs. For example, a sudden mortality improvement can be a windfall to the elderly – they enjoy extra years while escaping the corresponding extra support of the generation that went before.[41]

John Morrall provides reasoning similar to Arthur's in his analysis of the Occupational Safety and Health Administration (OSHA). Morrall is open to the argument that people besides the victims and their families would like to prevent occupational deaths and injuries. He is open because he finds that others do pay more for social security, welfare, workers' compensation, Medicare, and Medicaid in the wake of such deaths and injuries.

Morrall even points out some interesting "policy implications." Since the costs to others of nonfatal respiratory disease among cotton textile workers are greater than the costs of fatal accidents among construction workers, society may have "a greater financial interest" in reducing the former. What about nonfinancial interests – the psychological pain suffered by the kindhearted from learning about preventable deaths on the job?

Some noneconomists have thought these external costs significant. But Morrall concludes that "it remains to be shown that the quantitative significance of such beliefs [is] important relative to the feelings of the direct beneficiaries of occupational health and safety programs (the workers) and the financial stake that the public has in reducing the social costs of occupational illnesses and injuries." For his own part, Morrall thinks these psychological external effects either "trivial or ambiguous."[42]

Selfish assumptions are second nature to many economists. Economists believe that more money is always better than less, because more money means one can buy more goods and services. An example: a couple of decades ago a very well-paid economist and I were watching our sons play soccer. He said to me, "You know those country stores that have a little dish with pennies next to the cash register with a sign that says 'Take a few if you need them; leave a few if you don't?' I always take them. Who leaves them?"

Avoiding Controversy through "Scientific" Neutrality

One reason economists cannot quickly reject analyses such as those of Arthur and Morrall is that they want to build a science; to begin discriminating between tastes means opening up a can of worms. People will disagree; the cost–benefit analysis will not get off the ground. To argue about tastes is like arguing about values. It is no way to build a science of economics, or any other social science.

When I taught a few weeks of basic economic principles in a policy course, one of the works I used was an introductory text written by Richard Lipsey and Peter Steiner.[43] Very early in their book, the authors distinguish between positive statements "basically about matters of fact" and normative statements "based on a value judgment." They are particularly good here and throughout the text in showing that many value judgments rest on factual assumptions that can be investigated. (For example, many people think rent control is good *because* it provides more decent housing for poor people at a more attainable price.)

Nevertheless, Lipsey and Steiner give an example of a value disagreement when "reasonable people" would simply have "to agree to disagree." The text says that, although one person may believe that we should be charitable to all human beings including the inhabitants of China, someone else may say, "You ought not to be charitable toward the Chinese because my moral principles dictate that you should be charitable only toward Christians." Lipsey and Steiner say: "If both sides insist on holding to their views on charity, even if both are perfectly reasonable, there is no civilized way of forcing either to admit error."[44]

But why would the second person say one should be charitable only to Christians? Presumably because he is himself a Christian, and he understands his views on charity to be a correct interpretation of Christ's teaching. If this is so, the next step should be an examination of the teachings of Christ. These teachings may show no support for the view that people should be charitable only toward Christians, at which point reasonable people would not agree to disagree but would agree that the second person's value judgment was unreasonable.

Amartya Sen, a Nobel laureate economist who is nonetheless one of the discipline's most thoughtful critics, argues that a value judgment can be called basic only if it is supposed to apply under all conceivable circumstances. Most value judgments are nonbasic and can be addressed by evidence and argument. Moreover, even though some value judgments are demonstrably nonbasic, none is demonstrably basic. Jones might always produce an argument or a hypothetical situation that would convince Smith that what Smith thought was a basic value for him was in fact nonbasic. Thus, Sen concludes, "It seems impossible to rule out the possibility of fruitful scientific discussion on value judgments."[45]

Economists hope to avoid thorny problems by simply taking preferences as they find them. The underlying belief seems to be that one can avoid controversial value judgments if one refuses to make value judgments. But this procedure does not avoid controversial value judgments. Suppose that W. B. Arthur does find a large number of young workers who believe that their welfare increases when old people die. Suppose also that we are doing a cost–benefit analysis of a health program especially effective in reducing the risk of death for those between 65 and 75. It is a fairly expensive program, but it looks as if the willingness to pay of the elderly, together with that of their friends, family, and kindhearted members of the public at large, is great enough to pay for the medical costs. Adding the social security fund losses that Arthur mentions, however, makes costs exceed benefits, and so the program is abandoned. Is this not controversial?

Suppose the losers from the life extension are not social security taxpayers but, instead, greedy heirs despondent over measures that lengthen the lives of their eventual benefactors; or white racists who feel psychological costs from the benefits of a sickle cell anemia program. Should one conclude that lifesaving programs that are in the public interest from the point of view of all but certain heirs and racists might cease to be in the public interest if those heirs and racists were sufficiently greedy or prejudiced?

Perhaps some of the heirs and racists themselves would acknowledge that their gains from others' deaths should not influence a public policy that might lead to those deaths. For example, some people might believe that their welfare would go up if their rich uncles died, and yet not wish for them to die. And some who might wish that their rich uncles would die might quite consistently think that such wishes should not be entitled to public recognition.

Criminal justice programs provide another case in which the failure to make value judgments is more controversial than the willingness to do so. One study figured that the benefits of a Job Corps program that reduced the amount of stolen property should be considered

> a benefit to those other than Corps-members, but part of its value should be viewed as a cost to Corps-members, who no longer receive the income from stealing. The social benefit of a reduction in stolen property (the difference between the Corps-member's cost and everybody else's benefit) is the decrease in property value associated with the operations of fences, the damage to stolen property, and the loss of legal titles.[46]

In other words, it is only because stolen goods are "hot" or damaged, and thus not worth as much to criminals as to victims, that there are any societal costs at all from stolen property.[47] A theft of money, for example, produces no costs for these cost–benefit economists. In Charlottesville, Virginia, a blind man once had his wallet stolen three times in three months. The losses to him would be seen as balanced by the gains to the thief. Other applied studies have treated this issue in the same way, and their methodology enjoys the support of some of the best economic theorists.[48]

These applied methodologies are often presented in a matter-of-fact manner without the slightest hint that they might be controversial.[*] These economists are doing what they were taught to do: treat preferences in an "even-handed," nonjudgmental manner. But most of the rest of the world will think that one who tries to adopt a nonjudgmental, amoral perspective when looking at an immoral act becomes an apologist for the crime. Jeffrey Sedgwick has noted the older term for a criminal, an "outlaw." One who breaks the law puts himself outside the law and, for so long as he does so, outside society. The gains to outlaws from their illicit activities can thus safely be ignored when judging society's welfare.[49]

Some economists seem unable to appreciate the pleasures that goodwill and good character bring to those who possess these traits. As noted above, Gordon Tullock argued that burglars should steal if the benefits of doing so exceed the costs. He did acknowledge, however, that society may have an interest in subjecting individuals to "indoctrination" so as to increase the "conscience" costs when they break the law. Tullock further argued that we should spend more on indoctrination only if this proves a "lower-cost method of reducing the crime rate than the use of policemen and prisons."[50]

Consider the following, however: if a stranger returns, untouched, a missing wallet, we feel better than if a policeman returns it after catching a thief, because in the first case we see some evidence that we live among honest and friendly people. The stranger himself, as well as others, may genuinely gain from knowing that he behaved in

---

[*] In the first edition of this book, the reaction of readers to this discussion was varied. One public administration graduate student thought it unfair to suggest that most economists would count the benefits to thieves in their cost–benefit work since he could not believe "that most economists would go this far." A smart, well-read economist could not believe that I would exclude all benefits to thieves. He reminded me that the thief could be a mother stealing from the rich to feed her children.

an honorable way. This the Tullock argument ignores. Indeed, the principal problem he saw with reliance on indoctrination is that "the badly indoctrinated" gain "a distinct advantage over the well indoctrinated."[51] By indicating that only "indoctrination" can make conscience costs take hold and by ignoring conscience costs when giving advice about when individuals should break the tax law, Tullock suggested that conscience costs are unnatural or irrational even if they are socially useful.

But perhaps the pain of conscience is not unnatural for mankind, the animal that can blush. And perhaps the pleasure that comes from doing the right thing is natural for such a social animal. Aristotle's gentleman, for example, is not selfless. But he is "a man who wishes to live with himself; for he does so with pleasure, since the memories of his past acts are delightful." He perceives "his own goodness, and such perception is pleasant in itself."[52]

To be sure, some economists are embarrassed by what their model produces in the criminal justice field. Richard Nelson, for example, correctly notes that this view of the costs of crime will seem "clearly absurd" to most of us, But Nelson offers only a few brief sentences setting forth his "biases" on legitimate interests.[53] On the more general issue of illegitimate tastes, Ezra Mishan's cost–benefit text has a "note" in the back in which he suggests that one should exclude from calculations losses because of envy of others' good fortune or because of displeasure at association with members of other ethnic groups.

Mishan argues that an implicit ethical constitution should sometimes take precedence over utility calculations. Yet even an economist as willing and able as Mishan to make judgments about the quality of tastes is unwilling to let his thoughts in the note influence the body of the text. When Mishan discusses valuing lifesaving programs, for example, he mentions, without so much as a reference to his note, the need to include the preferences of those who would gain financially or psychologically when others die.[54]

Higher Tastes

The previous section argued that some death-wishing and crime-blessing tastes should not be recognized when considering public programs. What about tastes that seem higher or better? Should they be highlighted or encouraged in some way? It seems most contemporary economists say "No."

I have argued above that, for the most part, businesses provide useful information that helps consumers decide which goods and services they want. But the larger issues of a possible information bias or welfare loss because of heavy advertising of only goods and services receive little attention in the mainstream economic literature. After all, there are many possible noneconomic sources of happiness, such as good friends, a happy marriage, well-brought-up children, improving one's community, achieving well-deserved respect from good judges of character.

Profit seekers rarely, if ever, have incentives to encourage customers to pay much attention to these other possible sources of happiness. Advertisements highlighting them are drowned out by businesses that offer things that people can buy. For example, images of the retired football star Tony Romo, sitting at a desk on a gorgeous beach, suggest that enjoyable parties with handsome friends will be furthered by serving Corona beer. Another ad suggests that you are sure to be included in the party if you use the right wrinkle-away cream.

An especially awful over-the-top ad shows a well-to-do neighborhood on an idyllic summer day: a couple is jogging; a little girl does chalk drawings on her driveway; a father is pitching a baseball to his son. Suddenly the chalk bounces from a noisy vibration, the baseball drops, and the peaceful scene is interrupted by a fleet of red, loud Mercedes-Benz cars roaring through the neighborhood. It's as if their happy, comfortable lives together were missing that special ingredient – a new car to show off to the neighbors and another large monthly payment to worry about![55] The ad ends by warning viewers not to settle: "Mercedes-Benz – the best or nothing."

In his book *The Costs of Economic Growth*, Ezra Mishan argues that commercial advertising teases our senses and taps repeatedly at our greed, vanity, and lusts; because business propaganda emphasizes the "mundane and the material," it should be balanced by noncommercial attempts to influence tastes "for the better."[56]

Economists can become uncharacteristically emotional when reacting to arguments such as Mishan's. Robert Solow says, "It is a very fine line between analytical statements about the creation of wants by advertising and elaborate indications that one believes one's own tastes to be superior to those of the middle classes."[57] And William Baumol states, "I must sharply disagree with the implications of Scitovsky's view [much like Mishan's], for at its worst it offers unrestricted license to the bluenoses and those who would impose on myself and others their own standards of good taste and good behaviour."[58]

In a volume that resulted from the work of a study group composed primarily of theologians and other noneconomists, William Vickrey seems at least properly troubled by the problem:

> Advertising almost inevitably...produces changes in the fundamental preferences of the individual himself. [...] What is the place, in the broad scale of values, of activity designed to change the opinions, preferences, and ideals of individuals? We can hardly rest content to leave the decisions, as to how much effort is to be devoted to various kinds of educational and propaganda effort, to be determined by the financial support of those who are interested, either commercially or emotionally.
>
> This would imply that the ability of an idea or a program to command financial support would be the prime measure of the importance attached to its propagation. Such a proposition seems morally indefensible as an absolute standard, and defensible as a practical standard only in the absence of alternatives. But no alternative seems available, unless it is to lump this with other social values to be determined in part or in whole by methods outside the sphere of economics.[59]

Probably more common than Vickrey's ambivalence is Dean Worcester's conclusion that "too little time is likely to be devoted to advertising and to entertainment because government authorities, which may or may not be responsive to consumer interests, insist on a larger than optimal amount of public service programs."[60] Similarly, Robert Ayanian has said, "Clearly the vast majority of advertising in American society is for goods that the American people both want and need."[61]

Why are economists so defensive when someone suggests that commercial advertising may leave many consumers with an exaggerated opinion of the importance of goods and services to human happiness? There are a number of reasons for this. First, potential professional recruits very quickly learn that, in evaluative economics, the best thing that can be said about a policy is that consumers want it. Most of those who find this worldview uncongenial are likely to choose other professions. Thus, economics has a disproportionately large number of people who subscribe to a consumer sovereignty standard for public policy.

Second, those in the profession also learn that, if consumer tastes can be assumed to be stable and real, economists can show themselves to be quite useful to policy makers. On the other hand, if an economist abandons this assumption, he calls into question the value of the competitive market and of many of his own professional tools.

If we trust consumer sovereignty, we should be very concerned when economists locate inefficiencies, but, if consumers' tastes are distorted and unbalanced because of one-sided propaganda, economic efficiency becomes much less important. Indeed, its very meaning becomes ambiguous. Two thoughtful mainstream economists have called the treatment of consumer tastes "the Achilles heel of neoclassical economics."[62] It is thus not surprising that economists protect this weak spot with such vigor.

Third, as seen in the chapter on incentives, assuming self-interested behavior can point the way to good public policy. In his book offering sensible ways to reduce pollution, Charles Schultze is right to focus on redirecting economic incentives. In the middle of the book, however, he waxes philosophical, praising economic incentives because they "reduce the need for compassion, patriotism, brotherly love, and cultural solidarity as motivating forces behind social improvement." Schultze goes on to say, "Harnessing the 'base' motive of material self-interest to promote the common good is perhaps *the* most important social invention mankind has yet achieved."[63] He suggests what Kenneth Arrow has argued, namely that altruism is a scarce resource that society should avoid depleting recklessly.

But, as Ronald Sharp has argued, the self-interested economic incentive model does not fit much of our social life. An act of friendship

> cannot be understood as spending and thus depleting some allegedly limited supply (of, say, favors, good will, emotion, or, more generally, friendship itself). It is, rather, an act of giving, in which there is no thought for increasing or decreasing one's own capital – even though, paradoxically, it will lead to increase. We do not use up our friendly emotions by feeling them; on the contrary, we intensify them. "There is nothing

more productive of joy," says Cicero, "than the repayment of kindness."[64]

Studies support Cicero. Repaying brings pleasure, and more pleasure than being repaid.[65]

One cannot run an economy on patriotism, brotherly love, and cultural solidarity, but we don't need to husband them. There is good evidence that demonstrating these generally beneficial emotions will further increase them. For example, people are more likely to help a driver struggling to change a tire if they've seen someone helping another stranded driver with a flat tire some miles earlier.[66]

Arrow says that an economist sees himself as "the guardian of rationality, the ascriber of rationality to others, and the prescriber of rationality to the social world."[67] But economists do not really think reason is very powerful. It cannot, for example, determine the good things in life. The good things depend on each individual's idiosyncratic preferences. If idiosyncratic preferences move us, reason cannot be their source, for reason is not idiosyncratic.

———————

Tastes are not simply a matter of differing natures and arbitrary, inexplicable variations in preference (you like vanilla chocolate ice cream; I like chocolate). In some cases, tastes can be evaluated. There may be differences about whether it is fair to describe certain tastes as "low," "crude," "brutish," or "vicious" or about whether other tastes deserve praise such as "high," "civilized," "educated," or "enlightened." But in many cases there will be no such differences. And there are no disagreements in which A says a certain taste is "brutish and vicious" while B maintains that it is "enlightened" and "civilized."[68]

Many of us wish that we had different tastes. We make comments such as "I wish I had taken my piano lessons more seriously and really learned how to play," or "I wish I could learn to like Shakespeare." The verb "learn" is significant. We find Shakespeare hard, but, if we have lucked upon the right teacher, we can come to understand his depth. And, if we are really lucky, we will have learned that he is considered a genius all over the world.

For example, Paul Cantor, when attending the World Shakespeare Congress, describes "the edifying sight of a Czech scholar speaking in English in Tokyo to an audience from several different nations about the reception of Shakespeare in the Slavic world – and not merely making sense but providing genuine insights into the power of *Macbeth*."[69] Cantor says: "As far as I can tell, the only people intent on questioning the timelessness of Shakespeare's plays today are literature professors in the English-speaking world."

It takes knowledge to appreciate all kinds of activities, common as well as cultured. Friends like to go to a fancy Chinese restaurant with John because, knowing their general tastes, he can pick out a meal they will like better than they can themselves. If they want to see a baseball game, they go with Chris, because he knows why the third baseman moved a little to the right with a tie score, two out, and nobody on in the bottom of the tenth. They go backpacking with Nicholas because he notices and can explain more than they, and Nicholas in turn looks forward to trips with Rebecca because she knows more than he.

Agreement on a fixed hierarchy among differing activities with their accompanying pleasures is less likely than agreement among practitioners of a single activity. Natures and capacities differ, and no one can know all the contenders well enough to be able to rank the activities with confidence. But the absence of total chaos in the usage of words such as "crude" and "civilized" can save us from the nihilism involved in assuming that all choices are equal. As Leo Strauss has argued in another context, "If we cannot decide which of two mountains whose peaks are hidden by clouds is higher than the other, cannot we decide that a mountain is higher than a molehill?"[70]

There are probably very few cultures that don't have admirable aspects. We can do justice to diversity by calling attention to those aspects. But we don't have to make believe that "no one culture is intrinsically superior to another." High school students in my community and all over the country are now being told that "understanding" this "truth" is a measure of successful educational achievement.[71] Tell it to the swimmers trying to get here from Cuba or Haiti or the boat people who set out from Vietnam. United States flags were visible in Tiananmen Square in 1989 and in Hong Kong in 2019. A desire for life, liberty, and the pursuit of happiness is not only a Western value.[72]

As the political theorist Joseph Cropsey has argued, consumer sovereignty, individualism, or the importance of each of us as a unique phenomenon cannot be the bulwark of human dignity. What dignifies human beings "proceeds from their common relation to nonhuman things. [...] Their dignity is the attribute of their common nature, of what they possess jointly, not severally, and it inheres in what elevates them above nonhumanity rather than in what merely distinguishes them from each other."[73]

What does elevate humans above other social animals? In the 1988 PBS series *The Mind*, zoologist Jane Goodall says it is speech "that freed humans from the present," permitting them a past and a future. Aristotle agrees that speech is decisive. It permits reasoning about justice, which is necessary if large numbers of humans are to live well together. Justice is one of Aristotle's four cardinal virtues. The others are courage, moderation, and prudence or practical wisdom. Aristotle thinks agreement about these virtues should be easy; any man who would be happy would need at least a modicum of each of them.

No one would call another blessed who

> is afraid of the flies buzzing around him, abstains from none of the extremes when he desires to eat or drink, kills his dearest friends for a trifle, and similarly regarding the things connected with the mind, is as senseless and as thoroughly deceived [by a false perception of things] as a child or a madman.[74]

It is simply true that one needs a modicum of courage to live a good life. Imagine an eight-year-old child who is petrified as he walks through a shopping mall. He is constantly looking behind him. When his mother says "Stop that," he tells her: "There could be a man with a knife about to stab me." Doesn't she say, "Yes, dear, that could happen, but it is very, very unlikely"? She goes on: "That has never happened in this shopping center."

You cannot live a good life if you don't have enough courage to ignore that hypothetical danger. If someone is a gluttonous drunk and would kill his dearest friend for a trifle, he will not have friends. No one would want to be a friend to someone who is so immoderate that he would always put his own interests over the friend's. Don't we need friends to live a good life?[75]

Reason is obviously necessary for practical wisdom. A madman cannot make decisions likely to make him happy. Isn't there something especially horrible about losing one's mind? I know of an adult man whose mother recently asked him, "How long have I known you?" Judy can lose a leg and still be Judy. But her mind? In 1846 Abraham Lincoln wrote a poem when an intelligent youth from his home town went insane. Part of it said

And here's an object more of dread,
Than ought the grave contains –
A human form, with reason fled,
While wretched life remains.[76]

John Stuart Mill makes a long and interesting argument for the distinction between high and low pleasures. In the course of his argument he states that "men often, from infirmity of character, make their election for the nearer good, though they know it to be the less valuable."[77] But mainstream economists are quick to reject this part of their inheritance from a distinguished ancestor. Martin Bronfenbrenner has quoted the long passage of Mill's in which this sentence is found and has suggested that it is an "exquisite and labored amalgam of priggish condescension, intellectual snobbery, and what Bentham would call *ipse dixitism.*"[78]

What ways of life would Mill encourage? Well, he thought that there were two principal causes of "unsatisfactory" lives: "selfishness" and a "lack of mental cultivation." Today's economists think selfishness moves humans and is unavoidable, and their neutrality between tastes means no special nudge toward mental cultivation. Bronfenbrenner has little advice of his own. He favors "propaganda and public enlightenment for the lower cost cultural activities." What should be avoided at all costs is becoming "an unemployable intellectual." Ah, we definitely don't want a Socrates.

The Route to Happiness

In their work, the usual assumption of most economists is that an increase in income per capita will mean an increase in people's happiness or life satisfaction.[79] A minority of economists have disputed this assumption. For example, some research finds that, within a society, richer people are happier. But over time the rich and others do not become happier still as economic growth continues. Moreover, people in reasonably well-developed countries are not less happy than those in very well-developed countries.[80]

Those economists who are more skeptical about the gains from economic growth are the ones who suggest that humans are on a hedonic treadmill. Any gains in income, and thus happiness, are temporary, and we tend to return to the previous level. Some more recent research, however, thinks the treadmill school is wrong. These scholars, sometimes using a larger data set, find that people in rich countries are happier than those in less rich countries and that a country's population becomes happier as real income increases.[81]

Given the attention paid to economic growth in almost any political election, it would seem that there would be no dispute about whether gains in real income bring gains in happiness. After all, we never see politicians promising that, if elected, they will try very hard to be sure that wages do not increase! Yet some studies have found that in many countries, including the United States, gains in real income have not increased happiness.[82]

Robert Frank leads a group of economists who think they can explain the weak association between income and happiness gains. Frank believes that, although Adam Smith was worthy of his reputation, Charles Darwin was worthier still. Indeed, Frank thinks Darwin was the real founder of economics, because he saw that it is relative income and status that bring the good things in life, not absolute income.

Frank argues that what's good for the individual may not be good for the group. Holding a child's entry into kindergarten until a later age should help him excel in sports. But, if all parents with athletic children do the same, there will be no gain. If one job applicant buys an expensive suit to get a leg-up on competition, the money will be wasted if his top competitors also buy an expensive suit. When we buy a more expensive car to gain the admiration of neighbors, little will be gained if, a year later, our purchase leads our neighbors to trade in their perfectly good cars to buy a later model of our car. If we spend more money on cosmetic surgery so as to look better than our rivals, we will not gain an advantage if they also do the same.

Frank thinks that pursuit of "rival goods" to best local competitors ends up being counterproductive. They will be trying to best you, and, collectively, only a few can be at the top. He suggests we adopt very high progressive consumption taxes on the rich and use the revenue to improve nonrival goods such as infrastructure, parks, and other collective consumption goods. The rich won't really be harmed by the higher taxes, because the richest person will still be the richest despite the higher taxes he pays. His rivals will also be taxed highly, so he will still end up with the highest status.

Frank is interesting, and makes an important point that his profession should pay more attention to, but he chooses the examples that will help his case.[83] Other examples call it into question. If we want high status in a local area, why don't family doctors move to West Virginia, where they will not be competing with rich people in banking and finance for the biggest house in the neighborhood? Why are property values higher if you have a smaller house in a very nice neighborhood with large houses rather than the same house in a less nice neighborhood – even when both have good schools?

If you undertake a little cosmetic surgery and spend more on clothes so as to look your best, why do your efforts hurt the community as a whole? Doesn't the whole community gain if many others imitate you? Isn't it more enjoyable to walk the streets in a city with well-dressed and attractive people, rather than be surrounded by slovenly men and women?

I believe absolute income and relative income are both important to happiness. Several of the best studies described above show that absolute income gains matter. Moreover, it seems obvious that we become habituated to, and thus less grateful, for the good things our twenty-first-century capitalism churns out. Suppose a 21-year-old college student in 1940 visited the apartment of a 21-year-old college student in 2020. Imagine the wonders he would see: Central heating and air-conditioning, a microwave, a large color television with 160 channels – with good sound and a clear picture.

And, of course, the ubiquitous smartphone. It can be taken anywhere you want, even outside (and it would not be a shared "party line"!). The phone is also something called a personal computer, which can make a dinner reservation and get directions to the restaurant. You can play games on it and send a message to a friend across town, and the friend will get the message instantly.

Will Wilkinson adds, "Prior to the advent of modern sanitation and medicine, multitudes suffered from frequent low-grade bacterial infections and wandered around with toothaches and other chronic maladies." In time we learned to pay less attention to these serious problems, because, "as Martin Seligman writes, 'this process of [habituation] is an inviolable neurological fact of life. Neurons are wired to respond to novel events.'"[84]

Economic happiness aside, sustained economic growth serves social and political health. It is associated with greater tolerance, fairness, and democratic values. It is also associated with citizens' willingness to increase spending on publicly supported education and poverty reduction.[85] Larry Summers believes that slow growth rates help explain the "surly and dysfunctional" politics in the developed world.[86]

Despite the good that economic well-being provides, the burgeoning happiness studies show that many people trade some economic strength for noneconomic goods that are more important to happiness. One sign of this is the increase in investments in ventures that deliberately put up with suboptimal profitability in order to do good.

There is some evidence that socially responsible investment (SRI) now makes up one-fifth of the funds under professional management in the United States. This is up from one-ninth in 2012. Firms meeting SRI criteria invest in renewable energy and Third World development and avoid cigarette companies and heavily polluting companies. A Morgan Stanley survey found that millennials are much more interested than other investors in SRI companies; so the movement seems likely to grow.[87]

A concern with happiness will now lead us away from economics toward psychology and political philosophy. Before changing direction, I should acknowledge that there is a small economic literature on happiness. Of course, Robert Frank and his critics are centrally concerned with whether economic growth brings happiness. The impressive young scholars Justin Wolfers and Betsy Stevenson always seem to investigate interesting subjects, and happiness is one of them.

Princeton's Alan Krueger wrote occasionally on happiness. The research of Dartmouth's David Blanchflower really focuses on happiness. But he is lonely. The few studies by economists are dwarfed, for example, by what is going on within positive psychology. In 2000 PsycINFO cataloged 39 papers in which the title included the words "positive psychology." In 2017 there were 550. Similar searches for "happiness" showed growth from 70 to 194 and for "well-being" from 334 to 1598.[88]

In almost every happiness study done by psychologists, what is central is connection – to friends, spouses, religious institutions, charitable and recreational groups. Harvard's Dan Gilbert, sometimes called Professor Happiness, says

> We know that the best predictor of human happiness is human relationships and the amount of time that people spend with

family and friends. We know that it's significantly more important than money and somewhat more important than health.
That's what the data shows.[89]

Other researchers have found that "those with close social ties and
unhealthful lifestyles (such as smoking, obesity, and lack of exercise)
actually lived longer than those with poor social ties but more healthful
living habits."[90] Strong connections to other human beings are scarcer
than one might think. Studies show that 47 percent of adults in the
United States are lonely and that the mortality rate of the lonely is
comparable to that of those who smoke 15 cigarettes a day.[91]

One study of Twitter users looked at 6 million posts to find
what most often followed phrases such as "I wish," "I want," and "I
love." The most common desires were for love, time, and good relationships. There was longing for better friends, and healthy, long-term
relationships. The saddest and most frequent of all tweets: "I wish
someone cared."[92]

One activity that has shown great potential to address loneliness
is voluntarism. This activity is not explained by narrow self-interest as
economists usually understand it. But it clearly increases the happiness of
both the volunteer and those helped. Empathy is wired within us. It is not
simply a ruse feigned to gain approval from others. Stanford researchers
use magnetic resonance imaging (MRI) to watch people's brains as they
look at people getting hurt; the spectators' MRI images are a lot like
images "of people experiencing the pain firsthand."[93] Moreover, children too young to understand the concept of altruism are upset when
others feel pain, and they "try to help or comfort the afflicted."[94]

Survey data show that volunteers are 42 percent more likely to
be very happy than non-volunteers.[95] Over 600 people in our community of 146,000 perform volunteer work. One hundred participate in the
"Meals on Wheels" program, donating a few hours a week and driving
expenses to take a hot meal to elderly people who cannot cook for
themselves and who live alone.

As one volunteer testified: "You get so attached to the people on
your route. As soon as I started it, I got hooked. Now I really look
forward to it." Another volunteer, 74 years old herself, says, "I have 18
stops to make and everybody wants to talk. Often, I'm the only person
who stops by. If you could just see how grateful they are, you'd know
why I've been doing this for two years."[96]

This program is a perfect example of the sort of in-kind redistributive program economists typically attack. The charge would go like this. "Why have a separate bureaucracy charged with one small thing: delivering hot meals to the elderly? What is so special about a *hot* meal, anyway? Why not give the elderly the money we spend on the program to do with as they wish? They can use the money to buy Stouffer's frozen dinners if they want a hot meal, and they will still have money left over."

This analysis misses a lot. The most important thing the volunteers bring the elderly is not the hot meal but the human contact and the sense that someone cares. Volunteers can do this more convincingly than bureaucrats. More generally, more volunteers mean more public benefits can be secured without the inefficiency costs of bureaucracy and taxes. And, if people get their pleasure from giving others pleasure, society obviously gains.

Voluntarism can increase dramatically with just a little nudge from government. This was shown by the George H. W. Bush administration. During his 1991 State of the Union address, Bush maintained that Americans could find meaning by participating in the "Thousand Points of Light" voluntarism program in their communities. In 1995 the *Los Angeles Times* published a "scathing account" of the Points of Light national foundation (which received federal funding), maintaining that most of the money went for consultants and glitzy conferences. But there were very encouraging results at the local level.

Bush frequently mentioned points of light in his speeches, and the program attracted considerable media attention. Bush personally recognized daily volunteers for their efforts in programs such as caring for infants with AIDS or combating adult illiteracy. He signed 1020 "daily points of light" letters during his administration, and until his death he continued to sign letters recognizing Points of Light volunteers or agencies.[97] Volunteerism in America had been declining since 1974, but a Gallup survey showed an increase of 23 percent during Bush's presidency.[98]

Many of us spend large portions of our adult lives at jobs. Economists usually see work and leisure as trade-offs. We work to get money so that we can have leisure. We saw in Chapter 5, however, that more empirically oriented economists can't help but notice that, even if they get government support, unemployment makes people miserable.

Arthur Brooks is one economist who objects more broadly to the idea of a work–leisure trade-off. He provides evidence showing that 89 percent of Americans say they are very satisfied or somewhat satisfied with their jobs. Even 87 percent of people who self-identify as working class say they are very or somewhat satisfied. When asked if they would continue working even if they had enough money to live as comfortably as they would like, 69 percent of Americans say "Yes." Brooks says:

> Imagine two workers who are identical in every way – same income, education, age, sex, family situation, religion and politics – but the first is satisfied with his or her job and the second is not. The first person will be 28 percentage points more likely to say that he or she is very happy in life.[99]

So what makes for a good job? The European Social Survey finds people in well-paying jobs are happier but "a number of other aspects of jobs are strongly predictive of happiness." When summarizing, the work–life balance was listed first; but the factors that came next were job variety and learning new things.[100]

Let me get personal for a moment and then show some other evidence echoing my experience. A particular kind of learning – the required thesis at Princeton for the AB degree – changed my preferences and my life.

When I was growing up, almost all the men I knew were in business – my father, my uncle, and all their friends. In high school I was a B+ student; in college a B–/C+ student. I got into Princeton because I was class president and performed reasonably well in high school sports. At Princeton, I wandered through a variety of courses – a little of this, a little of that – working hard but achieving and retaining little.

But I lucked out. Princeton required every undergraduate to write a senior thesis. I hated the idea, but it was an absolute requirement. I wrote on the controversy about federal aid to higher education. My older brother had a job outside Washington, and I stayed with him during school breaks. I learned where in the library to find what Congress was up to, managed to get some good interviews on Capitol Hill, and got into some juicy files of lobbyists on the issue. To my amazement, I received an A on the thesis, and it was put up for the prize for the best thesis in the history department. I was very proud of my achievement.

The success of my thesis enabled me to win fellowships to Cornell, where I had the great fortune at the masters level to learn from the powerful mind and welcoming personality of the economist Alfred Kahn. Kahn left me impressed with the usefulness of applied normative microeconomics. I'm still impressed.

Then I had still more good fortune. A friend told me I should audit an undergraduate course with Allan Bloom, a brilliant man and unparalleled teacher, with some real knowledge of what a liberal education was. Bloom introduced me to the battle of the books through the great works of political philosophy. In time, Bloom's teaching enabled me to see that applied economics was a branch of utilitarianism. In studying the ground-moving history of political thought, I learned that utilitarianism was just one of many contending worldviews, and not the most impressive one.

I had still more luck when I landed at the University of Virginia. My department let me teach courses that, to put it mildly, were not standard within my discipline of political science. My career has enabled me to teach and befriend some very gifted students and write a couple of books that people I admire think are good ones. I learned a whole lot along the way. I'm sure I have been much happier with my career and life than I would have been had I gone into business.* The Princeton required thesis made everything that followed possible.

Thirty years after I graduated from Princeton, the required thesis was at the center of a row among Princetonians. A retired, chaired history professor, Lawrence Stone, published in the *Princeton Alumni Weekly* a call to end the mandatory senior thesis. The professor noted that supervision of each thesis took an inordinate amount of professors' time, and that most of the students seemed to have no interest in writing one. He suggested that participation in an eight-person senior seminar should be allowed in lieu of a thesis.

The proposal stimulated 11 letters to the editor, all opposed. One self-described weak and lazy student – Steven Biss, class of '87 – took lots of seminars because they were the easiest way to "blow off two or three hours" before practice or a big party. Stone's proposal would do an injustice to the weak and lazy students by letting them

---

* I should note here that I am a wholehearted supporter of private enterprise. Profit-seeking businesses make us wealthy and help keep us strong and free. They typically make money by providing goods and services at a fair price. Moreover, many successful people in business do lots of good through their charitable giving. But business was not the right place for me.

avoid "the shackles of the senior thesis." Writing his thesis, Biss "for the first time in his life" had to endure a period of introspection and sustained analysis. The result was "a document of which I could be proud."

The first and most striking of the letters came from George P. Shultz and Sidney Drell, a distinguished physicist. Shultz, who served as secretary of labor under President Nixon and secretary of state under President Reagan, was often described in the press as "relaxed," "easy-going," "soft-spoken," "stable," "thoughtful."[101] But Professor Stone's proposal had gotten him riled up. The two writers explained that writing a thesis was far and away the best part of their Princeton education.

> That experience was our key to a new world; it provided the incentive to move on to graduate work and formed the basis of our professional careers. [...] Don't give it away – unless you also want to give up on the large majority of students who, like ourselves before our theses, do not yet know what they are missing.

A few months later Professor Stone wrote to renounce his proposal. He had had no idea that so many students had written their theses only under compulsion, yet had learned from them and were "forever proud of what they achieved." A year after that Shultz and his wife gave Princeton $1 million to set up a fund to support senior theses in the field of public policy.[102] These Princeton stories show the existence and importance of changes in tastes. They also provide evidence that learning can be an important part of the route to happiness.

In 1974 one of the leading philosophers of the twentieth century, Robert Nozick, published *Anarchy, State, and Utopia*. It became known as one of the greatest philosophical defenses of libertarianism. Fifteen years later Nozick wrote that he now found the earlier book "seriously inadequate," voicing this opinion in a book called *The Examined Life*. He explains that

> there is a loss...when we are directed through life by the not fully mature picture of the world we formed in adolescence or young adulthood. [...] [E]xamination and reflection are not just *about* the other components of life; they are added *within* a life alongside the rest, and by their presence call for a new overall pattern that alters how each part of life is understood.[103]

Nozick says his later book reflects "now what is important in life." He has "no doubt" that his current understanding will change further through time.[104] Philosophers and Princetonians can look back on how learning and reflection have changed their lives. But one does not need a Princeton degree or a philosophy PhD to see that learning brings about changes in tastes.

About 32 million American adults cannot read.[105] Decades ago *The Daily Progress* in Charlottesville featured an article about a 40-year -old man who was illiterate until the Charlottesville branch of the Literacy Volunteers of America taught him how to read. Now, he said, "you can find me most anywhere reading. I'm learning about things that I never knew had been going on." He especially enjoyed history. He was then reading about the 1920s but planned "to catch up with the rest, too."[106]

Learning also enables the pleasures of a job well done. It makes bakers good bakers and air-conditioning repair people good at their job as well. Both occupations yield big smiles from customers, which demonstrate appreciation and admiration. "Earned success" has been found to bring happiness in a host of occupations that don't pay particularly well. "Americans who feel they are successful at work are twice as likely to say they are very happy overall as people who don't feel that way."[107]

One of the most exciting developments in the social sciences in the last few decades is the growth of positive psychology. It focuses on the brighter side of humanity. We have seen that family and friends are very important to happiness. But what else? Proponents of positive psychology introduce a new vocabulary. There is discussion of elevation, awe, admiration, and gratitude.

Jonathan Haidt is a leader in the movement. He looks at elevation in particular. In one experiment, some students are asked to "think of a specific time when you saw a manifestation of humanity's 'higher' or 'better' nature." Others are asked to "think of a specific time when you were making good progress towards a goal" – a condition that has been found to elicit happiness. The two groups reported different "physical feelings and motivations":

> Elevated participants were more likely to report physical feelings in their chests, especially warm, pleasant, or "tingling"

feelings, and they were more likely to report wanting to help others, to become better people themselves, and to affiliate with others. [...] Happiness energized people to engage in private or self-interested pursuits, while elevation seemed to open people up and turn their attention outwards, towards other people.

Haidt's students also felt elevation after viewing a ten-minute video about Mother Teresa. The findings about elevation have been reproduced in small groups in India and Japan.[108]

Another emotion that is beginning to attract the attention of psychologists is awe, which might be brought on by any number of things, including a natural wonder such as the Grand Canyon. But, for our purposes, we need to focus on awe at the wonders of humanity. In his *Theory of Moral Sentiments*, Adam Smith sketches the sort of person he believes we humans are in awe of:

The man of the most perfect virtue, the man whom we naturally love and revere the most, is he who joins, to the most perfect command of his own original and selfish feelings, the most exquisite sensibility both to the original and sympathetic feelings of others. The man who, to all the soft, the amiable, and the gentle virtues, joins all the great, the awful, and the respectable, must surely be the natural and proper object of our highest love and admiration.[109]

Smith would probably say that we Americans understand the beauty of the soft and amiable virtues, but it is harder for us to see the grandeur in the ancient ones of "self-government and self-command; fortitude, magnanimity, independency upon fortune."[110] But, on reflection, we can admire people who do the right thing even at great personal cost.

Smith's virtues include Aristotle's: prudence, moderation, courage, and justice. In the last two books of the *Theory of Moral Sentiments*, VI and VII, Smith emphasizes virtuous character. One commentator says that "he seems to look forward to a revival of ancient Greek ethics."[111] Smith would be delighted by the growing school of "virtue ethics," in which discussions of character and Aristotle are central. Virtue ethics challenges long-standing moral systems such as deontology (duty systems) and consequentialist systems such as utilitarianism.

Cynics say "the man of the most perfect virtue" does not exist. Smith might say maybe we would never see one. Perfection is indeed rare. But you can know the better by keeping your eye on the best. The men and women we look up to – those we admire, respect, and honor – have many of these virtues. Even as a child we can spot admirable peers. In my childhood pickup baseball games, there were always arguments about whether someone was safe or out. In time, we ended up agreeing that, no matter what team he was on, Johnny Clement should decide. We could see that he was the fairest.

At our best, we want to become more like Johnny Clement, or his adult equivalent. In this quest we are helped by what Smith calls our "impartial spectator." When we reflect on our behavior, and endeavor to be calm and disinterested, the impartial spectator appears within us. We attempt to be two people – both an "impartial spectator" and the person being judged.[112]

As an anonymous wit once said, "The secret of life is honesty and fair dealing. If you can fake that, you've got it made." Smith might say that's funny but not really true. In many of us, our impartial spectator won't shut up. For example, we do not feel at ease upon receiving an unearned compliment. The impartial spectator gnaws at us when we try to deceive ourselves, and we will not really be happy until we are honest. Smith says: "We want not only to be loved but to be lovely." Certainly, many of us can come to believe, without outside intervention, that our past behavior was wrong, and we can try to make amends for it.[113]

Further Reflections

The mainstream economic literature on information and changing tastes provides little useful policy guidance on the matters it focuses on and avoids the most important questions. Large numbers of Americans spend more than they think they should and save too little. Many think they are overweight and wish they ate less. Most smokers say they would like to stop. In cases such as these, it is clear that the economist's methodological preference for revealed preference does not reveal actual preferences.

People often have an internal conflict between passion and reasoned resolution. I doubt that most overweight Americans would object if cafeterias put salads at the start of the cafeteria line and cakes at the end. It could make some difference. So too could expecting that employees would want to save something for retirement, while not requiring them to do so.

One of the co-authors of the book *Nudge* is a distinguished economist. This book addresses in a thoughtful way a number of small changes that would enable consumers to do what they want to do: let their reasoned resolution rule. But I doubt that the book is on the undergraduate syllabi of large numbers of economics courses.

Forty-seven percent of Americans say they are lonely – a huge number! I doubt that many of these know that people who volunteer feel great joy and become less lonely. For a trivial amount of money, George H. W. Bush made this fact known to millions of Americans. Those who began to volunteer because of Bush's nudge are no doubt grateful.

Economists are again likely to complain: "Look, we never said we had all the answers. Let other disciplines add what Rhoads wants." But economists are not really so modest. They advocate for economic efficiency. They advocate for programs in which the benefits exceed the costs. They tend to believe that only equity considerations should qualify these recommendations. This stance flows from a belief in consumer sovereignty. "Consumers should get what they want if they are willing to pay the costs. Isn't that what democracy is?" Not really. As Buchanan told us: as citizens, we act on the basis of values; as consumers, we act on the basis of tastes.

Besides, assuming neutrality between tastes means that the wishes of greedy heirs can make costs exceed benefits for some lifesaving programs for the elderly; and it can mean the losses/costs to thieves from successful crime-fighting programs should influence policies in a way that they should not. I doubt very much that the public would tolerate such methodologies if they knew their details.

I can hear the howls. "Are we really going to get into the business of deciding whose tastes are higher?" To make some progress, we don't need to. We can ask people to rank *their own* tastes. For example, we can ask them if their taste for time spent volunteering is higher than their taste for the fourth beer every weekday night. More generally, my guess is that people will rank their benevolent tastes above their selfish desires.

We have seen that economists can make their data reach conclusions if they assume the benefits to a person are those that the person enjoys. Benefits to the individual are assumed to be self-interested ones.

More fundamentally, most economists seem to believe that selfish desires dominate human behavior. But we have seen that increases in economic power through raises and economic growth are not the best way to achieve happiness. Better to cultivate friends and family and continue learning.

If I could underline for emphasis just one part of this chapter, it would be the comparison of John Stuart Mill's worldview to that of Martin Bronfenbrenner. Mill was as much a political economist as a philosopher. His *Principles of Political Economy* was the leading economics textbook for 40 years. In it he expanded on the ideas of David Ricardo and Adam Smith. He helped develop economic principles that remain important today: economies of scale, opportunity cost, and comparative advantage in trade.[114]

Bronfenbrenner recoils from Mill's argument for favoring higher tastes, accusing Mill of "priggish condescension" and "intellectual snobbery."[115] Mill can be better understood, however, as anticipating today's happiness researchers. He wanted people to lead more satisfactory lives and believed the main impediments are selfishness and lack of mental cultivation. No wonder so many of today's economists would side with Bronfenbrenner! They take it as given that selfishness moves humans, and that encouraging higher tastes (learning) would violate their prized stance of scientific neutrality.

Economists are wrong on both counts. We have seen that mitigating selfishness and continued learning are both important steps toward happiness. One major indicator that selfish motives do not dominate us is the growing number of investors who give up some economic returns so as to further their political ends. And economic success is by no means the surest route to happiness. Good friends and loving families are.[116] Selfishness loses friends and destroys loving families. Acting on altruism and compassion stimulates these virtues further rather than using them up. Aristotle and Smith recommend practicing the virtues so that they become habitual and argue that being praiseworthy is more important than garnering praise.

Many contemporary economists would say that Mill's *Political Economy* is not really economics. But arguments such as his can be found throughout the history of mainstream economic thought. Adam Smith's concern with character is found in *The Wealth of Nations* as well as *The Theory of Moral Sentiments*. Smith was concerned that the

manufacturing process of his day could leave the ordinary worker
"stupid and ignorant,"

> not only incapable of relishing or bearing a part in any rational
> conversation, but of conceiving any generous, noble, or tender
> sentiment, and consequently of forming any just judgment con-
> cerning many even of the ordinary duties of private life...
> A man without the proper use of the intellectual faculties of
> a man, is, if possible, more contemptible than even a coward,
> and seems to be mutilated and deformed in a still more essential
> part of the character of human nature. Though the state was to
> derive no advantage from the instruction of the inferior ranks of
> people, it would still deserve its attention that they should not
> be altogether uninstructed.[117]

If Smith be thought dated, hear Alfred Marshall, a successor to
Mill who is generally considered the "father of neoclassicism." Marshall
said: "The power of rightly using such income and opportunities, as
a family has, is in itself wealth of the highest order, and of a kind that is
rare in all classes."[118] He maintained that "the discussion of the influence on general well-being which is exerted by the mode in which each
individual spends his income is one of the most important of those
applications of economic science to the art of living."[119]

Marshall encouraged "wisely ordered magnificence" – philanthropic expenditures on objects such as public parks and art collections.
Such expenditures, at once "free from any taint of personal vanity on the
one side and envy on the other," would make available "an abundance
of the higher forms of enjoyment for collective use."[120]

Marshall, an Englishman, suggested using awards such as knight-
hoods and the Queen's Award to Industry to encourage the development
of public-regarding behavior. He had no doubt that men are capable of
much more unselfish service than they typically show, and that "the
supreme aim of the economist is to discover how this latent social asset
can be developed most quickly and turned to account most wisely."[121]

Marshall's great contemporary, P. H. Wicksteed, distinguished
tastes further by noting that certain kinds of pleasures increased the
capacity for future enjoyment. Intellectual, literary, artistic, and scientific enjoyment demand at some point "painful effort and discipline."
But, with greater study, one's pursuit of these activities increases
"hedonistic capacity," which is not true of most other activities.

Like Marshall, Wicksteed believed that individual welfare could be increased if people could be induced to change their expenditure patterns. He noted, though, that commercial activity often brought about change of the wrong kind: the "action of the economic forces, unguided and unchecked, naturally favours the growth not only of a class of ministers to vice, but of a class of persons who live by enabling people to get another drop out of the squeezed orange of today's capacity for enjoyment, reckless of its reactions upon tomorrow."[122]

Still later, A. C. Pigou's pioneering *Economics of Welfare* argued that consumption patterns could exercise either an "elevating" or a "debasing" influence. He unabashedly declared the satisfactions connected with literature and art "ethically superior to those connected with the primary needs." A man "attuned to the beautiful in nature or art, whose character is simple and sincere, whose passions are controlled and sympathies developed," was "himself an important element in the ethical value of the world."[123]

Finally, consider the views of Frank Knight, an influential teacher at the University of Chicago in the 1930s and 1940s and a staunch proponent of free markets. Knight was particularly insightful about our aspiration for different, higher wants.

> The chief thing which the common-sense individual actually wants is not satisfactions for the wants which he has, but more and *better* wants. The things which he strives to get in the most immediate sense are far more what he thinks he ought to want than what his untutored preferences prompt. This feeling for what one *should* want, in contrast with actual desire, is stronger in the unthinking than in those sophisticated by education. It is the latter who argues himself into the "tolerant" (economic) attitude of *de gustibus non disputandum*... [T]he true achievement is the refinement and elevation of the plane of desire, the cultivation of taste. And let us reiterate that all this is true *to the person acting,* not simply to the outsider, philosophizing after the event.[124]

Knight was concerned about the effects of advertising and salesmanship on people's tastes:

> Ethically, the creation of the right wants is more important than want-satisfaction. With regard to the facts in the case, we

may observe that business is interested in the fact of change in wants more than in the character of the change, and presumably effects chiefly those changes which can be brought about more easily and cheaply. Our general moral teaching would indicate that it is easier to corrupt human nature than to improve it, and observation of the taste-forming tendencies of modern marketing methods tends perhaps to confirm the view and to substantiate a negative verdict on individualistic activity of this sort.[125]

Among the important adverse effects of salesmanship and economic rivalry is their tendency to work against the appreciation of the "free goods." They thus tend to undermine the "fairly established consensus that happiness depends more on spiritual resourcefulness, and a joyous appreciation of the costless things of life, especially affection for one's fellow creatures, than it does on material satisfaction."[126]

By quoting at length these great figures of the past, I do not mean to suggest that they would necessarily agree with each other in all respects or with what is argued here. But the overlapping message of the great economists I quote is that economics should add to its appreciation for the growth that capitalism and markets give us a profound understanding of their weaknesses in elevating tastes and making them more public regarding.

Where are the modern equivalents of these economic titans? As seen earlier in this chapter, Amartya Sen certainly believes in fruitful discussions of values and believes they can change; he also thinks that true choice in the developing world requires more education, which may lead to new tastes.[127] Arthur Brooks loves liberty and markets but finds that selfish assumptions do not reflect much behavior and are not likely to lead to happiness.

Deirdre McCloskey shows that ideas, not selfishness, move men and women; McCloskey's impressive corpus shows that our high goals of liberty, ethics, and equality are promoted through capitalism or (McCloskey's preferred term) free enterprise. In the wide range of authors he interviews on EconTalk and in his writing on Adam Smith, Russ Roberts shows his love for microeconomics and the importance he places on literature and virtues beyond its bounds. Robert Frank thinks his recommended high consumption taxes on the rich will lead to the provision of more collective consumption goods, such as infrastructure and public parks. Because of large gaps in my knowledge, I'm sure I must be neglecting others who should be added to this list.

But if representatives of the discipline were asked to name 30 contemporaries whose work was both excellent and representative of the concerns of a very large number of economists, I don't think any of those I list would be under consideration. Even those I list are not quite where the major figures of earlier generations were.

Major economists of the past (and, presumably, their best students) thought it was part of their task to remind their readers that there are high and low pleasures, that many of the high ones require reason and the sometimes painful acquisition of knowledge, that we aspire to tastes better than our current ones, and that such aspirations are sometimes hindered by profit-seeking businesses that cater to vices and overemphasize the importance of what money can buy. Today's economists are more likely to feel a professional obligation to combat such sentiments than to support them.

These striking differences reflect changes in the nature of the discipline and the way it educates its practitioners. Economics today is much more technical and much more insular. The older economists read widely beyond economics, and they felt the need to respond when one such as Thomas Carlyle said they were professing a "pig philosophy."[128] Because they were both broader and deeper, the older economists were less likely to forget that economic man is not the total man.

Today's graduate student in economics rarely studies closely any subject besides recent economics and mathematics. He is unlikely to know that even those contemporary philosophers who are utilitarian are more likely to side with Mill and praise the "incomparably more fecund" higher pleasures than they are to side with Bentham with his unwillingness to distinguish high from low.[129] He is also unlikely to know that the great economists of the past held views like those quoted earlier. Courses in the history of economic thought or political economy do not lead to the best jobs, and they attract few students.

Earlier chapters made use of the results of technical studies, so I would not wish to deny there have been fruits from recent developments in the discipline. Nonetheless, much of what is interesting in economics requires little technique and is not really new. One need not "progress" beyond Adam Smith to learn to appreciate markets and the power of economic incentives. In the *Wealth of Nations* one can even find a rough outline of the contemporary discipline's views on the roles for the market, national government, and local government.

One of the most pernicious effects of the modern project to make economics more "scientific" is the accompanying tendency to ridicule all beliefs that are "empty of empirically verifiable content."[130] The older economists knew that good economics, like good politics, can settle for less certainty than that.[131]

8 REPRESENTATIVES, DELIBERATION, AND POLITICAL LEADERSHIP

with Russell Bogue

Economists' Views

Welfare and cost–benefit economists make recommendations about good (i.e., consumer-preferred) policy. They have no explicit teaching about the desirable characteristics of the policy process or of political institutions. Nonetheless, there is an implicit teaching. Because externalities exist and preferences differ, some sort of political process that aggregates and weighs individuals' preferences is necessary. But consumers are assumed to have clear preferences. As E. J. Mishan has said, "All...the economic data used in a cost–benefit analysis, or any other allocative study, ...is based on this principle of accepting as final only the individual's estimate of what a thing is worth to him at the time the decision is to be made."[1] Moreover, consumers not only know what they want, but they should get what they want. In William Baumol's words, "It is essential...that the pattern of public intervention be designed very explicitly in terms of the desires of the public."[2]

As Chapter 7 indicated, in applied economic studies the desires of the public are determined by deducing preferences for government-provided goods from market decisions, or, in the absence of such decisions, from public polls. This assumes that participation in discussion and deliberation prior to decision does nothing to improve public policy. It thus ignores one of the principal functions of and arguments for representative political bodies.

Moreover, deliberation aside, welfare and cost–benefit economics leave no room for independent representatives or political leadership. By advocating that public policy be based on consumer "willingness to pay," welfare and cost–benefit economists silently assume the desirability of passive representatives;[3] if political judgment or leadership is needed at all, it is only to find the best tactical route for implementing the policy desires of today's consumers.

On these questions, the explicit teaching of most public choice political economists differs little from the implicit teaching of their cost–benefit cousins. The good representative is a clerk-like aggregator of consumers' preferences.[4] Nevertheless, although cost–benefit economists seem to assume that there are some such representatives willing to implement the consumer-desired programs the economists' studies recommend, the public choice economists seem certain that no such representatives exist.

The public choice economists believe that representatives seek personal economic and political benefits rather than broader public ones.[5] In the early public choice literature it was sometimes suggested that the selfish desire for reelection would lead representatives to give their electorates more or less what they wanted.[6] But later articles emphasized that "rational" voter ignorance makes politicians' support of inefficient special-interest legislation politically profitable. It also allows representatives to feather their nests with money from interest groups seeking governmental favors.[7] Demonstrating an ideological proximity to their cost–benefit peers, public choice scholars have even coined a less than complimentary term – "shirking" – for instances in which representatives fail to do as their constituents order.[8]

As mentioned earlier, one traditional argument for representative democracy focused on the potential for deliberation to produce better policy than would mere aggregation. Since public choice economists assume that representatives are ruled by narrow self-interest, they do not believe that much if any deliberation (i.e., reasoning on the merits) takes place in representative assemblies.

In light of their views on the motives and products of representative assemblies, it is not surprising that some public choice economists began to wonder if bodies such as the US Congress cannot be improved upon. Several suggested that we rely much more on public referenda and less on legislative decisions. For example, more than a decade before he became chairman of the Federal Trade Commission, James Miller proposed allowing voters to use home computers to directly register their decisions on public issues.

When voters felt that they did not know enough to cast a knowledgeable vote on any particular issue, they could delegate proxy on that issue to someone else who they thought would vote as they would if they knew more.[9] Economists such as Gordon Tullock supported Miller's proposal, and others have suggested different forms of referenda and "direct democracy" devices.[10] These early ideas have been given new life in recent economic literature. Wikipedia includes a long entry on "liquid democracy," a "sort of voluntary direct democracy";[11] James Green-Armytage has revived arguments for the viability of proxy voting;[12] and others have examined the conditions under which such systems might be effective.[13]

Some public choice economists support more direct forms of democracy but believe that it would be tremendously costly for everyone to become informed enough to make Miller's system work well. Dennis Mueller, Robert Tollison, and Thomas Willett, for example, note that, although computers have reduced the costs of casting votes, technology has also increased the complexity of public issues. The total amount of time needed to enable the general public to cast votes based on reasonable levels of information is at least as high as in earlier eras. These three economists favor a representative system of government because, through the division of labor, it reduces the time costs of informed decisions. They propose a more democratic form of representation, however – one whereby legislators would not be elected but chosen at random from the voting populace as a whole.[14]

Most recently, economists such as Bryan Caplan have challenged the prevailing consensus, suggesting a new take on the rational ignorance of voters discussed in Chapter 4: rational irrationality, or the idea that the low cost of political participation encourages systematically biased voting. Previously, some public choice economists suggested that the rational ignorance of voters would be randomly distributed across the policy spectrum, with mistakes canceling each other out until the well-informed voter's policy preferences were adopted. Caplan claims that ignorance is not random but, instead, biased in certain directions.

Because a single vote is almost never decisive, voters suspend their rational analysis – so crucial in consumer markets – and succumb to the charms of their preferred worldview, regardless of its practical implications. In economic terms, the political arena is unique, in that irrational behavior carries a low cost, allowing citizens to entertain, with apparent abandon, delusions and presumptions they would otherwise mute.[15]

Caplan uses the 1996 Survey of Americans and Economists on the Economy (SAEE) to identify several areas – such as free trade, the inefficiency of price controls, and labor-saving technologies – in which the public routinely rejects the consensus of economists. As explained in Chapter 4, economists believe that economic growth and a higher standard of living depend on labor-saving technology.

The public is frequently skeptical of such technology. Chapters 4 and 5 also explained why economists think that, over time, our capitalist system has increased real incomes for the average American family. The public seems skeptical. When asked in 1996 whether average family incomes had gone up more rapidly than the cost of living over the preceding 20 years, 70 percent of the public said "No," while only 22 percent of economists said "No"; when asked whether a recent price increase in gasoline was the result of normal supply and demand or oil companies seeking greater profits, 73 percent of the public said oil companies seeking greater profits, while 85 percent of economists said supply and demand.[16]

Ilya Somin, a law professor grappling, like Caplan, with the implications of widespread voter ignorance, has suggested decentralization as a method of combating voter irrationality by encouraging "foot voting." When citizens express their support for various public policy measures by physically moving into jurisdictions that enact these measures, they are more likely to invest the time and resources into becoming better-informed and more rational "consumers" of public policy. Still, Somin, like Caplan, is skeptical of making government more responsive to a populace wholly ignorant of most of the policies that govern their lives.[17]

Caplan's arguments amount to a critique of the traditional view of economists that the voter, like the consumer, should determine policy – that his preferences and his desires should rule our political life.

The Political Function of Citizens

Despite their differences, most cost–benefit and public choice economists seek a public policy determined less by elected representatives and more by ordinary Americans. As the *Federalist Papers* tell us, the Founding Fathers rejected direct forms of democracy because their reading of history and of human nature told them that direct democracy had not and would not produce stable, effective governments.

The ancient republics of Greece and Italy "were continually agitated..., kept in a state of perpetual vibration between the extremes of tyranny and anarchy." Although their "countenance" was more democratic than ours, their "soul" was more oligarchic. When decisions were made by the people as a whole, a skillful orator was able to appeal to the passions and "rule with as complete a sway as if a scepter had been placed in his single hand."[18]

The founders believed that the people are everywhere prone to "irregular passions" and "temporary errors and delusions." Therefore, even though "the republican principle demands that the deliberate sense of the Community should govern the conduct of those to whom they entrust the management of their affairs," it should not be interpreted to "require an unqualified complaisance to every sudden breeze of passion." Because the "interests" of the people are sometimes at variance with their "inclinations," it is advisable "to refine and enlarge the public views by passing them through the medium of a chosen body of citizens, whose wisdom may best discern the true interest of their country and whose patriotism and love of justice will be least likely to sacrifice it to temporary or partial considerations."[19]

James Madison and Alexander Hamilton believed that the true friend of democracy would support representative institutions that could preserve democracy by guarding against its excesses.[20] Lincoln, who saw and condemned "wild and furious passions" and "worse than savage mobs," agreed completely.[21] Even Jefferson, though defending the right of the people to instruct their representatives and emphasizing popular control of government, supported nonetheless a government wherein the "natural aristocracy" held office. The people were "competent judges of human character," capable of electing the "good and wise." But the representatives' independent judgment would be essential, for "the mass of individuals composing the society" are "unqualified for the management of affairs requiring intelligence above the common level."[22]

Jefferson did emphasize that there were "portions of self-government" for which the people were "best qualified" – "concerns...under their eye" such as "the care of their poor, their roads, police, elections, nomination of jurors, administration of justice in small cases," and such.[23] When Tocqueville visited America nearly half a century after the Constitution took effect, he applauded the widespread interest among the citizenry in filling the nearly "innumerable" offices concerned with these local problems.

While warning against plebiscitary democracy at higher levels, he thought town meetings and other municipal institutions a bulwark of liberty. Tocqueville supported public participation for reasons quite different from those of public choice economists, however. Widespread participation was not meant to provide an outlet for narrow self-interest but was, rather, a means of tempering it. Municipal government in America provided a way of "interesting the greatest possible number of persons in the Common weal." It gave people a taste for liberty at the same time as it taught them the art of self-government.[24]

Candid public discussion of the people's weaknesses is not a characteristic of politicians in the last 50 years. The former governor of Wisconsin, Scott Walker, has stated that the Founding Fathers were "ordinary people" who "risked their lives for the freedoms we hold dear today" – though few citizens of modern America have the desire (or ability) to draft a governing constitution.[25] Jimmy Carter, in his inaugural address, spoke to his audience as though they were gods:

> You have given me a great responsibility – to stay close to you, to be worthy of you, and to exemplify what you are. [...] Your strength can compensate for my weakness, and your wisdom can help to minimize my mistakes.[26]

Donald Trump, in his inaugural address, seemed to think he was the titular head of a direct democracy rather than the president in a constitutional republic. Trump said that his inauguration would be remembered as the day "the people became the rulers of this nation again," describing the oath of office as "an oath of allegiance to all Americans."[27] This was not true. In actuality, the oath of office – which he had taken just a moment earlier – affirmed that he would "faithfully execute the Office of the President of the United States, and will to the best of [his] ability, preserve, protect, and defend the Constitution of the United States."

But, politicians aside, many knowledgeable people still publicly support the founders' skepticism of public wisdom. Prominent journalists on both the left and right have espoused a more limited reliance on the public for democratic governance. George Will has criticized conservative politicians for introducing ways to undermine the independence of the Supreme Court – for example, Senator Ted Cruz's proposal to subject justices to recall elections. For Will, injecting the Supreme Court with populist sentiment ignores the principle of limited government, in which even the legislature cannot have its way at all times.[28]

Paul Krugman – a Nobel-Prize-winning economist and left-leaning pundit – seems to disagree with the views of most economists, writing that high office is "about changing the country for the better" – hardly a ringing endorsement of the idea that the people should be in control of their elected officials at all times.[29] Recently, Justice Ruth Bader Ginsburg has opposed those on the left who favor expanding the size of the Supreme Court so it would be less likely to interfere with public sentiments in favor of fundamental changes.[30]

The results of polls testing the US public's political knowledge lend support to these views. In 2011 many Americans could not distinguish fact from fiction regarding the Patient Protection and Affordable Care Act ("Obamacare"), one of the hallmark legislative achievements of President Obama's first term. Only a quarter of Americans could answer 70 percent or more of polling questions correctly, with a full third getting less than half correct. For example, nearly six in ten believed that the law created a government-run insurance plan alongside private ones (it didn't).[31]

That same year *Newsweek* polled 1000 respondents on basic civics and found that only 29 percent could name the current vice president.[32] On foreign policy questions the results were no better: a 2009 study in the *European Journal of Communication* found that only 58 percent of Americans could describe the Taliban – the terrorist group that their country had been fighting for eight years. Almost two-thirds were unable to identify the Kyoto Protocol as a climate change treaty. In this study, Americans ranked behind their European counterparts on every polled subject.[33]

Tocqueville thought democracies had great difficulty in subduing "the desires of the moment with a view to the future." This vice was particularly dangerous to the conduct of foreign affairs and the public finances. The more direct the democracy, the greater the danger.

> The disastrous influence that popular authority may sometimes exercise upon the finances of a state was clearly seen in some of the democratic republics of antiquity, in which the public treasure was exhausted in order to relieve indigent citizens or to supply games and theatrical amusements for the populace.[34]

The president and Congress have not done wonders with the public finances in recent years. But irrational public pressures may explain much of the record. In 2012, according to a Pew Research Center poll, Americans ranked the "budget deficit" third on their list of policy priorities, behind such broad categories as "the economy" and "jobs." When asked about 18 different areas in which the government could decrease spending, however, Americans were reluctant to make fiscal sacrifices in 16 of those areas; the percentage of respondents who favored increasing spending was higher than the percentage of respondents who supported a budget cut. Only for the categories of "aid to world's needy" and "unemployment aid" were the numbers of deficit hawks greater than those who preferred higher spending.[35]. We should therefore not be especially surprised when the individuals tasked with representing public opinion do not deal responsibly with public finances.[36]

Representatives, Deliberation, and Political Leadership

Tullock said that "the traditional response of students of politics to the obvious ignorance of the voters has been to lecture the voters on their duty to learn more."[37] To the contrary, in our country at least, the traditional response has been representation. In the new science of politics expounded by Hamilton and Madison it was precisely this "scheme of representation" that "promise[d] the cure." As mentioned earlier, the founders expected elected representatives to be wiser and more virtuous than the average voter. In addition, the powerful offices created by the Constitution, with their fixed and fairly lengthy terms, would appeal to able men, those who "possess most wisdom to discern, and most virtue to pursue the common good of the society."[38]

The founders knew, of course, that "enlightened statesmen will not always be at the helm."[39] But they thought that the large commercial republic they established would encourage quite ordinary representatives to behave in a more statesmanlike manner. In small republics there are few factions and interests, and it is easy for a single faction to compose a majority and proceed to oppress the minority. In a large commercial republic, however, even within an individual congressional district, there are a large variety of limited and specific interests. To win an election, candidates

> must appeal to diverse interests and win wide popular support. The ability to win such an election inclines the successful candidate toward the decent and moderate quality of representation which the system requires. Moreover, representatives from such districts need not be the captive of any one group but rather can find some elbowroom for statesmanship in the very confusion of factions.[40]

Even a representative from a district dominated by a single faction soon finds that he must cooperate with representatives with different constituencies if he is to obtain even a portion of what he wants. Thus, the large republic's legislative process encourages temperaments predisposed to consider the needs of others and the "permanent and aggregate interests of the Community."[41]

The founders thought that the "deliberate sense" of the community should guide democratic representatives.[42] But they did not think the "deliberate sense" could be known without deliberation. In 1796 Madison said, "This House, in its legislative capacity, must exercise its reason, it must deliberate; for deliberation is implied in legislation."[43]

The deliberative process makes possible a "refin[ing] and enlarg[ing]" of the public's views. As Woodrow Wilson later argued, such a process goes beyond mere bargaining among interests or aggregating preferences.

> Common counsel is not aggregate counsel. It is not a sum in addition, counting heads. It is compounded out of many views in actual contact; it is a living thing made out of the vital substance of many minds, many personalities, many experiences; and it can be made up only by the vital contacts of actual conference, only in face to face debate, only by word of mouth and the direct clash of mind with mind.[44]

In Wilson's perspective, such deliberation was important, not just because it produced better policy but also because legislative discussion was an important source of "instruction and elevation of public opinion."[45] Such instruction and elevation were, for Wilson, the essence of political leadership, and this led him to emphasize a side of the statesman's art wholly outside the range of interest of most economists, namely political rhetoric. The people possess fundamental values and aspirations, but the statesman must give these coherent direction by providing explicit ideas, policies, and programs. As one commentator notes, under such a system republican institutions and politicians become "molders of a public mind, not simply reflectors of popular demands. [...] Such a democracy is both agent and educator of its citizens."[46]

Lincoln also found leadership and rhetoric crucial:

> With public sentiment nothing can fail; without it, nothing can succeed. Consequently, he who moulds public sentiment goes deeper than he who enacts statutes or pronounces decisions. He makes statutes and decisions possible or impossible to be executed.[47]

Throughout his career Lincoln used his gift for rhetoric to try to calm the public's unjust passions. In the 1830s, when lynchings of both slaves and abolitionists became commonplace, he sought to make a "reverence for the laws" the "political religion of the nation."[48] When the Civil War neared its end, he fought vengeful passions with a policy of "malice toward none" and "charity for all."[49] And, of course, in his great debates with Stephen Douglas, Lincoln never ceased to remind his fellow citizens that consumer sovereignty – or, as Douglas put it, popular sovereignty – was not a sufficient principle for public policy.[50]

Lincoln noted that the principles of the Declaration of Independence required not only government by consent of the governed but also respect for individuals' unalienable rights to life, liberty, and the pursuit of happiness.[51] He said that people outside the territories could not justly remain indifferent about whether citizens in the territories voted for or against slavery. To adopt a stand of moral indifference would be to enshrine in the body politic the pernicious doctrine that "there is no right principle of action but *self-interest*."[52]

The beginning of this chapter noted that welfare and cost–benefit economists are concerned with the substance of policy rather than the policy process. But in fact, as we have seen, for them the substance of good policy is no more than whatever the consumers want. Lincoln spent much of his life fighting this doctrine. He believed that only a principled concern with substance could be sufficient. Good policy never ignores public opinion, but it also never ignores good ends. This means that strong public feelings and inclinations should sometimes be seen as danger signals rather than as guideposts for policy.

These views held by historic American statesmen are not archaic. Some recent students of politics continue to emphasize the importance of deliberation in lawmaking, of independent judgment in representation, and of leading and educating through public rhetoric.[53] W. Arthur Lewis, a Nobel-Prize-winning economist whose work on the economics of development is far removed from the literature discussed in this book, defends such a perspective by noting that citizens judge a politician "only to a limited extent by his accordance with their preconceived ideas. Rather a great political leader is judged like a great composer: one looks to see what he has created."[54]

When V. O. Key Jr., published his landmark *Public Opinion and American Democracy* in 1961, he felt it necessary to respond to those such as Walter Lippmann who despaired of the future of democracy because of the influence on policy of ignorant mass opinion. Key was less pessimistic, not because he believed that the mass of the public was in fact well informed but because he believed that the public was content with a role in which its electoral and other participation fixed only the "range of discretion within which government may act or within which debate at official levels may proceed." This left room to maneuver for the opinion leaders and political activists, who, on the whole, behaved responsibly.[55]

John Kennedy seemed to go even further than Madison, Wilson, and Lincoln when discussing the appropriate independence of elected representatives. "We must on occasion lead, inform, correct *and even ignore constituent opinion,* if we are to exercise fully that judgment for which we were elected."[56] If representatives believe that it is legitimate to exercise independent judgment during their elected terms, outcomes may be different from those recommended by cost–benefit economists in a host of policy areas.[57]

Consider lifesaving programs, for example. One economist has proposed allowing each taxpayer to decide how to divide his tax dollars between various government health programs.[58] But, inevitably, the media publicize the plight of some patient groups more than others. Those groups whose needs have been publicized in an effective way will already receive more private contributions than others equally as needy. Instead of correcting for the inadvertent injustice to those whose plight is not made known to benefactors, a public policy determined by consumer willingness to pay would accentuate it.

Policy toward lifesaving programs may also affect the goodwill and cohesion that exist among the citizenry. Tocqueville worried about the atomizing effect of American individualism and materialism because he believed that a society without cohesive qualities could not preserve political liberty. In his work on the value of life, Ezra Mishan calmly predicts that an atomizing process is under way: "The gradual loosening of emotional interdependence should cause the magnitude of the [psychological external costs of] bereavement...to decline."[59] W. B. Arthur's work, discussed in Chapter 7, assumes that the atomizing process has already progressed to the point at which younger citizens' welfare improves when older citizens die earlier.

Should a political representative merely adjust his value for life downward if the people's preferences change toward callousness or indifference in this way? Believing that a reverence for life and a concern for our fellow citizens are political goods in a democracy, he may instead want to try to extend the people's feelings and make them more public-regarding by, for example, promoting voluntarism and charitable giving.

The merits of deliberation are manifest both in theory and in practice. Indeed, critics of Caplan's public choice arguments contend that voter irrationality may have triggered "some foolish national debate in recent years," but comparatively little "foolish national policy." Considering the counterproductive economic ideologies that many voters hold, the United States is surprisingly friendly to markets and trade. Some see this discrepancy as evidence that deliberative policy makers are slowly and imperfectly doing the job of filtering the chaff from public opinion: taking the good and leaving the bad, as best they can.[60]

Further Reflections

Most economists seem to believe that the citizens' views on public policy should be decisive. For such economists, everything depends on the political capability of ordinary citizens. This is paradoxical, because economists realize that consumers often have poor knowledge of politics. Almost any microeconomist can cite cases in which consumers are clearly misinformed about the actual effects of popular price controls or environmental programs.

Economists believe consumers' preferences are revealed most accurately in the market, and they thus prefer benefit estimates deduced from revealed preferences for a private good. But, if these estimates are not available (and they very often are not), polling seems acceptable to many, if not most.[61] As suggested in Chapter 7, economists tend to insist that what some call ignorance others call wisdom. And, by equating democracy with consumer sovereignty, they often come to believe that a good democrat has no alternative to plebiscitary democracy.

Chapter 4 showed why public choice economists believe that political ignorance on the part of the public is rational and thus intractable. Some public choice economists have suggested institutional reforms that address the problem, such as letting the private sector perform more government functions and decentralizing others.[62] These suggestions are helpful, but even their proponents would acknowledge that they address only a small part of the awesome information problem that public choice theory has revealed.

Still, the intractability of the political ignorance problem has not led public choice economists to reassess the contemporary discipline's fundamental presuppositions. Like their colleagues, they have a personal commitment to and a professional stake in consumer sovereignty. And, as we have seen, they often favor more direct forms of democracy. I believe these forms would compound dramatically the risks posed by the political ignorance of ordinary citizens.

Tullock suggested that voter initiatives and referenda may make it easier for the voter to make up his mind than the current system, whereby a single vote must cover the entire scope of governmental activity. He thus concluded that such changes may actually ease the information problem for the voter.[63] But a single citizen's vote is no more likely to decide the outcome when being cast on initiatives than it is when voting for candidates. Thus, unless the initiative process makes politics seem much more interesting to the average voter, the ignorance outlined earlier will control policy without being transformed.

In states where the initiative and the referendum have been used, voters continue to exhibit only an intermittent interest in and rudimentary knowledge of politics. In California, for example, well-financed special interests usually spearhead the effort to get the petition signatures necessary to place initiatives on the ballot. One reporter tells of hurrying commuters in one subway station being pressed to sign three separate petitions at the bottom of a single escalator.[64] One California pollster later questioned those who had signed a petition on a complicated oil conservation measure.

> Most of them couldn't remember signing the petitions, and of those who did the majority didn't in any way connect signing the petition with the oil controversy then raging through the state. And among the signers of the petition, about half were for the measure they qualified for the ballot and half against it![65]

Official handbooks intended to educate the citizenry on the initiative issues usually justify political scientist Raymond Wolfinger's description of them as "fifty or sixty pages of absolutely impenetrable prose." Wolfinger says that he does not read California's handbook, and he does not know anybody who does except to see who is for or against a proposition.[66] Although he noted the popularity of the initiative process among the California citizenry, the late California pollster Mervin Field said the following about voters' knowledge of the issues:

> Voters seldom have clearly defined opinions about most measures, even on the eve of voting. Many have a limited and even erroneous understanding of the issues and opinions of this type are often subject to quick change under the pressure of massive propaganda and emotional appeals.[67]

Voter ignorance is understandable given the length of some ballot initiatives. From 2000 to 2006 46 initiatives were put on the ballot in California. Of these, 15 were over 5000 words long, and eight had over 10,000 words. In some cases, the wording of initiatives was so confusing that voters inadvertently voted against their stated preferences.[68]

These difficulties highlight another consequence of voter ignorance, on the "supply side" of legislation. Because initiatives are typically citizen-led, they suffer from a lack of proficiency in the research and drafting stages. The state legislature has access to research and technical staff, the testimony of relevant parties, and the accumulated expertise of years of statutory construction. Proposers of ballot initiatives seldom possess such resources. On issues of public morality or social policy – such as gay marriage – the process of direct legislation may be appropriate. But most modern public policy issues require a level of complexity and technical expertise that can be found only in a representative body devoted to lawmaking. Despite their reliance on the work of subcommittees, representatives frequently report that they have too little knowledge of the bills on which they have to vote. The problem would obviously be compounded for citizens who must make a living in some other way.[69]

When voter knowledge of issues is rudimentary or nonexistent, Miller's and Green-Armytage's proposals to allow voters to give an expert their proxy would do little to remedy the knowledge problem. If, for example, voters know little about economics and if they have neither the desire nor incentive to learn more about it, they cannot be expected to choose in any meaningful sense between contending economic "experts." Those chosen are likely to be entertaining demagogues.

Our current political process sometimes produces such representatives as well. But, after elections, presidents and congressmen have time to reassess positions. And they generally turn to distinguished economists to help them do so. Luminaries such as Ben Bernanke, Larry Summers, and Gregory Mankiw would not find it as easy to contribute to the political process under Miller's scheme.

Perhaps the greatest weakness of initiatives is their inability to build consensus.[70] After an election, the legislative process provides at least a chance for communication and consensus building. When compromises result, even those who oppose an enacted measure feel that some attention has been paid to their views. Initiatives and referenda, on the other hand, tend to divide the population into warring camps.[71] Fifty-one percent is enough to pass a measure, but, as Lincoln emphasized, it often takes the goodwill and cooperation of far more than this if statutes are to be enforceable.[72]

Unlike proposals to expand the use of initiatives, the randomly chosen representative system would provide for some sort of legislative, integrative process. But the typical representative would have no more interest in politics than the average voter. Thrown in the midst of a host of issues and complicated legal language, many would probably do what their staffs suggest they do. Since their terms would be fixed, there would be no electoral incentive to master the issues. Nor would representatives' incomes be affected by such mastery. They could, however, be affected by their votes on special-interest legislation.

One suspects that representatives would be offered lucrative jobs later or other benefits in exchange for votes. The temptations for these representatives, used to lower salaries back home, would be great indeed. The proponents of the representative-by-lot system have noted these potential problems, but these institutional economists have no institutional solution. In an uncharacteristically vague way they simply say that "care would have to be taken to insulate the legislators from lobbying pressures and to see that they cast informed votes."[73]

The randomly chosen representative system would make representatives more like average Americans. But it would mean that very few Americans would have anything at all to do with their government.[74] There would be no campaigns, no elections, no visits to the home district by the representative. Unable to seek reelection, representatives would have no incentive to attend to any mail received from ordinary citizens.

Congressional scholars suggest that the citizenry want access to two-way communication with, and character or judgment ("a good person") from, their representatives more than they want agreement with their incompletely formed policy preferences.[75] With a randomly chosen legislature, citizens would clearly get less of the first two than they now do. And one suspects that the average voter still thinks the representative he *selects* through an electoral process has a better-than-average character even if the voter does not think the representative belongs among the natural aristocracy.

This, of course, the public choice economists deny. They tend to see representatives as narrowly self-interested:[76] distributors of favors to groups that can get them reelected and collectors of cash contributions for themselves or of patronage for businesses in which they have an interest. More than a little of this sort of behavior goes on. But economists do not present systematic evidence supporting the adequacy or comprehensiveness of this view of representatives. Indeed, one systematic study of the subject found, to the surprise of the economists who authored it, that ideology seemed to explain much more congressional voting than economic self-interest did.[77] Most public choice economists, however, simply assume that representatives are narrowly self-interested like everyone else, and they then deduce that, if they are rational, they will behave in a self-interested way.

Congressional scholarship paints a more complicated picture. Some scholars do think that the desire for reelection explains most congressional behavior.[78] But others point out that many congressmen seek out particular committees because of their general policy concerns.[79] Representatives who seek power within Congress voluntarily leave committees that can help them get reelected for others that cannot, such as the House Rules Committee.[80] The rules and customs of the Congress sometimes seem designed to constrain rather than serve the reelection impulse.

There is also evidence that deliberation is important to Congress.[81] Bernard Asbell followed Edmund Muskie daily for more than a year to see how the Senate really worked. He found senators who insisted that real senatorial power was dependent on "doing your work and knowing what you're talking about."[82] And, for committees, it depended on a reputation for thoroughness, or comprehension, or reliability for fairness and accuracy, and for good judgment. He found a lobbyist who was surprised at the nature of the recently opened subcommittee markup sessions:

> The whole operation is much more subtle than I thought...
> I imagined, when they were behind closed doors, that the decisions would be much faster, You know, the chairman names the issue, everybody's already made up his mind or made his trades, and they vote. But it's not like that. There's a real *process*.[83]

With respect to lobbying, Asbell himself decided that 99 percent of it was not "parties, weekend hosting and passing plain white envelopes, but trying to persuade minds through facts and reason." Asbell also expressed surprise to find senatorial committee members open to arguments from across the aisle and clearly involved "in the difficult technical challenges of writing a clean air law."[84]

Although in recent days polarization has depressed congressional productivity and bipartisan inclinations, examples of deliberation abound. In 2013 *The Washington Post* reported on Representative Bob Goodlatte (R-Va.), then chairman of the House Judiciary Committee, which is responsible for most of the immigration-related legislation. According to the *Post*, Goodlatte's expertise and commitment to deliberative, incremental progress had won the respect of his peers.[85]

Former Speaker of the House Paul Ryan (R-Wis.), who had served as the chair of both the House Budget Committee and the Committee on Ways and Means, remembers advice he received from an ideological rival, Representative Barney Frank (D-Mass.), when Ryan was new to the House: "If you want to be effective...do not be a generalist. Don't spread yourself too thin. Specialize in two or three things, study up, and know those issues better than anyone else. Get yourself on the relevant committees, know everything there is to know about your issues, and then you can start setting policy in those areas."[86]

Ryan took this advice to heart: he was regarded as one of the foremost budget policy experts in the House. According to political scientist Dan Palazzolo, among Democrats, Representative Henry Waxman (Calif.) "used oversight and legislative power to challenge misinformation deployed by powerful corporate interests."[87] Such politicians represent the enduring value of having a deliberative temperament when considering legislation.

Joseph Bessette presents compelling evidence corroborating such findings. Sifting through 29 case studies of policy enactments in the post-war period up to 1980, he concludes that the presence of deliberation (either on the floor or in committees) holds up as the best explanation for the passage of many of the laws. Taking the least promising example – the Food Stamps Act of 1964, contemporaneously hailed as the result of interest group bargaining – Bessette recounts the evidence of deliberation: impassioned speeches on the floor of the House, high attendance at committee hearings, appeals to long-standing traditions, ideological arguments, and the use of statistical evidence. He concludes that the bill's passage was attributable to "the reasoned judgment" by the vast majority of House Democrats "that the administration's program constituted good public policy."[88]

Economists rarely refer to any of this congressional literature. Their view of the representative comes mostly from deductions, not from data. Similarly, the voter ignorance problem is treated in an abstract, conceptual way. James Buchanan and Bryan Caplan are some of the few public choice economists who have systematically studied some poll results. Buchanan was also one of the few to propose constitutional amendments to impede Congress's inclination to spend beyond tax revenues – usually with public support in almost all areas.[89]

The founders and Tocqueville viewed direct democracy with great alarm because they had studied the results where it had been tried. Economists do not interpret that history differently; they simply do not mention it. Lippmann and Key, as well as Madison and Tocqueville, saw that the political ignorance and the strong passions of the people were powerful forces that could bring down democratic regimes.

Economists rarely cite such authors, and presumably do not read them. They see ignorance as an interesting analytical puzzle.

Madison discussed the instability and "calamities" resulting from the six-month terms for representatives in some of the states of his day.[90] Jefferson agreed, arguing that the strong state governments he desired to counterpoise federal power would necessitate fewer representatives serving longer terms.[91] Economist James Miller, however, would have his proxy representatives recallable instantly.[92] And, without so much as a bow toward Madison or Jefferson, Ryan Amacher and William Boyes argue for more frequent elections of representatives.[93]

They, together with Kenneth Greene and Hadi Salavitabar, claim to have tested the Madisonian argument that representative democracies work better in large, heterogeneous jurisdictions than in small ones.[94] They note that contemporary economists have argued that decentralized, homogeneous governments, not the large heterogeneous ones, are the most responsive to voters. The test of both sets of authors consists in discovering the types of jurisdictions that are most responsive to voters' policy views. These authors find that representatives from large, heterogeneous jurisdictions behave in a less responsive, more independent fashion. Thus, the economists are declared right, and Madison wrong.

The Madison test bears no relation to the original, however. He never claimed that representatives in large republics would be more responsive. Minorities could sleep more easily in large republics because representatives would *not* so quickly respond to a majority faction's whim. Madison's argument for a large republic was like that of Jefferson. In small societies the schisms are too "violent" and "convulsive." Only in large republics will "a majority be found in *its councils,*" *free* from "local egoisms" and "particular interests."[95]

The classic controversy in the literature on representation pits those who see representatives as delegates, mere agents, against those who see them as independent trustees.[96] Economists who have written on representation give no sign that they know of the controversy. For Miller, the "ideal of representation" demands instant recall,[97] and, for Amacher and Boyes, "less responsive" equals "less representative."[98] Economists writing in the cost–benefit literature seem to agree entirely. Thus, for example, Thomas Schelling argues that consumer sovereignty in public policy is derivable from the principle "No taxation without representation."[99]

Economists claim to speak for the people. But the people themselves are not sure that they want to govern directly. When asked if congressmen should follow their own best judgment or the feelings and opinions of their district, the public appears closely divided. In 2013 public opinion of Congress was at historically low levels: a paltry 10 percent had confidence in the institution itself, with 17 percent expressing approval of their representatives.[100]

Some of the reasons specified for such lopsided disapproval – 28 percent because of a lack of compromise, 21 percent because of a lack of progress – indicate that the public was frustrated with the inability of representatives to compromise, to overcome differing opinions in order to reach consensus.[101] This appears to be evidence that the public prefers a trustee model of governance, especially given the deep ideological divides in the country that were the fount of such gridlock.

But earlier polling data suggest otherwise: 94 percent of Americans believe that public opinion should be consulted whenever a decision is made – not just at election time – and 81 percent believe that leaders should use public opinion polls to guide their decision-making process (compared to 18 percent who believe that such polls distract elected officials "from doing what they think is right").[102]

What emerges from such conflicting data is a tall order for American government: lawmakers must act as both deliberative thinkers, capable of compromise, and responsive representatives, bound to the views of their constituencies. On this issue, as on many others, the American public seems to want to have it both ways.

Our current system of representation seems well suited to the public it represents. That public has only a little interest in and knowledge of the issues of politics. Students of voting, however, find some evidence that "voters do have knowledge about the issues that they themselves raise in canvassing their likes and dislikes of parties and candidates." Sometimes people vote on the basis of a candidate's (or a party's) stance on a policy issue important to them, but more often they vote on the basis of their assessment of a candidate's experience, integrity, judgment, or capacity for leadership.[103]

Voters who, like John Stuart Mill, care more about the competence of candidates than about their issue stances are served well by a system that makes representatives accountable to the public but gives them considerable room to exercise their independent judgment during their term in office. Our system has worked fairly well for over 200 years, and it enjoys "that veneration which time bestows on everything, and without which perhaps the wisest and freest governments would not possess the requisite stability." [104]

James Madison, the author of the aforementioned words, promulgated a new science of politics only after reading the greatest theorists of free government, reflecting on contemporary and historical experience, and carefully considering all sides of relevant issues. The new science of politics promulgated by economists proposing constitutional restructuring of government falls well short of meeting those standards.

9 CONCLUSION

Economists spend most of their time studying human behavior in the marketplace. There they find that materialistic motives and narrow self-interest can explain almost all of what they observe and that, with the help of free markets and flexible prices, these motives usually lead to the efficient production of valued goods and services. As economists have begun to study the world beyond the marketplace, they have brought the lessons learned from it with them.

But these lessons do not always apply elsewhere. Some economists notice this discrepancy and are puzzled. They search for explanations for the "apparent irrationality" of philanthropy, for example. But such anomalies usually remain anomalies and are repressed during evaluative work, in which economists equate an individual's policy preferences with his financial self-interest. By this criterion, all citizens who pay social security taxes are declared gainers when the elderly die earlier.

Although economists often assume materialistic motives even when they are apparently absent, most of us prefer that such motives sometimes be ignored even when present. Polls show that about a half of Americans think they themselves buy more than they need, and three-quarters think we should learn to derive pleasure from nonmaterial experiences. Although some earlier economists thought aspirations for higher tastes significant, today's economists tend to ignore such aspirations.

They hope to avoid thorny value questions by taking tastes and preferences as they find them. Aspirations aside, treating preferences in a nonjudgmental way does not avoid controversy; when weighing costs and benefits, such treatment can sometimes make decisive the gains to the criminal from crime or the costs to the malevolent from lifesaving.

Even if money and narrow self-interest were the route to individual well-being, the well-being of society requires more. The most ingenious rechanneling of self-interest cannot overcome all inefficiencies caused by free riders. Ethics, goodwill, and civility can. There is some evidence that reminders of one's civic responsibilities and examples of or experience with altruistic acts can change behavior for the better. But economists largely ignore such external-benefit-generating possibilities even though these benefits are important to the achievement of societal well-being as economists themselves define it.

Many of my readers will remain unconvinced by my argument that there are cases in which some tastes can reasonably be considered to be higher than others. Perhaps they would change their mind if we further consider externalities in our valuation. Although dogfighting is a felony in all 50 states, "it continues to occur in every part of the country and in every type of community."[1] A newsletter, *Pit Dog*, keeps devotees up to date, with pictures and reports such as the following:

> One hour and a half. Scout working a down dog for 15 minutes, occasionally stopping to lick, then going back to chewing Buck. Mike starts encouraging the dog to kill Buck... Queenie's front legs gone now and her time to go, but she goes across like a dog should... She reminds me of a seal walking, her front legs just flapping.[2]

Would it be fair to call the taste for dogfighting a low taste? Would it be meddlesome if we concluded that we did not want our children to think it okay for some people to get their kicks out of seeing animals cruelly destroyed? Economists tend to ignore negative externalities created by bestiality as well as positive ones created by civic duty and goodwill, because they call into question views of the world that emphasize money and self-interest and because they complicate empirical work. But perhaps the most important reason is the way the discipline educates its practitioners. Economists' technical education leaves them unlikely to look for intangible externalities and poorly equipped to weigh their significance if they should bump into them.[3]

244 / The Limits of Economics

The late Kenneth Boulding suggested a reason why young economists rarely collect their own data: Today's graduate departments in economics rarely teach them how. Boulding also points out the dangers of forming conclusions about how the world works without ever confronting it directly:

> The successes of economics should not blind us to the fact that its subject matter is a system far more complex than the systems which are studied by the natural scientists, for instance, and we must recognize that our most elegant models can be no more than the crudest of first approximations of the complex reality of the systems which they purport to represent. If we educate out of our students that almost bodily sense of what the real world is like even though we may see it through a glass darkly, a trait which was so characteristic of the great economists of the past, something of supreme value will be lost.[4]

As Boulding suggests, many of today's practitioners of the worldly science, even the policy analysts, are remarkably unworldly. Those who write on particular welfare programs seldom interview those eligible for assistance and try to develop for themselves a sense of how welfare recipients live. Moreover, few ever mention sociologists who have done so.

Those who write on the largest political questions too often fail to approach their task with humility and trepidation, in full awareness of the high stakes involved. Their work rarely reflects on human nature or on the lessons of history. It does not ponder "violent" and "convulsive" schisms in politics, such as in Syria or Lebanon, and ask what institutions best build consensus and support for law. It does not note Hitler's early popularity in Germany and discuss the case for supreme courts that look to standards beyond consumer sovereignty. Indeed, it rarely refers to political theorists who have reflected on these matters.

Knowledge of some subjects, such as math, requires only a good theoretical mind. Knowledge of others, such as love, requires experience. It may make sense to ask a 12-year-old prodigy for help with a calculus problem, but a college student looks elsewhere for advice about problems with his girlfriend. Politics and public policy are more like love than math. Good answers to even general questions, such as how and when to restructure institutions, require a judgment that can come only with experience of the regime in question and with some knowledge of history.

The criticisms made in the last two chapters, however, should not overshadow the lessons economists taught us in earlier chapters. This book's central message is not anti-economics. I think economists should read more outside economics, and most people should read more within it.

First and foremost, economists teach us to respect markets. As Thomas Schelling has said, "Nothing distinguishes economists from other people as much as a belief in the market system."[5] Economists continue to think there is much truth in Adam Smith's view that, although a businessman seeks only his own interest, the invisible hand of the market leads him to promote society's interest nonetheless. Indeed, economists are more certain than some businessmen that the profit-seeking entrepreneur promotes the public welfare regardless of his philanthropic activity. As Boulding has said, economics "makes people appreciate the productivity of the commonplace, of exchange and finance, of bankers and businessmen."[6]

There is no reason to defer to economists' pronouncements about human nature or good constitutions, but markets are another matter. If economists possess expertise on anything, it is a knowledge of how markets work. They know that, in the private sector, firms' managers and owners reap the rewards when they efficiently respond to consumer demand. They think that governmental processes do not have mechanisms as powerful for promoting efficiency. Final proof of such a global judgment may always elude us. But Chapter 4 showed that it is not just theory; there is suggestive evidence that economists have properly evaluated the comparative efficiency of the two allocative mechanisms. To the skeptical but less knowledgeable noneconomist, it should be reassuring that this pro-market judgment is shared by both liberal and conservative economists.

It is not reassuring enough, however. Noneconomists almost always have reservations. They are troubled by profits, middlemen, and speculators. I briefly responded to these concerns in Chapter 4. But my brief responses are not conclusive, for one can always find examples of private-sector blunders. The noneconomist wonders if government could not have prevented them. Or she sees exciting opportunities, and wonders if government cannot somehow help take advantage of them. Of the private-sector blunders, economists can only suggest that there will be fewer of them in the market than in government, since those who commit them lose income. As for the public sector, economists usually say that government can improve the general climate for innovation but is incapable of identifying (and supporting) the products that will be commercial winners in the future.

Robert Samuelson puts it this way: "Through its tax laws, government can help create a climate for risk-taking. It ought to prey on the greed in human nature and the industriousness in the American character. Otherwise, stand aside."[7] But one more quotation from someone supporting the economic mainstream is not likely to convince the unconvinced. Economists realize this and throw up their hands. Albert Rees says that "much of the public hostility to our economic system comes from ignorance of it."[8] Charles Schultze declares that he is increasingly convinced that "no one but economists (and not all of them) really understands" how a market system works.[9] And Alain Enthoven says of economists' work in government: "The economic theory we are using is the theory most of us learned as sophomores. The reason Ph.D.'s are required [is] that many economists do not believe what they have learned until they have gone through graduate school."[10] Arguments that say "You would agree with me if you knew more" insult one's readers and invite their scorn. But I can understand the temptation. Most people who systematically study the allocative problems of all societies, and the way markets solve them, come away with increased respect for markets.[11] I ask only that my noneconomist readers test this proposition for themselves.

If economists are right about markets, greater respect for their allocative mechanisms will mean an increase in valued goods, services, or leisure. These are significant benefits in their own right, but perhaps not the most important ones. An economy that functions well can help foster political stability by building confidence in the system as a whole. Increasing efficiency and facilitating expansion in the economy can make possible an improved standard of living for workers and the elderly, stronger defenses, and a cleaner environment too. Political differences are usually more manageable in such circumstances.

Much of the sound advice economists offer on more specific questions also flows from their knowledge of markets. From studying markets they learn that resources are scarce and our ends multiple. Thus, to worry about costs is to care about benefits – benefits forgone in other sectors. Dedicated public professionals, eager to achieve their policy goals, sometimes need to be reminded of such opportunity costs.

By studying markets, economists also learn that spending decisions should not be determined by looking at the intrinsic importance of a function, since they require a weighing of marginal cost and marginal benefit. Those setting public-sector priorities may need reminding. And, of course, markets show the power of material incentives to coordinate human activity in a productive way. Many of the new regulatory programs rely on detailed laws and regulations to achieve their objectives. Economists convincingly show that using economic incentives instead can give us cleaner air, safer workers, and far lower bills besides.

Study of the market also led to the development of the enormously useful concepts of externality and public or collective consumption goods. Economists first determined that competitive markets produced efficient outcomes because production in all sectors continued up to the point at which the marginal costs of production equaled the benefits to the last consumer. But then Marshall and Pigou noted cases in which some societal costs of production were not reflected in firms' supply curves and in which some societal benefits were not reflected in consumers' demand curves. Useful work on market failure and on the functions of government soon followed.

Economists know that the market is an efficient mechanism to allocate scarce resources to valued goods and services, and they know that material incentives are the fuel that makes the market work. Most of what economists contribute to public policy deliberations can be traced to their knowledge of the utility of the mechanism and the power of the fuel. Their attachment to the mechanism and to the materialistic motive is thus quite understandable.

But a healthy polity requires more than an efficient economy, and there is no automatic mechanism that will produce health in a polity as regularly as the market produces efficiency in the economy. A healthy polity must find a way to deal with powerful political passions that are not always as harmless as most market desires. It must promote institutions that build consensus and strengthen ethical standards. Rather than continually giving narrow self-interest its head, it must sometimes seek to make narrow self-interest less narrow. And it must find a way to compensate for the market's overemphasis on the things money can buy as the route to human happiness.

We should not expect economic studies to reflect common views about high and low or unethical tastes. When uncertainties abound they will tend to emphasize monetary benefits and ignore less tangible ones. Since their focus is on narrow self-interest, they will not think about the need to foster military courage through special forms of honor or about ways to encourage ethics, civility, and altruism through appeals to the better sides of our natures.

There is no necessary contradiction, however, between great respect for markets responding to personal preferences (Chapter 4) and pursuits and virtues that enable men and women to thrive (Chapter 7). Adam Smith can be one of our guides. Crony capitalism does not bring us closer to the higher ends Smith, Marshall, and Knight sought than does free enterprise. Because it is unfair, crony capitalism takes us away from the higher ends. Economic growth brings plenty and leisure; both are compatible with human thriving.[*]

When I wrote the first edition of this book in 1985, my critique could not draw on flourishing schools of thought. That is no longer true. Now we are blessed with positive psychology, which considers emotions such as elevation, awe, admiration, and gratitude, and virtue ethics, which focuses on human character and human virtues. Economists who read in these literatures can begin to find their way back to the economics of Smith, Marshall, and Knight.

"But how can I do that? I have to learn all this math in order to get my PhD!" So, after you get your PhD (and tenure) you can try to convince your colleagues that the vast majority of our students will not become economic theorists, so they don't need the mathematics that would help them improve theory. For mathematics, some econometrics will suffice. Encourage them to get some perspective on their discipline

---

[*] In one way my critique of economics has been unfair. Traditionally, economics has been in the very ambitious valuation business. Economists would, for example, try to determine what consumers would pay to reduce the risk of death on the job. Most of my criticism has been about how economists value things. Recently a number of economists have been simply trying to look at effectiveness; for example, how much, if at all, would students' reading and math scores improve if there were smaller class sizes? Economists' quantitative methods are probably better than other social scientists', and they are less ideological. So they do important work on this sort of effectiveness issue. They are also very inventive. One study, for example, was able to show that the introduction of E-ZPass (electronic) toll collection "reduced prematurity and low birth weight among mothers within 2 kilometers (km) of a toll plaza by 10.8 percent and 11.8 percent, respectively, relative to mothers 2–10 km from a toll plaza" (Janet Currie and Reed Walker, "Traffic congestion and infant health: evidence from E-ZPass," *American Economic Journal: Applied Economics*, 2011, 3(1): 65–90).

by reading in positive psychology,[12] virtue ethics, and the history of economics and of political philosophy.

———————

This is not a book that focuses on current policy. The writing was finished days after the 2020 elections, and the book will not appear until the fall of 2021. Election-year politicking does not necessarily foreshadow what will be discussed in the following years' Congress. The uncertainty is increased with the recent elections because of the pandemic overshadowing them. I hope that, by the second half of 2021, Covid-19 will be in the rearview mirror, and we will be on the way out of the recession. Nevertheless, since throughout 2020 essentially all Democrats and an increasing number of Republicans have been focused on industrial policy, it seems likely that that will be a subject in the air.

Joe Biden's industrial proposals include a cross-country high-speed railroad system, a proposal that Obama also supported as president. We have seen that the new high-speed railroad system in California has hemorrhaged money and accomplished little or nothing. A cross-country system is likely to run into huge costs and even greater problems.[13] Biden also seeks to spend $400 billion on materials and products made in the United States. As part of his proposed effort to create manufacturing jobs, Biden also proposes adding a special tax for companies that move jobs overseas and giving a tax credit to companies that bring manufacturing back from overseas.[14]

Republican senators such as Marco Rubio and Josh Hawley have echoed Biden's (and Donald Trump's) call to bring manufacturing jobs back to the United States. Josh Hawley is wildly excited about the potential of government to improve our economic performance, an argument he links with dismal and inaccurate statistics about how the average worker has not had a real raise in 30 years.[15]

In his excellent book *The American Dream Is Not Dead*, AEI economist Michael Strain corrects Hawley: real wages for the typical worker increased 34 percent over the last three decades.[16] Economists are essentially united in their opposition to the buy-American movement. Strain summarizes their critique:

> Protectionism and industrial policy, including buy-American mandates, raise consumer prices and the prices of goods businesses use for production, reducing domestic competitiveness.

> They invite corruption and cronyism, and can increase the
> burden on taxpayers for government procurement. They lead
> to diplomatic friction and invite retaliation. The US trade war
> with China probably hurt manufacturing employment – the
> intended beneficiary – in addition to serving as a drag on the
> economy overall.[17]

In mentioning "corruption and cronyism," Strain suggests that there is
an equity issue in industrial policy, not just the efficiency one that was
discussed at length in Chapter 4. We have seen that economists cannot
agree on issues of distribution of income or what they call vertical
equity. But it is easier to see violations of "horizontal equity," and
economists are united, all other things being equal, in their support for
horizontal equity. With industrial policy, government ends up subsidizing some firms and industries and ignoring others. As discussed in
Chapter 4, Solyndra got a subsidy that other battery makers did not
get. There was no competitive process that chose Solyndra. This pattern
of subsidy violated horizontal equity.

Economists also have a long memory about the failures of US
industrial policy over the last four decades. More recent research from the
United Kingdom finds that subsidies to firms there have been "an almost
unmitigated failure." Two economists from the London School of
Economics report disappointing results in automobiles, aviation, ship-
building, machine tools, electrical engineering, computers, and textiles.[18]

Strain says mid-wage manufacturing jobs are shrinking as a share
of total employment, but they are shrinking in almost every developed
country. He notes, however, that "a new middle is taking its place. Its
fastest growing occupations include health technologists and technicians,
heating and air conditioning mechanics and installers, computer support
specialists, and self-enrichment education teachers, among others."[19]

In addition to his $400 billion for industrial policy, Biden has
also proposed $300 billion for research and development to "spur
domestic innovation and support domestic production."[20] As indicated
in Chapter 4, many economists would support an increase in federal
spending on research and development – especially on basic research.
Benjamin Jones and Larry Summers note that Einstein's general relativity
"was an essential tool underlying the global positioning system (GPS).
[...] The connections between basic research and its ultimate applications appear broad, deep, and hard to predict."[21]

How much influence will mainstream economics have on the Biden presidency? *The Economist* weighed in a month before the presidential election.[22] It foresaw a moderate increase in taxes on the rich and business and a 2 to 3 percent increase in public spending "especially on green infrastructure...and industrial policy." It hoped for a rollback of the Trump administration's most "reckless regulatory decisions," such as limiting the EPA's ability to reduce the use of coal. But it feared that out-of-control "left-wing [regulatory] appointees" could do serious damage to business. It worried that the Biden industrial policy would protect old industries and insulate them from healthy competition from abroad.

With respect to this book's themes, *The Economist* noted that "Mr. Biden's long career does not exactly suggest much enthusiasm for economics." Evidence for this conclusion can be gleaned from the confirmation hearings Biden chaired when Stephen Breyer was nominated to the Supreme Court. Breyer is the most economically literate justice on the Court; he came to the hearing having published a book, *Breaking the Vicious Circle*, in which he argued for consideration of marginal cost and marginal benefit in risk regulation. Indeed, he called the "single-minded pursuit" of complete risk elimination one of the three major problems in American risk management practices. Of the Republicans and Democrats who quizzed Breyer, Biden was the most unhappy about Breyer's use of an "economic model...in judicial decision-making."[23]

Still, President Biden could not pay less attention to mainstream economic thinking than President Trump did. During his term the economic advice he received came primarily from Larry Kudlow and Peter Navarro, neither of whom is a mainstream economist. I think many, maybe most, economists believe there is too much regulation of business; Trump dismantled some of this and prevented some expansion. Some economists would credit him for this. But I don't think there was much input from economists about what should go and what should stay. Deregulation changes at the Federal Drug Administration brought about more generic drug competition, and the consumer price index for prescription drugs became negative for the first time in 46 years.[24]

There were a host of areas where Trump voiced support for an initiative without economic analysis and without first alerting people who would need to carry out the initiative. As I wrote these words on September 26, 2020, I read at my breakfast table that, at Trump's direction and without economic analysis, the federal government was to send drug discount cards worth $200 to 33 million people on

Medicare. A White House insider said this was "a last minute thing that is still being worked out." It sounded as if the money was to come from Medicare, which is struggling financially and, as early as 2022, may not be able to meet its projected obligations. So far as I can tell, nothing ever came of Trump's directive on drug discount cards.[25]

Final Thoughts

In the nineteenth century Adam Smith's description of the wonderful results made possible by markets and the invisible hand began to be questioned. A number of economists have insisted that supply and demand would create economic efficiency only if there were easy entry for new producers and if consumers had perfect information. But, in many markets, new producers don't have easy entry and consumers rarely know as much about product defects as their producers do. Businesses thus have market power, which calls into question market outputs. Since there is neither pure competition nor perfect information, there are "imperfections" in the market.

Deirdre McCloskey, a polymath who began as an economic historian, lists 108 of these "briefly fashionable but never measured...'imperfections.'" They have been accumulating for well over two centuries![26] No wonder some newly minted economists think good outcomes won't come from unadjusted markets. But McCloskey points out that we have no measurements documenting the losses in consumer well-being from great market power or imperfect consumer information. Many of the imperfections are just left as a rain cloud producing gloom.

Can government improve the situation? Some economists think so. But, as this book has explained, the government's record on improving market outcomes is not so good. There is more that could be said. The antitrust case against IBM for monopolizing computer sales was eventually withdrawn as being "without merit." Along the way, from 1969 to 1982, the case produced tens of thousands of exhibits and a paper trail of 30 million sheets.[27] By the time the suit was abandoned, foreign competition had increased, and minicomputers had been developed and marketed by many smaller firms.

Or take the information problem. When I first studied economics, George Akerlof's 1970 paper "The market for lemons: quality uncertainty and the market mechanism" seemed to be on every syllabus. It eventually may have helped win Akerlof a Nobel Prize in 2001. Akerlof noted, for example, that car dealers usually know if a vehicle has been in a collision or used as a rental car, but potential customers do not.

In the 50 years since Akerlof wrote, the federal government has passed laws requiring dealers to give customers more information. But, over time, the private sector has provided much more information than the government requires. For example, third parties such as Carfax add to accidents and rental use – records on mileage, maintenance, and number of previous owners for the car you are thinking of buying. As explained in Chapter 7, the automakers now make available for their models online arcane information that some customers think is important – such as turning radius.

So, given the imperfections, how should we feel about our market outcomes? McCloskey notes that, in 1800, a town's general store had true monopoly power. It was too hard to travel to other towns to bring real competition. Because of improvements in transportation there was less monopoly power in 1900, still less in 1950. There is even less today, now that the information revolution joins better transportation and makes it possible to comparison-shop without leaving your living room.

More important still, in the United States per capita incomes have risen from roughly $3 a day in 1800 to $120 a day in 2010.[28] Economists Benjamin Jones and Lawrence Summers make the same point but present the standard of living data somewhat differently: "US income per-capita is currently 25 times its level in 1820."[29] These results came from "pretty competitive markets" producing "exchange tested betterment."[30] Maybe "pretty competitive markets" filled by private enterprise are not so bad.

I am not saying "Don't change anything." I agree with Paul Krugman (see Chapter 4) that there is something "remarkable" and "amazing" about how well markets "organize economic activity." I side with Larry Summers, who thinks that reformers concerned about equity should first look at getting rid of tax dodges. Michael Strain at AEI (*The American Dream Is Not Dead*) and Richard Reeves at Brookings (*Dream Hoarders*) make some suggestions for reform that are worth considering. Of the more ambitious proposals, Jonathan Gruber and Simon Johnson's *Jump-Starting America* is intriguing.[31]

Readers who think my suggestions for possible improvement vague are right. Again, this book does not focus on current policy debates. Even if it did, those debates will look different when the book is published. In any case, I would not support a particular policy without giving it a lot more thought and analysis than I can do here. What I can say is that Strain, Reeves, and Gruber are thoughtful economists who make suggestions worthy of more thought and analysis.

I also think that, when discussing economic inequality, we should calm down a little. As I try to show in Chapter 5, it's more complicated than the mainstream press lets on. Covid-19 hit the economy hard. It has been especially tough on low-income workers. But, in time, it will be behind us. Michael Strain shows that, in the four years before Covid-19 hit, usual weekly earnings for the bottom 10 percent grew by 20 percent, "one third faster than growth at the median." Income inequality "has stopped growing and might even be declining."[32]

Taking a broader look, is there evidence that people are happier when there is less income inequality? Arthur Brooks shows that the answer is "No." They are happier in countries where there is more mobility but not where there is more equality of income.[33] This should not be so surprising. We would have more income equality if people such as Bill Gates and Jeff Bezos and Oprah Winfrey were Swiss rather than American. Do we really think we would be better off?

William Nordhaus, a Nobel Prize winner, finds that, of the welfare gains that flow from innovation, the innovators get 2.2 percent. The rest of us, consumers, get 97.8 percent.[34] Does that seem so unfair? Deirdre McCloskey is right. When judging free enterprise, or, if you will, capitalism, we should take the long view. When I do, my feelings are of gratitude. We are so lucky to have economic and political regimes based on the same first principle: liberty.[35] I am also happy to learn that the virtue ethicists think gratitude is a virtue,[36] and that positive psychology finds that feeling grateful makes one happy.[37]

NOTES

Introduction

1. David R. Henderson, ed., *The Concise Encyclopedia of Economics* (Carmel, IN: Liberty Fund, 2007).
2. John Brandl, "Review of Steven E. Rhoads *The Economist's View of the World*," *Public Budgeting & Finance*, 1986, 6(2): 115–116.
3. Joseph E. Stiglitz, "A democratic socialist agenda is appealing: no wonder Trump attacks it," *Washington Post*, May 8, 2019.
4. Alex Tabarrok, "The economics of sawdust," Marginal Revolution, June 2, 2008.
5. Tabarrok, "The economics of sawdust"; Joel Millman, "Sawdust shock: a shortage looms as economy slows," *Wall Street Journal*, March 3, 2008; "Sawdust," Wikipedia.
6. Tabarrok, "The economics of sawdust."
7. On China, see *The Washington Post*, October 3, 1981; December 30, 1977; December 10, 1975; and February 6, 1982; and *The New York Times*, August 16, 1979; on the Soviet Union, see *The Washington Post*, July 13, 1977; November 2, 1981; November 28, 1981; June 16, 1983; and July 27, 1983.
8. The first statement is that of Paul McCracken, former chairman of the Council of Economic Advisers. McCracken also noted that, even on the council, most of his time was spent on microeconomic questions; see William Allen, "Economics, economists and economic policy: modern American experiences," *History of Political Economy*, 1977, 9(1): 48–88, 70–3. The second statement was made by an unnamed Harvard economist; see Steven Kelman, *What Price Incentives? Economists and the Environment* (Boston: Auburn House Publishing, 1981), 1 1n.

Chapter 1 Opportunity Cost

1. Kenneth J. Arrow, *The Limits of Organization* (New York: Norton, 1974), 17.
2. Richard Lipsey and Peter Steiner, *Economics* (New York: Harper & Row, 1978), 228. Lipsey and Steiner note that the "view that public control was needed to save an industry from the dead hand of third-rate, unenterprising private owners was commonly held about the British coal industry and was undoubtedly a factor leading

to its nationalization in 1946." One British commission reported as follows: "It would be possible to say without exaggeration of the miners' leaders that they were the stupidest men in England; if we had not had frequent occasion to meet the owners." Economist Sir Roy Harrod saw it differently, arguing that the contrast between the run-down state of the mines in Wales and their advanced state in Derbyshire was explained by the Derbyshire's mines' impressive (coal) capacities, not their management's.

3. "Briefing: The future of jobs," *The Economist*, January 18, 2014, 25.
4. *Congressional Quarterly Almanac*, 1971, 135.
5. Allen, "Economics, economists and economic policy," 70.
6. Jill Lawless, "Final Concorde flight lands at Heathrow," *Washington Post*, October 24, 2003.
7. Allen V. Kneese and Charles Schultze, *Pollution, Prices and Public Policy* (Washington, DC: Brookings Institution Press, 1975), 85, 90. The incentive approach will be discussed more fully in Chapter 3.
8. Steven E. Rhoads, *Policy Analysis in the Federal Aviation Administration* (Lexington, MA: Lexington Books, 1974), 106.
9. Frank S. Levy, Arnold Meltsner, and Aaron Wildavsky, *Urban Outcomes* (Berkeley: University of California Press, 1974), 154–7, 238. For a discussion of how economists and engineers understand "efficiency" differently, see Douglas Anderson, *Regulatory Politics and Electric Utilities: A Case Study in Political Economy* (Boston: Auburn House Publishing, 1981), 100–1.
10. Charlotte Allen, "Bullet train to nowhere," *Weekly Standard*, September 12, 2016.
11. Michael Barone, "The not-inevitable candidate and his not-feasible pet project," *Washington Examiner*, June 12, 2019.
12. Clifford Winston, "On the performance of the US transportation system: caution ahead," *Journal of Economic Literature*, 2013, 51(3): 773–824.
13. *Chicago Tribune*, "Trump pushes infrastructure plans but Congress blocked Obama on the issue," November 11, 2016.
14. Ashley Halsey III, "Trump promised $1 trillion for infrastructure, but the estimated need is $4.5 trillion," *Washington Post*, March 10, 2017.
15. Ralph Vartabedian, "Cost for California bullet train system rises to $77.3 billion," *Los Angeles Times*, March 9, 2018; Ralph Vartabedian, "California bullet train cost surges by 2.8 billion: 'worst case scenario has happened,'" *Los Angeles Times*, January 16, 2018; Allen, "Bullet train to nowhere"; *Washington Post*, "Crazy train," November 14, 2011.
16. Bent Flyvbjerg, "Megaprojects," EconTalk, May 25, 2015.
17. Josh Dawsey, "Trump cools to idea of taking on welfare programs, seeing little chance of success in Congress," *Washington Post*, January 5, 2018.
18. Clifford Winston, "Winston on transportation," EconTalk, October 14, 2013; Winston, "On the performance of the US transportation system"; Diane Whitmore Schanzenbach, Ryan Nunn, and Greg Nantz, "If you build it: a guide to the economics of infrastructure investment" (Washington, DC: Hamilton Project, Brookings Institution, 2017); Gilles Duranton, Geetika Nagpal, and Matthew Turner, "Transportation infrastructure in the US," Working Paper 27254 (Cambridge, MA: National Bureau of Economic Research, 2020).
19. Randal O'Toole, "Paint is cheaper than rails: why Congress should abolish New Starts," Policy Analysis 727 (Washington, DC: Cato Institute, 2013), 6.
20. O'Toole, "Paint is cheaper than rails"; Kate Lowe and Sandra Rosenbloom, "Federal New Starts programs: what do new regulations mean for metropolitan areas," Urban Institute, March 2014.

21. Conor Dougherty, "Candidates in a rare accord, on this upgrading infrastructure," *New York Times*, September 19, 2016.
22. *New York Times*, "Obama's 2013 State of the Union address," February 12, 2013.
23. *New York Times*, "Obama's economics speech at Knox College," July 24, 2013.
24. Donald Trump, "Bridges in danger," *Morning Joe show*, MSNBC, December 18, 2015.
25. Mike Baker and Joan Lowy, "Thousands of bridges at risk of collapse in freak accidents," *Washington Post*, August 26, 2013; Ashley Halsey III, "US has 63,000 bridges that need significant repairs; local governments turn to Congress," *Washington Post*, April 25, 2014.
26. Barry B. LePatner, *Too Big to Fall: America's Failing Infrastructure and the Way Forward* (New York: Foster Publishing, 2010).
27. Research assistant Wendy Morrison, interview with LePatner, 2013.
28. NACE International, "Highways and bridges," www.nace.org/Corrosion-Central /Industries/Highways-and-Bridges.
29. Chris Edwards, "Crumbling infrastructure?," *National Review*, March 20, 2013.
30. John Mendeloff, *Regulating Safety: An Economic and Political Analysis of Occupational Safety and Health Policy* (Cambridge, MA: MIT Press, 1979), 69.
31. Rhoads, *Policy Analysis in the Federal Aviation Administration*, 18–21; Steven E. Rhoads (ed.), *Valuing Life: Public Policy Dilemmas* (Boulder, CO: Westview Press, 1980), 2.
32. *Washington Post*, June 23, 1986.
33. Jonathan Rosenfeld, "Improving roadway designs for traffic safety," *National Law Review*, October 23, 2017.
34. W. Kip Viscusi, "Pricing lives for corporate risk decisions," *Vanderbilt Law Review*, 2015, 68(4): 1117–1162, 1139–42; Rhoads, Valuing Life.
35. Emily Goff, "How to fix America's infrastructure," Heritage Foundation, June 2, 2014.
36. Ashley Halsey III, "Lahood urges more states to ban phone use by drivers," *Washington Post*, June 8, 2012.
37. Greg Ip, *Foolproof: Why Safety Can Be Dangerous and How Danger Makes Us Safe* (New York: Little, Brown, 2015), ch. 4.
38. Tammy O. Tengs, Miriam E. Adams, Joseph S. Pliskin, Dana Gelb Safran, Joanna E. Siegel, Milton C. Weinstein, and John D. Graham, "Five-hundred life-saving interventions and their cost-effectiveness," *Risk Analysis*, 1995, 15(3): 369–390.
39. R. Jeffrey Smith, "Chernobyl report surprisingly detailed but avoids painful truths, experts say," *Washington Post*, August 27, 1986.
40. Richard Wilson and Edmund A. C. Crouch, *Risk–Benefit Analysis*, 2nd ed. (Cambridge, MA: Harvard University Press, 2001), 115–16.
41. Comptroller General, "Report to the Congress of the United States: environmental, economic, and political issues impede Potomac River cleanup efforts," B-202338, no. 117241, 1981.
42. Angus Phillips, "Nose deep in figures, GAO can't see the river for the cesspool," *Washington Post*, February 14, 1982.
43. Gardner M. Brown Jr. and Jason F. Shogren, "Economics of the Endangered Species Act," *Journal of Economic Perspectives*, 1998, 12(3): 3–20.
44. Julian L. Simon and Aaron Wildavsky, "Species loss revisited," *Society*, 1992, 30(1): 41–46.
45. Testimony of Dr. T. Eisner, before Senate Subcommittee on Environmental Protection, April 10, 1992, 9–12; David W. Ehrenfeld, "The conservation of non-resources," *American Scientist*, 1976, 64(6): 648–656.

46. Simon and Wildavsky, "Species loss revisited."
47. R. Alexander Pyron, "Species die. Get over it," *Washington Post*, November 26, 2017; Chris Thomas, *Inheritors of the Earth: How Nature Is Thriving in an Age of Extinction* (London: Allen Lane, 2017), cited in *The Economist*, "Crucibles of cosmopolitan creation," August 5, 2017.
48. *The Economist*, "Why extinctions aren't what they used to be," August 5, 2017.
49. John Koprowski, "The Mt. Graham Red Squirrel Research Program," University of Arizona Conservation Research Laboratory, 2017, https://cals.arizona.edu /research/redsquirrel/mgrs-projhistory.html; Tony Davis, "Endangered red squirrels might be unable to recover from Arizona wildfire," *Arizona Daily Star*, October 19, 2017; University of Arizona, "Mount Graham red squirrel census," 2010, http:// mgio.arizona.edu/sites/mgio/files/mgrscensus2010.pdf.
50. William Baxter, *People or Penguins: The Case for Optimal Pollution* (New York: Columbia University Press, 1974).
51. R. Alexander Pyron, "We don't need to save endangered species. Extinction is part of evolution," *Washington Post*, November 22, 2017.
52. Abraham Lincoln, "The repeal of the Missouri Compromise and the propriety of its restoration: speech at Peoria, Illinois, in reply to Senator Douglas, October 16, 1854," in Roy Basler, ed., *Abraham Lincoln: His Speeches and Writings* (Cleveland, OH: World Publishing, 1946): 283–324, 301–4.
53. Laurence H. Tribe, "Ways not to think about plastic trees," in Laurence H. Tribe, Corinne Schelling, and John Voss, eds., *When Values Conflict: Essays on Environmental Analysis, Discourse, and Decision* (Cambridge, MA: Ballinger Publishing, 1976): 61–91.
54. Robert Dorfman, "An afterword: humane values and environmental decisions," in Tribe, Schelling, and Voss, *When Values Conflict*: 153–173.
55. Emily Ekins, "Cato/YouGov poll: 92% support police body cameras, 55% willing to pay more in taxes to equip local police," Cato Institute, January 5, 2016.
56. R. J. Reinhart, "Public split on basic income for workers replaced by robots," Gallup, February 26, 2018.
57. Emily Ekins, "Large majorities support key Obamacare provisions, unless they cost something," Cato Institute, March 2, 2017.
58. Steven E. Rhoads, *The Economist's View of the World: Government, Markets, and Public Policy* (New York: Cambridge University Press, 1985), 23.
59. Kneese and Schultze, *Pollution, Prices and Public Policy*.

Chapter 2 Marginalism

1. A. H. Maslow, *Motivation and Personality* (New York: Harper & Row, 1954), ch. 5, 107.
2. Richard B. McKenzie and Gordon Tullock, *The New World of Economics* (Homewood, IL: Irwin, 1981), 331–8.
3. See Kenneth Boulding, *Beyond Economics* (Ann Arbor, MI: University of Michigan Press, 1970), 220.
4. See Jack A. Meyer, *Health Care Costs Increases* (Washington, DC: American Enterprise Institute, 1979), 12.
5. Joseph Newhouse, Charles Phelps, and William B. Schwartz, "Policy options and the impact of national health insurance," *New England Journal of Medicine*, 1974, 290 (24): 1345–1359. See also a Rand Corporation study that found that medical expenses were 50 percent higher for those with complete health insurance coverage.

The study also suggested that cost sharing may not have an adverse effect on health: *Washington Post*, December 17, 1981, 8.

6. Charles Fried, "Difficulties in the economic analysis of rights," in Gerald Dworkin, Gordon Bermant, and Peter G. Brown, eds., *Markets and Morals* (Washington, DC: Hemisphere, 1977): 175–195, 188–9.

7. This economic point of view is covered in more depth in Chapter 5.

8. Fried, "Difficulties in the economic analysis of rights," 191.

9. *Washington Post*, "From an editorial by John E. Curley Jr., president of the Catholic Health Association, in an issue of The Catholic Health World," July 19, 1985.

10. Michael Cooper, "Economics of need: the experience of the British health service," in Mark Perlman, ed., *The Economics of Health and Medical Care: Proceedings of a Conference of the International Economic Association* (New York: Wiley, 1973): 89–107, 89–99, 105.

11. Cooper, "Economics of need," 91–3.

12. Martin S. Feldstein, *Economic Analysis for Health Efficiency* (Amsterdam: North Holland, 1967) [cited in Cooper, "Economics of need"].

13. Robin Hanson, "Cut medicine in half," Cato Unbound, September 10, 2007. See also Jonathan Skinner, "Causes and consequences of geographic variation in health care," in Mark V. Pauly, Thomas G. McGuire, and Pedro Pita Barros, eds., *Handbook of Health Economics*, vol. 2 (Oxford: North Holland, 2012): 45–94.

14. Donald M. Berwick and Andrew D. Hackbarth, "Eliminating waste in US health care," *Journal of the American Medical Association*, 2012, 307(14): 1513–1516.

15. Institute of Medicine, *Best Care at Lower Cost: The Path to Continuously Learning Health Care in America* (Washington, DC: National Academies Press, 2013), 14.

16. Katherine Baicker, Sarah L. Taubman, Heidi Allen, and Mira Bernstein, "The Oregon experiment: effects of Medicaid on clinical outcomes," *New England Journal of Medicine*, 2013, 368(18): 1713–1722.

17. White House, "President Obama meets with Senate leaders," December 15, 2009. See also White House, "Nurses join President Obama on health care reform," July 15, 2009; White House, "President Obama and President Clinton discuss health care," September 24, 2013; and White House, "President Obama speaks on the Affordable Care Act," November 6, 2013.

18. Charles Silver and David A. Hyman, *Overcharged: Why Americans Pay Too Much for Health Care* (Washington, DC: Cato Institute, 2018), 286. See also " Sarah L. Taubman, Heidi Allen, Bill J. Wright, Katherine Baicker, and Amy N. Finkelstein, "Medicaid increases emergency-department use: evidence from Oregon's health insurance experiment," *Science*, 2014, 343(6168): 263–268; and Amy N. Finkelstein, Sarah L. Taubman, Heidi Allen, Bill J. Wright, and Katherine Baicker, "Effect of Medicaid coverage on ED use: further evidence from Oregon's experiment," *New England Journal of Medicine*, 2016, 375(16): 1505–1507.

19. Donald Gould, "Some lives cost too dear," *New Statesman*, 1975, 90(2331): 633–634, 634.

20. *Washington Post*, June 23, 1978, A2.

21. The FAA's policy guidance process is discussed in more detail in Steven E. Rhoads, "Policy guidance for the FAA's engineering and development programs," AVP-110, (Washington, DC: Federal Aviation Administration, 1974), mimeo. The quantitative objectives established by the FAA represented that agency's version of the federal government's management by objectives (MBO) system. This management tool, previously used in business and in some governments, was brought to the federal government in the presidency of Richard Nixon. MBO systems that focus on end products are fine if an identified unit is responsible for the outcome and if it,

for example, is asked to achieve as much as it did the preceding year with less money. MBO systems can also be useful tools for scheduling and following through on the particular tasks that must be accomplished to implement a program that will further an objective. Specific end product or process objectives may even help a well-led bureaucracy do more than staff paper studies had suggested was possible. But an objective-setting process such as the FAA's will not serve in these ways. No single FAA unit is responsible for meeting broad agency goals such as "Reduce general aviation accidents by 10 percent." Moreover, even if there were a unit head who controlled all programs affecting general aviation, the FAA could not hold him accountable. Since little thought has been given to whether the funded programs affecting general aviation could reasonably be expected to reduce general aviation accidents by 10 percent, there is no way to know whether a manager achieving an 8 percent reduction should be praised or blamed.

The National Advisory Commission on Criminal Justice Standards and Goals has used a flawed goal- and priority-setting process like that of the FAA. See the discussion in Jeffrey Sedgwick, "Welfare economics and criminal justice policy" (PhD dissertation, University of Virginia, 1978), ch. 7.

Noneconomist professionals can sometimes recommend priority-setting systems that are truly bizarre; see also C. R. Simpson, "Municipal budgeting: a case of priorities," *Governmental Finance*, August 1976, 12–19.

22. Jimmy Carter, "The president's news conference," American Presidency Project, April 15, 1977. See also *Congressional Quarterly Almanac 1977*.

23. Kenneth Boulding, "Economics as a moral science," in his *Economics as a Science* (New York: McGraw-Hill, 1970): 117–138, 134.

24. Alexis de Tocqueville, *Democracy in America*, 2 vols. (New York: Random House, 1945 [1835]), I, 51.

25. David A. Mauer, "New beginnings," *Charlottesville Daily Progress*, February 6, 1994.

26. De Tocqueville, *Democracy in America*, I, 45.

27. Kneese and Schultze, *Pollution, Prices and Public Policy*, epilogue.

28. James M. Buchanan, "Economics and its scientific neighbors," in Sherman Krupp, ed., *The Structure of Economic Science: Essays on Methodology* (Englewood Cliffs, NJ: Prentice-Hall, 1966): 166–183, 168.

29. John Maher, *What Is Economics?* (New York: Wiley, 1969), 146–8.

30. McKenzie and Tullock, *The New World of Economics*, ch. 2.

Chapter 3 Economic Incentives

1. Charles Schultze, *The Public Use of Private Interest* (Washington, DC: Brookings Institution Press, 1977), 1–16. See the revised 2010 edition of these pivotal essays, and read more about the legacy of Schultze's work in George Eads, "Remembering Charlie Schultze," George Washington University, Regulatory Studies Center, November 8, 2016.

2. Environmental Protection Agency, "The origins of EPA," www.epa.gov/history/origins-epa.

3. Lester Lave and Gilbert Omenn, *Clearing the Air: Reforming the Clean Air Act* (Washington, DC: Brookings Institution, 1981), 9. See also R. Shep Melnick, "Deadlines, common sense, and cynicism," *Brookings Review*, 1983, 2(1): 21–24. For recent examples of deadline postponements, see the history of power plant effluent limits (https://eelp.law.harvard.edu/2018/07/power-plant-effluent-limits)

and steam electric power-generating effluent guidelines (www.epa.gov/eg/steam-electric-power-generating-effluent-guidelines-rule-reconsideration), and read about the relaxation of emission standards during the coronavirus pandemic in Lisa Friedman, "EPA, citing coronavirus, drastically relaxes rules for polluters," *New York Times*, March 26, 2020 [updated April 14, 2020].

4. Larry Ruff, "Federal environmental regulation," in Leonard Weiss and Michael Klass, eds., *Case Studies in Regulation: Revolution and Reform* (Boston: Little, Brown, 1981): 235–261, 246. For a brief history of the court's involvement in environmental regulation, see James E. McCarthy and Claudia Copeland, "EPA regulations: too much, too little, or on track?," Congressional Research Service, December 30, 2016.

5. Ruff, "Federal environmental regulation," 254.

6. As quoted in Ruff, "Federal environmental regulation," 254. For a brief look at the current complexity of effluent guidelines, see Environmental Protection Agency, "Learn about effluent guidelines," www.epa.gov/eg/learn-about-effluent-guidelines. A recent example of plant-level adjustments in a different area of environmental regulation can be seen in the attempted use of waivers by President Trump's EPA to exempt oil refineries from biofuel blending requirements: see Stephanie Kelly, "Congressional watchdog to review Trump administration's use of biofuel waivers," Reuters, January 10, 2020.

7. Bernard Asbell, *The Senate Nobody Knows* (Baltimore: Johns Hopkins University Press, 1978), 318–26; see also 175, 188, 363. This information disadvantage seems to continue with a 2016 Congressional Research Service review concluding: "In revising proposed rules, EPA often relied on data submitted by industry and other stakeholders, acknowledging that it had inadequate or incomplete data when it proposed the rules" (McCarthy and Copeland, "EPA regulations").

8. See Herman E. Daly and Joshua Farley's explanation for the reasoning behind choosing this tax level in their textbook *Ecological Economics: Principles and Applications* (Washington, DC: Island Press, 2004), 376–8. For a discussion on some of the difficulties of establishing a tax equal to the marginal level of harm to society, see *The Economist*, "Pigouvian taxes," August 19, 2017.

9. For a complete theoretical discussion of the cap-and-trade concept, see Steven C. Hackett, *Environmental and Natural Resources Economics: Theory, Policy, and the Sustainable Society* (New York: M. E. Sharpe, 2010), 227–36.

10. For an example of how buying and selling emission permits under the cap-and-trade system has affected the steel industry in the European Union, read Chris Bryant, "How the steel industry made millions from the climate crisis," *Washington Post*, November 25, 2019.

11. Environmental Protection Agency, "Economic incentives," www.epa.gov/environmental-economics/economic-incentives.

12. Under the US Sulfur Dioxide Trading Program, this is exactly how things played out, because firms with extremely high costs of control often purchased allowances instead of resisting regulation in court. See Richard Schmalensee and Robert N. Stavins, "Lessons learned from three decades of experience with cap and trade," *Review of Environmental Economics and Policy*, 2017, 11(1): 59–79.

13. Kneese and Schultze, *Pollution, Prices and Public Policy*, 89.

14. General Accounting Office, "A market approach to air pollution control could reduce compliance costs without jeopardizing clean air goals," Report PAD-82-15 (Washington, DC: US Government Printing Office, 1982), esp. 25–6; Robert Crandall, *Controlling Industrial Pollution: Economics and Politics of Clean Air* (Washington, DC: Brookings Institution Press, 1983), ch. 3;

Robert Crandall and Paul Portney, "The free market and clean air," *Washington Post*, August 20, 1981; Kneese and Schultze, *Pollution, Prices and Public Policy*, 99.

15. In China, market-based approaches lead to greater increases in environmental efficiency than command-and-control approaches: Rong-hui Xie, Yi-jun Yuan, and Jing-jing Huang, "Different types of environmental regulations and heterogeneous influence on 'green' productivity: evidence from China," *Ecological Economics*, 2017, 132: 104–112. In the empirical literature, it is often difficult to assess the impacts of tax- or permit-based systems versus mandates because many countries and regions use a combination of strategies. For a theoretical explanation of why market-based programs should be more efficient than command-and-control regulations, see Hackett, *Environmental and Natural Resources Economics*, 227–36.

16. Kneese and Schultze, *Pollution, Prices and Public Policy*, 90. A 2012 study of countries in the European Union shows a strong negative relationship between environmental taxes and pollution: see Bruce Morley, "Empirical evidence on the effectiveness of environmental taxes," *Applied Economics Letters*, 2012, 19(18): 1817–1820.

17. Betty Atkins, "Strong ESG practices can benefit companies and investors: here's how," NASDAQ, June 5, 2018. For empirical evidence on sustainability leading to a competitive advantage, see Neeraj Gupta and Christina C. Benson, "Sustainability and competitive advantage: an empirical study of value creation," *Competition Forum*, 2011, 9(1): 121–136; and Silvia Cantele and Alessandro Zardini, "Is sustainability a competitive advantage for small businesses? An empirical analysis of possible mediators in the sustainability–financial performance relationship," *Journal of Cleaner Production*, 2018, 182: 166–176. For a more complete discussion of the growing impact of sustainability on business practices, see Chris Laszlo and Nadya Zhexembayeva, *Embedded Sustainability: The Next Big Competitive Advantage* (Abingdon: Taylor & Francis, 2017); and McKinsey and Company, "The business of sustainability," October 1, 2011.

18. For more on this example, see *National Journal*, October 10, 1981, 1818.

19. For an example of effluent standards varying by time of year, see the EPA's requirement that gasoline sold from June 1 through September 15 of each year meets lower volatility standards to limit the harmful emissions that increase during warmer months. Available at Environmental Protection Agency, "Gasoline Reid vapor pressure," www.epa.gov/gasoline-standards/gasoline-reid-vapor-pressure.

20. *Washington Post*, May 31, 1976, A16.

21. *New York Times*, "Climate and energy experts debate how to respond to a warming world," October 7, 2019.

22. Alanna Petroff, "These countries want to ban gas and diesel cars," CNN Business, September 11, 2017.

23. Christopher Marquis and John Almandoz, "New Resource Bank: in pursuit of green," Case Study Analysis 412-060 (Cambridge, MA: Harvard Business Publishing, 2011), 11.

24. Chris Mooney and Juliet Eilperin, "Senior Republican statesmen propose replacing Obama's climate policies with a carbon tax," *Washington Post*, February 8, 2017.

25. Kelman sees this objection to selling a "license to pollute" as central for many environmentalists (*What Price Incentives?*, 44).

26. *Congressional Record*, US Senate, November 2, 1971, 117(30), 38, 829.

27. Kelman, *What Price Incentives?*, 44–53, 69–77, 112.

28. Kelman, *What Price Incentives?*, 110–14.

29. Lester Lave and Eugene Seskin, "Death rates and air quality," *Washington Post*, November 12, 1978.

30. *Los Angeles Times*, December 30, 1971.
31. Emma Newburger, "'Hit them where it hurts': several 2020 Democrats want a carbon tax on corporations," CNBC, September 20, 2019.
32. Newburger, "'Hit them where it hurts.'"
33. Mooney and Eilperin, "Senior Republican statesmen propose."
34. Mooney and Eilperin, "Senior Republican statesmen propose."
35. Thomas Pyle, "There's nothing conservative about a carbon tax," *National Review*, March 23, 2017.
36. Zack Coleman and Eric Wolff, "Why greens are turning away from a carbon tax," Politico, December 9, 2018.
37. Emily Cadei, "The tax hike even Republicans are embracing," OZY, April 10, 2015.
38. Department of Transportation, "Corporate average fuel economy (CAFE) standards," last modified August 11, 2014.
39. Wharton University of Pennsylvania, "The unintended consequences of ambitious fuel-economy standards," February 3, 2015.
40. Rebecca Beitsch, "Trump administration rolls back Obama-era fuel efficiency standards," The Hill, March 31, 2020.
41. Matthew Daly, "Democrats decry 'pandemic of pollution' under Trump's EPA," Associated Press, May 20, 2020.
42. Wharton University of Pennsylvania, "The unintended consequences."
43. Wharton University of Pennsylvania, "The unintended consequences."
44. University College London, "British carbon tax leads to 93% drop in coal-fired electricity," January 27, 2020.
45. Brad Plumer and Nadja Popovich, "These countries have prices on carbon. Are they working?," *New York Times*, April 2, 2019.
46. Environmental Defense Fund, "How economics solved acid rain," last modified September 2018.
47. David Greene [interview with David Kestenbaum], "Why the government sells flood insurance despite losing money," NPR, "Planet Money" podcast audio, September 13, 2017.
48. Eli Lehrer, "Dead in the water: the federal flood insurance fiasco," *The Weekly Standard*, January 28, 2013, 13–15.
49. Noel King and Nick Fountain, "Episode 797: flood money," NPR, "Planet Money" podcast audio, September 29, 2017.
50. Darryl Fears and Steven Mufson, "Trump revokes order on flood-risk planning," *Washington Post*, August 16, 2017, A3; Eli Lehrer, "Curious fiscal sense," *The Weekly Standard*, February 22, 2016, 18–19.
51. Joel Achenbach and Mark Berman, "Population centers grow too close to disaster-risk areas," *Washington Post*, October 16, 2017, A3.
52. Achenbach and Berman, "Population centers grow too close."
53. *The Economist*, "Coastal cities and climate change: you're going to get wet," June 15, 2013, 27–28.
54. *The Economist*, "Coastal cities and climate change."
55. Lehrer, "Curious fiscal sense."
56. *The Economist*, "Coastal cities and climate change."
57. Brady Dennis, "US flood insurance program struggling," *Washington Post*, July 17, 2017, A1, A4.
58. Dennis, "US flood insurance program struggling."
59. Steve Goldstein, "Does US bear some of the blame for the flooding?," *Philadelphia Inquirer*, July 18, 1993, D1–2.
60. Goldstein, "Does US bear some of the blame for the flooding?"

61. Alisa Chang and Noel King, "National Flood Insurance Program will pay out billions for a few properties," NPR, "All Things Considered" podcast audio, September 21, 2017.
62. Chang and King, "National Flood Insurance Program will pay out billions."
63. King and Fountain, "Episode 797: flood money."
64. Dennis, "US flood insurance program struggling."
65. Dennis, "US flood insurance program struggling."
66. Helen Dewar, "Senate panel increases aid to flood area," Washington Post, July 31, 1993, A8.
67. Dewar, "Senate panel increases aid to flood area."
68. Rosalind S. Helderman and Paul Kane, "Boehner [missing] spending-bill rebellion," Washington Post, September 23, 2011.
69. Ross Kerber, "Floods may turn tide on insurance reform," Washington Post, August 3, 1993, A4.
70. Sheldon Richman, "Federal flood insurance: managing risk or creating it?," Regulation: The Cato Review of Business & Government, 1993, 16(3): 15–16.
71. Richman, "Federal flood insurance"; Washington Post, "A troubled program continues" [editorial], August 4, 2018, A12.
72. Jane Dunlap Norris, "Dedication of levee is timely," The Daily Progress, May 1, 1989, A1, A12.
73. Norris, "Dedication of levee is timely"; The Daily Progress, "Scottsville is Thacker's great legacy" [editorial], February 24, 2016, C6.
74. Robert Brickhouse, "Dike is Scottsville salvation," The Daily Progress, A1, A8.
75. Brickhouse, "Dike is Scottsville salvation."
76. Pat Wechsler, "Plan [missing] for Scottsville," The Daily Progress, 1977.
77. Wechsler, "Plan [missing] for Scottsville."
78. The Daily Progress, "Scottsville is Thacker's great legacy"; Norris, "Dedication of levee is timely."
79. David Conrad and Larry Larson, "We knew what to do about floods. We didn't do it," Washington Post, September 3, 2017, B1, B3.
80. Kenneth J. Cooper, "$2 billion fund for disaster relief recommended," Washington Post, December 15, 1994, A17.
81. Lehrer, "Curious fiscal sense."
82. Conrad and Larson, "We knew what to do about floods."
83. Conrad and Larson, "We knew what to do about floods."
84. Conrad and Larson, "We knew what to do about floods."
85. Michael Grunwald, "High, mostly dry on Midwest rivers," Washington Post, June 25, 2001, A1, A5.
86. Conrad and Larson, "We knew what to do about floods."
87. Elizabeth Rush, "For those living by the water's edge, it may be time to move," Washington Post, September 17, 2017, B2.
88. Rush, "For those living by the water's edge."
89. Rush, "For those living by the water's edge."
90. David Schrank, Bill Eisele, and Tim Lomax, 2019 Urban Mobility Report (Bryan, TX: Texas A&M Transportation Institute, 2019).
91. Schrank, Eisele, and Lomax, 2019 Urban Mobility Report.
92. Jonathan I. Levey, Jonathan J. Buonocore, and Katherine von Stackelberg, "Evaluation of the public health impacts of traffic congestion: a health risk assessment," Environmental Health, 2010, 9, article 65.
93. Mary Snow and Pat Smith, "Congestion pricing won't work, New Yorkers say, Quinnipiac University poll finds; voters say scrap elite school test, increase

diversity," Quinnipiac University, April 2, 2019; Luz Lazo and Emily Guskin, "Poll: Washington-area residents widely oppose paying a toll to drive into downtown DC," *Washington Post*, May 17, 2019.

94. Camila Domonoske, "City dwellers don't like the idea of congestion pricing – but they get over it," NPR, May 7, 2019.

95. Domonoske, "City dwellers don't like the idea of congestion pricing."

96. Christina Anderson, Winnie Hu, Weiyi Lim, and Anna Schaverien, "3 far-flung cities offer clues to unsnarling Manhattan's streets," *New York Times*, February 26, 2018.

97. Gilbert White, *Strategies of American Water Management* (Ann Arbor, MI: University of Michigan Press, 1969) [cited in Robert K. Davis and Steven Hanke, "Pricing and efficiency in water resource management," in Arnold C. Harberger, ed., *Benefit Cost Analysis 1971* (Chicago: Aldine, 1972): 271–295, 276]. For an interesting discussion of economist Alfred Kahn's uses of incentives and marginalism in reforming New York State's electric utility rate structure, see Douglas Anderson, *Regulatory Politics and Electric Utilities* (Boston: Auburn House Publishing, 1981), ch. 4. Telephone directory assistance is another case of a quasi-public service where scarce resources are wasted frivolously when provided free. In 1977 the Chesapeake and Potomac Telephone Co. found directory assistance calls fell 59 percent when a 10-cent charge was instituted for each assistance call beyond the first six per month: *Washington Post*, March 9, 1977, A12.

98. Antonio Martino, "Measuring Italy's underground economy," *Policy Review*, 1981, 16: 87–106.

99. See William Nordhaus and Alice Rivlin's discussion of this in Department of Commerce, Office of the Secretary, "Regulatory reform seminar: proceedings and background papers" (Washington, DC: US Government Printing Office, 1978), 60–1.

Chapter 4 Government and the Economy

1. E. C. Pasour Jr., and J. Bruce Bullock, "Energy and agriculture: some economic issues," in William Lockeretz, ed., *Agriculture and Energy* (New York: Academic Press, 1977): 683–693.

2. Some economists do not like the potential Pareto improvement concept, and they would argue that economic efficiency is obtained only if the compensation of losers actually takes place and thus there are no losers. When cost–benefit studies talk of economic efficiency benefits, however, they usually use the potential Pareto understanding of economic efficiency. Charles Schultze reflects this literature when he says that "[a]n efficient move is, by definition, one in which gains exceed losses": *The Public Use of Private Interest*, 22. Edgar Browning and Jacqueline Browning's popular public finance text also states that government expenditure and tax packages that make some citizens worse off may nonetheless be economically efficient; *Public Finance and the Price System*, 2nd ed. (New York: Macmillan, 1983), 31–3. For more on Pareto optimality and economic efficiency, see E. J. Mishan, *Cost–Benefit Analysis* (New York: Praeger, 1976); and Mark Blaug, *Economic Theory in Retrospect* (Cambridge: Cambridge University Press, 1978), 618–39.

3. Kenneth J. Arrow and Frank H. Hahn, *General Competitive Analysis* (San Francisco: Holden-Day, 1971), vi–vii.

4. Leonard E. Read, "I, pencil: my family tree," *The Freeman*, December 1958; as quoted in Milton Friedman and Rose Friedman, *Free to Choose* (New York: Avon Books, 1979): 3–5.

5. Friedman and Friedman, *Free to Choose*, 7. My discussion of "the pencil" draws heavily on this work.

6. Leonard E. Read, "I, pencil," Foundation for Economic Education, https://fee.org /resources/i-pencil.

7. In their text, Browning and Browning provide the following interesting example of free rider behavior: "In 1970...General Motors tried to market pollution control devices for automobiles at $20 (installed) that could reduce the pollution emitted by 30 to 50 percent... GM withdrew the device from the market because of low sales. This was simply the large-group free rider problem at work. Everyone might have been better off if all drivers used the device, but it was not in the interest of any single individual to purchase it because the overall level of air quality would not be noticeably improved as a result of one person's solitary action" (*Public Finance and the Price System*, 28).

8. See Bryan Caplan, *The Myth of the Rational Voter: Why Democracies Choose Bad Policies* (Princeton, NJ: Princeton University Press, 2007), esp. 135–41.

9. E. S. Savas, "Refuse collection," *Policy Analysis*, 1977, 3(1): 49–74. Corroborative studies in three countries are summarized in E. S. Savas, "Public vs. private refuse collection: a critical review of the evidence," *Urban Analysis*, 1979, 6(1): 1–13.

10. See the discussion of the study in the *Washington Post*, October 10, 1975, A1.

11. It would come as no surprise to public choice scholars to learn that the potential savings had long been hidden from view by estimating distant employee retirement costs at less than one-third of the real figure; *Washington Post*, August 24, 1976, A4. Also on the federal contracting question, see the *Washington Post*, April 11, 1981, A2; November 29, 1977, A18; November 22, 1977, D7; December 30, 1977, A5. For a description of bureaucracy's attempt to preserve its monopoly on information by deliberately refusing to collect useful output information, see the discussion of New York police response times in the *New York Times*, January 10, 1978, B1. Sometimes, however, the problem is politicians blocking administrators seeking efficiency improvements. In 1978 a General Services Administration (GSA) attempt to obtain competitive bidding on overhead projectors was blocked when 80 members of Congress received complaints from the projector industry and wrote the GSA; *Washington Post*, August 25, 1978, A9.

12. See Douglass North and Roger Miller, *The Economics of Public Issues* (New York: Harper & Row, 1980), ch. 15; Roger S. Ahlbrandt Jr., "Efficiency in the provision of fire services," *Public Choice*, 1973, 16(1): 1–15; *Washington Post*, October 11, 1981; also see, on contracting and government efficiency, Louis De Alessi, "An economic analysis of government ownership and regulation: theory and evidence from the electric power industry," *Public Choice*, 1979, 19(1): 1–42; E. S. Savas, *Privatizing the Public Sector* (Chatham, NJ: Chatham House, 1982); Donald Fisk, *Private Provision of Public Services: An Overview* (Washington, DC: Urban Institute, 1978); Robert Spann, "Public versus private provision of governmental services," in T. E. Borcherding, ed., *Budgets and Bureaucrats: The Sources of Government Growth* (Durham, NC: Duke University Press, 1977): 71–89; *Washington Post*, November 5, 1980, B1; Robert W. Poole Jr., *Cutting Back City Hall* (New York: Universe, 1981); James Bennett and Manuel Johnson, *Better Government at Half the Cost: Private Provision of Public Services* (Aurora, IL: Green Hill, 1981). For a cautionary note on contracting, see this report: California Tax Foundation, *Contracting Out Local Government Services in California* (Sacramento: California Tax Foundation, 1981). Charles Goodsell has written what he calls "a public administration polemic," in which he argues that the studies on the comparative efficiency of government and business are

mixed and inconclusive: *The Case for Bureaucracy: A Public Administration Polemic* (Chatham, NJ: Chatham House, 1983). Although Goodsell does discuss some early studies by economists, he cites none published after 1979. He also fails to cite any of the sources listed in this note. Some of these review the literature thoroughly, and all but one of these were published at least two years before Goodsell's book appeared.

13. See E. S. Savas, *Privatization in the City: Successes, Failures, Lessons* (Washington, DC: Congressional Quarterly Press, 2005), esp. 89–90, 116.

14. Savas, *Privatization in the City.*

15. *The Daily Progress*, "Charlottesville to privatize trash collection," June 5, 1999.

16. Lisa Rein, "Fairfax employees run up odometers to keep their cars," *Washington Post*, September 24, 2006.

17. Savas, *Privatization in the City*, 53–4; also see Stephen Goldsmith, *The Responsive City: Engaging Communities through Data-Smart Governance* (San Francisco: Jossey-Bass, 2014).

18. Bradley Graham, "Cohen at a crossroads after base closing loss," *Washington Post*, May 19, 1998.

19. Christopher Lee, "Army weighs privatizing close to 214,000 jobs," *Washington Post*, November 3, 2002.

20. Herman Schwartz, "Small states in big trouble: the politics of state reorganization in Australia, Denmark, New Zealand and Sweden in the 1980s," *World Politics*, 1994, 46(4): 527–555.

21. Pew Charitable Trusts, "Subsidyscope: transportation," last modified May 31, 2013, www.pewtrusts.org/-/media/legacy/uploadedfiles/pcs_assets/2009/subsidys cope_transportation_sector.pdf.

22. Dierdre McCloskey and Art Carden, *Leave Me Alone and I'll Make You Rich: How the Bourgeois Deal Enriched the World* (Chicago: University of Chicago Press, 2020).

23. Joseph Vranich, *End of the Line: The Failure of Amtrak Reform and the Future of America's Passenger Trains* (Washington, DC: AEI Press, 2004), 5.

24. Chris Edwards and Peter J. Hill, "Cutting the Bureau of Reclamation and reforming water markets," Downsizing the Federal Government, February 1, 2012.

25. Robert D. Behn, "For US '81 outlays, there's no tomorrow," *New York Times*, September 30, 1981, 31.

26. *Washington Post*, September 14, 1979, A1.

27. *San Francisco Chronicle*, "The US keeps paying twice," August 15, 1984.

28. Dale Russacoff, "A license to print money, part II," *Washington Post*, April 19, 1990.

29. Pete Earley, "Criminals fail to pay full debt to society," *Washington Post*, September 20, 1983

30. Earley, "Criminals fail to pay full debt to society"; Saundra Torry, "Unpaid federal fines drift into oblivion, disorganization," *Washington Post*, September 16, 1989.

31. Larry Margasak, "GAO: Pentagon wasting tickets," *Washington Post*, June 9, 2004.

32. Jonathan Weisman, "IRS opting not to go after many scofflaws," *Washington Post*, March 20, 2004.

33. Robert Reich, *The Next American Frontier* (New York: Times Books, 1983); Lester Thurow, *The Zero-Sum Society: Distribution and the Possibilities for Change* (New York: Penguin Books, 1981), esp. 96, 132; *Newsweek*, "The road to lemon socialism," April 25, 1983; and Barry Bluestone and Bennett Harrison, *The Deindustrialization of America* (New York: Basic Books, 1982). Felix

Rohatyn's positions are discussed in Jeremy Bernstein, "Profiles: allocating sacrifice," *New Yorker*, January 23, 1983, 45–78. Over 30 industrial policy bills were introduced in the 98th Congress. The Democratic Caucus of the US Senate and the Democratic majority of the House Banking Committee's Subcommittee on Economic Stabilization both endorsed industrial policy plans. The provisions of some of these bills and the ideas of the authors cited here are surveyed in Richard McKenzie, "National industrial policy: an overview of the debate," Backgrounder 275 (Washington, DC: Heritage Foundation, 1983). For more recent evidence, see the rest of this section and accompanying endnotes.

34. Robert D. Hershey Jr., "Synfuels Corp. is running on empty," *New York Times*, August 25, 1985; Steven Mufson, "Before Solyndra, a long history of failed government energy projects," *Washington Post*, November 12, 2011; Wikipedia, "Synthetic Fuels Corporation," https://en.wikipedia.org/Synthetic_Fuels_Corporation.
35. J. Raloff, "Congress kills the US Synfuels Corp," *Science News*, January 11, 1986; Wikipedia, "Synthetic Fuels Corporation."
36. E. J. Dionne Jr., "Beneath the rhetoric, an old question: Bush Clinton debate frames classic choice: how much government?," *Washington Post*, August 31, 1992.
37. Robert J. Samuelson, "Selling Supercar," *Washington Post*, October 13, 1993.
38. Matt Pressman, "Tesla is obstructed by anti-free-market laws in numerous US states," CleanTechnica, August 3, 2019; Antony Ingram, "Why can't we buy cars that can get 60, 70, 80 miles per gallon?," Green Car Reports, April 28, 2014.
39. Alison Vekshin and Mark Chediak, "Solyndra's $733 million plant had whistling robots, spa showers," *Bloomberg*, September 28, 2011; Carol D. Leonnig and Joe Stephens, "Solyndra's ex-employees tell of high spending, factory woes," *Washington Post*, September 22, 2011.
40. Office of Inspector General, Department of Energy, "The Department of Energy's Loan Guarantee to Solyndra, Inc.," Special Report: 11–0078-I (Washington, DC: Department of Energy, 2015). When Solyndra faced financial difficulties, the Department of Energy changed the loan terms to allow the company to continue receiving taxpayer funds: Carol D. Leonnig, "Energy Department knew Solyndra had violated its loan terms: but more funding was approved for the solar company," *Washington Post*, September 29, 2011.
41. Steven F. Hayward, "President Solyndra," *The Weekly Standard*, October 3, 2011; Carol D. Leonnig, Joe Stephens, and Alice Crites, "Obama's focus when visiting cleantech companies raises questions," *Washington Post*, June 25, 2011; Carol D. Leonnig and Joe Stephens, "Venture capitalists play key role in Obama's Energy Department," *Washington Post*, February 14, 2012.
42. Peter Thiel, *Zero to One: Notes on Startups, or How to Build the Future* (London: Virgin Books, 2014).
43. Thiel, *Zero to One*, 164–71.
44. *Washington Post*, "No fun in the sun," November 18, 2011; also see Carol D. Leonnig and Joe Stephens, "Obama's green car push struggles to pass go," *Washington Post*, December 8, 2011.
45. Joe Stevens and Carol D. Leonnig, "Energy Department failed to sound alarm as Solyndra solar company sank," *Washington Post*, November 11, 2011.
46. Joe Stevens and Carol D. Leonnig, "Energy Department finalizes $4.7 billion in solar loans," *Washington Post*, October 1, 2011.
47. Raloff, "Congress kills the US Synfuels Corp."
48. Mufson, "Before Solyndra."
49. Heather Long, "Remember Bush's 2002 steel tariffs? His Chief of Staff warns Trump not to do the same," *Washington Post*, March 6, 2016.

50. John Lancaster, "Military moves with political overtones," *Washington Post*, September 3, 1992.

51. Fareed Zakaria, "The GOP has lost its economic soul," *Washington Post*, December 6, 2019.

52. N. Gregory Mankiw, *Principles of Economics*, 6th ed. (Mason, OH: Southwestern Cengage Learning, 2010), ch. 9; Paul Krugman and Robin Wells, *Economics*, 3rd ed. (New York: Worth Publishers, 2013), ch. 8.

53. University of Pennsylvania economist Michael Wachter, as quoted in *Business Week*, July 4, 1983, 61; Alfred Kahn, "The relevance of industrial organization," in John V. Craven, ed., *Industrial Organization, Antitrust and Public Policy* (Boston: Kluwer-Nijhoff, 1983): 3–17, 16.

54. *The Economist*, "Abenomics: overhyped, underappreciated," July 30, 2016.

55. Krugman and Wells, *Economics*, 121–2; also see *The Economist*, "State your business: China's highflying private sector faces an advance by the state," December 8, 2018.

56. Richard B. McKenzie, "Industrial policy," in Henderson, *The Concise Encyclopedia of Economics*, www.econlib.org/library/Enc1/IndustrialPolicy.html.

57. In the comment by David R. Henderson, "Industrial policy: democratic economists speak out," on McKenzie, "Industrial policy," in *The Concise Encyclopedia of Economics*.

58. Alfred Kahn, "America's Democrats: can liberalism survive inflation?," *The Economist*, March 7, 1981, 22–25. The first three quotes are from the *Washington Post*, July 3, 1983, G1, G4; the last Schultze quote is from *Business Week*, July 4, 1983, 57. See as well Charles Schultze, "Industrial policy: a dissent," *Brookings Review*, 1983, 2(1): 3–12. Liberal economists Joseph Pechman and Francis Bator have also been described as "dubious" about "whether industrial policy is more than a slogan": *Washington Post*, June 10, 1983, D8, D11. It also seems unlikely that Arthur Okun would have supported the most common industrial policy proposals. In his well-known book, Okun notes that we expect taxpayer money to be treated with respect and caution, and he thus doubts that government could respond flexibly enough to organize economic activity in areas where experimentation and innovation are important: *Equality and Efficiency: The Big Tradeoff* (Washington, DC: Brookings Institution, 1975), 60–1.

59. Roberta Rampton and Mark Hosenball, "In Solyndra note, Summers said Feds 'crappy' investor," Reuters, October 3, 2011. There is a school that takes a much more benign view of government industrial policy. Mariana Mazzucato, a political philosopher who now works in political economy, speaks for this school in *The Entrepreneurial State: Debunking Public vs. Private Sector Myths* (London: Anthem Press, 2013). The book presents evidence that government support played an outsized role in much recent technological change. The same argument is made by noneconomists Michael Shellenberger and Ted Nordhaus, "The boom in shale gas? Credit the feds," *Washington Post*, December 17, 2011. Cato Foundation scholars, on the other hand, provide evidence that even government *general* financing of science and research has accomplished little in the United States, and may in fact have been counterproductive. Patrick J. Michaels makes this argument and cites research by his Cato colleague, Terence Kealey, in "Who should fund science?," *Philadelphia Inquirer*, April 10, 2017. The dissenters from the economists' opposition to industrial policy proposals have made no headway among mainstream economists. In light of the dismal results of government interventions set forth above, it would seem that the sorts of industrial policies typically proposed by politicians are not worthy of support.

60. See the coverage of the studies in Bruce Bartlett, "Enterprise zones: a bipartisan failure," Fiscal Times, January 10, 2014.
61. Dan Wells, "The Trump administration said these tax breaks would help distressed neighborhoods. Who's actually benefiting?," Washington Post, June 6, 2019.
62. Eric Wesoff, "Trump budget request boosts nuclear, clean coal – while solar, ARPA-E and energy R&D are cut," PV Magazine USA, February 11, 2020.
63. A recent case of this is North Sea oil. For years the North Sea was not considered a good bet for finding oil. In the 1960s a gas deposit found off the Netherlands stimulated some interest. But, after 29 dry holes, eight of the nine exploration groups abandoned their activities. The consensus among geologists was that there was no oil to be found. One group continued to explore, and we now know that the North Sea is a major oil province, with 16 billion barrels of reserves already discovered. Potential recoverable reserves are estimated at 40 billion barrels or more.
    Richard R. Nelson and Richard N. Langlois give these other examples: "Strange as it now seems to us, aviation experts were once divided on the relative merits of the turboprop and turbojet engines as power plants for the aircraft of the future; and the computer industry was by no means unanimous that transistors – or later, integrated circuits – were to be the technology of the future" ("Industrial innovation policy: lessons from American history," Science, 1983, 219(4586): 814–818, 815).
64. Richard R. Nelson, The Moon and the Ghetto: An Essay on Public Policy Analysis (New York: Norton, 1977), 120.
65. Nelson, The Moon and the Ghetto, 120; Nelson and Langlois, "Industrial innovation policy," 815, 817.
66. Rick Weiss, "In recognizing surprise, researchers go from A to B to discovery," Washington Post, January 26, 1998.
67. Stanford University, "Nathan Rosenberg, Stanford professor and expert on the economic history of technology, dead at 87," September 1, 2015; Washington Post, "Don't write off the salad shooter," June 12, 1974; Rick Weiss, "Nobel Prize vindicates US scientist," Washington Post, October 7, 1997.
68. George Will provides this quote and more startling surprises from Matt Ridley's How Innovation Works: And Why It Flourishes in Freedom: George Will, "Innovation's secret sauce: freedom," Washington Post, October 8, 2020.
69. Sarah DiGiulio, "These ER docs invented a real Star Trek Tricorder," Mach, NBC News, May 10, 2017.
70. Laura Shin, "Using fungi to replace Styrofoam," New York Times, April 13, 2009; Emily Gosden, "IKEA plans mushroom-based packaging as eco-friendly replacement for polystyrene," Telegraph, February 24, 2016. Also see Ashley Halsey III, "Plastic bottles may become part of roads surface: new asphalt mixes could pave way for cheaper, more durable streets," Washington Post, October 29, 2018.
71. Jon Gertner, "George Mitchell: the father of fracking," New York Times Magazine, December 2013; Leighton Walter Kille, "The environmental costs and benefits of fracking: the state of research," Journalist's Resource, October 26, 2014; Kevin Begos, "CO2 emissions in US fall to 20 year low", Phys.org, August 16, 2012; Bjorn Lomborg, "Innovation vastly cheaper than green subsidies," The Globe and Mail, July 15, 2013.
72. David Koenig, "US expected to be world's top oil producer," Associated Press, July 14, 2018.
73. Kahn, "America's Democrats," 25. Also see Amitai Etzioni, "The MITIzation of America?," Public Interest, 1983, 72: 44–51, 46–7; Robert J. Samuelson, "The

policy peddlers," *Harper's*, June 1983: 60–65, 62; and George Eads, "The political experience in allocating investment: lessons from the United States and elsewhere," in Michael Wachter and Susan Wachter, eds., *Toward a New US Industrial Policy?* (Philadelphia: University of Pennsylvania Press, 1981): 472–479.

74. Leonnig, Stephens, and Crites, "Obama's focus."

75. Tyler Cowen, *The Complacent Class: The Self-Defeating Quest for the American Dream* (New York: St. Martin's Press, 2017).

76. Drew Desilver, "Fact tank: our lives in numbers," Pew Research Center, August 7, 2018.

77. Erik Brynjolfsson, Felix Eggers, and Avinash Gannamaneni, "Using massive online choice experiments to measure changes in well-being," Working Paper 24514 (Cambridge, MA: National Bureau of Economic Research, 2018); Chad Syverson, "Challenges to mismeasurement explanations for the US productivity slowdown," *Journal of Economic Perspectives*, 2017, 31(2): 165–186; Martin S. Feldstein, "Underestimating the real growth of GDP, personal income, and productivity," *Journal of Economic Perspectives*, 2017, 31(2): 145–164; Philippe Aghion, Antonin Bergeaud, Timo Boppart, Peter J. Klenow, and Huiyu Li, "Missing growth from creative destruction," Working Paper 24023 (Cambridge, MA: National Bureau of Economic Research, 2017).

78. Caplan, *The Myth of the Rational Voter.*

79. Arguments in this section are not meant to ignore the controversy over how much more recent growth has done for higher-income Americans as compared to average Americans. This issue, together with other equity issues, will be discussed in Chapter 5.

80. Jay Shambaugh and Ryan Nunn, "American markets need more competition and more new businesses," Hamilton Project, Brookings Institution, June, 13, 2018; Lee Ohinian [discussion with Russ Roberts], "The future of freedom, democracy and prosperity," EconTalk, June 29, 2015.

81. Cowen, *The Complacent Class.* Additionally, the high cost of housing in areas with the most productive and highest wage jobs discourages Americans from moving to these jobs and these locations. Government policies such as regulatory barriers are partially to blame for these high housing prices, seen especially in high-productivity cities such as New York City and San Francisco.

82. TV History, "Television history: the first 75 years," www.tvhistory.tv/tv-prices.htm.

83. Mark Perry, "The 'good old days' are today: today's home appliances are cheaper, better, and more energy efficient than ever before," American Enterprise Institute, August 3, 2014.

84. Adam Smith, *An Inquiry into the Nature and Causes of the Wealth of Nations* (London: W. Strahan and T. Cadell, 1776), book IV, ch. 2.

85. Caplan, *The Myth of the Rational Voter*, 65.

86. William B. Walstad and Max Larsen, "Results from a national survey of American economic literacy," Gallup Organization, 1992.

87. If the government spending is paid for by compulsory taxes rather than debt, it fares no better by the economists' standard of consumer sovereignty. Those who would have spent, not saved, the money taxed away would obviously require a higher-than-market return on their investment before they agreeing to give up their private consumption. (Otherwise they would have planned to save their money, not spend it.)

88. On speculation, see Armen Alchian and William Allen, *University Economics: Elements of Inquiry*, 3rd ed. (Belmont, CA: Wadsworth, 1972), ch. 10. For

congressional concern about manipulation of the coffee market, see the
Washington Post, March 15, 1977, A1. For Department of the Interior economists'
devices for dealing with congressional misunderstanding of speculation, see
Christopher Leman and Robert Nelson, "Ten commandments for policy
economists," *Journal of Policy Analysis and Management*, 1981, 1(1): 97–117, 102.

89. *Washington Post*, May 3, 2012.
90. Alan S. Blinder, "In defense of the oil companies," *Washington Post*, September 3,
    1990; also see Benjamin Zycher, "In defense of price gouging and racketeering,"
    American Enterprise Institute, August 7, 2014; and Fox News, "Hurricane Harvey
    price gouging complaints include $99 for water," August 26, 2017.
91. Chuck Schumer and Bernie Sanders, "Limit corporate stock buybacks," *New York
    Times*, February 4, 2019.
92. Brad Hershbein, David Boddy, and Melissa Kearney, "Nearly 30% of workers in
    the US need a license to perform their job: it is time to examine occupational
    licensing practices," Brookings, January 27, 2015; Morris M. Kleiner, "Why
    license a florist?," *New York Times*, May 28, 2014.
93. Campbell Robertson, "A clash over who is allowed to give you a brighter smile,"
    New York Times, May 25, 2013.
94. *The Economist*, "How to rig an economy: occupational licensing blunts competi-
    tion. It may also boost inequality," February 17, 2018.
95. *The Economist*, "Not enough lawyers?," September 3, 2011.
96. *The Economist*, "How to rig an economy."
97. See, for example, this letter to the editor in the *Washington Post*, from
    Gail Mackiernan, "Mr. Kavanaugh's loyalties," August 15, 2018.
98. *The Economist*, "Licence to kill competition: America should get rid of oppressive
    job licensing," February 17, 2018; also see Brink Lindsey and Steven M. Teles, *The
    Captured Economy: How the Powerful Enrich Themselves, Slow Down Growth,
    and Increase Inequality* (Oxford: Oxford University Press, 2015).
99. See *Regulation*, "Professional licensure: one diagnosis, two cures," 1983, 7(5): 11–13.
100. Hershbein, Boddy, and Kearney, "Nearly 30% of workers in the US need
     a license."
101. Jared Meyer [interview with Maureen Olhausen], "FTC sets its sights on occupa-
     tional licensing," Forbes, April 17, 2017.
102. *The Economist*, "Grudges and kludges," March 4, 2017.
103. Luigi Zingales, *A Capitalism for the People: Recapturing the Lost Genius of
     American Prosperity* (New York: Basic Books, 2012).
104. Elizabeth Bailey, in John J Siegfried, ed., *Better Living through Economics*,
     (Cambridge, MA: Harvard University Press, 2010).
105. Thomas Gale Moore, "Trucking deregulation," in Henderson, *The Concise
     Encyclopedia of Economics*, www.econlib.org/library/Enc/TruckingDeregulation
     .html.
106. Elizabeth E. Bailey, "Air-transportation deregulation," in Siegfried, *Better Living
     through Economics*: 188–202, 196.
107. See George Eads, "Competition in the domestic trunk airline industry: too much or
     too little?," in Almarin Phillips, ed., *Promoting Competition in Regulated Markets*
     (Washington, DC: Brookings Institution, 1975): 13–54; for evidence on consumer
     savings since deregulation, see Theodore Keeler, "The revolution in airline regula-
     tion," in Weiss and Klass, *Case Studies in Regulation*: 53–85; John Meyer, Clinton
     V. Oster, Benjamin A. Bermin, Ivor Morgan, and Diana L. Strassmann, *Airline
     Deregulation: The Early Experience* (Boston: Auburn House Publishing, 1981);
     and *Regulation*, 1982, 6(2): 52.

108. IGM Forum, "Taxi competition," September 29, 2014.

109. Ashley Halsey III, "The fight over tight flights," *Washington Post*, February 25, 2018.

110. Ted S. Warren and Amy Held, "The FAA declined to regulate seat size and pitch on airlines," NPR, July 5, 2018; Halsey, "The fight over tight flights"; David Schaper, "Tired of tiny seats and no legroom on flights? Don't expect it to change," NPR, July 12, 2018.

111. Ashley Halsey III, "FAA bill could cut excessive air fees," *Washington Post*, September 19, 2018.

112. See Russ Roberts [podcast conversation with Richard Epstein], "Cruises, first-class travel, and inequality," EconTalk, June 27, 2016.

113. Scott McCartney, "How much of your $355 ticket is profit for airlines?," *Wall Street Journal*, February 15, 2018.

114. Warren and Held, "The FAA declined to regulate seat size and pitch"; Halsey, "The fight over tight flights"; Schaper, "Tired of tiny seats and no legroom on flights?"

115. For the politics of antitrust, see Tony Romm and Elizabeth Dwoskin, "Big tech faces antitrust review: House plans broad look at industry, growing consensus on Hill that regulation is lax," *Washington Post*, June 4, 2019; James Hohmann, "Monopolies, mergers emerge as major issues for Democrats," *Washington Post*, April 2, 2019.

116. See Frank H. Easterbrook, "Breaking up is hard to do," *Regulation*, 1981, 5(6): 25–31, esp. 31. Also see Robert J. Samuelson, "Some cautious words about merger mania," *Washington Post*, December 1, 1981, D6.

117. Alan Reynolds, "The return of antitrust?," *Regulation*, 2018, 41(1): 24–30. For a recent argument that antitrust makes it easier for larger businesses to increase their market power, see Mark Jamison, "Three myths about antitrust," blog post, American Enterprise Institute, September 2, 2020.

118. Steven Pearlstein, "Is Amazon getting too big?," *Washington Post*, July 28, 2017.

119. Pearlstein, "Is Amazon getting too big?"

120. Marc Fisher, "Why Trump went after Bezos: two billionaires across a cultural divide," *Washington Post*, April 5, 2018; later a *Washington Post* headline said "Microsoft lands huge Pentagon cloud contract: Amazon is spurned for $10 billion deal after Trump voices opposition," October 26, 2019. Also see Mark Jamison, "Are regulatory attacks on Big Tech politically motivated?," American Enterprise Institute, September 30, 2019.

121. For a serious argument supporting intervention to prevent the T-Mobile and Sprint merger, see discussion in *The Economist*, May 5, 2018.

122. Tyler Cowen, *Big Business: A Love Letter to an American Anti-Hero* (New York: St. Martin's Press, 2019); James Pethokoukis [interview with Tyler Cowen], American Enterprise Institute, May 20, 2019.

123. See Russ Roberts [podcast conversation with Timothy Taylor], "Government vs. business," EconTalk, February 1, 2016.

124. Jessica Sidman, "Underfed: good staff is in short supply, and restaurants are getting desperate," *Washington City Paper*, June 5, 2013; Peter Romeo, "10 states open investigation into restaurants' no poaching pacts," Restaurant Business Online, July 10, 2018.

125. Adriana D. Krugler. "The effects of employment protection in Europe and the USA," Opuscle 18 (Barcelona: Centre de Recerca en Economia Internacional, 2007); Steven Pearlstein, "French take to the streets to preserve their economic fantasy," *Washington Post*, March 22, 2006; *The Economist*, "Working man's burden," February 6, 1999; Edward Cody, "Overload of regulatory do's and don't's is stifling France's growth, critics say," *Washington Post*, April 17, 2013.

126. Casey B. Mulligan, "Why 49 is a magic number," *New York Times*, January 2, 2013.
127. Adam Nossiter, "Macron takes on France's Labor Code, 100 Years in the making," *New York Times*, August 4, 2017.
128. Unemployment figures computed by my research assistant, Brooke Henderson, from Organisation for Economic Co-operation and Development (OECD) long-term unemployment rate data, accessed 13 August 2018.
129. Robert H. Frank, *Luxury Fever: Money and Happiness in an Era of Excess* (Princeton, NJ: Princeton University Press, 1999), 274.
130. Joseph Stiglitz, as quoted in Frank, *Luxury Fever*, 274.
131. Lawrence H. Summers, "Growth not austerity is best remedy for Europe," *Financial Times*, April 29, 2012.
132. Barbara Palmer, "Does anyone labor at the Labor Department?," *Washington Post*, January 8, 1981.
133. John M. Goshko, "'Cut things not people' is rallying cry at State as funding shortfall looms," *Washington Post*, October 29, 1987.
134. See, for example, Governor Jim Gilmore's letter to state employees March 13, 2001.
135. United States International Trade Commission, "A review of recent developments in the US automobile industry including an assessment of the Japanese voluntary restraint agreements," Publication 1648 (Washington, DC: USITC, 1985).
136. *Washington Post*, May 23, 1982, F2.
137. Doron P. Levin, "General Motors to cut 70,000 jobs; 21 plants to shut," *New York Times*, December 19, 1991.
138. Jason L. Kopelman and Harvey S. Rosen, "Are public sector jobs recession-proof? Were they ever?," Working Paper 240 (Princeton, NJ: Princeton University, Griswold Center for Economic Policy Studies, 2014).
139. Lawrence H. Summers, "Taxing robots won't solve joblessness," *Washington Post*, March 7, 2017.
140. Caplan, *The Myth of the Rational Voter*, 53, 66–7.
141. Roberts, "Government vs. business."
142. See Wikipedia, "Subsidized housing in the United States."
143. Edgar Olsen, "We don't need more housing projects," *Washington Post*, October 11, 2016. Also see Edgar Olsen, "Getting more from low income housing assistance," Hamilton Project Discussion Paper 2008–13 (Washington, DC: Brookings Institution, 2008).
144. *St. Louis Post Dispatch*, "Missouri's king of tax credits plays shell game with campaign donations," January 18, 2014.
145. See the discussion in Roland McKean, "Divergences between individual and total costs within government," *American Economic Review*, 1964, 54(3): 243–249.
146. Russ Roberts [podcast with Brink Lindsey and Steve Teles on their book *The Captured Economy*], EconTalk, November 30, 2017; also see Robin Feldman and Evan Frondorf, *Drug Wars: How Big Pharma Raises Prices and Keeps Generics off the Market*, (Cambridge: Cambridge University Press, 2017).
147. William Allen, "Economics, economists and economic policy: modern American experiences," *History of Political Economy*, 1977, 9(1): 48–88, 52.
148. Alan S. Blinder, *Advice and Dissent: Why America Suffers When Economics and Politics Collide* (New York: Basic Books, 2018).
149. Caplan, *The Myth of the Rational Voter*, 53.
150. Samuelson, "The policy peddlers," 63.
151. Sifan Liu and Joseph Parilla, "Hidden entrepreneurs: what crowdfunding reveals about startups in metro America," Brookings Foundation, September 18, 2018.

152. *The Economist*, "Innovation prizes: and the winner is…," August 7, 2010.
153. *The Economist*, "Innovation prizes."
154. *The Economist*, "Innovation prizes."
155. Email from Allen Lynch, September 24, 2018.
156. I used this east European example over many years in my classes, but I cannot find the *Charlottesville Daily Progress* article that describes this situation.
157. Russ Roberts [podcast with Casey Mulligan], "Cuba," EconTalk, October 24, 2016.
158. Joseph E. Stiglitz, "Explaining 'democratic socialism,'" *Washington Post*, May 9, 2019.
159. Krugman and Wells, *Economics*, 121.
160. Paul Kane, "Senate votes to privatize its failing restaurants," *Washington Post*, June 9, 2008.

Chapter 5 Economists and Equity

1. Rasmussen Reports, "Republicans think US spends too much on welfare, Democrats disagree," July 12, 2018.
2. *The Economist*, "Inequality illusions," November 30, 2019.
3. Stephen Rose, "How different studies measure income inequality in the US: Piketty and company are not the only game in town" (Washington, DC: Urban Institute, 2018); Robert J. Samuelson [discussing another Rose study], "The rise of the upper-middle-class," *Washington Post*, August 17, 2020.
4. See Aparna Mathur, "Sanders' inequality tax trap," American Enterprise Institute, October 4, 2019.
5. Jeff Stein, "Sanders tax plan targets large firms with big gaps in pay," *Washington Post*, October 1, 2019.
6. Alex Edmans, "Why we need to stop obsessing over CEO pay ratios," Harvard Business Review, February 23, 2017.
7. Daron Acemoglu, "Survey of executive pay IGM economic experts panel," IGM Forum, January 31, 2012.
8. Robert J. Samuelson, "The $100 trillion question: what to do about wealth?," *Washington Post*, May 5, 2019.
9. Sylvain Catherine, Max Miller, and Natasha Sarin, "Social security and trends in inequality," February 29, 2020, https://ssrn.com/abstract=3546668.
10. *The Economist*, "Inequality illusions," 13.
11. Investopedia, updated March 3, 2020; also see Emmanuel Saez and Gabriel Zucman, "Wealth inequality in the United States since 1913: evidence from capitalized income tax data," *Quarterly Journal of Economics*, 2016, 131(2): 519–578.
12. Bruce D. Meyer and James X. Sullivan, "Annual report on US consumption poverty: 2017," American Enterprise Institute, November 1, 2018.
13. Isabel V. Sawhill and Christopher Pulliam, "Lots of plans to boost tax credits: which is best?," Brookings Institute, January 16, 2019.
14. Executive Office of the President, *Economic Report of the President: Together with the Annual Report of the Council of Economic Advisers* (Lanham, MD: Bernan Press, 2019), 20.
15. David Leonhardt, "Upward mobility has not declined, study says," *New York Times*, January 23, 2014.
16. William McBride, "Thomas Piketty's false depiction of wealth in America," Tax Foundation, August 4, 2014.
17. Lawrence H. Summers, "The inequality puzzle," *Democracy Journal*, 2014, 33: 91–99.

18. David Leonhardt, "In climbing income ladder, location matters," *New York Times*, July 22, 2013; W. Bradford Wilcox, Joseph Price, and Jacob Van Leeuwen, "The family geography of the American dream: new neighborhood data on single parenthood, prisons, and poverty," Institute for Family Studies, October 17, 2018.

19. Benjamin Austin, Edward Glaeser, and Lawrence H. Summers, "Saving the heartland: place-based policies in 21st-century America," *Brookings Papers on Economic Activity*, 2018, 49(1): 151–232. After this report was issued, Summers suggested consideration of another idea: the federal government could "provide extra support to public education and community colleges in areas where joblessness is high or has recently risen. We no longer share a common lived experience" (larrysummers.com, October 9, 2019).

20. Lawrence M. Mead, "Overselling the Earned Income Tax Credit," *National Affairs*, 2014, 21: 20–33; Nicholas Eberstadt, *Men without Work: America's Invisible Crisis* (West Conshohocken, PA: Templeton Press, 2016); Robert J. Samuelson, "Jobless by choice – or pain," *Washington Post*, November 27, 2016. The effects of the EITC on drawing women into the workforce seem much more favorable: Bruce D. Meyer, "The effects of the Earned Income Tax Credit and recent reforms," *Tax Policy and the Economy*, 2010, 24(1): 153–180.

21. Arthur Brooks, *Gross National Happiness: Why Happiness Matters for America – and How We Can Get More of It* (New York: Basic Books, 2008).

22. Russ Roberts [interview with Edward Glaeser], "Edward Glaeser on joblessness and the war on work," EconTalk, March 26, 2018; Edward Glaeser, "Mission: revive the Rust Belt: we should subsidize employment, not joblessness, and target efforts where they are most needed," *City Journal*, August 2018.

23. Cowen, *The Complacent Class*.

24. Jonathan Rothwell, "The biggest economic divides aren't regional, they're local (just ask parents)," *New York Times*, February 12, 2019; see also Samuel J. Abrams, "Hey, college graduates: don't dismiss rural America," *New York Times*, July 21, 2019.

25. Yvette Brazier, "How sitting in traffic jams can harm your health," Medical News Today, August 29, 2016.

26. University of California, Berkeley, School of Public Health, "Nurtured by nature," Wellness Letter, March 2019. See also MaryCarol R. Hunter, Brenda W. Gillespie, and Sophie Yu-Pu Chen, "Urban nature experiences reduce stress in the context of daily life based on salivary biomarkers," *Frontiers of Psychology*, 2019, 10: article 722; *Washington Post*, "Health news: "being near green spaces helps adults fend off depression, and it may work for kids too," January 23, 2018.

27. Eugenia C. South, Bernadette C. Hohl, Michelle C. Kondo, John M. MacDonald, and Charles C. Branas, "Effect of greening vacant land on mental health of community-dwelling adults: a cluster randomized trial," *JAMA Network Open*, 2018, 1(3): e180298.

28. Okun, *Equality and Efficiency*, 97.

29. Edgar Browning, "How much more equality can we afford?," *Public Interest*, 1976, 43: 90–110, esp. 95.

30. Okun, *Equality and Efficiency*, 97.

31. Okun, *Equality and Efficiency*, 47, 109.

32. Okun, *Equality and Efficiency*, 97.

33. See George Shultz's comments in George Break, George P. Shultz, and Paul A. Samuelson, "The role of government: taxes, transfers, and spending," in Martin S. Feldstein, ed., *The American Economy in Transition* (Chicago: University of Chicago Press, 1980): 617–674, 660–1.

34. Trading Economics, "United States GDP annual growth rate," https://tradingeco
nomics.com/united-states/gdp-growth-annual.
35. Thomas Sowell, "Thoughts and Details on Poverty," *Policy Review*, 1981, 17:
11–25, 20; Thomas Sowell, *"Trickle Down" Theory and "Tax Cuts for the Rich"*
(Stanford, CA: Hoover Institution Press, 2012).
36. Kahn, "America's Democrats," 22. Also see Kenneth Boulding, "Economic progress as a goal of economic life," in A. Dudley Ward, ed., *Goals of Economic Life*
(New York: Harper & Row, 1953): 52–83, esp. 76.
37. During the 2020 presidential campaign Vice President Joseph Biden and Senator
Elizabeth Warren both argued that productivity gains no longer led to wage
increases. Economist Michael Strain shows this is not true in "Wages are based
more on productivity, less on exploitation," Bloomberg, December 31, 2019.
38. Milton Friedman and Paul A. Samuelson discuss *The Economic Responsibility of
Government* (College Station, TX: Center for Education & Research in Free
Enterprise, Texas A&M University, 1980), 24.
39. Kahn, "America's Democrats," 24.
40. Wikipedia, "Middle-out economics."
41. Russ Roberts [interview with Gabriel Zucman], "Inequality, growth, and distributional national accounts," EconTalk, September 7, 2017.
42. Lindsey and Teles, *The Captured Economy*.
43. Zlati Meyer, "Regulations and permit headaches keep food trucks from cruising
down Easy Street," *USA Today*, June 12, 2018; F. Will, "The land of the free and
the home of the rent-seekers," *Washington Post*, August 13, 2019.
44. Paul Avelar, "Braiding initiative seeks to untangle restrictions on natural hair
braiders," Institute for Justice, August 2014; Nick Sibilla, "How hair braiding
explains what's gone wrong with America's economy," Forbes, January 29, 2015.
45. Summers, "The inequality puzzle."
46. Edward C. Prescott, "Why do Americans work so much more than Europeans?,"
Federal Reserve Bank of Minneapolis Quarterly Review, 2004, 28(1): 2–13.
47. Lawrence H. Summers, "What I do support in a new tax plan," LarrySummers.
com, October 26, 2017.
48. Toluse Olorunnipa, "Warren's ambitious agenda relies on a massive wealth tax
that the rich may evade," *Washington Post*, May 22, 2019.
49. See the brief discussion of their research in *The Economist*, "Repairing the safety
net: the welfare state needs updating," July 14, 2018.
50. N. Gregory Mankiw, "Defending the one percent," *Journal of Economic
Perspectives*, 2013, 27(3): 21–34, 21.
51. The most recent year available when Mankiw wrote.
52. Mankiw, "Defending the one percent," 21.
53. Patricia Kanngiesser and Felix Warneken, "Young children consider merit when
sharing resources with others," *PLOS ONE*, 2012, 7(8): 1–5.
54. Jonathan Haidt, *The Righteous Mind: Why Good People Are Divided by Politics
and Religion* (New York: Vintage Books, 2013), ch. 8.
55. Matt Weidinger, "One government agency knows you just got a job. So why does
another keep paying you unemployment checks?," American Enterprise Institute,
July 3, 2019.
56. Dave Yost, "Auditor of State Takes on Food Stamp Fraud, Offers Recommendations
to ODJFS" [received by Michael Colbert], Ohio State Auditor's Office, January 10,
2012.
57. Judith Meyer, "Feds ask Maine to hold off on photo EBT card plan," *Lewiston Sun
Journal*, April 25, 2014.

58. Patrice Lee Onwuka, "Trump saves taxpayers $2.5 billion by directing food stamps to the truly needy," Independent Women's Forum, July 29, 2019.

59. Channa Joffe-Walt, "Unfit for work: the startling rise of disability in America," NPR, March 27, 2013.

60. Stephen Ohlemacher, "Improper payments by federal agencies reach a record $125B," Associated Press, March 17, 2015.

61. Leonard E. Burman, "Tax evasion, IRS priorities, and EITC precertification," statement of Leonard E. Burman before the United States House of Representatives Committee on Ways and Means; on waste, fraud, and abuse, Urban Institute, February 1, 2017.

62. Natasha Sarin and Lawrence H. Summers, "Shrinking the tax gap: approaches and revenue potential," Tax Notes, November 18, 2019.

63. Natasha Sarin and Lawrence H. Summers, "Yes, our tax system needs reform. Let's start with this first step," Washington Post, November 17, 2019.

64. Abraham Lincoln, "Lincoln's reply at Ottawa, August 21, 1858," in Paul M. Angle, ed., The Complete Lincoln–Douglas Debates of 1858 (Chicago: University of Chicago Press, 1991): 119–120.

65. See, for example, Ilya Somin, "How liberals learned to love federalism," Washington Post, July 12, 2019.

66. Marc F. Plattner, "American democracy and the acquisitive spirit," in Robert A. Goldwin and William A. Schambra, eds., How Capitalistic Is the Constitution? (Washington, DC: American Enterprise Institute for Public Policy Research, 1982): 1–21.

67. Thomas Jefferson, "Second inaugural address" [Washington, DC, March 4, 1805), available at https://avalon.law.yale.edu/19th_century/jefinau2.asp.

68. James Madison, "The same subject continued" [Federalist Paper no. 10; 1787], in Clinton Rossiter, ed., The Federalist Papers (New York: Signet Classic, 2003): 71–79.

69. Founders Online, "From Thomas Jefferson to John Adams, 28 October 1813," National Archives, https://founders.archives.gov/documents/Jefferson/03-06-02-0446.

70. Founders Online, "From Thomas Jefferson to James Madison, 28 October 1785," National Archives, https://founders.archives.gov/documents/Jefferson/01-08-02-0534.

71. James G. Wilson, "The unconstitutionality of eliminating estate and gift taxes," Cleveland State Law Review, 2000, 48(4): 780–788.

72. Founders Online, "From John Adams to James Sullivan, 26 May 1776," National Archives, https://founders.archives.gov/documents/Adams/06-04-02-0091.

73. Founders Online, "From George Washington to Richard Henderson, 19 June 1788," National Archives, https://founders.archives.gov/documents/Washington/04-06-02-0304.

74. Okun, Equality and Efficiency.

75. Plattner, "American democracy and the acquisitive spirit," 19.

76. Greg Rosalsky, "If a wealth tax is such a good idea, why did Europe kill theirs?," NPR, "Planet Money" podcast audio, February 26, 2019.

77. Alan Viard, "Wealth taxation: an overview of the issues," Aspen Institute Economic Strategy Group, October 3, 2019; Lawrence H. Summers and Natasha Sarin, "Be very skeptical about how much revenue Elizabeth Warren's wealth tax could generate," Washington Post, June 28, 2019; The Economist, "What if America introduces a wealth tax?," July 6, 2019.

78. Olorunnipa, "Warren's ambitious agenda relies on a massive wealth tax."

79. Rafael Badziag, *The Billion Dollar Secret: 20 Principles of Billionaire Wealth and Success* (St Albans: Panoma Press, 2019); Hillary Hoffower, "An entrepreneur who interviewed 21 billionaires says the key difference between them and millionaires is how they answer a simple question about money," Business Insider, June 17, 2019.
80. Sarah Berger, "Here's what CEOs actually do all day," CNBC, June 20, 2018.
81. Jonathan M. Ladd, Joshua A. Tucker, and Sean Kates, "2018 American Institutional Confidence Poll" (Washington, DC: Georgetown University, Baker Center, 2018).
82. Douglas Holtz-Eakin, David Joulfaian, and Harvey S. Rosen, "The Carnegie conjecture: some empirical evidence," *Quarterly Journal of Economics*, 1993, 108(2): 413–435.
83. *The Economist*, "A hated tax but a fair one," November 23, 2017. Also see Henry Aaron, "To reduce inequality, tax inheritances," Brookings Institution, November 15, 2019 [a version of the article also appeared in *The New York Times*, October 15, 2019]. See also Matt O'Brien, "If it weren't for the estate tax, the majority of the superwealthy's money would never be taxed," *Washington Post*, February 11, 2019.
84. Reuters, "House passes repeal of estate tax, but veto vow makes it dead on arrival," *Washington Post*, April 16, 2015.
85. Chye-Ching Huang and Chloe Cho, "Ten facts you should know about the federal estate tax," Center on Budget and Policy Priorities, October 30, 2017.
86. Peter Lindert and Jeffrey Williamson, "Unequal gains: American growth and inequality since 1700," Vox, June 16, 2016.
87. Robert Bellafiore, "Summary of the latest federal income tax data, 2018 update", Tax Foundation, November 13, 2018.
88. Sandy Baum and Sarah Turner, "'Free tuition' is the opposite of progressive policymaking," *Washington Post*, May 5, 2019; Matthew M. Chingos, "Report: who would benefit most from free college?," Brookings Institution, April 21, 2016.
89. Richard Vedder, "The case against free college tuition," Forbes, April 12, 2018; for surprising evidence that giving poor families income helps their children achieve better educational outcomes than Headstart, see Grover "Russ" Whitehurst, "This policy would help poor kids more than universal pre-K does," *Washington Post*, July 28, 2016.
90. Adam Looney, "Up front: how progressive is Senator Elizabeth Warren's loan forgiveness proposal?," Brookings Institution, April 24, 2019.
91. James C. Capretta, "An ObamaCare tax worth keeping: the levy on 'Cadillac' plans will help counter perverse tax incentives," *Wall Street Journal*, July 19, 2018. Another provision in US tax law requires employers that give cushy untaxed health benefits to their top executives to give the same benefits to their ordinary workers. This certainly sounds as though it helps the little guy, but most economists believe expensive tax-free benefits are mainly a boon to a company's highest-paid employees. They pay for an expensive house and an expensive automobile out of their own funds, and are delighted with an expensive health care policy for which most of the costs are paid for by company funds. Lower middle-income families have a lower middle-income home and a lower middle-income car; employers are forced to give them a Cadillac-type health plan when many of them would prefer that some of the subsidy for their health care be given to them in cash. See Mark Warshawsky [discussion], "Compensation, health care costs, and inequality," EconTalk, January 2, 2017.
92. Kahn, "America's Democrats," 24.

93. Kahn, "America's Democrats," 24.
94. Bruce Jepsen, "Big employers win delay for Obamacare's Cadillac tax once again," Forbes, January 23, 2018.
95. Alan S. Blinder, "Taxing unemployment benefits is a *good* idea," *Washington Post*, December 15, 1982, A27. For other economist supporters, see Charles Schultze, cited in *Public Interest*, 1983, 71, 151; and Robert J. Samuelson, *Washington Post*, February 10, 1981, C4.
96. Browning and Browning, *Public Finance and the Price System*, 145.
97. Daniel Hamermesh's review of more than a dozen studies shows "a substantial consensus that higher UI benefits do induce people to remain unemployed longer": Daniel Hamermesh, "Transfers, taxes and the NAIRU," Working Paper 548 (Cambridge, MA: National Bureau of Economic Research, 1980), 15.
98. Blinder, "Taxing unemployment benefits is a *good* idea."
99. Charles Schultze, Edward Fried, Alice Rivlin, and Nancy Teeters, *Setting National Priorities: The 1973 Budget* (Washington, DC: Brookings Institution, 1972), 241n. Also see Browning and Browning, *Public Finance and the Price System*, 144; and Hamermesh, "Transfers, taxes and the NAIRU," 15.
100. R. Glenn Hubbard, "The Tax Cuts and Jobs Act and investment: progress, not perfection," American Enterprise Institute, October 2, 2019.
101. Laura Kusisto, "Rent controls gain support in cities," *Wall Street Journal*, February 5, 2018.
102. Jovana Rizzo, "Rangel not only famous rent-stabilized tenant," The Real Deal: New York Real Estate News, July 15, 2008; James Fanelli, "Rent-stabilized apartments are being occupied by millionaires, records show," DNA Info, April 30, 2014; Krugman and Wells, *Economics*, 132.
103. Richard M. Alston, J. R. Kearl, and Michael B. Vaughan, "Is there a consensus among economists in the 1990s?," *American Economics Review*, 1992, 82(2): 203–209.
104. For a general discussion, see Rebecca Diamond, "Report: what does economic evidence tell us about the effects of rent control?," Brookings Institution, October 18, 2018; see also *Washington Post*, "Rent control has returned: economists, not populists, are correct about the policy's effects" [editorial], September 22, 2019.
105. Max Ehrenfreund, "A 'very credible' new study on Seattle's $15 minimum wage has bad news for liberals," *Washington Post*, June 26, 2017.
106. Noam Scheiber, "They said Seattle's higher base pay would hurt workers: why did they flip?," *New York Times*, October 22, 2018.
107. Andrew Van Dam, "It's not just paychecks: the surprising society-wide benefits of raising the minimum wage," *Washington Post*, July 8, 2019.
108. Van Dam, "It's not just paychecks."
109. Charles Lane, "We don't need a one-size-fits-all federal minimum wage," *Washington Post*, May 13, 2019.
110. Quoted in Ehrenfreund, "A 'very credible' new study."
111. Lynda Gorman, "Minimum wages," in Henderson, *The Concise Encyclopedia of Economics*, www.econlib.org/library/Enc/MinimumWages.html.
112. David Card and Alan Krueger, "Minimum wages and employment: a case study of the fast food industry in New Jersey and Pennsylvania," *American Economic Review*, 1994, 84(4): 772–793.
113. Gwen Ifill, interview with Alan Krueger, *News Hour*, PBS, November 10, 2015; Rachel Greszler, "A fifteen dollar minimum wage: bad news for low income workers," *Washington Times*, January 21, 2019.

114. Christina D. Romer, "The business of the minimum wage," *New York Times*, March 2, 2013.
115. Bureau of Labor Statistics, "Characteristics of minimum wage workers, 2017," March 2018.

Chapter 6 Externalities and the Government Agenda

1. The quotation is from the subtitle of a book by Gordon Tullock, *Private Wants, Public Means: An Economic Analysis of the Desirable Scope of Government* (New York: Basic Books, 1970). Tullock's "main analytical tool" is "the economics of externalities" (v). He says, "Traditionally, the decision between governmental provision of the good or service and private provision of the good or service has turned on rather irrational considerations." Tullock believes economics and in particular the externality concept provide "the necessary theory for making a genuinely scientific decision on this problem" (259). Although that claim is grander than most, this chapter will show that economists frequently use the externality concept to evaluate government involvement. For other examples, besides those given here, see my *Policy Analysis in the Federal Aviation Administration*, 16, chs. 4–6, and citations on 141–2, nn. 55, 56. For another provocative example, see Otto Davis and Andrew Whinston, "Economic problems in urban renewal," in Edmund Phelps, ed., *Private Wants and Public Needs* (New York: Norton, 1965), 140–153.
2. The landmark article on the market's ability to take account of externalities is Ronald Coase, "The problem of social cost," *Journal of Law and Economics*, 1960, 3: 1–44.
3. Actually, as Tullock shows, customers would almost certainly lose more than businesses gained if the increase in production and the lower price were not permitted (see *Private Wants, Public Means*, ch. 7). Some economists call these economically efficient effects on others "pecuniary externalities," which they distinguish from the "real," or "technological," inefficient externalities. Other economists would reserve the term "externality" for real or technological third-party effects. Distinguishing "pecuniary" from "real" externalities can be difficult without substantial knowledge of economics. For more on the subject, see Tullock, *Private Wants, Public Means*; Roland McKean, *Efficiency in Government through Systems Analysis: With Emphasis on Water Resource Development* (New York: Wiley, 1958), 136–49; and E. J. Mishan, *Cost–Benefit Analysis* (New York: Praeger, 1976), ch. 16.
4. They are efficient pecuniary third-party effects. See preceding note.
5. Justin Jouvenal, "Intrigue deepens over bizarre attack on Rand Paul," *Washington Post*, December 8, 2017.
6. For more on this, see James M. Buchanan and W. Craig Stubblebine, "Externality," *Economica*, 1962, 29(116): 371–384. Also see Roland McKean, "Property rights within government and devices to increase governmental efficiency," *Southern Economic Journal*, 1972, 39(2): 177–186.
7. *Washington Post*, July 8, 1982, A13. Repeated July 29, 1982, A21. In part because of governmental pressure, the chemical industry has done much to minimize the adverse effects of its products on the environment and has come up with useful metrics to measure the progress. See National Academy of Engineering, "The chemical industry," chapter 5 in *Industrial Environmental Performance Metrics: Challenges and Opportunities* (Washington, DC: National Academies Press, 1999): 85–106. But its understandable concern with high profits means cleaning the environment cannot be its paramount interest.

8. *Washington Post*, June 3, 1983, A19.

9. *Washington Post*, June 3, 1983.

10. Lawrence White, *The Regulation of Air Pollutant Emissions from Motor Vehicles* (Washington, DC: American Enterprise Institute, 1982), 14.

11. "General aviation" is a catchall designation encompassing all civil aviation not legally defined as commercial air carriers. It includes instructional, personal, business, and agricultural aircraft. Somewhat confusingly, it also includes some transport for hire, such as "air taxis" and certain charter and contract companies.

12. See W. Stephen Dennis, "User fees: does general aviation already pay 'fair share'?," Airport Journals, January 1, 2006.

13. This bogus spillover GDP benefit of government expenditure is frequently used as a justification for programs. When a cut in the National Endowment for the Arts budget was proposed in 1981, Theodore Bickel warned of the economic effects on taxi drivers and restaurants (ABC radio news, February 14, 1981). What these businesses lose others will gain when the money is spent elsewhere. Also note Alfred Marcus's misuse of this sort of "benefit" in "Environmental Protection Agency," in James Q. Wilson, ed., *The Politics of Regulation* (New York: Basic Books, 1980): 267–303, 280.

14. Quoted in Rhoads, *Policy Analysis in the Federal Aviation Administration*, 43.

15. For a fuller discussion of economists' responses to general aviation arguments, see my *Policy Analysis in the Federal Aviation Administration*, esp. ch. 6. National defense is one of the arguments used to support proposed government-directed industrial policies that would assist "critical strategic" industries such as steel. Marginalism is at the core of economist Charles Schultze's rebuttal: "The national defense/essential industry argument is usually presented in an all or nothing mode, as though, in the absence of import protection, the affected industry would disappear. In fact, what is almost always at stake is a much less dramatic change in the industry's fortunes, of a magnitude that is irrelevant to national defense. Whether, for example, the domestic steel industry meets 80 percent of the nation's peacetime needs, as it does now, or only 60 percent is of no significance to the nation's security" ("Industrial policy: a dissent," 9).

16. Robert Puentes, Adie Tomer, and Joseph Kane, "A new alignment: strengthening America's commitment to passenger rail," Brookings Institution, March 1, 2013.

17. Kirsten Korosèc, "Amtrak funding slashed in half under Trump spending plan," Fortune, February 13, 2018.

18. Puentes, Tomer, and Kane, "A new alignment."

19. Korosec, "Amtrak funding slashed in half."

20. *Washington Post*, October 1, 1978, A5.

21. Amtrak, "California Zephyr," www.amtrak.com/california-zephyr-train.

22. All these arguments except that pertaining to energy are taken from *The New York Times*, December 30, 1970, 1, 29.

23. Amtrak actually boasts that, on its Northeast corridor, 92 percent of travelers have college degrees, and their average household income is $170,000 a year: Brent Gardner, "Trains for the 1%," US News & World Report, October 4, 2016.

24. See Christopher Zook, Francis Moore, and Richard Zeckhauser, "'Catastrophic' health insurance: a misguided prescription?," *Public Interest*, 1981, 62: 66–81, 80.

25. Glenn Blomquist, "Traffic safety regulation by NHTSA," Government Regulation Working Paper 16 (Washington, DC: American Enterprise Institute, 1981), 10.

26. See, e.g., Blomquist, "Traffic safety regulation by NHTSA"; and Albert Nichols and Richard Zeckhauser, "Government comes to the workplace: an assessment of OSHA," *Public Interest*, 1977, 49: 39–69.

27. See Ilya Somin, *Democracy and Political Ignorance: Why Smaller Government Is Smarter* (Stanford, CA: Stanford University Press, 2013) for an interesting discussion by a law professor who has been heavily influenced by economics. One survey shows that Americans trust local government more than federal and state government: Rasmussen Reports, "Americans still have more faith in local government than in feds, states," June 11, 2013.

28. In a letter Alfred Kahn quite correctly pointed out that reasoning about externalities would lead one to believe that the functions should be provided supranationally. Most economists do not mention this possibility, presumably because our supranational bodies have little power and because, as with income distribution and cost–benefit analysis, the profession seems to have accepted the convention that the nation is the most appropriate unit for analyzing welfare gains and losses.

29. See, e.g., Mark V. Pauly, "Income redistribution as a local public good," *Journal of Public Economics*, 1973, 2(1): 35–58.

30. "When Florida first ran out of federal relief for its thousands of Haitian refugees, it notified each of them that they might find additional help from any of 10 other states. At the same time, Texas officials printed brochures with the warning that state welfare payments are the nation's second lowest, after Mississippi, and show no signs of rising" (*Washington Post*, June 14, 1982, A5).

31. Justin Jouvenal, "Homeless say booming cities have outlawed their right to sleep, beg and even sit," *Washington Post*, June 2, 2016.

32. Heather McDonald, "San Francisco gets tough with the homeless," *City Journal*, Autumn 1994.

33. David Holmstrom, "Cities get tougher on homeless, as number of street dwellers rises," *Christian Science Monitor*, December 14, 1994.

34. Rachel Uranga, "One city's key to keeping its California paradise: arrest the homeless," Fusion, June 22, 2016.

35. René Sanchez, "Exasperated cities move to curb or expel the homeless," *Washington Post*, October 30, 2002.

36. *The Guardian*, "Bussed out: how America moves its homeless," December 20, 2017.

37. Maya Kosoff, "Amazon crushes a small tax that would have helped the homeless," Vanity Fair, June 12, 2018.

38. *Washington Post*, June 14, 1982, A5.

39. For a more extended discussion of externalities and federalism, see George Break, *Financing Government in a Federal System* (Washington, DC: Brookings Institution, 1980), esp. ch. 3; and Browning and Browning, *Public Finance and the Price System*, ch. 15. The Brownings suggest that the federal share under several matching grant programs is too high. For example, they doubt that 90 percent of the benefits of the federal interstate highway program go to nonstate residents. Similarly, they think it unlikely that 75 percent of the benefits from sewage waste treatment systems go to nonresidents (480).

40. For an example from the policy literature of economists using externalities to help determine what unit of government should have program responsibility, see David Harrison Jr., and Paul Portney, "Making ready for the Clean Air Act," *Regulation*, 1981, 5(2): 24–31. The subject is also briefly treated in *Regulation*, 1982, 6(2), 54; and *Regulation*, 1982, 6(1), 3.

41. For one case in which federal subsidies have led local decision makers to spend money where "nobody in their right mind" would spend it, see *The Washington Post*, January 4, 1982, 1, 4–6.

42. Joseph E. Aldy, "Eliminating fossil fuel subsidies," Innovative Approaches to Tax Reform Proposal 5 (Washington, DC: Hamilton Project, Brookings Institution, 2013).

43. Bjorn Lomborg, "Green energy is the real subsidy hog," *Wall Street Journal*, November 11, 2013.
44. From a speech at the Conservative Political Action Conference, as transcribed by Elliott Negin, "EPA chief Pruitt even violates his own principles," Union of Concerned Scientists, April 26, 2015.
45. Eric Pianin, "Bush plans to shift some EPA enforcement to states," *Washington Post*, July 22, 2001.
46. Kenlyn Duncan, "Out-of-state pollution is hurting Marylanders" [letter to the editor], *Washington Post*, August 7, 2017.
47. Robert Pear, "Reagan's plans for budget cuts angering states," *New York Times*, December 24, 1984.
48. Mary McGrory, "Cuomo and Buchanan duke it out," *Washington Post*, June 23, 1985.
49. Mary McGrory, "Making butter a luxury," *Washington Post*, February 7, 1985. See also Tom Wicker, "This is still one nation," *New York Times*, February 13, 1985.
50. Allen V. Kneese, *Measuring the Benefits of Clean Air and Water* (Washington, DC: Resources for the Future, 1984).
51. Cass R. Sunstein, *The Cost–Benefit Revolution* (Cambridge, MA: MIT Press, 2018), 45; W. Kip Viscusi, "Pricing lives for corporate and governmental risk decisions," *Journal of Benefit–Cost Analysis*, 2015, 6(2): 227–246; W. Kip Viscusi, "The value of life," in Steven N. Durlauf and William E. Blume, eds., *The New Palgrave Dictionary of Economics*, 2nd ed. (London: Palgrave Macmillan, 2008), https://doi.org/10.1057/978-1-349-95121-5_1323-2.
52. Acting general counsel Molly J. Moran and assistant secretary for transportation policy Carlos Monje to secretarial officers and modal administrators of the US Department of Transportation, August 8, 2016, Office of the Secretary of Transportation, "Guidance on treatment of the economic value of a statistical life (VSL) in US Department of Transportation analyses: 2016 adjustment." For more on the current estimations of VSL, see Thomas J. Kniesner and W. Kip Viscusi, "The value of a statistical life," in *Oxford Research Encyclopedia of Economics and Finance*, July 2019, 10.1093/acrefore/9780190625979.013.138.
53. Todd C. Frankel, "The government has spent decades studying what a life is worth. It hasn't made a difference in the COVID-19 crisis," *Washington Post*, May 23, 2020.
54. Cass R. Sunstein, "The stunning triumph of cost–benefit analysis," Bloomberg, September 12, 2012.
55. Jonathan H. Addler, "Supreme Court smacks EPA for ignoring costs, but mercury rule likely to persevere," *Washington Post*, June 30, 2015.
56. Cass R. Sunstein, "Why companies reject Trump's deregulation theology," Bloomberg, January 9, 2019. See also Juliet Eilperin and Brady Dennis, "The EPA is about to change a rule cutting mercury pollution. The industry doesn't want it," *Washington Post*, February 17, 2020.
57. Lisa Heinzerling, "Cost-nothing analysis: environmental economics in the age of Trump," *Colorado Natural Resources, Energy & Environmental Law Review*, 2019, 30(2): 287–305. See also critiques by NYU Law School professor Richard Revesz in "Donald Trump's toolkit: how the president has used OMB, an obscure but important federal agency," *The Economist*, March 7, 2020.
58. Sunstein, *The Cost–Benefit Revolution*, 209.
59. Sunstein, *The Cost–Benefit Revolution*, 209.
60. Susan Dudley, Glenn C. Blomquist, Richard B. Belzer, and Timothy Brennan, "Consumer's guide to regulatory impact analysis: ten tips for being an informed policymaker," *Journal of Benefit–Cost Analysis*, 2017, 8(2): 187–204.

61. Dudley *et al.*, "Consumer's guide." A landmark paper in the field of behavioral economics was written by the psychologists Daniel Kahneman and Amos Tversky, "Judgement under uncertainty: heuristics and biases," *Science*, 1974, 185(4157): 1124–1131. For a discussion of how these concepts apply to decisions about energy efficiency, see Cristina Cattaneo, "Internal and external barriers to energy efficiency: which role for policy interventions?," *Energy Efficiency*, 2019, 12(5): 1293–1311. Ted Gayer has shared his concerns with the influence of behavioral economics on federal cost–benefit analysis: Ted Gayer, "A better approach to environmental regulation: getting the costs and benefits right," Hamilton Project Discussion Paper 2011–06 (Washington, DC: Brookings Institution, 2011).

62. For examples and explications of behavioral economics, see David Laibson, "Golden eggs and hyperbolic discounting," *Quarterly Journal of Economics*, 1997, 112(2): 443–478; Sendhil Mullainathan and Eldar Shafir, *Scarcity: Why Having Too Little Means So Much* (New York: Times Books, 2013); and Emmanuel Lee, "Behavioural science, rationality and public policy," Behavioraleconomics.com, November 24, 2017.

63. Pew Research Center, "Little public support for reductions in federal spending" (Washington, DC: Pew Research Center, 2019).

64. Ted Gayer and W. Kip Viscusi, "Overriding consumer preferences with energy regulations," *Journal of Regulatory Economics*, 2013, 43(3): 248–264; Ted Gayer and W. Kip Viscusi, "Resisting abuses of benefit cost analysis," *National Affairs*, 2016, 27: 59–71.

65. Ted Gayer, "Energy efficiency, risk and uncertainty, and behavioral public choice," Brookings Institution, March 6, 2015.

66. Gayer, "Energy efficiency."

67. Bill Clinton, "Regulatory planning and review," Executive Order 12866 of September 30, 1993, *Federal Register*, 1993, 58(190).

68. Gayer and Viscusi, "Overriding consumer preferences with energy regulations," 260.

69. FINRA Investor Education Foundation, "The state of US financial capability: The 2018 National Financial Capability Study" (Washington, DC: FINRA Investor Education Foundation, 2019), 27.

70. Federal Reserve System, "Consumer credit – G.19," July 8, 2020.

71. For example, see chairman of the board of management Kurt-Ludwig Gutberlet, "Energy efficiency is the key to implementing the energy transition in Germany," in *Group Annual Report 2011* (Munich: BSH Hausgeräte GMBH, 2011): 28–31.

72. Jonathan Wiener, "Unplugged: energy guide vs. Energy Star," Earth Justice, May 24, 2011.

73. Marla C. Sanchez, Richard E. Brown, Carrie Webber, and Gregory K. Homan, "Savings estimates for the United States Environmental Protection Agency's ENERGY STAR voluntary product labeling program," *Energy Policy*, 2008, 36(6): 2098–2108; Franz Fuerst and Pat McAllister, "Eco-labeling in commercial office markets: do LEED and Energy Star offices obtain multiple premiums?," *Ecological Economics*, 2011, 70(6): 1220–1230; Omar I. Asensio and Magali A. Delmas, "Nonprice incentives and energy conservation," *Proceedings of the National Academy of Sciences of the United States of America*, 2015, 112(6): E510–E515; Stephanie Heinzle and Rolf Wüstenhagen, "Disimproving the European Energy Label's value for consumers? Results from a consumer survey," discussion paper (St. Gallen: University of St. Gallen, 2010); and Gicheol Jeong and Yeunjoong Kim, "The effects of energy efficiency and environmental labels on appliance choice in South Korea," *Energy Efficiency*, 2015, 8(3): 559–576.

74. Lucas W. Davis and Gilbert E. Metcalf, "Does better information lead to better choices? Evidence from energy-efficiency labels," *Journal of the Association of Environmental and Resource Economists*, 2016, 3(3): 589–625.
75. Ted Gayer, phone conversation with Steve Rhoads, June 2020.

Chapter 7 The Economist's Consumer and Individual Well-Being

1. On the market production of information see George Stigler, "The economics of information," *Journal of Political Economy*, 1961, 69(3): 213–225; and Friedman and Friedman, *Free to Choose*, 213.
2. *Washington Post*, June 19, 1981, C15; *Washington Post*, January 15, 1982, A14. There are also examples of companies withholding information from their employees about the long-term health risks of their firm's occupations. See Steven Kelman, *Regulating America, Regulating Sweden* (Cambridge, MA: MIT Press, 1981), 57; *Washington Post*, April 17, 1982, A21.
3. Brian Elbel, Rogan Kersh, Victoria L. Brescoll, and L. Beth Dixon, "Calorie labeling and food choices: a first look at the effects on low-income people in New York City," *Health Affairs*, 2009, 28(Supplement 1): https://doi.org/10.1377/hlthaff.28.6.w1110.
4. Aaron Yelowitz, "Menu mandates and obesity: a futile effort," Policy Analysis 789 (Washington, DC: Cato Institute, 2016).
5. American Academy of Family Physicians, "New report shows US obesity epidemic continues to worsen," October 15, 2018.
6. Brian Vastag and N. C. Aizenman, "New York's plan to curb soda size stirs new controversy over obesity," *Washington Post*, June 3, 2012.
7. Michael O'Hare, "Information strategies as regulatory surrogates," in Eugene Bardach and Robert Kagan, eds., *Social Regulation: Strategies for Reform* (San Francisco: Institute for Contemporary Studies, 1982): 221–236, 229.
8. Ben Guarino and Eli Rosenberg, "Don't fret over cancer warning ordered for coffee," *Washington Post*, March 31, 2018.
9. Thomas C. Frohlich and Vince Calio, "Nine of the most totally misleading product claims," *Time*, May 21, 2014.
10. Wikipedia, "False advertising," https://en.wikipedia.org/wiki/False_advertising.
11. Claude S. Colantoni, Otto A. Davis, and Malati Swaminuthan, "Imperfect consumers and welfare comparisons of policies concerning information and regulation," *Bell Journal of Economics and Management Science*, 1976, 7: 602–615, 613; also see Schwartz and Wilde, "Intervening in markets," 668; Walter Y. Oi, "The economics of product safety," *Bell Journal of Economics and Management Science*, 1973, 4: 3–27; and Victor Goldberg's critique of Oi's paper, and Oi's rejoinder, in *Bell Journal of Economics and Management Science*, 1974, 5: 683–695. Despite the fancy mathematical models used, the empirical situation is so unclear that Oi ended this exchange of opinion by referring to his own preference for throwaway pop bottles even though he knew they were more likely to explode.
12. Steven Kelman, "Regulation and paternalism," *Public Policy*, 1981, 29(2): 219–254, 229.
13. Richard Nelson, "Comments on Peltzman's paper on automobile safety regulation," Working Paper 5–13 (New Haven, CT: Institution for Social and Policy Studies, Yale University, 1976): 15.

14. Kelvin Lancaster, "A new approach to consumer theory," *Journal of Political Economy*, 1966, 74(2): 132–157, 149–50. For an example of economists building on Lancaster's work, see Colantoni, Davis, and Swaminuthan, "Imperfect consumers and welfare comparisons."

15. Jerome Rothenberg, "Welfare comparisons and changes in tastes," *American Economic Review*, 1953, 43(5): 885–890, 887, emphasis in original.

16. *Washington Post*, "Gambler's vows: for bettor or worse," July 9, 1974.

17. *Daily Progress*, May 30, 1981, B10. Note also a recent study of psychiatrists that found that a majority of the small minority of therapists who repeatedly had sexual intercourse with patients believed that their conduct "was bad for both therapist and patient": *Washington Post*, September 1, 1983, A3.

18. Centers for Disease Control and Prevention, "Cigarette smoking among US adults hits all-time low," November 14, 2019.

19. Jonathan Gruber, "Smoking's 'internalities': given smokers' future preferences, lawmakers should raise cigarette taxes," *Regulation*, 2002, 25(4): 52–57, 52.

20. Reto Odermatt and Alois Stutzer, "Smoking bans, cigarette prices and life satisfaction," *Journal of Health Economics*, 2015, 44: 176–194.

21. Irving Kristol, *Two Cheers for Capitalism* (New York: Mentor Books, 1978), 82.

22. First results were reported in a Louis Harris poll in the *Washington Post*, September 18, 1978, A4; the second from a Harris poll in the *Washington Post*, May 23, 1977, A10. Other polls have found that far more Americans think we are less happy because of increased affluence than think we are happier. Low-income respondents do not equate happiness with economic well-being any more than do high-income respondents: Jennifer Hochschild, "Why the dog doesn't bark: income, attitudes and the redistribution of wealth," *Polity*, 1979, 11(4): 478–511, 509.

23. James B. Stewart, "Facebook has 50 minutes of your time each day. It wants more," *New York Times*, May 12, 2016.

24. Cited in Tibor Scitovsky, *The Joyless Economy* (Oxford: Oxford University Press, 1978), 163–4.

25. James M. Buchanan, "Individual choice in voting and the market," *Journal of Political Economy*, 1954, 62(4): 334–343, 336.

26. David Friedman, "Economics and evolutionary psychology," in Roger Koppl, ed., *Evolutionary Psychology and Economic Theory* (Bingley: Emerald, 2005): 17–33.

27. Richard H. Thaler and Cass R. Sunstein, *Nudge: Improving Decisions about Health, Wealth, and Happiness* (London: Penguin Books, 2009); Danny Vinik, "Obama's retirement fail," Politico, June 7, 2018. At the urging of economists, the Pension Protection Act of 2006 gave businesses incentives to automatically enroll employees in retirement savings plans: John Beshears, James Choi, David Laibson, Brigitte C. Madrian, and Brian Weller, "Public policy and saving for retirement: the autosave features of the Pension Protection Act of 2006," in Siegfried, *Better Living through Economics*: 274–290.

28. Will Wilkinson, "Why opting out is no third way," *Reason*, October 2008: 64–69.

29. Friedman, "Economics and evolutionary psychology."

30. David Laibson, "Golden eggs and hyperbolic discounting," *Quarterly Journal of Economics*, 1997, 112(2): 443–478.

31. Ashoka Mody, Franziska Ohnsorge, and Damiano Sandri, "Precautionary savings in the Great Recession," *IMF Economic Review*, 2012, 60(1): 114–138.

32. Paul Davidson, "Americans are sitting on record cash savings amid pandemic and uncertain economy," *USA Today*, August 10, 2020.

33. For articles supporting the learning explanation, see Robert H. Frank, Thomas D. Gilovich, and Dennis T. Regan, "Do economists make bad citizens?," *Journal of*

Economic Perspectives, 1996, 10(1): 187–192; Adam Grant, "Does studying economics breed greed?," Psychology Today, October 22, 2013; and Robert H. Frank, Thomas D. Gilovich, and Dennis T. Regan, "Does studying economics inhibit cooperation?," *Journal of Economic Perspectives*, 1993, 7(2): 159–171. For articles supporting the predisposition side, see Bruno S. Frey and Stephan Meier, "Are political economists selfish and indoctrinated? Evidence from a natural experiment," *Economic Inquiry*, 2003, 41(3): 448–462; and John R. Carter and Michael D. Irons, "Are economists any different, and if so, why?," *Journal of Economic Perspectives*, 1991, 5(2): 171–177.

34. Frank, Gilovich, and Regan, "Does studying economics inhibit cooperation?," 162.

35. Gordon Tullock, "More thought about demand revealing," *Public Choice*, 1982, 38(2): 167–170, 167.

36. James M. Buchanan, *Public Finance in Democratic Process: Fiscal Institutions and Individual Choice* (Chapel Hill, NC: University of North Carolina Press, 1967), 198. Also see Bruce Bolnick, "Toward a behavioral theory of philanthropic activity," in Edmund Phelps, ed., *Altruism, Morality and Economic Theory* (New York: Russell Sage, 1975): 197–224, 198.

37. William Breit, "Income redistribution and efficiency norms," in Harold Hochman and George Peterson, eds., *Redistribution through Public Choice* (New York: Columbia University Press, 1974): 3–21, esp. 11, 18.

38. Bolnick, "Toward a behavioral theory," esp. 198–9. For discussion of other economists who have seen altruism as being "silly" or "irrational," see Gerald Marwell and Ruth Ames, "Economists free ride, does anyone else?," *Journal of Public Economics*, 1981, 15(3): 295–310, 299.

39. "For the purposes of predictive science, the elements in individual utility functions must be specified in clear, recognizable and measurable terms. Application of the *homo economicus* construction for empirical or predictive purposes requires something like the assumption of net wealth maximization as a surrogate for maximization of consumption more broadly achieved" (Geoffrey Brennan and James M. Buchanan, "The normative purpose of economic 'science': rediscovery of an eighteenth century method," *International Review of Law and Economics*, 1981, 1 (2): 155–166, 162). See also Richard McKenzie, *The Limits of Economic Science* (Boston: Kluwer-Nijhoff, 1983); and Ronald Coase, "Economics and contiguous disciplines," *Journal of Legal Studies*, 1978, 7(2): 201–211.

40. Gordon Tullock, "Does punishment deter crime?," *Public Interest*, 1974, 36: 103–111, 106; Gordon Tullock, *The Logic of the Law* (New York: Basic Books, 1971), esp. 164–5, 213. Also see sociologist Serapio Zalba's comments in Simon Rottenberg, ed., *The Economics of Crime and Punishment* (Washington, DC: American Enterprise Institute, 1973): 58–62, 62.

41. W. B. Arthur, "The economics of risks to life," *American Economic Review*, 1981, 71(1): 54–64, 55, 61.

42. John Morrall III, "OSHA after ten years," Working Paper 13 (Washington, DC: American Enterprise Institute, 1981). Like Arthur, Albert Nichols and Richard Zeckhauser's analysis of OSHA makes no mention of psychological external costs to the kindhearted: "OSHA after a decade: a time for reason," in Weiss and Klass, *Case Studies in Regulation*: 202–234, esp. 208–9.

43. Lipsey and Steiner, *Economics*.

44. Lipsey and Steiner, *Economics*, 17–19.

45. Amartya Sen, *Collective Choice and Social Welfare* (San Francisco: Holden-Day, 1970), 64. Also see 56–63.

46. David Long, Charles Mallar, and Craig Thornton, "Evaluating the benefits and costs of the Job Corps," *Journal of Policy Analysis and Management*, 1981, 1(1): 55–76, 61.

47. Some economists have noted that an additional crime may lead to other societal costs in the form of additional expenditures to protect oneself from crimes: James M. Buchanan, *The Limits of Liberty: Between Anarchy and Leviathan* (Chicago: University of Chicago Press, 1975), 122.

48. Timothy Hannan, "The benefits and costs of methadone maintenance," *Public Policy*, 1976, 24(2): 197–226, 200–1; Gary Becker, "Crime and punishment: an economic approach," *Journal of Political Economy*, 1968, 76(2): 169–217; Richard Posner, *Economic Analysis of Law* (Boston: Little, Brown, 1972), 357–9. In a more recent review article, Mark Cohen notes that some economists count the lost wages and freedom as costs to the criminal, while others argue for a "social constraint" and refuse to count such costs in their cost–benefit work: Mark A. Cohen, "The 'cost of crime' and benefit–cost analysis of criminal justice policy: understanding and improving upon the state-of-the-art," 2016, https://ssrn.com/abstract=2832944.

49. Jeffrey Sedgwick, "Welfare economics and criminal justice policy," PhD dissertation (Charlottesville, VA: University of Virginia, 1978), 156–7.

50. Tullock, *Logic of the Law*, 254.

51. Tullock, *Logic of the Law*, 254–5.

52. Aristotle, *Nicomachean Ethics*, in Richard McKeon, ed., *Introduction to Aristotle* (New York: Modern Library, 1947), book IX, chs. 4 & 9, 502, 514. See also Adam Smith, *The Theory of Moral Sentiments*, D. D. Raphael and A. L Macfie, eds. (Indianapolis: Liberty Classics, 1976 [1759]), III.2.1–III.2.6.

53. Nelson, *The Moon and the Ghetto*, 151.

54. Mishan, *Cost–Benefit Analysis*, 312–15, 385–8.

55. See Autoshow, "Mercedes-Benz 2017 summer event commercial," June 1, 2017, www.youtube.com/watch?v=v8QpbNJWYEk.

56. E. J. Mishan, *The Costs of Economic Growth* (New York: Praeger, 1967), 130, 119.

57. Robert Solow, "A rejoinder," *Public Interest*, 1967, 9: 118–119, 119.

58. William Baumol, *Welfare Economics and the Theory of the State* (Cambridge, MA: Harvard University Press, 1969), 29.

59. William Vickrey, "Goals of economic life: an exchange of questions between economics and philosophy," in Ward, *Goals of Economic Life*: 148–177, 159.

60. Dean Worcester Jr., *Welfare Gains from Advertising: The Problem of Regulation* (Washington, DC: American Enterprise Institute, 1978), 124. For additional mainstream reaction to the Galbraith–Mishan argument, see Abba Lerner, "The economics and politics of consumer sovereignty," *American Economic Review*, 1972, 62(1/2): 258–266, 258; and William Breit and R. L. Ransom, *The Academic Scribblers* (New York: Holt, Rinehart & Winston, 1971), 169–70, 200.

61. Robert Ayanian, "Does advertising persuade consumers to buy things they do not need?," in M. Bruce Johnson, ed., *The Attack on Corporate America: The Corporate Issues Sourcebook* (New York: McGraw-Hill, 1978): 236–239, 239.

62. Mancur Olson and Christopher Clague, "Dissent in economics: the convergence of extremes," *Social Research*, 1971, 38(4): 751–776. Also see Steven Kelman, *What Price Incentives?*, 19–20.

63. Schultze, *The Public Use of Private Interest*, 17–18, emphasis in original.

64. Ronald Sharp, *Friendship and Literature: Spirit and Form* (Durham, NC: Duke University Press, 1986), 94.

65. Maria G. Janicki, "Beyond sociobiology: a kinder and gentler evolutionary view of human nature," in Charles Crawford and Catherine Salmon, eds., *Evolutionary Psychology, Public Policy and Personal Decisions* (Mahwah, NJ: Psychology Press, 2004): 49–68.

66. Peter Singer, "Altruism and commerce: a defense of Titmuss against Arrow," *Philosophy and Public Affairs*, 1973, 2(3): 312–320, 319.

67. Kenneth Arrow, *The Limits of Organization* (New York: Norton, 1974), 16. Also see McKenzie and Tullock, *The New World of Economics*, chs. 1 & 21.

68. For somewhat different arguments on the general subject of this and the following paragraphs, see David Braybrooke, "From economics to aesthetics: the rectification of preferences," *Nous*, 1974, 8(1): 13–24; and Scitovsky, *The Joyless Economy*, esp. pt. II. Also see Steven Kelman, "Cost–benefit analysis: an ethical critique," *Regulation*, 1981, 5(1): 33–40, 38.

69. Paul Cantor, "Playwright of the globe," *Claremont Review of Books*, 2006, 7(1): 34–40.

70. Leo Strauss, "What is political philosophy?," *Journal of Politics*, 1957, 19(3): 343–368, 351.

71. Tammy Poole, "School board adopts multicultural education policy," *Daily Progress*, November 22, 1991.

72. On this point, see the *Washington Post* editorial "Asian values," August 1, 1997.

73. Joseph Cropsey, "What is welfare economics?," *Ethics*, 1955, 65(2): 116–125, 124. See also Walter Berns, "The behavioral sciences and the study of political things: the case of Christian Bay's *The Structure of Freedom*," *American Political Science Review*, 1961, 55(3): 550–559.

74. *The Politics of Aristotle*, trans. Carnes Lord, 2nd ed. (Chicago: University of Chicago Press: 2013), book 7, ch. 1, 187.

75. Aristotle, *Nicomachean Ethics*, book III, chs. 6–9, 361–8.

76. Part of a longer poem, "My childhood-home I see again," in Abraham Lincoln, *Speeches and Writings*, vol. 1, *1832–1858* (New York: Library of America, 1989): 120–122.

77. John Stuart Mill, *Utilitarianism* (Indianapolis: Hackett, 1979 [1861]), 10.

78. Martin Bronfenbrenner, "Poetry, pushpin, and utility," *Economic Inquiry*, 1977, 15(1): 95–110, 98.

79. The typical measure for happiness is the response given by people who are asked survey questions such as "How happy would you say you are – very happy, somewhat happy or not very happy?" These sorts of responses seem to correlate pretty well with efforts to measure happiness by people's facial affect and reports of friends and acquaintances about how happy the subject seems. See Will Wilkinson, "In pursuit of happiness research: is it reliable? What does it imply for policy?," Policy Analysis 590 (Washington, DC: Cato Institute, 2007).

80. Richard A. Easterlin, "Explaining happiness," *Proceedings of the National Academy of Sciences*, 2003, 100(19): 11176–11183; Carol Graham, "The economics of happiness," in Durlauf and Blume, *The New Palgrave Dictionary of Economics*, 2nd ed., https://pdfs.semanticscholar.org/8d28/abb020d4b2604e9df53c24982ec119f2df43.pdf.

81. Betsy Stevenson and Justin Wolfers, "Economic growth and subjective well-being: reassessing the Easterlin paradox," Working Paper 14282 (Cambridge, MA: National Bureau of Economic Research, 2008); Wilkinson, "In pursuit of happiness research"; Helen Johns and Paul Ormerod, *Happiness, Economics and Public Policy* (London: Institute of Economic Affairs: 2012).

82. John F. Helliwell, Richard Layard, and Jeffrey D. Sachs, eds, *World Happiness Report 2019* (New York: Sustainable Development Solutions Network, 2019), as summarized in *The Economist*, "Economic growth does not guarantee happiness," March 21, 2019.

83. Frank, *Luxury Fever*; Robert H. Frank, *The Darwin Economy: Liberty, Competition, and the Common Good* (Princeton, NJ: Princeton University Press, 2011).

84. Quoted in Wilkinson, "In pursuit of happiness research," 9.

85. Benjamin M. Friedman, *The Moral Consequences of Economic Growth* (New York: Vintage Books, 2006), esp. 351.

86. Lawrence H. Summers, "The age of secular stagnation: what it is and what to do about it," Foreign Affairs, February 2016. Also see Friedman, *The Moral Consequences of Economic Growth*.

87. *The Economist*, "Generation SRI," November 25, 2017; Tony Mecia, "Feel-good investing," *Weekly Standard*, April 10, 2017.

88. Bryant Stone, "A call for the positive: why young psychological scientists should take positive psychology seriously," Association for Psychological Science, August 29, 2018.

89. Claudia Dreifus, "The smiling professor," *New York Times*, April 22, 2008.

90. Jane E. Brody, "Social interaction is critical for mental and physical health," *New York Times*, June 12, 2017, quoting John Robbins, *Healthy at 100: How You Can – at Any Age – Dramatically Increase Your Life Span and Health Span* (New York: Random House, 2006).

91. John Murphy, "New epidemic affects nearly half of American adults," MDLinx, January 11, 2019; *The Economist*, "Mind and body: the reason loneliness could be bad for your health," February 24, 2011.

92. Anasse Bari, Julian De Niro, and Melanie Tosik, "What do people say they want on Twitter?," *Washington Post*, December 16, 2018.

93. *Washington Post*, "I feel your pain. No, Really," April 8, 2003.

94. Ann Waldron, review of Morton Hunt, *The Compassionate Beast: What Science Is Discovering about the Humane Side of Humankind* (New York: William Morrow, 1990), in *Washington Post*, July 3, 1990.

95. Brooks, *Gross National Happiness*, 177. Also see Tyler J. VanderWeele, "Volunteering and human flourishing," Psychology Today, August 26, 2020.

96. *Daily Progress*, October 17, 1982, F1, and March 14, 1982, B1. See also Marissa J. Lang, "Among the gifts, companionship: eager volunteers pay Christmas visits to hundreds of homebound district seniors," *Washington Post*, December 26, 2019.

97. George H. W. Bush, "The Points of Light Movement" [the president's report to the nation] (Washington, DC: Government Printing Office, 1993), 47.

98. Micaela Connery, "A 'kinder, gentler' president: how George Herbert Walker Bush captured America with 'a thousand points of light,'" masters thesis (Charlottesville: University of Virginia, 2009).

99. Brooks, *Gross National Happiness*, 157–62.

100. Jan-Emmanuel De Neve and George Ward, "Does work make you happy? Evidence from the *World Happiness Report*," Harvard Business Review, March 20, 2017.

101. See, e.g., Bernard Gwertzman, "The Shultz method," *New York Times*, January 2, 1983.

102. *Princeton Alumni Weekly*, March 20, 1991; May 15, 1991; July 10, 1991; April 1, 1992.

103. Robert Nozick, *The Examined Life: Philosophical Meditations* (New York: Simon & Schuster, 1989), 11–15, emphases in original.

104. Nozick, *The Examined Life*, 18.
105. Valerie Strauss, "Hiding in plain sight: the adult literacy crisis," *Washington Post*, November 1, 2016.
106. Kathryn Leckie, "Reading class helped man learn what he's missed," *Daily Progress*, November 27, 1983. For a long letter, filled with "joy," from a 54-year-old woman newly able to read, see William Raspberry, "Gift of understanding," *Washington Post*, December 25, 1991. In the same year that Raspberry wrote, the University of Virginia's student-run radio station broadcast the following promotion: "Since 1972 we've been giving audiences music that they don't yet know they want."
107. Arthur Brooks, "A formula for happiness," *New York Times*, December 15, 2013.
108. Jonathan Haidt, "Elevation and the positive psychology of morality," in Corey L. M. Keyes and Jonathan Haidt, eds., *Flourishing: Positive Psychology and the Life Well-Lived* (Washington, DC: American Psychological Association: 2003): 275–289.
109. Smith, *The Theory of Moral Sentiments*, III.3.35.
110. Smith, *The Theory of Moral Sentiments*, VII.2.2.
111. Samuel Fleischacker, "Adam Smith's moral and political philosophy," in Edward N. Zalta, ed., *The Stanford Encyclopedia of Philosophy* (Stanford, CA: Stanford University Press, 2017), https://plato.stanford.edu/archives/spr2017/entries/smith-moral-political.
112. Smith, *The Theory of Moral Sentiments*, III.2.1–III.2.34.
113. Smith, *The Theory of Moral Sentiments*, III.2.1.
114. John Stuart Mill, *Principles of Political Economy*, vols. 2 & 3 of the *Collected Works of John Stuart Mill*, J. M. Robson, ed. (Indianapolis: Liberty Fund, 2006 [1848]).
115. Bronfenbrenner, "Poetry, pushpin, and utility," 98.
116. Groundbreaking research in Framingham, Massachusetts, shows that networks of friendship can range surprisingly far. If A's friend B becomes happier, A does as well. But gains in happiness by B's friend C also increase B's happiness, and thereby raise happiness for A. And happiness gains by C's friend D increase C's happiness, and thus B's happiness and thus A's happiness. A's happiness is thus increased by C's and D's even though he does not know either! The research shows that happiness spreads up to three degrees of separation. James H. Fowler and Nicholas A. Christakis, "Dynamic spread of happiness in a large social network: longitudinal analysis over 20 years in the Framingham Heart Study," *BMJ*, 2008, 337: a2338, https://doi.org/10.1136/bmj.a2338. This article originated the discussion, criticism, and follow-on research of the Framingham social network analysis. It has been cited by over 2100 other articles.
117. Smith, *The Wealth of Nations*, book V, ch. 1, 303, 308.
118. Alfred Marshall, *Principles of Economics: An Introductory Volume* (London: Macmillan, 1910), book VI, ch. 13, sect. 14, 599.
119. Marshall, *Principles of Economics*, book III, ch. 3, sect. 6, 114.
120. Marshall, *Principles of Economics*, book III, ch. 3, sect. 6, 113. Adam Smith was willing to go beyond encouragement to stimulate better expenditure patterns by the rich. He advocated higher tolls on luxury carriages than on freight wagons so that "the indolence and vanity of the rich" could "contribute in a very easy manner to the relief of the poor": *The Wealth of Nations*, book V, ch. 1, pt. III, art. 1, 246.
121. Marshall, *Principles of Economics*, book I, ch. 1, sect. 4, 8.
122. Philip Wicksteed, *The Common Sense of Political Economy*, Lionel Robbins, ed. (London: Routledge & Kegan Paul, 1950), book II, ch. 1, 431, 434.
123. A. C. Pigou, *The Economics of Welfare* (London: Macmillan, 1938), 13, 17, 18.

124. Frank Knight, *The Ethics of Competition* (London: Allen & Unwin, 1935), 22–3.
125. Knight, *The Ethics of Competition*, 52n,
126. Knight, *The Ethics of Competition*, 71.
127. Amartya Sen, *Development as Freedom* (New York: Knopf, 1999).
128. Thomas Carlyle, "'Pig philosophy,' a section of 'Jesuitism,'" in *Latter-Day Pamphlets* (Andover: Warren F. Draper, 1860): 400–403.
129. The words are Jack Smart's, from J. J. C. Smart, "An outline of a system of utilitarian ethics," in J. J. C. Smart and Bernard Williams, *Utilitarianism: For and Against* (Cambridge: Cambridge University Press, 1973): 3–76, 24.
130. The phrase is Roger Bolton's, in his exhaustive study "The economics and public financing of higher education: an overview," in *The Economics and Financing of Higher Education in the United States*, a compendium of papers submitted to the Joint Economic Committee, US Congress (Washington, DC: Government Printing Office, 1969): 11–104, 33. Deirdre McCloskey reaches a conclusion similar to mine in *The Rhetoric of Economics* (Madison, WI: University of Wisconsin Press, 1998).
131. Aristotle explains the necessary imprecision of political science: "A properly educated or cultivated person is one who 'searches for that degree of precision in each kind of study which the nature of the subject at hand admits.'" See Carnes Lord, *The Modern Prince: What Leaders Need to Know Now* (New Haven, CT: Yale University Press, 2004), ch. 3, 30–1.

Chapter 8 Representatives, Deliberation, and Political Leadership

1. Mishan, *Cost–Benefit Analysis*, 318.
2. Baumol, *Welfare Economics and the Theory of the State*, 29.
3. Thomas Schelling, "The life you save may be your own," in Samuel Chase, ed., *Problems in Public Expenditure Analysis* (Washington, DC: Brookings Institution, 1968): 127–162, 161. Leland Yeager dissents from many of his colleagues and makes a powerful case for deliberation in "Pareto optimality in policy espousal," *Journal of Libertarian Studies*, 1978, 2(3): 199–216.
4. James C. Miller III, "A program for direct and proxy voting in the legislative process," *Public Choice*, 1969, 7(1): 107–113; Kenneth Greene and Hadi Salavitabar, "Senatorial responsiveness, the characteristics of the polity and the political cycle," *Public Choice*, 1982, 38(3): 263–269; Ryan Amacher and William Boyes, "Cycles in senatorial voting: implications for the optimal frequency of elections," *Public Choice*, 1978, 33(1): 5–13. See also more recent work supporting the view that a greater number of representatives (and thus better representation of the public's views) is desirable: Emmanuelle Auriol and Robert J. Gary-Bobo, "The more the merrier? Choosing the optimum number of representatives in modern democracies," VoxEU, October 9, 2007.
5. James M. Buchanan and Gordon Tullock, *The Calculus of Consent: Legal Foundations of Constitutional Democracy* (Ann Arbor, MI: University of Michigan Press, 1965), 20.
6. See, e.g., Buchanan, *Public Finance in Democratic Process*, 176. Also see Duncan MacRae's discussion, *The Social Function of Social Science* (New Haven, CT: Yale University Press, 1976), 197.
7. Greene and Salavitabar, "Senatorial responsiveness," 263; Edgar Browning, "More on the appeal of minimum wage laws," *Public Choice*, 1978, 33(1): 91–93, 93; William Niskanen, "The pathology of politics," in Richard Selden, ed., *Capitalism and Freedom: Problems and Prospects* (Charlottesville, VA:

University of Virginia Press, 1975): 20–35; Julius Margolis, "Public policies for private profits: urban government," in Harold Hochman and George Peterson, eds., *Redistribution through Public Choice* (New York: Columbia University Press, 1974): 289–319, esp. 301; MacRae, *The Social Function of Social Science*, 197; Fred Gottheil, *Principles of Economics*, 7th ed. (Mason, OH: Southwestern Cengage Learning, 2013), 348–9.

Some notable economists have dissented from the prevailing consensus that interest groups distort consumer preferences and introduce inefficiencies in policy making. See, e.g., Donald Wittman, *The Myth of Democratic Failure: Why Political Institutions Are Efficient* (Chicago: University of Chicago Press, 1995), 76–86; and Gary S. Becker, "A theory of competition among pressure groups for political influence," *Quarterly Journal of Economics*, 1983, 98(3): 371–400.

8. See, e.g., Arman A. Alchian and Harold Demsetz, "Production, information costs, and economic organization," *American Economic Review*, 1972, 62(5): 777–795; Joseph P. Kalt and Mark A. Zupan, "Capture and ideology in the economic theory of politics," *American Economic Review*, 1984, 74(3): 279–300; and Joseph P. Kalt and Mark A. Zupan, "The apparent ideological behavior of legislators: testing for principal–agent slack in political institutions," *Journal of Law and Economics*, 1990, 33(1): 103–131.

9. Miller, "A program for direct and proxy voting."

10. Tullock, *Private Wants, Public Means*, 112–13. Martin Shubik has expressed reservations about Miller's proposal, but his suggested amendment to it (that legislation not become law unless passed in two public pollings at least six weeks apart) is a fairly minor one: "On Homo politicus and the instant referendum," *Public Choice*, 1970, 9(1): 79–84. William Niskanen has also discussed Miller's proposal sympathetically, though he supports other forms of referenda and "direct democracy" devices: "The pathology of politics"; and "Toward more efficient fiscal institutions," *National Tax Journal*, 1972, 25(3): 343–347.

11. See Wikipedia, "Liquid democracy." See also Steve Hardt's and Lia C. R. Lopes's examination of "liquid democracy" via social networks: "Google votes: a liquid democracy experiment on a corporate social network," Technical Disclosure Commons, June 5, 2015.

12. James Green-Armytage, "Direct voting and proxy voting," *Constitutional Political Economy*, 2015, 26(2): 190–220.

13. Gal Cohensius, Shie Manor, Reshef Meir, Eli Meirom, and Ariel Orda, "Proxy voting for better outcomes," Technion – Israel Institute of Technology, November 28, 2016.

14. Dennis Mueller, Robert Tollison, and Thomas Willett, "Representative democracy via random selection," *Public Choice*, 1972, 12(1): 57–68.

15. Caplan, *The Myth of the Rational Voter*, esp. 52–83, 114–27.

16. The Survey of Americans and Economists on the Economy was a collaborative project of *The Washington Post*, the Kaiser Family Foundation, and Harvard University (1996).

17. Somin, *Democracy and Political Ignorance*.

18. Alexander Hamilton, James Madison, and John Jay, *The Federalist Papers*, ed. Clinton Rossiter (New York: New American Library, 1961 [1788]), no. 9.

19. Hamilton, Madison, and Jay, *The Federalist Papers*, nos. 9, 10, 49, 58, 63, 71.

20. For a defense of this view, see Martin Diamond, Winston Fisk, and Herbert Garfinkel, *The Democratic Republic* (Chicago: Rand McNally, 1970), ch. 4. For a discussion of contending views, see Martin Diamond, "Conservatives, liberals, and the Constitution," in R. A. Goldwin, ed., *Left,*

Right and Center: Essays on Liberalism and Conservatism in the United States (Chicago: Rand McNally, 1965): 60–86.

21. Abraham Lincoln, "The perpetuation of our political institutions: address before the Young Men's Lyceum of Springfield, Illinois, January 27, 1838," in Roy P. Basler, ed., *The Collected Works of Abraham Lincoln*, 8 vols. (New Brunswick, NJ: Rutgers University Press, 1953): I, 108–115; also see "Speech in the Illinois Legislature, January 11, 1837," in *The Collected Works*: I, 61–69, 69.

22. Jefferson's letters to John Taylor, May 28, 1816; to Isaac Tiffany, August 26, 1816; to John Adams, October 28, 1813; and to Pierre Samuel du Pont de Nemours, April 24, 1816; all in Morton Frisch and Richard Stevens, eds., *The Political Thought of American Statesmen* (Itasca, IL: Peacock, 1973), 26–36. Also see Harvey C. Mansfield Jr., "Thomas Jefferson," in Morton Frisch and Richard Stevens, eds., *American Political Thought* (New York: Scribner, 1971): 23–50.

23. Jefferson's letter to John Adams, October 28, 1813, in Frisch and Stevens, *The Political Thought of American Statesmen*, 28.

24. De Tocqueville, *Democracy in America*, I, esp. 63, 70, 94–6, 265, 309–10.

25. Tom Kertscher, "Were the founding fathers 'ordinary people?,'" PolitiFact, July 2, 2015; see also Walker's speech at the conference for the Faith and Freedom Coalition, June 20, 2015: www.c-span.org/video/?326702-5/governor-scott-walker-rwi-faith-freedom-coalition-conference.

26. *Washington Post*, January 21, 1977, A17.

27. For the full text of Donald Trump's inaugural address, see www.whitehouse.gov/briefings-statements/the-inaugural-address.

28. See, e.g., George Will, "Some GOP candidates becoming unhinged over gay marriage ruling," *Washington Post*, July 1, 2015; and George Will, "On Obamacare, John Roberts helps overthrow the Constitution," *Washington Post*, June 25, 2015.

29. Paul Krugman, "In defense of Obama," Rolling Stone, October 8, 2014.

30. Caitlin Yilek, "Ruth Bader Ginsburg opposes Democratic proposal to add seats to Supreme Court," Washington Examiner, July 24, 2019.

31. Kaiser Family Foundation, "Pop quiz: assessing Americans' familiarity with the health care law" (Menlo Park, CA: Kaiser Family Foundation, 2011).

32. Andrew Romano, "How ignorant are Americans?," Newsweek, March 3, 2011.

33. James Curran, Shanto Iyengar, Anker Brink Lund, and Inka Salovaara-Moring, "Media system, public knowledge and democracy: a comparative study," *European Journal of Communication*, 2009, 24(1): 5–26.

34. De Tocqueville, *Democracy in America*, I, 222–3, 237–9.

35. Andrew Kohut, "Debt and deficit: a public opinion dilemma," Pew Research Center, June 14, 2012.

36. It is worth noting that not all economists agree with the consensus that voter ignorance poses significant problems for democratic representation. Donald Wittman, the most notable dissenter, has argued that voters need to know few specific details in order to make accurate judgments about the policy positions of their representatives. Just as consumers can use brand names and product reviews to make decisions about which items to buy, Wittman argues, voters can make sound electoral decisions by observing the party platform, endorsements, and interest group support of available candidates. Yet this argument is persuasive only – if at all – for the election of representatives. It does little to assuage concerns about political ignorance when the goal is to gauge voter opinion on specific policy issues. Most voters are informed enough not to vote for a candidate with opposite views from their own; but it is a long shot to argue from there that voters are

informed enough to consult regularly on defense spending, manufacturing regulations, or delicate questions of foreign policy. Wittman, *The Myth of Democratic
Failure*, 7–20. Caplan's work on voter irrationality provides strong reason to avoid
overt reliance on public opinion.

37. Tullock, *Private Wants, Public Means*, 115; also see 119.
38. Hamilton, Madison, and Jay, *The Federalist Papers*, nos. 9, 10, 57. Also see
    Diamond, Fisk, and Garfunkel, *The Democratic Republic*, 99–100; and
    Walter Berns, "Does the Constitution 'secure these rights'?," in Robert Goldwin
    and William Schambra, eds., *How Democratic Is the Constitution?* (Washington,
    DC: American Enterprise Institute, 1980): 59–78.
39. Hamilton, Madison, and Jay, *The Federalist Papers*, no. 10.
40. Diamond, Fisk, and Garfunkel, *The Democratic Republic*, 99–100.
41. Hamilton, Madison, and Jay, *The Federalist Papers*, no. 10; also see no. 51. On
    Madison's attempt to design a government in which representatives would be
    unlikely to act on narrow self-interest, see Robert J. Morgan, "Madison's analysis
    of the sources of political authority," *American Political Science Review*, 1981, 75
    (3): 613–625.
42. Hamilton, Madison, and Jay, *The Federalist Papers*, nos. 63, 71.
43. Joseph M. Bessette, *The Mild Voice of Reason: Deliberative Democracy and
    American National Government* (Chicago: University of Chicago Press, 1994).
44. Woodrow Wilson, *Constitutional Government in the United States* (New York:
    Columbia University Press, 1908), 104–5. The importance of deliberation to
    democracy was first emphasized by Aristotle, who believed that it was only when
    the people met together and discussed policy that their claim to rule could be taken
    seriously. As Ernest Barker notes, for Aristotle, "The people at large have the merit
    of a good collective judgment not as a static mass, but when they are dynamic – in
    other words when they assemble, and when the process of debate begins":
    Ernest Barker, *The Politics of Aristotle* (New York: Oxford University Press,
    1962), 126. Another famous statement from the founders' era was that of
    Edmund Burke: "Your representative owes you…his judgment… Government
    and legislation are matters of reason and judgment, and not inclination; and
    what sort of reason is that in which the determination precedes the discussion, in
    which one set of men deliberate and another decide, and where those who form the
    conclusion are perhaps three hundred miles distant from those who hear the
    argument?" *The Works of the Right Honorable Edmund Burke*, 3 vols. (Boston:
    Little, Brown, 1894), II, 95–6.
45. From Woodrow Wilson, *Congressional Government: A Study in American Politics*
    (Boston: Houghton Mifflin, 1885). Quoted in Harry Clor, "Woodrow Wilson," in
    Frisch and Stevens, *American Political Thought*: 191–217, 192.
46. Clor, "Woodrow Wilson," 194.
47. Abraham Lincoln, "First debate with Stephen Douglas at Ottawa, Illinois,
    August 21, 1858," in *The Collected Works*: III, 1–37, 27. See also *The Collected
    Works*, III, 29; and Benjamin P. Thomas, *Abraham Lincoln* (New York: Knopf,
    1952), 133.
48. Abraham Lincoln, "Perpetuation of our political institutions," in *The Collected
    Works*: I, 108–115.
49. Abraham Lincoln, "Second inaugural address" [Washington, DC, March 4, 1865],
    available at www.ourdocuments.gov/doc.php?flash=false&doc=38&page=
    transcript.
50. Although today's economists are likely to be opposed to rather than indifferent
    about slavery, this belief comes from sources other than their economics. Welfare

economics says society will have to determine property rights and distributions of income. In Lincoln's time slaves were property, not holders of rights. If the people in some states say this is just, there is nothing in welfare economics to declare them wrong. Leland Yeager dissented from fellow economists when he criticized over-reliance on the concept of Pareto optimality. He notes, "Akin to its indiscriminate respect for all values is the tendency of the Pareto approach to regard whatever emerges from market transactions as ethically valid (with qualifications about externalities and so forth)." See Yeager, "Pareto optimality in policy espousal." Also see Tullock's comments on South Africa: *Private Wants, Public Means*, 238.

51. In his first inaugural address Thomas Jefferson spoke of the "sacred principle, that though the will of the majority is in all cases to prevail, that will to be rightful must be reasonable."

52. Abraham Lincoln, "Speech at Peoria, Illinois, on the repeal of the Missouri Compromise, October 16, 1854," in *The Collected Works*: II, 246–283, emphasis in original.

53. Joseph M. Bessette, "Deliberation and the lawmaking process," in *The Mild Voice of Reason*: 150–181; Joseph M. Bessette, "Deliberation in American lawmaking," *Philosophy & Public Policy Quarterly*, 1994, 14(1/2): 18–24; V. O. Key Jr., *Public Opinion and American Democracy* (New York: Knopf, 1961), ch. 21; Hanna Pitkin, *The Concept of Representation* (Berkeley, CA: University of California Press, 1967), ch. 10, esp. 212; Carl Friedrich, "Deliberative assemblies," in *Constitutional Government and Democracy: Theory and Practice in Europe and America*, 4th ed. (Waltham, MA: Blaisdell, 1968); Duncan MacRae Jr., "Normative assumptions in the study of public choice," *Public Choice*, 1973, 16 (1): 27–41, 38–9; MacRae, *The Social Function of Social Science*, 194–200; Willmoore Kendall and George Carey, "The intensity problem and democratic theory," *American Political Science Review*, 1968, 62(1): 5–24, 23; Robert Axelrod, "The medical metaphor," *American Journal of Political Science*, 1977, 21: 430–432, 432; Geoffrey Vickers, "Values, norms and policies," *Policy Sciences*, 1973, 4(1): 103–111, 109.

54. W. Arthur Lewis, "Planning public expenditures," in Max F. Millikan, ed., *National Economic Development* (New York: National Bureau of Economic Research, 1967): 201–227, 207.

55. Key, *Public Opinion and American Democracy*, ch. 21, esp. 536, 539, 553–8.

56. John F. Kennedy, *Profiles in Courage* (New York: Cardinal, 1956), 14, emphasis added.

57. Herbert Storing argues that one of the great dangers of populism is that it undermines the statesman's "confidence in his own judgment, in the legitimacy of relying on his own judgment even in the face of popular disagreement": Herbert Storing, "American statesmanship: old and new," in Robert Goldwin, ed., *Bureaucrats, Policy Analysts, Statesmen: Who Leads?* (Washington, DC: American Enterprise Institute, 1980): 88–113, 103.

58. Charles Wolf's proposal, cited by Vincent Taylor, "How much is good health worth?," *Policy Sciences*, 1970, 1(1): 49–72, 69.

59. Mishan, *Cost–Benefit Analysis*, 318–19.

60. Daniel Casse, "Casting a ballot with a certain cast of mind" [review of *The Myth of the Rational Voter*, by Bryan Caplan], *Wall Street Journal*, July 10, 2007.

61. Schelling, "The life you save may be your own"; Mishan, *Cost–Benefit Analysis*, 162; Jan Paul Acton, *Evaluating Public Programs to Save Lives: The Case of Heart Attacks* (Santa Monica, CA: Rand Corporation, 1973).

62. Tullock, *Private Wants, Public Means*, ch. 5; and Dennis Mueller, *Public Choice* (Cambridge: Cambridge University Press, 1979), 124.

63. Tullock, *Private Wants, Public Means*, 120.

64. *Los Angeles Times*, March 26, 1982, 29.

65. Herbert Baus and William Ross, *Politics Battle Plan* (New York: Macmillan, 1968), 61; quoted in Eugene Lee, "California," in David Butler and Austin Ranney, eds., *Referendums* (Washington, DC: American Enterprise Institute, 1978): 87–122, 101–2.

66. Raymond Wolfinger, "Discussion," in Austin Ranney, ed., *The Referendum Device* (Washington, DC, American Enterprise Institute, 1981): 60–73, 63–4. Also see David Magleby's comments in *The Washington Post*, May 29, 1982, A11.

67. *Los Angeles Times*, March 26, 1982, 29. Field's views are significant, since pollsters profit from initiatives. Interest groups and newspapers need them to assess trends in public opinion prior to election day.

68. Tracy Westen, *Democracy by Initiative: Shaping California's Fourth Branch of Government*, 2nd ed. (Los Angeles: Center for Governmental Studies, 2008), 9.

69. Even when voter interest and knowledge are high, initiative proposals are often passed that include poorly thought-out provisions. Raymond Wolfinger notes that "Proposition 13 [which made increases in California property taxes much harder to achieve] included a number of secondary provisions that illustrate some interesting things about referendums. One such provision said that the assessed value of property was to be cut to what it was in 1975–1976, except that any piece of property sold after that date would be assessed at the sale price. In a building with twenty condominiums, each assessed in 1975–1976 for $50,000, if one were sold in 1979 for $125,000 then nineteen people would be paying taxes on $50,000 and the twentieth would be paying taxes on $125,000. That is an example of the kind of kicker often inserted in the language of propositions in California. The people knew what they were voting on, but few knew that the package they were voting on included things like this $125,000 versus $50,000 situation" (Wolfinger, "Discussion," 64–5).

70. See Richard Fenno on Congress's relative strengths in this regard: Richard F. Fenno Jr., *Home Style: House Members in Their Districts* (Boston: Little, Brown, 1978), 245. For more on the importance of consensus building as a criterion of a good governmental process, see Kendall and Carey, "The intensity problem and democratic theory"; and David Braybrooke, *Three Tests for Democracy: Personal Rights, Human Welfare, Collective Preference* (New York: Random House, 1968), esp. 202–7. On the failure of initiatives to encourage compromise, see Michael Malbin, "The false hope of law by initiative," *Washington Post*, January 7, 1978, 15.

71. Indeed, recent scholarship has suggested that deliberation of the sort discouraged by direct democracy may be crucial for creating the conditions necessary for consensus. Research shows that giving participants time to discuss divisive issues increases the likelihood that they will view the issue through the same ideological lens. Even though substantive agreement may not be reached, a type of "meta-agreement" can be reached – that is, agreement about the terms in which the issue should be described (liberal versus conservative, secular versus religious, etc.). This in turn means that each participant can choose a single preferred policy outcome that can be ranked in comparison to those of his peers, a condition that public choice economists call "single-peaked preferences." The results are more fruitful discussions and more legitimate compromises. Neglect such deliberation, however, and compromise can be harder to attain. Christian List, Robert Luskin, James Fishkin, and Iain McLean, "Deliberation, single-peakedness, and the

possibility of meaningful democracy: evidence from deliberative polls," *Journal of Politics*, 2012, 75(1), 80–95.

72. Some supporters of ballot initiatives have proposed further incorporating the legislature. This "indirect initiative" process varies by state, but it amounts to a cooperative effort between the citizens, who propose ballot initiatives, and the legislature, which must debate and ultimately pass them. In Massachusetts, for example, petitioners are incentivized to propose bills to the legislature – instead of putting them on the ballot to be voted on directly by the public – by a lower signature threshold. The legislature may then approve, amend, or reject the initiative by a majority vote. Other recommendations for incorporating the legislature include holding mandatory public hearings, requiring an impartial analysis of initiatives by a legislative analyst, allowing for negotiation between petitioners and the legislature, providing for legislative amendments to popularly passed initiatives, and providing drafting assistance. Such improvements may help to mitigate the effects of voter rational ignorance on public policy. Westen, *Democracy by Initiative*, 18–22; J. Fred Silva, "The California Initiative Process: background and perspective," occasional paper (San Francisco: Public Policy Institute of California, 2000), 37; Massachusetts Constitution amendment article XLVIII, initiative part 5 (statutes), part 4 (constitutional amendment), available at https://malegislature.gov/Laws/Constitution#cart048.htm.

73. Mueller, Tollison, and Willett, "Representative democracy via random selection," 65.

74. Key believes it is important that the general public feels that it shares in and participates in the political order: *Public Opinion and American Democracy*, 547–8.

75. Fenno, *Home Style*, 240–5. Also see the section later in this chapter suggesting considerable public support for independent representatives. If one knows little about the issues it may be quite rational to vote for the person who seems to have good character or judgment rather than the person who shares one's current uninformed predilections. When Jones says that Smith has good judgment, he suggests that he would probably agree with Smith if he knew what Smith has learned by participating in the legislative process.

76. See the section "Economists and the Selfishness Assumption." Also see Greene and Salavitabar, "Senatorial responsiveness." William Mitchell says, of economists who author public-finance texts, "Almost all…take a perverse pleasure in announcing that voters, politicians, bureaucrats, alike, are just like all the rest of us and that our continued supplies of public goods depend not on their good will but a fine appreciation of their self-interests as political actors": William Mitchell, "Textbook public choice: a review essay," *Public Choice*, 1982, 38(1): 97–112, 104.

77. James Kau and Paul Rubin, *Congressmen, Constituents and Contributors: Determinants of Roll Call Voting in the House of Representatives* (Boston: Martinus Nijhoff, 1982). Kau and Rubin find that both constituent ideology and the ideology of the representative are significant in explaining congressional votes. They also find that contributions from business-oriented political action committees do not influence the voting behavior of congressional recipients, but, even after controlling for economic factors, public interest lobbies do influence voting behavior (esp. 3–5, 45, 80, 93–4, 121–4). I am pleased to be able to balance my frequent criticisms of Gordon Tullock's work by noting here that he is the general editor of *Studies in Public Choice*, a series that found room for the unorthodox and interesting findings both of Kau and Rubin and of McKenzie's *The Limits of Economic Science* (briefly discussed in Chapter 9).

78. David Mayhew, *Congress: The Electoral Connection* (New Haven, CT: Yale University Press, 1974); and Morris Fiorina, *Congress: Keystone of the Washington Establishment* (New Haven, CT: Yale University Press, 1977).

79. Richard F. Fenno Jr., *Congressmen in Committees* (Boston: Little, Brown, 1973).

80. Bessette, "Deliberation in American lawmaking," 18–19; Fenno, *Congressmen in Committees*, 5.

81. This is documented at length in Bessette, "Deliberation in American lawmaking," and in Arthur Maass, *Congress and the Common Good* (New York: Basic Books, 1983).

82. Asbell, *The Senate Nobody Knows*, 267, 210.

83. Asbell, *The Senate Nobody Knows*, 370–1.

84. Asbell, *The Senate Nobody Knows*, 30, 42–3. Note also that John Manley attributed Wilbur Mills's preeminence on the House Ways and Means Committee to "influence" rather than "power." Manley says that "influence is, in essence, a means of *persuasion* that involves giving reasons or justifications for doing certain things and avoiding others, whereas power may be taken to mean the communication of decisions that activate obligations": John F. Manley, *The Politics of Finance: The House Committee on Ways and Means* (Boston: Little, Brown, 1970), 122. Also see Bessette, "Deliberation in American lawmaking."

85. Jenna Johnson, "House Judiciary Committee chairman well versed in immigration debate," *Washington Post*, June 23, 2013.

86. Paul Ryan, *The Way Forward: Renewing the American Idea* (New York: Twelve, 2014), 76.

87. Daniel J. Palazzolo, "Return to deliberation? Politics and lawmaking in committee and on the floor," in William Connelly, Jack Pitney, and Gary Schmitt, eds., *Is Congress Broken? The Virtues and Defects of Partisanship and Gridlock* (Washington, DC: Brookings Institution Press, 2017).

88. Bessette, *The Mild Voice of Reason*, esp. 74, 82, 87, 95–6, 98, 146–7.

89. Buchanan, *Public Finance in Democratic Process, The Limits of Liberty*.

90. Hamilton, Madison, and Jay, *The Federalist Papers*, no. 63.

91. John Dewey, ed., *The Living Thoughts of Thomas Jefferson* (Greenwich, CT: Fawcett, 1940), 58. Jefferson and other founders also emphasized that the most able and talented men would not be attracted to offices with very short terms and little power. Economists do not discuss this incentive.

92. Miller, "A program for direct and proxy voting," 373.

93. Amacher and Boyes, "Cycles in senatorial voting."

94. Ryan Amacher and William Boyes, "Politicians and polity: responsiveness in American government," *Southern Economic Journal*, 1979, 46(2): 558–567; Greene and Salavitabar, "Senatorial responsiveness."

95. Thomas Jefferson, "Letter to Monsieur d'Ivernois, Feb. 6, 1975," in Andrew Lipscomb, ed., *The Writings of Thomas Jefferson*, 20 vols. (Washington, DC: Thomas Jefferson Memorial Society, 1903): IX, 299–300, emphasis added. Also see Hamilton, Madison, and Jay, *The Federalist Papers*, no. 10.

96. Pitkin, *The Concept of Representation*, ch. 7.

97. Miller, "A Program for direct and proxy Voting," 373.

98. Amacher and Boyes, "Cycles in senatorial voting," 10.

99. Schelling, "The life you save may be your own," 161.

100. Elizabeth Mendes and Joy Wilke, "Americans' confidence in Congress falls to lowest on record," Gallup, June 13, 2013.

101. Lydia Saad, "Gridlock is top reason Americans are critical of Congress," Gallup, June 12, 2013.

102. Steven Kull, "American public says leaders should pay attention to opinion polls," Common Dreams, March 28, 2008.
103. Stanley Kelley, *Interpreting Elections* (Princeton, NJ: Princeton University Press, 1983), esp. 57, 163–5.
104. Hamilton, Madison, and Jay, *The Federalist Papers*, no. 49.

Chapter 9 Conclusion

1. American Society for the Prevention of Cruelty to Animals, "The criminal, underground world of dogfighting," www.aspca.org/animal-cruelty/dogfighting.
2. *Chicago Tribune*, September 1, 1974.
3. For a discussion of the necessity, and difficulty, posed by taking account of intangible externalities, see Chapter 10 of the 1985 edition of *The Economist's View of the World*.
4. Kenneth Boulding, "Economics and the future of man," in *Economics as a Science*: 139–157, 156.
5. Thomas Schelling, "Economic reasoning and the ethics of policy," *Public Interest*, 1981, 63: 37–61, 59.
6. Boulding, *Economics as a Science*, 136.
7. Robert J. Samuelson, "Micro revolution: compete or stand aside," *Washington Post*, October 21, 1980, D8.
8. Rees went on to say, "Most economists are more conservative on economic issues than, say, sociologists, because they do understand it": William McCleery, "A conversation with Albert Rees," *Princeton Alumni Weekly*, March 15, 1976.
9. Schultze, *The Public Use of Private Interest*, 76–7.
10. Alain Enthoven, "Defense and disarmament: economic analysis in the Department of Defense," *American Economic Review*, 1963, 53(2): 413–422, 422.
11. This is a theme in George Stigler, "The politics of political economists," *Quarterly Journal of Economics*, 1959, 73(4): 522–532.
12. See, for example, Tyler J. VanderWeele, "Activities for flourishing: an evidence-based guide," *Journal of Positive School Psychology*, 2020, 4(1): 79–91.
13. Scott Shackford, "Biden says high-speed rail will get millions of cars off the road. That's malarkey," Reason, March 16, 2020.
14. Justine Coleman, "Biden unveils plan to penalize companies that offshore jobs ahead of Michigan visit," The Hill, September 9, 2020.
15. Josh Hawley, "Americans are ready for a comeback. Congress must help unleash it," *Washington Post*, April 8, 2020; Bryan Riley, "Sen. Hawley is entitled to his opinion on trade, but not his own facts," National Taxpayers Union, May 5, 2020.
16. Michael R. Strain, *The American Dream Is Not Dead (But Populism Could Kill It)* (West Conshohocken, PA: Templeton Press, 2020); George Will, "Despite bipartisan lament, upward mobility lives on," *Washington Post*, March 12, 2020; Michael R. Strain, "What conservatism should look like after Trump," Bloomberg Opinion, November 12, 2019.
17. Michael R. Strain, "Bidenomics is a populist gridlock buster. Uh-oh," Bloomberg Opinion, July 14, 2020.
18. Stephen Broadberry and Tim Leunig, "The impact of Government policies on UK manufacturing since 1945," Evidence Paper 2 for Future of Manufacturing Project (London: Government Office for Science, 2013).
19. Strain, *The American Dream Is Not Dead*.
20. Strain, "Bidenomics is a populist gridlock buster."

21. Benjamin F. Jones and Lawrence H. Summers, "A calculation of the social returns to innovation," Working Paper 27863 (Cambridge, MA: National Bureau of Economic Research, 2020).

22. *The Economist*, "Joe Biden would not remake America's economy," October 3, 2020.

23. Committee on the Judiciary, "Nomination of Stephen G. Breyer to be an associate justice of the Supreme Court of the United States" (Washington, DC: Government Printing Office, 1995), 7.

24. Casey B. Mulligan, *You're Hired! Untold Successes and Failures of a Populist President* (Washington, DC: Republic Book Publishers, 2020).

25. Amy Goldstein, "President Trump's Medicare drug discount cards face uncertain path," *Washington Post*, October 15, 2020; Lenny Bernstein, "Health officials scramble to explain details of Trump's $200 drug discount card," *Washington Post*, September 25, 2020. For a more upbeat assessment of the Trump administration, see University of Chicago economist Casey Mulligan's *You're Hired!*.

26. Deirdre McCloskey, "The two movements in economic thought, 1700–2000: empty economic boxes revisited," *History of Economic Ideas*, 2018, 26(1): 63–95.

27. Jeremy Norman, "The antitrust case, US v. IBM, is tried and eventually withdrawn," History of Information.

28. Deirdre McCloskey, *Bourgeois Dignity: Why Economics Can't Explain the Modern World* (Chicago: University of Chicago Press, 2010).

29. Jones and Summers, "A calculation of the social returns to innovation."

30. See Deirdre McCloskey, "How growth happens: liberalism, innovism, and the Great Enrichment," deirdremccloskey.com, November 29, 2018; and McCloskey, "The two movements in economic thought"; also see John Mueller, *Capitalism, Democracy, and Ralph's Pretty Good Grocery* (Princeton, NJ: Princeton University Press, 1999).

31. Strain, *The American Dream Is Not Dead*; Richard V. Reeves, *Dream Hoarders: How the American Upper Middle Class Is Leaving Everyone Else in the Dust, Why That Is a Problem, and What to Do About It* (Washington, DC: Brookings Institution Press, 2017); Jonathan Gruber and Simon Johnson, *Jump-Starting America: How Breakthrough Science Can Revive Economic Growth and the American Dream* (New York: PublicAffairs, 2019).

32. Strain, *The American Dream Is Not Dead*.

33. Arthur C. Brooks, "What really buys happiness? Not income equality, but mobility and opportunity," *City Journal*, Summer 2007.

34. William D. Nordhaus, "Schumpeterian profits and the alchemist fallacy revised," Yale Economic Applications and Policy Discussion Paper 6 (New Haven, CT: Department of Economics, Yale University, 2005).

35. Americans still value liberty more than people in western Europe. When pollsters ask which is more important – "freedom to pursue life's goals without state interference" or "state guarantees [that] nobody is in need" – Americans favor freedom "by a 58 percent to 35 percent margin," according to a 2011 Pew survey. "In Europe, opinion was the opposite. Germans valued protections over freedom 62 percent to 36 percent. The results were similar for France, Britain and Spain." Robert J. Samuelson, "Is America really so exceptional?," *Washington Post*, September 22, 2013.

36. Kristján Kristjánsson, "An Aristotelian virtue of gratitude," *Topoi*, 2013, 34(2): 499–511; Wikiversity, "Virtues/gratitude," https://en.wikiversity.org/wiki/Virtues/Gratitude; Michael W. Austin, "The virtue of thankfulness," Psychology Today, November 22, 2010.

37. Sara B. Algoe, Jonathan Haidt, and Shelly L. Gable, "Beyond reciprocity: gratitude and relationships in everyday life," *Emotion*, 2008, 8(3): 425–429; Catherine Clifford discusses Jonathan Haidt's research in "Happiness expert: these are the 3 components of lasting happiness (and the mistakes people make)," *Health and Wellness*, CNBC, April 11, 2019; see also Arthur Brooks, "Choose to be grateful. It will make you happier," *New York Times*, November 22, 2015.

INDEX

Printed in the United States
by Baker & Taylor Publisher Services